CIM

STUDY TEXT

PROFESSIONAL CERTIFICATE IN MARKETING

PAPER 2

MARKETING ENVIRONMENT

In this September 2007 edition

- Easy to use presentation
- Fully updated for examinations in December 2007 and June 2008
- Material on key examinable topics
- Updated exam tips and case examples
- Material supporting assignment route

FOR EXAMS IN DECEMBER 2007 AND JUNE 2008

BPP LEARNING MEDIA

First edition 2002
Sixth edition September 2007

ISBN 9780 7517 4168 1 (previous edition 0 7517 2748 2)

British Library Cataloguing-in-Publication Data
A catalogue record for this book
is available from the British Library

Published by

BPP Learning Media
BPP House, Aldine Place
London W12 8AA

www.bpp.com/learningmedia

Printed in Great Britain by
WM Print
45-47 Frederick Street
Walsall
WS2 9NE

All our rights reserved. No part of this publication may be reproduced, stored in a retrieval system or transmitted, in any form or by any means, electronic, mechanical, photocopying, recording or otherwise, without the prior written permission of BPP Learning Media.

We are grateful to the Chartered Institute of Marketing for permission to reproduce in this text the syllabus, guidance notes and past examination questions. We are also grateful to Karen Beamish of Stone Consulting for preparing the assignment based assessment learning material.

©
BPP Learning Media
2007

Contents

Page

Introduction
The BPP Study Text – Syllabus – Websites– Guide to the assignment route – The exam paper .... iv – xxx

Part A The organisation and its environment
1 Introduction to organisations 3
2 Organisations as systems 27
3 The marketing environment and change 51

Part B The micro-environment
4 The micro-environment 63
5 Stakeholders 75
6 Pressure groups 89
7 The industry environment 101

Part C The macro-environment
8 The macro-environment 125
9 The social and cultural environments 141
10 The economic and international environments 165
11 The political and legal environments 193
12 The natural environment 213
13 The technical and information environments 231
14 Environmental challenges 255

Part D Environmental information systems
15 The marketing information system 283
16 Information systems and change 301

Question and Answer bank 327

Specimen paper and suggested answers 379

List of key concepts and Index 399

Review form and free prize draw

The BPP Study Text

Aims of this Study Text

> To provide you with the knowledge and understanding, skills and application techniques that you need if you are to be successful in your exams

This Study Text has been written around the **Marketing Environment** syllabus.

- It is **comprehensive**. It covers the syllabus content. No more, no less.
- It is targeted to the **exam**. We have taken account of the pilot paper, guidance the examiner has given and the assessment methodology.

> To allow you to study in the way that best suits your learning style and the time you have available, by following your personal Study Plan (see below)

You may be studying at home on your own until the date of the exam, or you may be attending a full-time course. You may like to (and have time to) read every word, or you may prefer to (or only have time to) skim-read and devote the remainder of your time to question practice. Wherever you fall in the spectrum, you will find the BPP Study Text meets your needs in designing and following your personal study plan.

> To tie in with the other components of the BPP Effective Study Package to ensure you have the best possible chance of passing the exam

INTRODUCTION

Recommended period of use	Elements of the BPP Effective Study Package
3-12 months before exam	**Study Text** Acquisition of knowledge, understanding, skills and applied techniques
1-6 months before exam	**Practice & Revision Kit (9/2007)** Tutorial questions and helpful checklists of the key points lead you into each area. There are then numerous Examination questions to try, graded by topic area, along with realistic suggested solutions prepared by marketing professionals in the light of the Examiner's Reports. The September 2007 edition will include the December 2006 and June 2007 papers.
From three months before the exam until the last minute	**Passcards** Work through these short memorable notes which are focused on what is most likely to come up in the exam you will be sitting..

Settling down to study

By this stage in your career you may be a very experienced learner and taker of exams. But have you ever thought about *how* you learn? Let's have a quick look at the key elements required for effective learning. You can then identify your learning style and go on to design your own approach to how you are going to study this text – your personal study plan.

Key element of learning	Using the BPP Study Text
Motivation	You can rely on the comprehensiveness and technical quality of BPP. You've chosen the right Study Text – so you're in pole position to pass your exam!
Clear objectives and standards	Do you want to be a prizewinner or simply achieve a moderate pass? Decide.
Feedback	Follow through the examples in this text and do the Action Programme and the Quick Quizzes. Evaluate your efforts critically – how are you doing?
Study plan	You need to be honest about your progress to yourself – don't be over-confident, but don't be negative either. Make your Study Plan (see below) and try to stick to it. Focus on the short-term objectives – completing two chapters a night, say – but beware of losing sight of your study objectives.
Practice	Use the Quick Quizzes and Chapter Roundups to refresh your memory regularly after you have completed your initial study of each chapter.

These introductory pages let you see exactly what you are up against. However you study, you should:

- **Read through the syllabus** – this will help you to identify areas you have already covered, perhaps at a lower level of detail, and areas that are totally new to you.

- **Study the examination paper section**, where we show you the format of the exam (how many and what kind of questions and so on).

INTRODUCTION

Key study steps

The following steps are, in our experience, the ideal way to study for professional exams. You can of course adapt it for your particular learning style (see below).

Tackle the chapters in the order you find them in the Study Text. Taking into account your individual learning style, follow these key study steps for each chapter.

Key study steps	Activity
Step 1 **Chapter Topic list**	Study the list. Each numbered topic denotes a **numbered section** in the chapter.
Step 2 **Introduction**	Read it through. It is designed to show you **why the topics in the chapter need to be studied** – how they lead on from previous topics, and how they lead into subsequent ones.
Step 3 **Explanations**	Proceed **methodically** through the chapter, reading each section thoroughly and making sure you understand.
Step 4 **Key Concepts**	**Key Concepts** can often earn you **easy marks** if you state them clearly and correctly in an appropriate exam.
Step 5 **Exam Tips**	These give you a good idea of how the examiner tends to examine certain topics – pinpointing **easy marks** and highlighting **pitfalls**.
Step 6 **Note taking**	Take **brief notes** if you wish, avoiding the temptation to copy out too much.
Step 7 **Marketing at Work**	Study each one, and try if you can to add flesh to them from your **own experience** – they are designed to show how the topics you are studying come alive (and often come unstuck) in the **real world**. You can also update yourself on these companies by going on to the World Wide Web.
Step 8 **Action Programme**	Make a very good attempt at each one in each chapter. These are designed to put your **knowledge into practice** in much the same way as you will be required to do in the exam. Check the answer at the end of the chapter in the **Action Programme Review**, and make sure you understand the reasons why yours may be different.
Step 9 **Chapter Roundup**	Check through it very carefully, to make sure you have grasped the **major points** it is highlighting.
Step 10 **Quick Quiz**	When you are happy that you have covered the chapter, use the **Quick Quiz** to check your recall of the topics covered. The answers are in the paragraphs in the chapter that we refer you to.
Step 11 **Illustrative question(s)**	Either at this point, or later when you are thinking about revising, make a full attempt at the **illustrative questions**. You can find these at the end of the Study Text, along with the **Answers** so you can see how you did.

INTRODUCTION

Developing your personal study plan

Preparing a study plan (and sticking closely to it) is one of the key elements in learning success.

First you need to be aware of your style of learning. There are four typical learning styles identified by Peter Honey and Alan Mumford. Consider yourself in the light of the following descriptions. and work out which you fit most closely. You can then plan to follow the key study steps in the sequence suggested.

Learning styles	Characteristics	Sequence of key study steps in the BPP Study Text
Theorist	Seeks to understand principles before applying them in practice	1, 2, 3, 7, 4, 5, 8, 9, 10, 11 (6 continuous)
Reflector	Seeks to observe phenomena, thinks about them and then chooses to act	
Activist	Prefers to deal with practical, active problems; does not have much patience with theory	1, 2, 8 (read through), 7, 4, 5, 9, 3, 8 (full attempt), 10, 11 (6 continuous)
Pragmatist	Prefers to study only if a direct link to practical problems can be seen; not interested in theory for its own sake	8 (read through), 2, 4, 5, 7, 9, 1, 3, 8 (full attempt), 10, 11 (6 continuous)

Next you should complete the following checklist.

Am I motivated? (a) ☐

Do I have an objective and a standard that I want to achieve? (b) ☐

Am I a theorist, a reflector, an activist or a pragmatist? (c) ☐

How much time do I have available per week, given: (d) ☐

- The standard I have set myself
- The time I need to set aside later for work on the Practice and Revision Kit
- The other exam(s) I am sitting, and (of course)
- Practical matters such as work, travel, exercise, sleep and social life?

Now:

- Take the time you have available per week for this Study Text (d), and multiply it by the number of weeks available to give (e)   (e) ☐
- Divide (e) by the number of chapters to give (f)   (f) ☐
- Set about studying each chapter in the time represented by (f), following the key study steps in the order suggested by your particular learning style

This is your personal **study plan**.

INTRODUCTION

Short of time?

Whatever your objectives, standards or style, you may find you simply do not have the time available to follow all the key study steps for each chapter, however you adapt them for your particular learning style. If this is the case, follow the skim study technique below (the icons in the Study Text will help you to do this).

Skim study technique

Study the chapters in the order you find them in the Study Text. For each chapter, follow the key study steps 1–2, and then skim-read through step 3. Jump to step 9, and then go back to steps 4–5. Follow through step 7, and prepare outline Answers to the Action Programme (step 8). Try the Quick Quiz (step 10), following up any items you can't answer, then do a plan for the illustrative question (step 11), comparing it against our answers. You should probably still follow step 6 (note-taking).

Moving on...

However you study, when you are ready to embark on the practice and revision phase of the BPP Effective Study Package, you should still refer back to this Study Text:

- As a source of **reference** (you should find the list of key concepts and the index particularly helpful for this)
- As a **refresher** (the Chapter Roundups and Quick Quizzes help you here)

A note on pronouns

On occasions in this Study Text, 'he' is used for 'he or she', 'him' for 'him or her' and so forth. Whilst we try to avoid this practice it is sometimes necessary for reasons of style. No prejudice or stereotyping accounting to sex is intended or assumed.

Syllabus

Aims and objectives

The *Marketing Environment* module equips participants to explain the nature of the marketing environment and its relevance for organisations and marketing practice. It provides knowledge of marketing information and its use in organisations, particularly in its application in the strategy and marketing planning processes. It aims to provide participants with a working knowledge of organisations and the various influences of their wider environments.

Participants will not be expected to have any prior qualifications or experience in a marketing role.

Learning outcomes

Participants will be able to:

- Distinguish between the types of organisation within the public, private and voluntary sectors, and understand their objectives and the influences upon them.

- Explain the main elements of an organisation's marketing environment and discuss the significance of current and future environmental challenges.

- Describe the interactions between the main elements of the marketing environment.

- Assess the potential impact on an organisation of key trends in the social, technical, economic, environmental, political, legal and ethical environments.

- Demonstrate an understanding of an organisation's micro-environment.

- Explain the process for collecting information about the marketing environment from relevant primary and secondary sources.

- Compare and contrast various techniques for collecting information about the marketing environment.

Knowledge and skill requirements

Element 1: The nature of the organisation and the impact of its environment (15%)	
1.1	Demonstrate a broad appreciation of the internal environment.
1.2	Explain the classification of private, public and voluntary organisations, their legal status and operational characteristics.
1.3	Assess comparative strengths and weaknesses of small/medium and large/global sized organisations.
1.4	State the meaning and importance of an organisation's mission and explain the nature and significance of the objectives pursued.
1.5	Identify the internal and external influences on the formulation of objectives and specify the key drivers for organisational change.
1.6	Explain the nature of open systems and the interface between organisations and their marketing environment.
1.7	Represent the organisation as an open system responding to changing environmental conditions.
1.8	Demonstrate the dynamic and complex nature of environmental change and its importance to the development of marketing strategy and planning.
1.9	Appreciate the potential significance of emerging environmental challenges to effective marketing in the present and the future.

Element 2: The micro-environment (20%)	
2.1	Describe the external and internal stakeholders that constitute the micro-environment within which organisations operate and their importance to the marketing process.
2.2	Explain the nature of the interactions between the organisation and its various stakeholders.
2.3	Demonstrate an awareness of key internal and external sources of information on the micro-environment.
2.4	Explain the significance of the range of pressure groups interested in the organisation and their potential impacts.
2.5	Specify the role of marketing in managing these pressure groups.
2.6	Explain the importance of monitoring competitors and industries and how the organisation assesses the strategic and marketing implications.
2.7	Examine the impact of competition policies on the organisation and its marketing environment.

INTRODUCTION

Element 3: The macro-environment (50%)	
3.1	Appreciate the importance of the macro-environment to the marketing process.
3.2	Awareness of key sources of information on the macro-environment.
3.3	Explain the social, demographic and cultural environments and, in general terms, their influence on and implications for marketing.
3.4	Explain the economic and international environments and, in general terms, their influence on and implications for marketing.
3.5	Explain the political and legislative environments and, in general terms, their influence on and implications for marketing.
3.6	Explain the natural environment and, in general terms, its influence on and implications for marketing.
3.7	Explain the importance of the technical and information environments and their actual and potential impacts on organisations, employment, marketing and communications.
3.8	Assess the potential significance of environmental challenges to marketing in the future: e.g. globalisation; single currency; information communication technology; and environmental decline.

Element 4: Environmental information systems (15%)	
4.1	Explain why information is important to organisations.
4.2	Explain the concept of a marketing information system and its key role in effective marketing decision-making.
4.3	Explain the importance of marketing research and the information benefits it can provide.
4.4	Identify key sources of internal and external information.
4.5	Utilise, interpret and present secondary and primary data in identifying environmental trends and estimating current demand.
4.6	Explain the techniques available for forecasting future demands and coping with the challenge of environmental change.
4.7	Explain the importance of information systems the continuing impact of new technologies.

Related skills for marketers

There is only so much that a syllabus can include. The syllabus itself is designed to cover the knowledge and skills highlighted by research as core to professional marketers in organisations. However, marketing is performed in an organisational context so there are other broader business and organisational skills that marketing professionals should also posses. The 'key skills for marketers' are therefore an essential part of armoury of the 'complete marketer' in today's organisations. They have been identified from research carried out in organisations where marketers are working.

'Key skills for marketers' are areas of knowledge and competency common to business professionals. They fall outside the CIM's syllabus, providing underpinning knowledge and skills. As such they will be treated as systemic to all marketing activities, rather than subjects treated independently in their turn. While it is not intended that the key skills are formally taught as part of programmes, it is expected that tutors will encourage participants to demonstrate the application of relevant key skills through activities, assignments and discussions during learning.

Using ICT and the Internet

Planning and using different sources to search for and select information; explore, develop and exchange information and derive new information; and present information including text, numbers and images.

Using financial information and metrics

Planning and interpreting information from different sources; carrying out calculations; and presenting and justifying findings.

Presenting information

Contributing to discussions; making a presentation; reading and synthesising information and writing different types of document.

Improving own learning and performance

Agreeing targets and planning how these will be met; using plans to meet targets; and reviewing progress.

Working with others

Planning work and agreeing objectives, responsibilities and working arrangements; seeking to establish and maintain co-operative working relationships; and reviewing work and agreeing ways of future collaborative work.

Problem solving

Exploring problems, comparing different ways of solving them and selecting options; planning and implementing options; and applying agreed methods for checking problems have been solved.

Applying business law

Identifying, applying and checking compliance with relevant law when undertaking marketing activities.

Assessment

CIM will normally offer two forms of assessment for this module from which centres or participants may choose: written examination and continuous assessment. CIM may also recognise, or make joint awards for, modules at an equivalent level undertaken with other professional marketing bodies and educational institutions.

Marketing journals

In addition to reading core and supplementary textbooks participants will be expected to acquire a knowledge and understanding of developments in contemporary marketing theory, practice and issues. The most appropriate sources of information for this include specialist magazines eg *Marketing*, *Marketing Week*, *Campaign* and *Revolution*; dedicated CIM publications eg *Marketing Business*; and business magazines and newspapers eg *The Economist*, *Management Today*, *Business Week*, *The Financial Times*, and the business pages and supplements of the quality press. A flavour of developments in academic marketing can be derived from the key marketing journals including:

- Admap
- European Journal of Marketing
- Journal of the Academy of Marketing Science
- Journal of Consumer Behaviour: An International Research Review
- Journal of Consumer Research
- Marketing Intelligence and Planning
- Journal of Marketing
- Journal of Marketing Management

Websites

The Chartered Institute of Marketing

www.cim.co.uk	CIM website with information and access to learning support for participants.
www.cim.co.uk/learningzone	Direct access to information and support materials for all levels of CIM qualification
www.cim.co.uk/tutors	Access for Tutors
www.shapetheagenda.com	Quarterly agenda paper from CIM

Publications online

www.ft.com	Extensive research resources across all industry sectors, with links to more specialist reports. (Charges may apply)
www.thetimes.co.uk	One of the best online versions of a quality newspaper.
www.economist.com	Useful links, and easily-searched archives of articles from back issues of the magazine.
www.mad.co.uk	Marketing Week magazine online.
www.brandrepublic.com	Marketing magazine online.
www.westburn.co.uk	Journal of Marketing Management online, the official Journal of the Academy of Marketing and Marketing Review.
http://smr.mit.edu/smr/	Free abstracts from Sloan Management Review articles
www.hbsp.harvard.edu	Free abstracts from Harvard Business Review articles
www.ecommercetimes.com	Daily enews on the latest ebusiness developments
www.cim.co.uk/knowledgehub	3000 full text journals titles are available to members via the Knowledge Hub – includes the range of titles above - embargoes may apply.
www.cim.co.uk/cuttingedge	Weekly round up of marketing news (available to CIM members) plus list of awards and forthcoming marketing events.

Sources of useful information

www.1to1.com	The Peppers and Rogers One-to-One Marketing site which contains useful information about the tools and techniques of relationship marketing
www.balancetime.com	The Productivity Institute provides free articles, a time management email newsletter, and other resources to improve personal productivity
www.bbc.co.uk	The Learning Zone at BBC Education contains extensive educational resources, including the video, CD Rom, ability to watch TV programmes such as the News online, at your convenience, after they have been screened
www.busreslab.com	Useful specimen online questionnaires to measure customer satisfaction levels and tips on effective Internet marketing research
www.lifelonglearning.co.uk	Encourages and promotes Lifelong Learning through press releases, free articles, useful links and progress reports on the development of the University for Industry (UFI)
www.marketresearch.org.uk	The Market Research Society. Contains useful material on the nature of research, choosing an agency, ethical standards and codes of conduct for research practice
www.nielsen-netratings.com	Details the current levels of banner advertising activity, including the creative content of the ten most popular banners each week (within Top Rankings area)
www.open.ac.uk	Some good Open University videos available for a broad range of subjects
www.direct.gov.uk	Gateway to a wide range of UK government information

INTRODUCTION

www.srg.co.uk	The Self Renewal Group – provides useful tips on managing your time, leading others, managing human resources, motivating others etc
www.statistics.gov.uk	Detailed information on a variety of consumer demographics from the Government Statistics Office
www.durlacher.com	The latest research on business use of the Internet, often with extensive free reports
www.cyberatlas.com	Regular updates on the latest Internet developments from a business perspective
http://ecommerce.vanderbilt.edu	eLab is a corporate sponsored research centre at the Owen Graduate School of Management, Vanderbilt University
www.kpmg.co.uk	The major consultancy company websites contain useful research reports, often free of charge
www.ey.com/uk	
www.pwcglobal.com	PricewaterhouseCoopers
http://web.mit.edu	Massachusetts Institute of Technology site has extensive research resources
www.adassoc.org.uk	Advertising Association
www.dma.org.uk	The Direct Marketing Association
www.theidm.co.uk	Institute of Direct Marketing
www.export.org.uk	Institute of Export
www.bl.uk	The British Library, with one of the most extensive book collections in the world
www.managers.org.uk	Chartered Management Institute
www.cipd.co.uk	Chartered Institute of Personnel and Development
www.emerald-library.com	Article abstracts on a range of business topics (fees apply)
www.w3.org	An organisation responsible for defining worldwide standards for the Internet

Case studies

www.1800flowers.com	Flower and gift delivery service that allows customers to specify key dates when they request the firm to send them a reminder, together with an invitation to send a gift
www.amazon.co.uk	Classic example of how Internet technology can be harnessed to provide innovative customer service
www.broadvision.com	Broadvision specialises in customer 'personalisation' software. The site contains many useful case studies showing how communicating through the Internet allow you to find out more about your customers
www.doubleclick.net	DoubleClick offers advertisers the ability to target their advertisements on the web through sourcing of specific interest groups, ad display only at certain times of the day, or at particular geographic locations, or on certain types of hardware
www.facetime.com	Good example of a site that overcomes the impersonal nature of the Internet by allowing the establishment of real time links with a customer service representative
www.hotcoupons.com	Site visitors can key in their postcode to receive local promotions, and advertisers can post their offers on the site using a specially designed software package
www.superbrands.org	Access to case studies on international brands

The Exam Paper

Format of the paper

Number of marks

Part A: A case study or scenario
Compulsory multi-part question relating to the case study   40
(Answer generally required in report format)

Part B: Three questions from a choice of six (20 marks each)   60
(Answer generally required in essay format)
                                                                   ___
                                                                   100

Analysis of past papers

The analysis below shows the topics which have been examined since the new syllabus was introduced.

December 2006

Part A (compulsory question worth 40 marks)

1. Water supply is a critical problem for developed and developing countries alike, although it presents a particular challenge to developing economies.

   (a) Define terms: charitable organisation; economic growth; export subsidies; global warming; lifestyle changes

   (b) Explain why opening up international trade would benefit a developing economy more effectively than debt relief

   (c) Explain why water demand increases faster than supply. Describe forecasting method for water supply/demand prediction

   (d) Compare effectiveness of regulation, persuasion, incentives in reducing demand

Part B (three questions, 20 marks each)

2. Example of: organisation's legal form/status; mission statement; internal environment; interrelationship with external environment; drivers for change.

3. Notes on: change in the mobile phone sector; nature of competition in the market and one preferred strategic response.

4. Information, client needs and fundraising issues for a charitable organisation caring for the elderly.

5. For a government agency/department of your choice, define: connected stakeholder, pressure group, market research; and analyse implications of each.

6. Explain challenge of technical/information environment for mail order company. Assess impact of recent developments.

7. From data given: draw a graph of sales growth; comment on accuracy of forecasting; discuss variables in qualitative forecast of future sales (in housing market).

What the examiner said

- This paper embraced the new 'generic marking' approach: 10% allocated to format and presentation; 45% to conceptual content; 30% for application; and just 15% to the more difficult

INTRODUCTION

area of evaluation and recommendations. This should guide candidates' priorities: marks for format and application alone give a solid platform for an overall mark.

- The key to an A/B grade paper was context, application and a very careful reading of the question requirements.
- The ability to justify points with examples and explanations is the key to very high marks.
- Weaker candidates failed to earn format marks by ignoring the use of grids for comparisons, or overlooking instructions for report, bullet point or graph format.
- Other general weaknesses include: lack of contextual detail, failure to read the question carefully, undeveloped repetition of case materials, and waffle rather than focus.

More specific comments will be noted in Exam Tips throughout the Text.

June 2006

Part A (compulsory question worth 40 marks)

1 An international airline is an example of a business under pressure from environmental pressure groups and public concern about carbon dioxide emissions and global climate change.

    (a)   Explain terms: taxation; voluntary regulation; globalisation; new energy technologies; teleconferencing

    (b)   Identify environmental pressure groups. Concerns of pressure groups and other stakeholders. Management of concerns through the marketing mix

    (c)   Forecasting techniques used to predict the impact of environmental change

    (d)   Impacts on marketing environment of implementing Kyoto Protocol

Part B (three questions, 20 marks each)

2 Importance of 'quality' information. Elements of effective Mk1S and benefits for competitive position.

3 Purpose of mission statement. External influences on organisational objectives. Promotional opportunities to change organisation image.

4 Arguments for/against discounted pricing through supermarket chain.

5 Notes for presentation on: importance/benefits of continuous marketing research; sources of info re micro environment.

6 Impact of social environment changes on demand for tourism. Tactics to stimulate demand.

7 Multinational food manufacturer as an open system. Effects of one opportunity and threat in macro environment.

What the examiner said

- Better scripts had a good structure: they addressed the question in a logical and ordered manner, and developed and gave examples of points. (Formal report format was generally not expected or required: don't waste time on it unless specifically asked.)
- Higher grade answers proposed appropriate marketing actions and backed them up with concise justifications. They set their answers in the required context, and used practical and topical examples.
- There are still weaknesses in reading questions carefully and addressing the 'keywords' and contexts set. Careful attention to topic keywords keeps answers relevant – and is crucial in deciding which optional questions you are best able to attempt.

INTRODUCTION

- Many candidates leave the compulsory question until last and, through poor time management, fail to do it justice. This is a critical element in passing the overall examination: plan to complete all four questions!
- Crucial marks were available simply for context and definition of key terms: do not neglect these aspects.

More specific comments will be noted in Exam Tips throughout the Text.

December 2005

Part A (compulsory question worth 40 marks)

1 Software developer Microsoft pursues aggressive competitive strategies which have exposed it to legal scrutiny and security attacks.

   (a) Significance of: monopoly partner; unfair competition; barriers to entry; patents and copyright
   (b) Impact of competition policies on marketing approach
   (c) Open/closed savings and open/closed systems
   (d) Explain corporate objectives

Part B (three questions, 20 marks each)

2 Strengths/weaknesses of voluntary or public sector organisation. Small v large business marketing advantages

3 Stakeholder/shareholder. Stakeholder group in cosmetics industry. Influence on marketing approach

4 Notes on: legal regulation; consumer protection; non-litigation to resolve disputes; role of government in legislative environment

5 Business cycle in construction industry. Forecasting timing point in business cycle. Need to understand business cycle

6 Macro-environmental challenges for an insurance company, and marketing action plan to overcome them

7 Primary/secondary, internal/external data. Contribution of MkIS to office equipment wholesaler. Sources of info to forecast supply/demand

What the examiner said

- Candidates should not waste time writing answers in report or memo format unless specifically required to so do!
- Answers need to be planned and developed with greater focus on answering all parts of the question in a balanced fashion.
- Attention must be given to topic keywords and instruction keywords, in order to avoid answering more than is required (eg. explain TWO terms out of four, or discuss the voluntary OR public sector – *not* compare the two).
- Specific marks are allocated to *contextualisation*: relating the question to the specific circumstances of the case study, and the firms or sectors referred to in each of the optional questions.
- *Definition* of key terms used in the question, where appropriate, earn at least 1 mark, whether formally required or not.

INTRODUCTION

- The ability to justify points by using concise practical *examples* is one of the ways to achieving high marks.

More specific comments will be noted in Exam Tips throughout the Text.

June 2005

Part A (compulsory question worth 40 marks)

1 the global marketing environment is vulnerable to risk and threats, including the SARS virus.
   - (a) Trade liberalisation and the case for expanded international trade
   - (b) SARS-like outbreak on a cruise line: forecasting techniques; impacts; marketing response
   - (c) Factors in economic growth rate; sources of info to monitor growth
   - (d) Raising stakeholder confidence, for tourism in China.

Part B (three questions, 20 marks each)

2 Objectives of public/private/voluntary sector. Issues changing business objectives

3 Interaction with stakeholders (travel/tourism sector). Use of pressure group for marketing advantage

4 Fragmented/concentrated industry. Competitor monitoring in a concentrated industry

5 Economic/technical/natural environments in an open system. Natural environment implications for a car manufacturer

6 Concept of MkIS. Impact of e-B2B, web, mobile communications

7 Implications of: sensing systems; market research; real-time on-line info; environmental audits; trade sources (within environmental info system)

What the examiner said

- Where organisational *context* was selected or related to, candidates produced a fuller and much more convincing answer.

- Increased reference to relevant academics and practitioners, including the use of practical examples, is welcome: this is the way to very high marks.

- Candidates must avoid forcing models which they know well (such as PESTLE or Porter's five forces) into answers where they are not relevant!

- Don't waste time providing answers in report format where not asked to do so (the examiner sees the headings/introductions etc as 'passing' and does not award them marks) – or *failing* to use the formats specified (brief, bullet point list etc).

December 2004

Part A (compulsory question worth 40 marks)

1. An international engineering, logistics and industrial equipment company has diversified its product portfolio and is considering moving into children's games.

    (a) Use of branding to develop the business
    (b) Outline marketing plan for new board game
    (c) Use of marketing mix to support the product

Part B (three questions, 20 marks each)

2. Unique characteristics of services affecting marketing. Role of people in providing customer value

3. Benefits of marketing to business organisations, consumers, society. Ethical and social responsibility issues

4. Importance of new products to household cleaning products manufacturer. Stages of new product development process

5. Promotional tools in FMCG market. Factors influencing choice of tools

6. Environmental factors in international soft drinks marketing. Effects on marketing mix

7. Importance of relationship marketing in consumer services. Role of ICT in maintaining long-term relationships.

June 2004

Part A (compulsory question worth 40 marks)

1. An international food company has introduced a new brand of cheese, which has had a short product life cycle, and is vulnerable to price pressure.

    (a) Market orientation and its importance
    (b) Adapting marketing mix for decline stage of product life cycle
    (c) Suggest consumer research methods to explore brand's lack of success

Part B (three questions, 20 marks each)

2. Segmentation, targeting and positioning. Evaluating commercial attractiveness of a market segment

3. SWOT and Ansoff. Uses in marketing planning

4. Marketing planning process. Marketing audit as appraisal of external environment

5. Use of technology in marketing communications. Different tools for B2B and B2C product launch

6. Selecting a market channel for a new FMCG. Advantages/disadvantages of Internet as direct channel

7. Approaching pricing decisions for a car manufacturer. Impact of Internet on price decisions.

INTRODUCTION

December 2003

Part A (compulsory question worth 40 marks)

1   Macdonalds

    (a)   Research methods and information sources
    (b)   Environmental analysis
    (c)   Legal environment
    (d)   Cultural preference

Part B (three questions, 20 marks each)

2   Dynamic and complex changes, impact on marketing strategy and planning
3   Customer and employee stakeholders
4   Impact on natural environment of political developments and technological breakthroughs
5   Marketing in public sector: marketing research, marketing information system, Delphi technique
6   Developments in technology, competitor environment, suppliers, government intervention
7   Macro and micro environment of a voluntary organisation

June 2003

Part A (compulsory question worth 40 marks)

1   Report for a travel agency on the global cruise market

    (a)   Forecasting methods
    (b)   Social and demographic trends
    (c)   Two alternative scenarios
    (d)   Evaluation of pressure group concerns

Part B (three questions, 20 marks each)

2   Voluntary sector objectives, stakeholders and culture
3   Pressure groups
4   ICT and competitive advantage in the car industry
5   The business cycle
6   The international environment
7   Marketing information system

December 2002

Part A (compulsory question worth 40 marks)

1   Enron

    (a)   Explanation of terms
    (b)   Lobbying
    (c)   Online trading
    (d)   Strengths and weaknesses of larger organisations

Part B (three questions, 20 marks each)

2   Open systems; Porter's five force analysis
3   Public sector v private sector marketing environment
4   Natural, international and cultural environments
5   Economic growth
6   Teleconferencing, deregulation green taxes, tariff cuts
7   Expansion of a business

Specimen paper

Part A

1. Extract from a book about the environment

    (a) Explain terms
    (b) Private sector objectives
    (c) Control
    (d) Stakeholder groups

Part B

2. Monitoring environment

3. Social or lifestyle trends

4. Government economic objectives and indicators

The Specimen paper and BPP's suggested answers are reproduced at the back of the Study Text.

Guide to the assignment route

- Aims and objectives of this guide
- Introduction
- Assignment route, structure and process
- Preparing for assignments: general guide
- Presentation
- Time management
- Tips for writing assignments
- Writing reports
- Resources to support assignment based assessment

Aims and objectives of this guide to the assignment route

- To understand the scope and structure of the route process
- To consider the benefits of learning through the assignment route
- To assist students in preparation of their assignments
- To consider the range of communication options available to students
- To look at the range of potential assignment areas that assignments may challenge
- To examine the purpose and benefits of reflective practice
- To assist with time-management within the assignment process

Introduction

At time of writing, there are over 80 CIM Approved Study Centres that offer the assignment route option as an alternative to examinations. This change in direction and flexibility in assessment was externally driven by industry, students and tutors alike, all of whom wanted a test of practical skills as well as a knowledge-based approach to learning.

At Stage 1, all modules are available via this assignment route. The assignment route is however optional, and examinations are still available. This will of course depend upon the nature of delivery within your chosen Study Centre.

Clearly, all of the Stage 1 subject areas lend themselves to assignment-based learning, due to their practical nature. The assignments that you will undertake provide you with an opportunity to be **creative in approach and in presentation.** They enable you to give a true demonstration of your marketing ability in a way that perhaps might be inhibited in a traditional examination situation.

The assignment route offers you considerable scope to produce work that provides existing and future **employers** with **evidence** of your **ability.** It offers you a **portfolio** of evidence which demonstrates your abilities and your willingness to develop continually your knowledge and skills. It will also, ultimately, help you frame your continuing professional development in the future.

It does not matter what type of organisation you are from, large or small, as you will find substantial benefit in this approach to learning. In some cases, students have made their own organisation central to their assessment and produced work to support their organisation's activities, resulting in subsequent recognition and promotion: a success story for this approach.

So, using your own organisation can be beneficial (especially if your employer sponsors you). However, it is equally valid to use a different organisation, as long as you are familiar enough with it to base your assignments on it. This is particularly useful if you are between jobs, taking time out, returning to employment or studying at university or college.

INTRODUCTION

To take the assignment route option, you are required to register with a CIM Accredited Study Centre (ie a college, university, or distance learning provider). **Currently you would be unable to take the assignment route option as an independent learner**. If in doubt you should contact the CIM Education Division, the awarding body, who will provide you with a list of local Accredited Centres offering the Assignment Route.

Structure and process

The **assignments** that you will undertake during your studies are normally set **by CIM centrally** and not usually by the study centre. All assignments are validated to ensure a structured, consistent, approach. This standardised approach to assessment enables external organisations to interpret the results on a consistent basis.

Each module at Stage 1 has one assignment, with four separate elements within it. This is broken down as follows.

- The **Core Section** is compulsory and worth 40% of your total mark.

- The **Elective Section** has four options, from which you must complete **two**. Each of these options is worth 25% of your total mark. Please note here that it is likely that in some Study Centres the option may be chosen for you. This is common practice and is done in order to maximise resources and support provided to students.

- The **Reflective Statement** is also compulsory. It is worth 10%. It should reflect what you feel about your learning experience during the module and how that learning has helped you in your career both now and in the future.

The purpose of each assignment is to enable you to demonstrate your ability to research, analyse and problem-solve in a range of different situations. You will be expected to approach your assignment work from a professional marketer's perspective, addressing the assignment brief directly, and undertaking the tasks required. Each assignment will relate directly to the syllabus module and will be applied against the content of the syllabus.

All of the assignments clearly indicate the links with the syllabus and the assignment weighting (ie the contribution each assignment makes to your overall marks).

Once your assignments have been completed, they will be marked by your accredited centre, and then **moderated** by a CIM External Moderator. When all the assignments have been marked, they are sent to CIM for further moderation. After this, all marks are forwarded to you by CIM (not your centre) in the form of an examination result. Your **centre** will be able to you provide you with some written feedback on overall performance, but **will not** provide you with any detailed mark breakdown.

Preparing for assignments: general guide

The whole purpose of this guide is to assist you in presenting your assessment professionally, both in terms of presentation skills and overall content. In many of the assignments, marks are awarded for presentation and coherence. It might therefore be helpful to consider how best to present your assignment. Here you should consider issues of detail, protocol and the range of communications that could be called upon within the assignment.

INTRODUCTION

Presentation of the assignment

You should always ensure that you prepare two copies of your assignment, keeping a soft copy on disc. On occasions assignments go missing, or second copies are required by CIM.

- Each assignment should be clearly marked up with your name, your study centre, your CIM Student registration number and ultimately at the end of the assignment a word count. The assignment should also be word-processed.

- The assignment presentation format should directly meet the requirements of the assignment brief, (ie reports and presentations are the most called for communication formats). You **must** ensure that you assignment does not appear to be an extended essay. If it does, you will lose marks.

- The word limit will be included in the assignment brief. These are specified by CIM and must be adhered to.

- Appendices should clearly link to the assignment and can be attached as supporting documentation at the end of the report. However failure to reference them by number (eg Appendix 1) within the report and also marked up on the Appendix itself will lose you marks. Only use an Appendix if it is essential and clearly adds value to the overall assignment. The Appendix is not a waste bin for all the materials you have come across in your research, or a way of making your assignment seem somewhat heavier and more impressive than it is.

Time management for assignments

One of the biggest challenges we all seem to face day-to-day is that of managing time. When studying, that challenge seems to grow increasingly difficult, requiring a balance between work, home, family, social life and study life. It is therefore of pivotal importance to your own success for you to plan wisely the limited amount of time you have available.

Step 1   Find out how much time you have

Ensure that you are fully aware of how long your module lasts, and the final deadline. If you are studying a module from September to December, it is likely that you will have only 10-12 weeks in which to complete your assignments. This means that you will be preparing assignment work continuously throughout the course.

Step 2   Plan your time

Essentially you need to **work backwards** from the final deadline, submission date, and schedule your work around the possible time lines. Clearly if you have only 10-12 weeks available to complete three assignments, you will need to allocate a block of hours in the final stages of the module to ensure that all of your assignments are in on time. This will be critical as all assignments will be sent to CIM by a set day. Late submissions will not be accepted and no extensions will be awarded. Students who do not submit will be treated as a 'no show' and will have to resubmit for the next period and undertake an alternative assignment.

Step 3   Set priorities

You should set priorities on a daily and weekly basis (not just for study, but for your life). There is no doubt that this mode of study needs commitment (and some sacrifices in the short term). When your achievements are recognised by colleagues, peers, friends and family, it will all feel worthwhile.

INTRODUCTION

Step 4   **Analyse activities and allocate time to them**

Consider the **range** of activities that you will need to undertake in order to complete the assignment and the **time** each might take. Remember, too, there will be a delay in asking for information and receiving it.

- Preparing terms of reference for the assignment, to include the following.
    1. A short title
    2. A brief outline of the assignment purpose and outcome
    3. Methodology – what methods you intend to use to carry out the required tasks
    4. Indication of any difficulties that have arisen in the duration of the assignment
    5. Time schedule
    6. Confidentiality – if the assignment includes confidential information ensure that this is clearly marked up and indicated on the assignment
    7. Literature and desk research undertaken

This should be achieved in one side of A4 paper.

- A literature search in order to undertake the necessary background reading and underpinning information that might support your assignment
- Writing letters and memos asking for information either internally or externally
- Designing questionnaires
- Undertaking surveys
- Analysis of data from questionnaires
- Secondary data search
- Preparation of first draft report

Always build in time to spare, to deal with the unexpected. This may reduce the pressure that you are faced with in meeting significant deadlines.

Warning!

The same principles apply to a student with 30 weeks to do the work. However, a word of warning is needed. Do not fall into the trap of leaving all of your work to the last minute. If you miss out important information or fail to reflect upon your work adequately or successfully you will be penalised for both. Therefore, time management is important whatever the duration of the course.

Tips for writing assignments

Everybody has a personal style, flair and tone when it comes to writing. However, no matter what your approach, you must ensure your assignment meets the **requirements of the brief** and so is comprehensible, coherent and cohesive in approach.

Think of preparing an assignment as preparing for an examination. Ultimately, the work you are undertaking results in an examination grade. Successful achievement of all four modules in a level results in a qualification.

INTRODUCTION

There are a number of positive steps that you can undertake in order to ensure that you make the best of your assignment presentation in order to maximise the marks available.

Step 1 Work to the brief

Ensure that you identify exactly what the assignment asks you to do.

- If it asks you to be a marketing manager, then immediately assume that role.
- If it asks you to prepare a report, then present a report, not an essay or a letter.
- Furthermore, if it asks for 2,500 words, then do not present 1,000 or 4,000 unless it is clearly justified, agreed with your tutor and a valid piece of work.

Identify whether the report should be **formal or informal**; who it should be **addressed to**; its **overall purpose** and its **potential use** and outcome. Understanding this will ensure that your assignment meets fully the requirements of the brief and addresses the key issues included within it.

Step 2 Addressing the tasks

It is of pivotal importance that you address **each** of the tasks within the assignment. **Many students fail to do this** and often overlook one of the tasks or indeed part of the tasks.

Many of the assignments will have two or three tasks, some will have even more. You should establish quite early on, which of the tasks:

- Require you to collect information
- Provides you with the framework of the assignment, i.e. the communication method.

Possible tasks will include the following.

- *Compare and contrast.* Take two different organisations and compare them side by side and consider the differences ie the **contrasts** between the two.

- *Carry out primary or secondary research.* Collect information to support your assignment and your subsequent decisions

- *Prepare a plan.* Some assignments will ask you to prepare a plan for an event or for a marketing activity – if so provide a step-by-step approach, a rationale, a time-line, make sure it is measurable and achievable. Make sure your actions are very specific and clearly explained. (Make sure your plan is SMART.)

- *Analyse a situation.* This will require you to collect information, consider its content and present an overall understanding of the situation as it exists. This might include looking at internal and external factors and how the current situation evolved.

- *Make recommendations.* The more advanced your get in your studies, the more likely it is that you will be required to make recommendations. Firstly **considering and evaluating your options** and then making justifiable **recommendations**, based on them.

- *Justify decisions.* You may be required to justify your decision or recommendations. This will require you to explain fully how you have arrived at as a result and to show why, supported by relevant information. In other words, you should not make decisions in a vacuum; as a marketer your decisions should always be informed by context.

INTRODUCTION

- *Prepare a presentation.* This speaks for itself. If you are required to prepare a presentation, ensure that you do so, preparing clearly defined PowerPoint or overhead slides that are not too crowded and that clearly express the points you are required to make.

- *Evaluate performance.* It is very likely that you will be asked to evaluate a campaign, a plan or even an event. You will therefore need to consider its strengths and weaknesses, why it succeeded or failed, the issues that have affected it, what can you learn from it and, importantly, how can you improve performance or sustain it in the future.

All of these points are likely requests included within a task. Ensure that you identify them clearly and address them as required.

Step 3 — Information search

Many students fail to realise the importance of collecting information to **support** and **underpin** their assignment work. However, it is vital that you demonstrate to your centre and to the CIM your ability to **establish information needs**, obtain **relevant information** and **utilise it sensibly** in order to arrive at appropriate decisions.

You should establish the nature of the information required, follow up possible sources, time involved in obtaining the information, gaps in information and the need for information.

Consider these factors very carefully. CIM are very keen that students are **seen** to collect information, **expand** their mind and consider the **breadth** and **depth** of the situation. In your *Personal Development Portfolio*, you have the opportunity to complete a **Resource Log**, to illustrate how you have expanded your knowledge to aid your personal development. You can record your additional reading and research in that log, and show how it has helped you with your portfolio and assignment work.

Step 4 — Develop an assignment plan

Your **assignment** needs to be structured and coherent, addressing the brief and presenting the facts as required by the tasks. The only way you can successfully achieve this is by **planning the structure** of your assignment in advance.

Earlier on in this unit, we looked at identifying your tasks and, working backwards from the release date, in order to manage time successfully. The structure and coherence of your assignment needs to be planned with similar signs.

In planning out the assignment, you should plan to include **all the relevant information as requested** and also you should plan for the use of models, diagrams and appendices where necessary.

Your plan should cover your:

- Introduction
- Content
- Main body of the assignment
- Summary
- Conclusions and recommendations where appropriate

Step 5 Prepare draft assignment

It is good practice to always produce a **first draft** of a report. You should use it to ensure that you have met the aims and objectives, assignment brief and tasks related to the actual assignment. A draft document provides you with scope for improvements, and enables you to check for accuracy, spelling, punctuation and use of English.

Step 6 Prepare final document

In the section headed 'Presentation of the Assignment' in this unit, there are a number of components that should always be in place at the beginning of the assignment documentation, including **labelling** of the assignment, **word counts**, **appendices** numbering and presentation method. Ensure that you **adhere to the guidelines presented**, or alternatively those suggested by your Study Centre.

Writing reports

Students often ask 'what do they mean by a report?' or 'what should the report format include?'.

There are a number of approaches to reports, formal or informal: some report formats are company specific and designed for internal use, rather than external reporting.

For continuous assessment process, you should stay with traditional formats.

Below is a suggested layout of a Management Report Document that might assist you when presenting your assignments. (Further guidance is given in Chapter 12 of this Text.)

- *A Title page* includes the title of the report, the author of the report and the receiver of the report
- *Acknowledgements* – this should highlight any help, support, or external information received and any extraordinary co-operation of individuals or organisations
- *Contents page* provides a clearly structured pathway of the contents of the report – page by page.
- *Executive summary* – a brief insight into purpose, nature and outcome of the report, in order that the outcome of the report can be quickly established
- *Main body of the report divided into sections, which are clearly labelled.* Suggested labelling would be on a numbered basis eg:
  - 1.0 Introduction
  - 1.1 Situation analysis
  - 1.1.1 External analysis
  - 1.1.2 Internal analysis
- *Conclusions* – draw the report to a conclusion, highlighting key points of importance, that will impact upon any recommendations that might be made
- *Recommendations* – clearly outline potential options and then recommendations. Where appropriate justify recommendations in order to substantiate your decision
- *Appendices* – ensure that you only use appendices that add value to the report. Ensure that they are numbered and referenced on a numbered basis within the text. If you are not going to reference it within the text, then it should not be there

INTRODUCTION

- *Bibliography* – while in a business environment a bibliography might not be necessary, for an **assignment-based report it is vital**. It provides an indication of the level of research, reading and collecting of relevant information that has taken place in order to fulfil the requirements of the assignment task. Where possible, and where relevant, you could provide academic references within the text, which should of course then provide the basis of your bibliography. References should realistically be listed alphabetically and in the following sequence

    - Author's name and edition of the text
    - Date of publication
    - Title and sub-title (where relevant)
    - Edition 1st, 2nd etc
    - Place of publication
    - Publisher
    - Series and individual volume number where appropriate.

Resources to support assignment based assessment

The aim of this guidance is to present you with a range of questions and issues that you should consider, based upon the assignment themes. The detail to support the questions can be found within your BPP Study Text and the 'Core Reading' recommended by CIM.

Additionally you will find useful support information within the CIM Student website www.cim.co.uk -: www.cimvirtualinstitute.com, where you can access a wide range of marketing information and case studies. You can also build your own workspace within the website so that you can quickly and easily access information specific to your professional study requirements. Other websites you might find useful for some of your assignment work include www.wnim.com - (What's New in Marketing) and also www.connectedinmarketing.com - another CIM website.

Other websites include:

www.mad.com	– Marketing Week
www.ft.com	– Financial Times
www.thetimes.com	– The Times newspaper
www.theeconomist.com	– The Economist magazine
www.marketing.haynet.com	– Marketing magazine
www.ecommercetimes.com	– Daily news on e-business developments
www.open.gov.uk	– Gateway to a wide range of UK government information
www.adassoc.org.uk	– The Advertising Association
www.marketresearch.org.uk	– The Marketing Research Society
www.amazon.com	– Online Book Shop
www.1800flowers.com	– Flower and delivery gift service
www.childreninneed.com	– Charitable organisation
www.comicrelief.com	– Charitable organisation
www.samaritans.org.uk	– Charitable organisation

xxix

INTRODUCTION

Part A
The organisation and its environment

Introduction to organisations

Chapter topic list

1. Organisations and their internal environment
2. Different types of organisation
3. Public sector organisations
4. Non-commercial organisations
5. Business organisations
6. Comparing different types of organisation

Syllabus content

- 1.1 Demonstrate a broad appreciation of the internal environment
- 1.2 Explain the classification of private, public and voluntary organisations, their legal status and operational characteristics
- 1.3 Assess comparative strengths and weaknesses of small/medium and large/global sized organisations

PART A   THE ORGANISATION AND ITS ENVIRONMENT

Introduction

This chapter is an overall introduction to the Study Text. We discuss the concept of the organisation and the similarities and differences between different types of organisation.

We start by showing what all organisations have in common and why there is a need for organisations. We introduce systems theory early on as it demonstrates how organisations differ from, but also relate to, the outside environment.

We then go on to discuss different types of organisation. You need to understand the differences between different types of organisation, particularly between **profit-making** and **non-profit-making** organisations and also the significance of the legal differences between organisations. The organisation structure will have a very significant impact upon marketing, since it affects the way organisations buy and supply goods.

Exam tip

The syllabus stresses the importance of communicating the concepts and implications of the marketing environment using a variety of relevant formats. Formats that may be requested in the exam include slides, notes for a talk, a checklist or a report. You must ensure that if you are asked for a particular format, you follow it; the examiner will not be impressed by an unstructured essay with long paragraphs if bullet point summaries (lists of several short points) have been requested. On the other hand, the examiner has complained, following 2005 sittings, that candidates waste time *adding* report or memo formats when this has not been requested! If no format is specified, a well-structured essay is the best option.

1 Organisations and their internal environment

FAST FORWARD

Organisations achieve results through the division of labour and co-operative efforts, which individuals cannot achieve alone.

Key concept

An **organisation** is a social arrangement for the controlled performance of collective goals.

Examples of organisations
A multinational company making and selling cars
An accountancy firm
A charity
A local authority
A trade union
An army
A political party

These organisations seem, on the surface, to be very different. They do different things and draw their resources from different sources. However, in contrast to other groups of people, such as the family, organisations have much in common.

They are social systems which:

- Are **preoccupied** with **performance**, and adherence to or improvement of standards
- Contain formal control systems
- Feature separation of tasks (or division of labour)
- Require an ordered environment (although this may not exist)
- Have a variety of objectives and goals, which the organisation exists to achieve

1.1 Why organisations exist

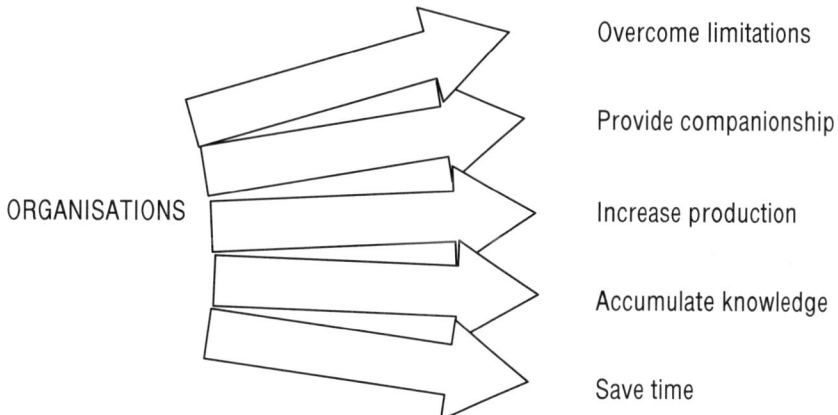

- Overcome limitations
- Provide companionship
- Increase production
- Accumulate knowledge
- Save time

1.2 Objectives

The relationship of individual and organisational objectives is very important.

(a) An organisation consists of people who **inter-react** with each other.

(b) The way in which people inter-react is **designed** and **ordered** by the **organisation** structure to achieve joint (organisational) objectives. Each individual has a view of what these organisational objectives are.

(c) Each person in the organisation has his or her own **personal objectives**.

(d) Organisational objectives must be **compatible** with the **personal objectives** of the individuals concerned if they are to be well-integrated members of the organisation.

1.3 Management's role

Management should:

- Recognise individuals' personal objectives
- Integrate individuals' objectives with those of the organisation
- Recognise individuals' different views of the organisation's objectives
- Integrate these different views
- Use human and material resources to achieve objectives most efficiently

1.4 Formal and informal organisations

FORMAL AND INFORMAL ORGANISATIONS	
Formal	**Informal**
• Formal constitution	• Spontaneous
• Planned division of responsibility	• Loose structure
• Procedures for personnel changes	• Difficult to determine membership
• Defined communication channels	• Flexibility
• Controlled by centres of power	• No apparent controls

Within every formal organisation there exists a complex informal organisation. The formal organisation is a prescribed structure of relationships and ideas. Informal organisation modifies this formal structure.

The informal organisation of a company is so important that a newcomer has to 'learn the ropes' before he can settle effectively into his job, and he must also become accepted by his fellow workers. Given an acceptable social atmosphere, the informal organisation:

(a) **Improves communications** by means of a 'bush telegraph' system

(b) **Helps co-ordinate** various individuals or departments and establishes unwritten methods for getting a job done. They may be more flexible and adaptable to required changes.

1.5 Authority, responsibility and power in organisations

Formal organisations need structures of authority and responsibility.

(a) **Authority**

Authority is the right to do something. In an organisation, it refers to the scope and amount of discretion given to a person to make decisions, by virtue of the position he or she holds in the organisation.

(b) **Responsibility**

Responsibility is the liability of a person to be called to account for exercising authority. It is a formal obligation to do something.

(c) **Accountability**

Accountability is the duty of an individual to report to a superior on how he has fulfilled his responsibilities.

(d) **Delegation**

Delegation is the process whereby a superior gives a subordinate the authority and responsibility to carry out a given aspect of the superior's own task. Delegation shapes the hierarchical structure of the formal organisation, where authority and responsibility are passed down the chain of command and accountability passes back up.

1.6 Organisation structure

Organisational *design or structure* implies a framework or mechanism with certain specific functions.

(a) **Linking**

The organisation links individuals in an established **network of relationships** so that authority, responsibility and communications can be controlled.

(b) **Grouping**

The organisation groups together the **tasks required** to fulfil the objectives of the organisation, and allocate them to suitable individuals or groups.

(c) **Authority**

Each individual or group is given the **authority** required to perform the allocated functions. The organisation controls behaviour and resources in the interests of the organisation as a whole.

(d) **Co-ordination**

The **objectives** and **activities** of separate units should be brought together, so that overall aims are achieved without gaps or overlaps in the flow of work required.

(e) **Facilitation**

Managers should **facilitate the flow of work**, information and other resources required, through planning, control and other systems.

1.7 The role of marketing

Key concept

Marketing is the management process responsible for identifying, anticipating and satisfying customer requirements profitably. (CIM)

Clearly the **customer** is at the centre of the definition. Marketing activity will depend on the requirements of **customers** and the **structure of markets**. It will take account of the longer-term factors affecting the customer base (such as population changes) or the market (such as technological factors).

However, as we shall see in Chapter 2, the marketer may be working for an organisation that is not primarily focused on the customer.

1.8 The internal environment

The 'internal environment' of a marketing organisation refers to all these interlinked sub-systems of the organisational system:

- The workforce/employees and employee relations
- Management and management 'style'
- Formal organisation structure
- Organisation culture (shared values and behaviours: 'the way we do things round here')
- The marketing role and interface
- Technology (equipment, systems and organisation of work)
- The internal value chain or processes

Exam tip

A question in December 2006 asked you to describe the internal environment of an organisation of your choice. The examiner's report noted that although this topic is seldom explicitly tested, it is part of the syllabus and deserves attention!

2 Different types of organisation

FAST FORWARD

Organisations can be analysed by **size, legal form** and **activity**.

WAYS OF CLASSIFYING ORGANISATIONS	
Ownership	Private and public sector
Control	Shareholders, managers and trustees
Activity	Retailers, manufacturers, hospitals
Legal structure	Partnership or limited company
Commercial or non-commercial objectives	Companies, non-profit making organisations, charities
Accountability	Shareholders, government
Sources of finance	Borrowing, the state, investments

Marketers need to be able to understand the effects of different types of organisation on **marketing operations**. Consider the following ways in which organisation structure can affect marketing.

(a) **Buyers**

Organisations are **buyers** of goods and services. A large multi-national is likely to buy in a very different way from a small sole trader. The large multi-national firm may have a substantial purchasing department, systems for assessing supplier reliability and a complex planning process. A small sole trader is unlikely to have such things.

(b) **Sellers**

Organisations are **suppliers** of goods and services. They need to respond to changes in consumer demand. The size, structure and resources of an organisation influence how quickly (if at all!) it is able to respond to marketing opportunities.

3 Public sector organisations

FAST FORWARD

Many **public sector organisations** have the primary goals of providing a service. A secondary goal is the efficiency and effectiveness with which resources are used.

Key concept

A **public sector organisation** is an organisation controlled directly and/or indirectly and/or funded by central and/or local government.

In most economies, ownership of organisations is vested either in the government or in private individuals and institutions. Governments make laws, and so provide the environment for activity in the private sector.

Some public sector organisations are supposed to have a commercial objective; others are not.

(a) Publicly-owned postal services will probably exist to **make a profit** out of mail services.
(b) The armed forces will not be profit-making organisations.
(c) Government departments provide services.

The distinguishing characteristics of the non-profit orientated public sector are as follows.

(a) The public sector can **command resources**.

(b) Ideas of **fairness** underpin service provision (for example, everybody should have the right to an education).

(c) The public sector is based on the idea of **equal rights**. Each individual should have the right of protection from invasion, and should be equal under the law.

Public sector organisations tend to have different **sources of revenue** from private sector organisations.

(a) Their revenue does not come from the sale of goods and services, but is **raised** directly from the **taxpayer**. It is then allocated towards socially desirable objectives.

(b) Revenue may be provided by **other public sector bodies**. Local authorities, for example, may derive some revenue from central government, some from local taxation.

(c) In the public sector, demand for services **cannot be rationed by charging a high price** (thereby restricting the number of people able to pay). Instead, the resources to provide services are restricted, and these restricted resources determine the volume of services provided.

Distinctions between the public and private sectors are becoming increasingly blurred. In particular, the marketing environment of each is becoming similar, as public services are exposed to greater competition.

3.1 Advantages and disadvantages of public sector organisations

Figure 1.1: Advantages and disadvantages of public sector organisations

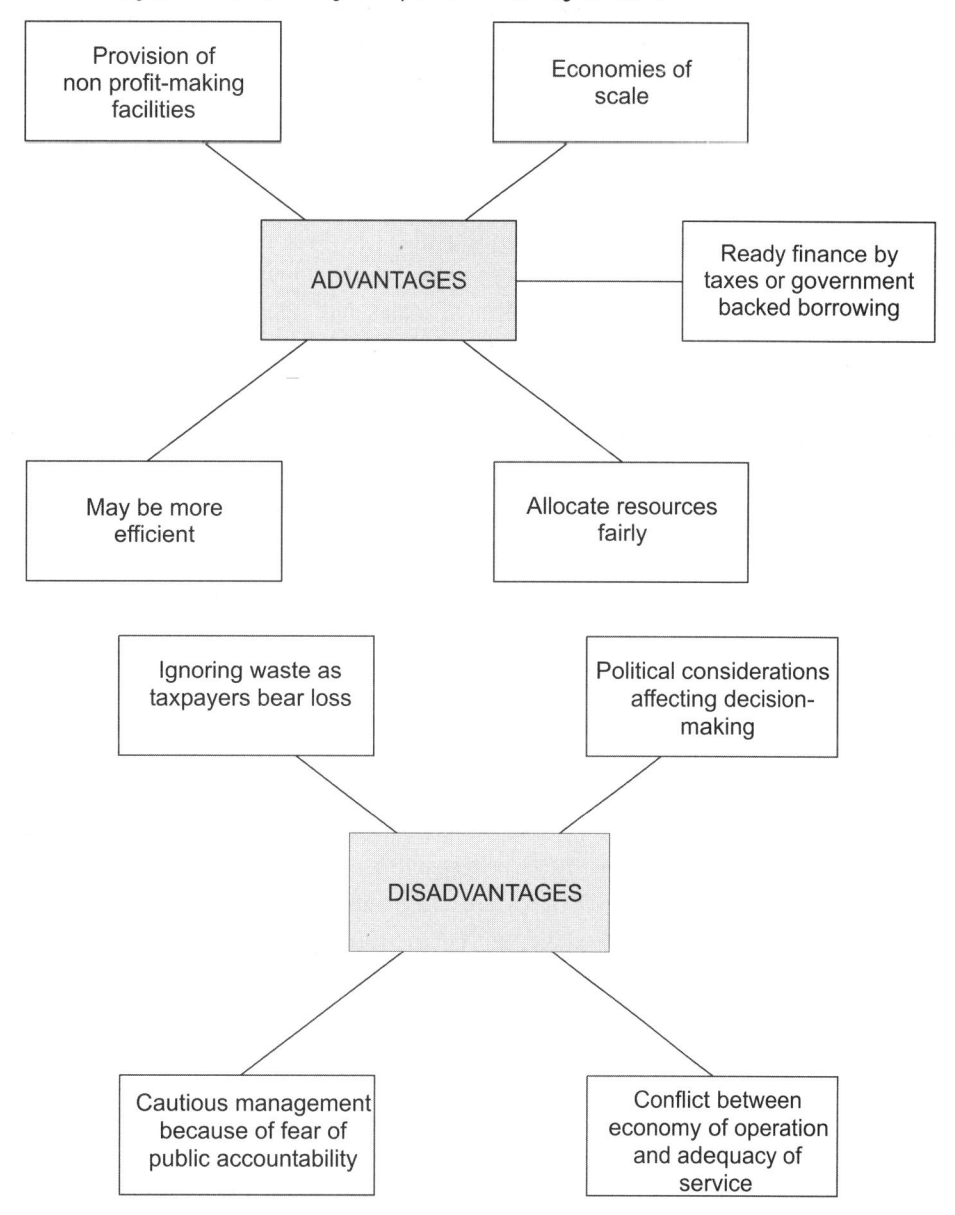

```
                Provision of                    Economies of
                non profit-making               scale
                facilities
                        \                   /
                         \                 /
                          \               /
                                                    Ready finance by
                          ADVANTAGES  ────────────  taxes or government
                                                    backed borrowing
                          /               \
                         /                 \
                        /                   \
                May be more                 Allocate resources
                efficient                   fairly


                Ignoring waste as           Political considerations
                taxpayers bear loss         affecting decision-
                                            making
                        \                   /
                         \                 /
                          \               /
                          DISADVANTAGES
                          /               \
                         /                 \
                        /                   \
                Cautious management         Conflict between
                because of fear of          economy of operation
                public accountability       and adequacy of
                                            service
```

3.2 Developments in the public sector

FAST FORWARD

> The boundaries between public and private sectors are altering with **privatisation** and the introduction of **market-based measures**.

Public sector bodies are ultimately accountable to the electorate. Four trends in the UK public sector are worthy of note.

(a) More public sector activities will be carried out away from the direct control of central government. Policy is determined by central government, but will be implemented by autonomous **executive agencies**, although such agencies are increasingly assuming a policy forming role also.

(b) Public bodies are more likely to become purchasers rather than providers of services. An obvious example is refuse collection. At one time directly managed by local authorities, this

PART A   THE ORGANISATION AND ITS ENVIRONMENT

      service is now often performed by private sector businesses on fixed-term contracts marked under **compulsory competitive tendering**.

(c) **Market-type structures** were introduced to public sector bodies by the 1979-1997 Conservative government in the UK. In the National Health Service internal market, hospitals have to compete for funds. Their immediate customers might have been **regional health authorities**, or general practitioners, who purchase services on behalf of the ultimate consumer of them, the patient.

(d) Full scale **privatisation** has been implemented in some industries. Public utilities such as the electricity and water industries have been privatised, meaning that overall ownership of the organisation has been transferred into private hands, usually via the issue of shares. These industries, however, are still subject to state regulation as many of them are monopolies or near-monopolies.

Public sector organisations all have an important **service element** to them. Many do not exist to make a profit, even though some are expected to cover at least a proportion of their costs through user fees.

Action Programme 1

Why should governments get involved in commercial activities?

Action Programme 2

In what areas of their activities will public sector organisations use marketing techniques?

Exam tip

> Exam questions in 2003, 2004 and 2005 have covered the similarities and the differences between marketing objectives in the public and private (and voluntary) sectors, or the strengths and weaknesses of public (or voluntary) sector organisations. A government agency or department (of your choice) was the focus of a question in 2006: you had to discuss various aspects of its marketing environment. Get to grips with this material!

4 Non-commercial organisations

FAST FORWARD

> Non-commercial organisations include trade unions, employers' organisations, professional associations, clubs and **charities**.

Some organisations do not exist to make a profit, but nor are they public services.

Some organisations make surpluses of revenue over expenditure resulting from activities such as running bars and dining rooms, insurance and sickness benefits, holiday clubs and savings clubs. The division and application of the surpluses depends on the organisation and its aims and objectives.

EXAMPLES OF NON-COMMERCIAL ORGANISATIONS	
Trade unions	Organisations of workers in trades or industries, protecting common interests, particularly pay and conditions
Employers' associations	Represent and promote business interests of their membership

1: INTRODUCTION TO ORGANISATIONS

EXAMPLES OF NON-COMMERCIAL ORGANISATIONS	
Motoring organisations	Provide services, particularly help with breakdowns
Professional associations	Membership requirements include passing exams and fulfilling ethical standards. May exercise control over professional practices and members' behaviour. Performance measured by prestige, value of qualifications
Charities	Have well-defined goals eg relieving poverty or suffering. Raise money by donations, charity shops and so on. Measure success by promoting beneficiaries' interests, raising public awareness and raising money

4.1 Strengths and limitations of non-commercial organisations

These vary widely but certain general features often occur (Figure 1.2).

Figure 1.2: Strengths and limitations of non-commercial organisations

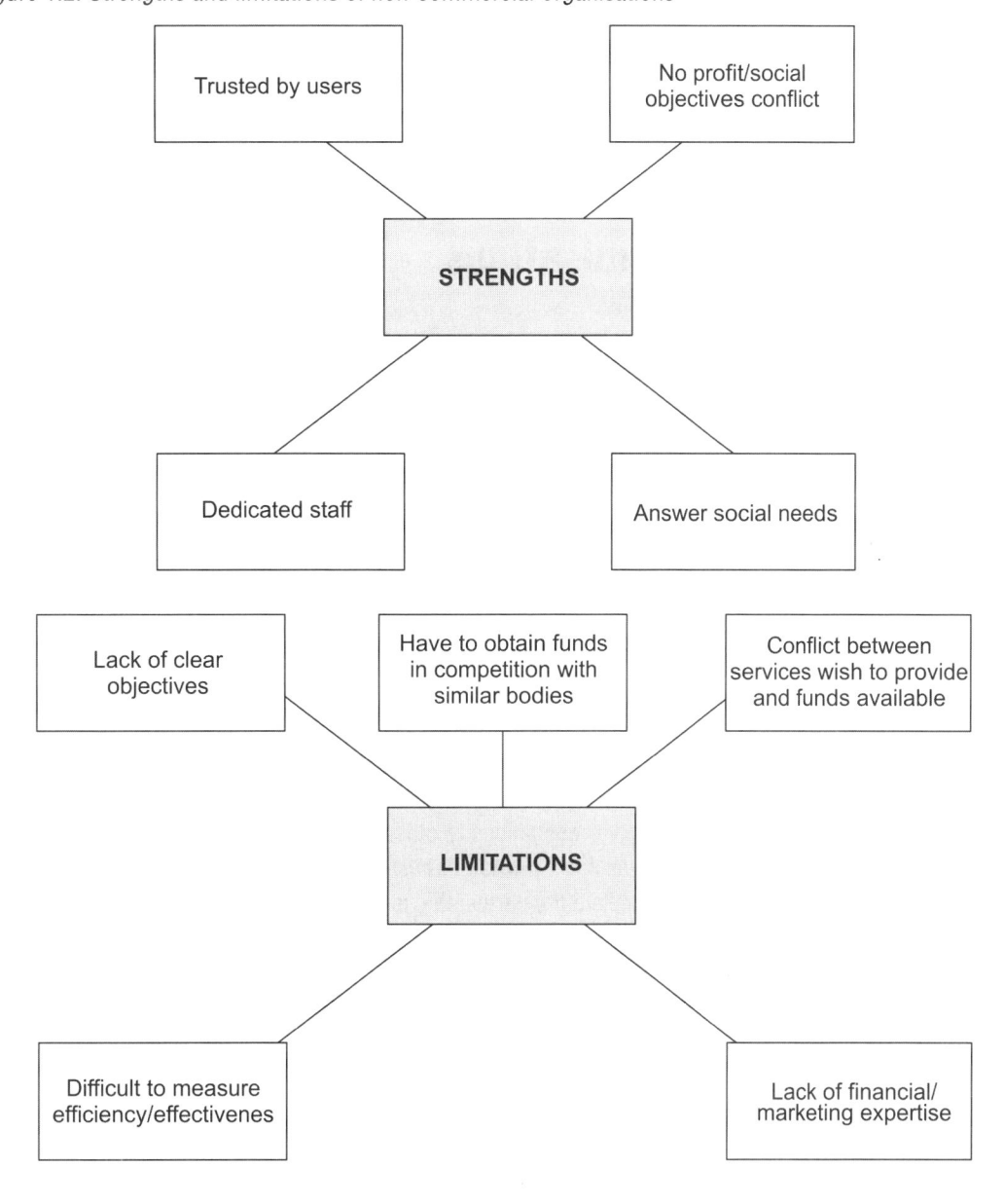

STRENGTHS
- Trusted by users
- No profit/social objectives conflict
- Dedicated staff
- Answer social needs

LIMITATIONS
- Lack of clear objectives
- Have to obtain funds in competition with similar bodies
- Conflict between services wish to provide and funds available
- Difficult to measure efficiency/effectivenes
- Lack of financial/marketing expertise

PART A   THE ORGANISATION AND ITS ENVIRONMENT

Action Programme 3

The Guidance Notes for this unit have highlighted the need for you to read a variety of publications, including Internet sources. We shall as a result have a number of Action Programmes throughout this Text which require research on the Internet.

As a start, look up the website of a major charity and consider how that charity is using its website to market itself to a person visiting the site for the first time.

We give the results of a review of the National Society for the Prevention of Cruelty to Children's website in the Action Programme Review at the end of the chapter.

[key skill for Marketers: Using ICT and the Internet]

The stakeholders of voluntary sector organisation (those who have an interest in the organisation's activities) will include members and donors. We consider stakeholders further in Chapter 5.

Exam tip

> Don't neglect voluntary organisations: questions were set on them, in both 2005 exams and in December 2006, when you were asked to discuss a range of environmental issues (client needs, information, fundraising) for an aged care charity.

5 Business organisations

FAST FORWARD

> Organisations have **goals**. Business organisations' primary goal is to provide a return on money invested. This they do by selling goods and services.

A **business organisation** exists to make a profit.

A key issue is the degree to which a business is a separate legal entity from its owners.

Key concepts

> A **sole tradership** is a business owned and run by one individual, perhaps employing one or two assistants and controlling their work. The individual's business and personal affairs are, for legal and tax purposes, identical.
>
> **Limited company** status, on the other hand, means that the business's debts and the personal debts of the business's owners (shareholders) are legally separate. The shareholders cannot be sued for the debts of the business unless they have given some personal guarantee. This is called **limited liability**.
>
> **Partnerships** are arrangements between individuals to carry on business in common with a view to profit. A partnership, however, involves obligations to others, and so a partnership will be governed by a partnership agreement. Unless it is a **limited liability partnership (LLP),** partners will be fully liable for debts and liabilities, for example if the partnership is sued.

Sole traderships and partnerships are concentrated in the small business sector. Most businesses of any size are limited companies. Some small businesses are limited companies, too, but often the owner must give a personal guarantee to the bank for loans to the business.

1: INTRODUCTION TO ORGANISATIONS

5.1 Sole traders

FAST FORWARD

Sole traderships and **partnerships** tend to be small. They have the advantage of privacy and flexibility, but the disadvantages of vulnerability and unlimited liability, except in the case of **limited liability partnerships (LLPs)**.

A sole trader owns and runs a business, contributes the capital to start the enterprise, runs it with or without employees, and earns the profits or stands the loss of the venture.

EXAMPLES OF SOLE TRADERS	
Retail	Local newsagents
Service industries	Plumbers, hairdressers
Manufacturing and craft industries	Tailoring

5.1.1 Advantages and disadvantages of being a sole trader

Figure 1.3: Advantages and disadvantages of sole tradership

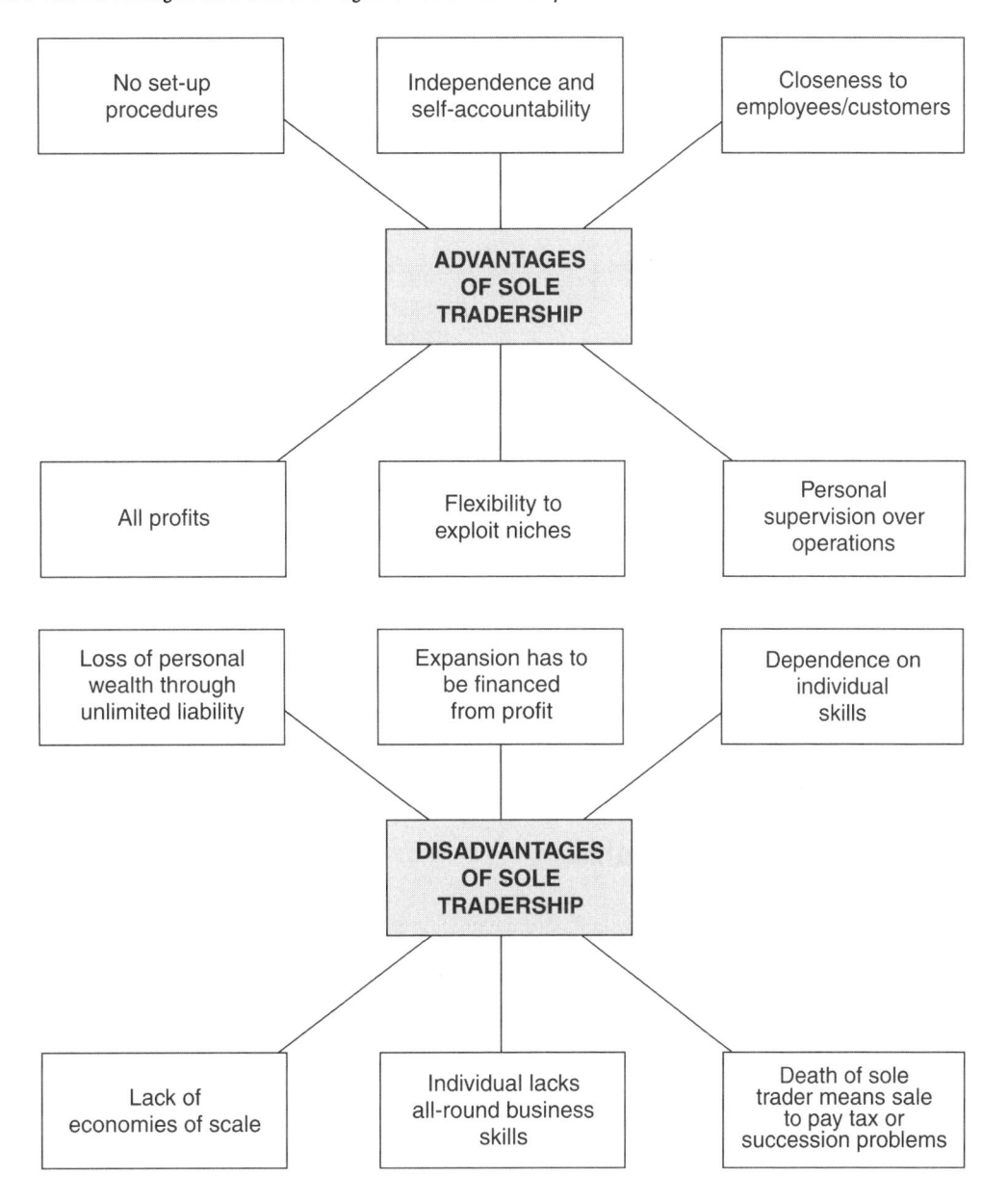

ADVANTAGES OF SOLE TRADERSHIP
- No set-up procedures
- Independence and self-accountability
- Closeness to employees/customers
- All profits
- Flexibility to exploit niches
- Personal supervision over operations

DISADVANTAGES OF SOLE TRADERSHIP
- Loss of personal wealth through unlimited liability
- Expansion has to be financed from profit
- Dependence on individual skills
- Lack of economies of scale
- Individual lacks all-round business skills
- Death of sole trader means sale to pay tax or succession problems

13

PART A   THE ORGANISATION AND ITS ENVIRONMENT

5.2 Partnerships

A partnership is an arrangement between two or more individuals to carry on a business on an agreed basis. Partnerships are found in similar fields to those operated by sole traders, where there are two or more joint owners, and in many professions. Many accountancy firms operate as Limited liability Partnerships (LLPs).

Figure 1.4: Advantages and disadvantages of partnership

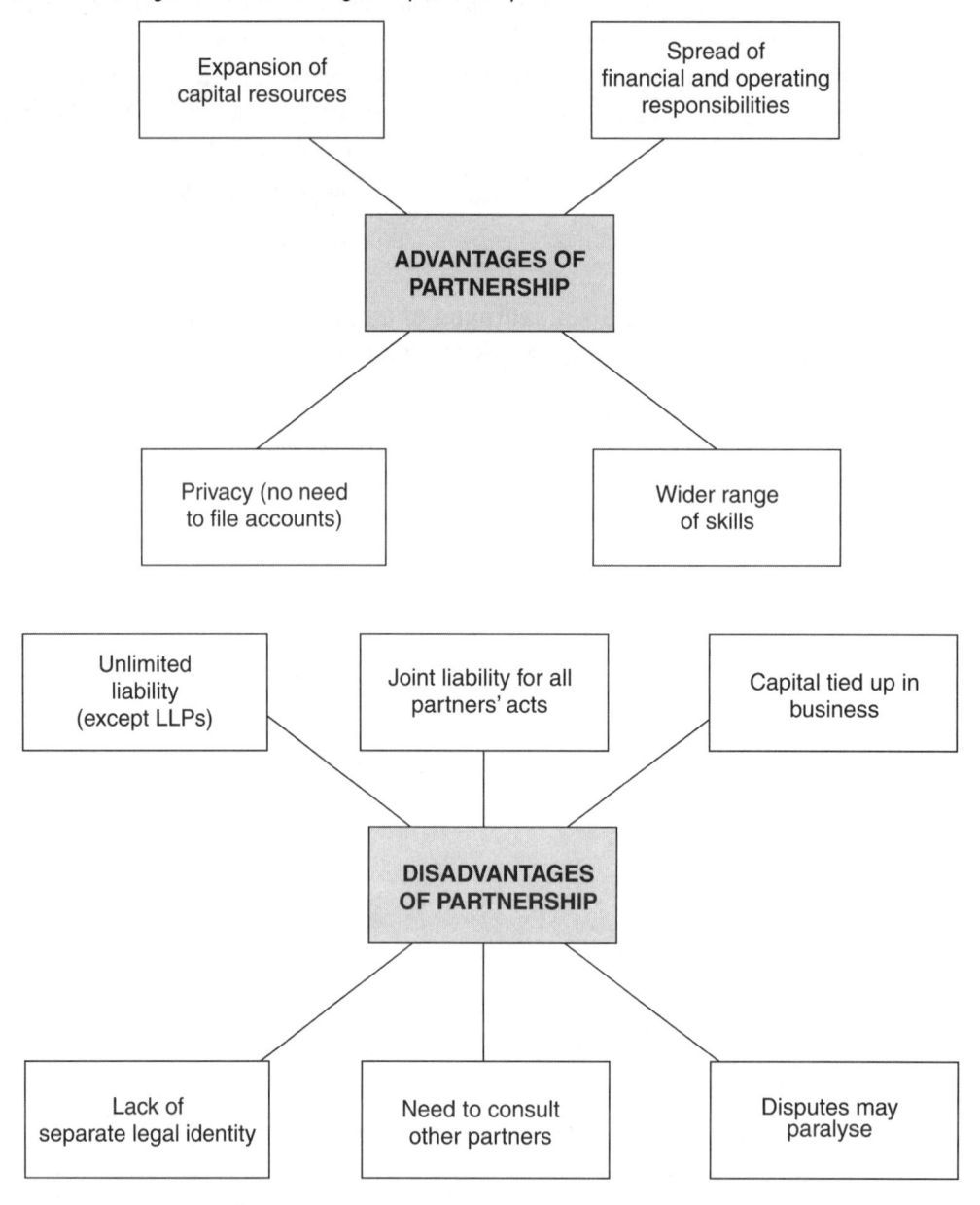

ADVANTAGES OF PARTNERSHIP
- Expansion of capital resources
- Spread of financial and operating responsibilities
- Privacy (no need to file accounts)
- Wider range of skills

DISADVANTAGES OF PARTNERSHIP
- Unlimited liability (except LLPs)
- Joint liability for all partners' acts
- Capital tied up in business
- Lack of separate legal identity
- Need to consult other partners
- Disputes may paralyse

5.3 Limited companies

> **FAST FORWARD**
>
> **Limited companies** separate, in theory, ownership from control. The main difference between **private** limited companies and **public** limited companies is that the latter can offer their shares to the general public.

The limited company has a **separate legal personality**. The liability of its shareholders for the debts of the company only extends to the capital they contributed.

The **ownership** and **control** of a limited company are legally separate, even though they may be vested in the same individual or individuals.

(a) Shareholders are the **owners**, but have limited rights, as shareholders, over the day-to-day running of the company. They provide capital and receive a return.

(b) **Directors** are appointed to run the company on behalf of shareholders. In practice they have a great deal of autonomy.

Figure 1.5: Advantages and disadvantages of limited liability status

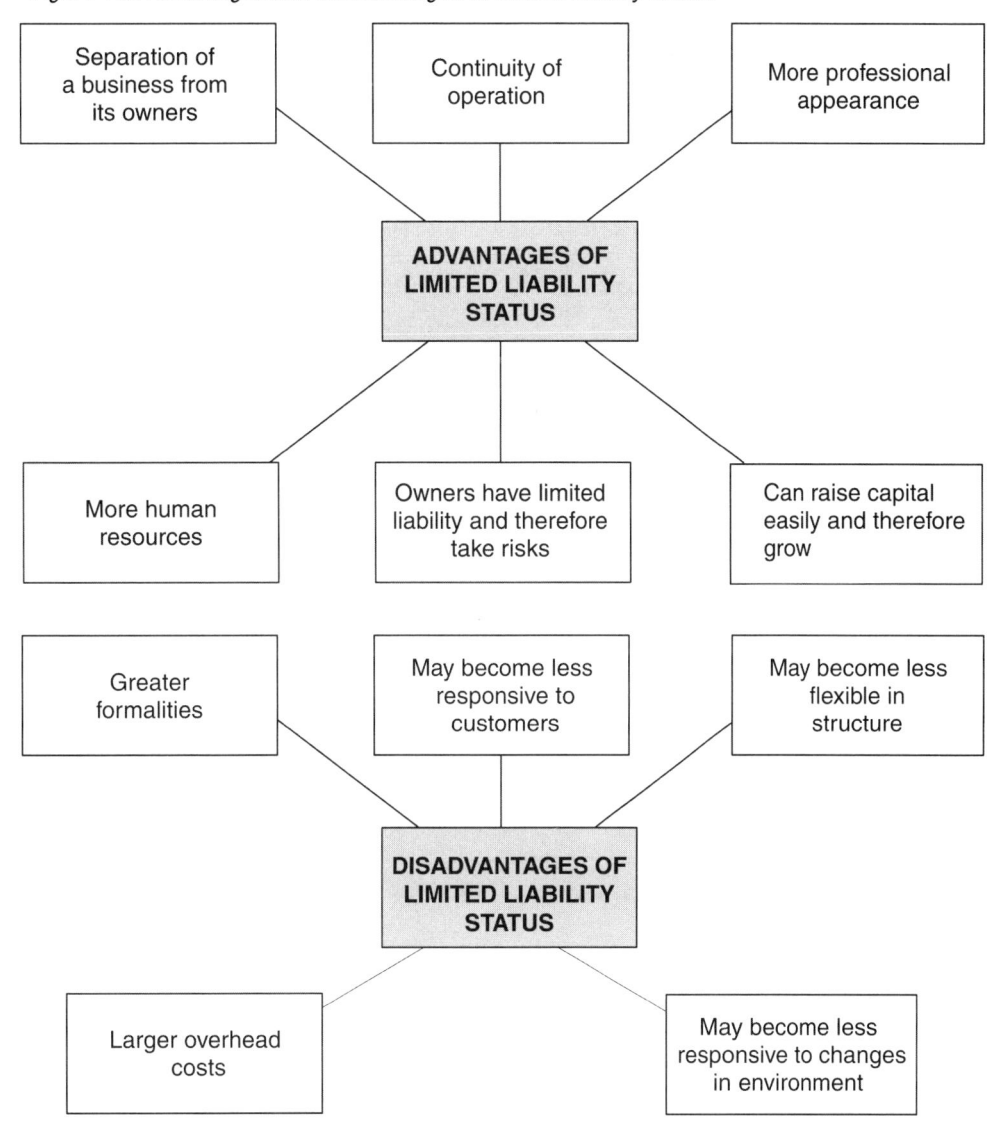

```
┌─────────────────┐    ┌─────────────┐    ┌─────────────────┐
│ Separation of   │    │ Continuity  │    │ More professional│
│ a business from │    │ of operation│    │ appearance      │
│ its owners      │    │             │    │                 │
└─────────────────┘    └─────────────┘    └─────────────────┘
              \              |              /
               ┌──────────────────────────┐
               │   ADVANTAGES OF          │
               │   LIMITED LIABILITY      │
               │   STATUS                 │
               └──────────────────────────┘
              /              |              \
┌─────────────┐    ┌──────────────────┐    ┌────────────────┐
│ More human  │    │ Owners have      │    │ Can raise      │
│ resources   │    │ limited liability│    │ capital easily │
│             │    │ and therefore    │    │ and therefore  │
│             │    │ take risks       │    │ grow           │
└─────────────┘    └──────────────────┘    └────────────────┘

┌─────────────┐    ┌──────────────────┐    ┌────────────────┐
│ Greater     │    │ May become less  │    │ May become less│
│ formalities │    │ responsive to    │    │ flexible in    │
│             │    │ customers        │    │ structure      │
└─────────────┘    └──────────────────┘    └────────────────┘
              \              |              /
               ┌──────────────────────────┐
               │   DISADVANTAGES OF       │
               │   LIMITED LIABILITY      │
               │   STATUS                 │
               └──────────────────────────┘
              /                             \
      ┌──────────────┐              ┌─────────────────┐
      │ Larger       │              │ May become less │
      │ overhead     │              │ responsive to   │
      │ costs        │              │ changes in      │
      │              │              │ environment     │
      └──────────────┘              └─────────────────┘
```

In the UK, limited companies come in two types: **private limited companies** (eg X Limited) and **public limited companies** (eg X plc). They differ as follows.

(a) **Ownership**

Most private companies are owned by only a small number of shareholders. Public companies generally are owned by a wider proportion of the investing public.

(b) **Finance**

A private company's share capital will normally be provided by the founder or promoter, business associates of the founder or employer or venture capitalists.

A public company's share capital, in addition, can be raised from the public directly, or through institutional investors, using recognised markets.

Many companies start in a small way, often as family businesses which operate as private companies, then grow to the point where they can invite the public to subscribe for shares. The new capital thus made available enables the firm to expand its activities and achieve the advantages of large scale operation.

5.3.1 Control of limited companies

In the UK, the **Board of Directors** controls management and staff, and is accountable to the shareholders, but it has responsibilities to both groups, to owners and to employees alike (figure 1.6).

Figure 1.6: The division of power in limited companies

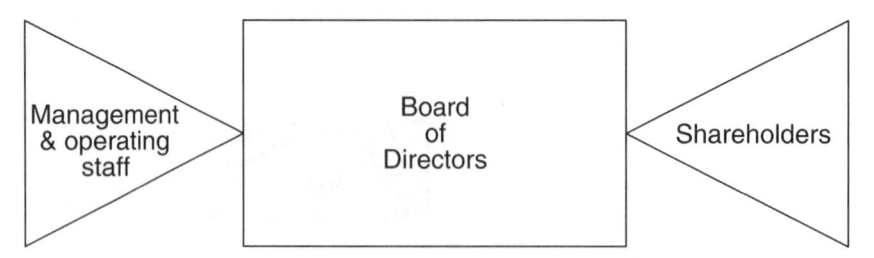

Management & operating staff ⟷ Board of Directors ⟷ Shareholders

(a) **Shareholders** may be large institutional investors, such as insurance companies and pension funds. They may be private individuals. Employees can also become shareholders.

(b) **Directors** are often **shareholders**. Executive directors participate in the daily operations of the organisation.

(c) **Operational management** usually consists of career managers who are recruited to operate the business, and are accountable to the board.

Action Programme 4

Florence Nightingale runs a successful and growing small business, as a sole trader. She wishes to expand the business and has her eyes on Scutari Ltd, a small private limited company in the same line. After the acquisition, she runs the two businesses as if they were one operation, making no distinction between them. What problems might this cause?

5.4 Franchises

In franchising, the owner of the name of a product or a retail group (the **franchisor**) sells the right to distribute the product or operate under the store name to a **franchisee**. The **franchisee** has independence to sell the product or run the shop as a separate venture. The Body Shop is an example of a franchise operation.

Figure 1.7: Advantages of franchising

ADVANTAGES OF FRANCHISING
- Easier to raise capital as using known name
- Avoid administrative set-up costs
- Avoid initial marketing and brand establishment costs
- Ability to sell franchise via franchisor
- Can use franchisor's marketing resources

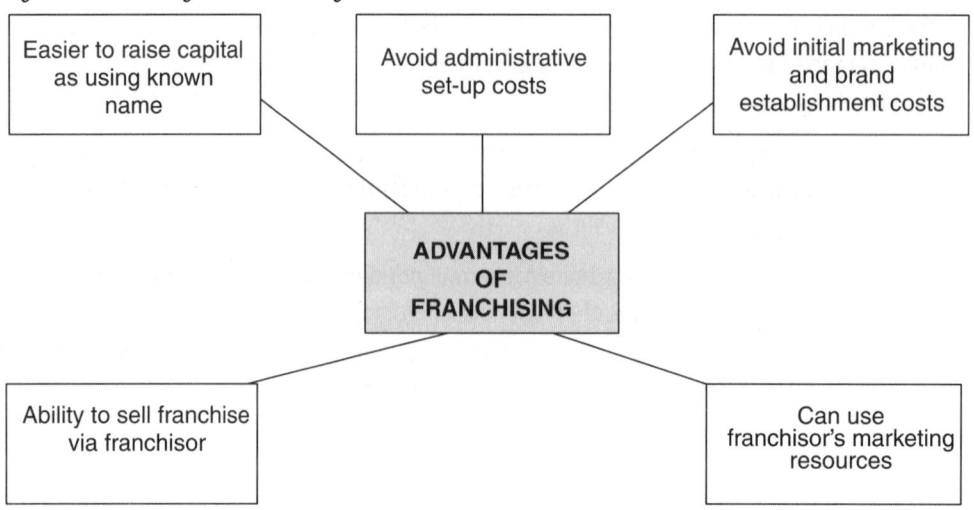

5.5 Business activities

Business organisations can also be classified by type of activity.

EXAMPLES OF BUSINESS ACTIVITIES	
Manufacturing	Acquisition of raw materials and by use of labour and technology turning them into products
Extractive/raw materials	Extraction and refining of raw materials
Energy	Conversion of one resource (coal) into another (electricity)
Retailing/distribution	Delivering goods to the end consumer
Services	See below

5.5.1 Service industries

Services are distinguished from products.

(a) **Services are intangible**.

A service cannot be seen, touched or displayed. Money transmission is a service which customers pay for and which is performed by banks, but the customer does not have anything material to show as a result.

(b) **Services are inseparable**.

In general, services cannot be stored since the production and consumption of a service cannot be separated. For example, when you have dental treatment, the service is consumed as it is produced.

(c) **Services are heterogeneous**.

The quality of the service product is highly dependent on the quality of the person providing it (eg the actors in a play).

Examples of services:

- Retailing and distribution
- Transport and communications
- Banking and finance
- Public administration and defence (including the army)
- Business services
- Public services, such as education and medicine

Exam tip

> A question in the December 2006 exam gave you the opportunity to compose your own 'mini case study' (ie a description of an organisation and its environment) for an organisation of your choice. The matters to be covered (briefly) were: the organisation's legal form or status; its mission statement; the nature of its internal environment and its interrelationship with the external environment and its key drivers of change. You may like to prepare notes for such a 'case study', as a way of gathering together useful information on a few 'organisations of your choice'.

PART A   THE ORGANISATION AND ITS ENVIRONMENT

6 Comparing different types of organisation

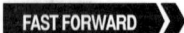

> **FAST FORWARD**
>
> In contrasting different types of organisation
>
> - the ease of formation
> - the way and ease with which finance is raised
> - size, and hence
> - economies of scale,
>
> are issues for comparison. Your syllabus requires you to understand the strengths and weaknesses of each type of formation.

We shall now draw together the different types of organisation and compare them on the basis of certain criteria.

6.1 Ease of formation

How do you set up an organisation, especially a business organisation?

6.1.1 Sole tradership

It might appear easy to set up a sole tradership. After all, a sole trader is not operating under limited liability, and so does not have to endure the legal procedures and expense of setting up a limited company.

That said, a sole trader cannot avoid bureaucratic irritation and legal regulations. At some stage attention has to be paid to matters such as taxation, health and safety and planning permission.

None of these requirements are unique to sole tradership but they do indicate that being a sole trader is no guarantee of avoiding bureaucratic procedures.

6.1.2 Partnerships

Partnerships in theory are just as easy to form as sole traders. However, the partners are bound by the terms of the partnership agreement, and there may be restrictions on changing it. A partnership does not necessarily end with the departure of one of the partners, as new partners can be brought in.

6.1.3 Limited companies

As limited liability status confers significant legal benefits, there is greater regulation over the formation and status of limited companies than over partnerships and sole traders.

There are two ways of acquiring limited company status.

(a) Two or more individuals and/or companies agree to set up a company. Appropriate documents are drawn up and the company is registered.

(b) Companies may be purchased **'off the shelf'** in which all the work of setting up the company has been done, although the documents that define the company have to be altered.

6.1.4 Non-commercial bodies

Most **public sector bodies** are established by legislation, or by delegated authority given to a minister.

Laws will govern the formation of **trade unions**. To be effective in a work context, a trade union has to be recognised as such by the employer.

Charities will also be subject to special rules governing their incorporation.

6.2 Raising finance

6.2.1 Sole tradships

Raising finance:

- The sole trader's own savings
- The sole trader's family and friends, or any other interested parties
- The bank (overdraft or loan finance)
- The profits of the business

A sole trader's business and personal affairs are legally the same. A lender, though interested primarily in the affairs of the business, has the benefit that the trader's domestic assets provide additional security.

Overdraft finance can be withdrawn at any time by the bank. Too many businesses use it for long-term investment, whereas overdraft finance is only really suitable for short-term fluctuations.

A **loan** is more secure, from the bank's point of view. It enables the unincorporated business to predict the likely repayments. However, these do not alter according to the conditions of trade.

6.2.2 Partnerships

Similar considerations arise for partnerships. New partners are generally expected to contribute additional capital to the partnership when they join. The other main source of finance for a partnership is the **revenues and profits** of the business itself. Otherwise they have to rely on bank finance.

6.2.3 Limited companies

Limited companies restrict the liability of the shareholders to the amount they initially invested in the company. For this reason, companies are able to raise money through **issuing shares**.

A share signifies that the owner of the share has an interest, as owner, in the company. It is a form of property which can be transferred to another person, subject to any restrictions imposed by the constitution of the company.

Share capital can be raised in different ways.

- Privately
- Publicly, by offering the shares for sale on the stock market

There are restrictions regarding the offer of shares for sale to the public. There must be a **prospectus**, which is subject to detailed rules as to what it contains.

6.2.4 Public sector bodies

Public sector institutions can command resources raised through **general taxation**. Some also charge for services. The government does not raise taxes specifically for investment or current spending: they are collected into a consolidated fund. The total of government spending therefore contains both short-term and long-term items. Resources are limited by the government's overall financing requirement.

6.2.5 Charities

Charities raise funds through a variety of methods including:

- Donations
- Legacies
- Membership fees
- Grants
- Fundraising activities

- Commercial operations such as shops
- Loans

One definition of a not-for-profit organisation is that it seeks to cover its costs; **profits** are only made as a means to an end such as providing a service, or accomplishing some socially or morally worthy objective.

6.3 Size

Many of the consequences of differences in size between organisations are bound up with the concept of **economies of scale**.

Key concept

> **Economies of scale** are factors which cause average cost to decline in the long run as output of a firm increases.

6.4 Internal economies of scale

6.4.1 Technical economies

Technical economies arise in the **production process**.

Large undertakings can make use of larger and more specialised machinery. If smaller undertakings tried to use similar machinery, the costs would be excessive because the machines would become obsolete before their physical life ends (ie their economic life would be shorter than their physical life). Obsolescence is caused by falling demand for the product made on the machine, or by the development of newer and better machines.

Indivisibility of operations is also important.

(a) Some operations must be carried out at the same cost, regardless of whether the business is small or large; these are fixed costs and **average fixed costs always decline as production increases**.

(b) Similarly, other operations' costs vary a little, but not proportionately, with size (ie they are 'semi-fixed' costs).

(c) Some operations are not worth considering below a certain level of output (eg expensive advertising campaigns).

6.4.2 Commercial or marketing economies

Buying economies may be available, reducing the cost of material purchases through bulk purchase discounts.

Stockholding becomes more efficient. The most economic quantities of inventory to hold increase with the scale of operations.

6.4.3 Financial economies

Large firms may find it easier to obtain loan finance at attractive rates of interest. It is also feasible for them to sell shares to the public via a stock exchange.

Action Programme 5

The above list is not exhaustive. Can you add to it?

6.5 External economies of scale

External economies of scale occur as an **industry** grows in size. Here are two examples.

(a) A large **skilled labour force** is created and educational services can be geared towards training new entrants.

(b) **Specialised ancillary industries** will develop to provide components, transport finished goods, trade in by-products, provide special services and so on. For instance, law firms may be set up to specialise in the affairs of the industry.

6.6 The effect of size

The extent to which both internal and external economies of scale can be achieved will vary from industry to industry, depending on the conditions in that industry. In other words, big-sized firms are better suited to some industries than others.

(a) **Internal economies of scale**

These are potentially more significant than external economies to a supplier of a product or service for which there is a **large consumer market**. A firm in such an industry may have to grow to a certain size in order to benefit fully from potential economies of scale, and thereby be cost-competitive and capable of making profits and surviving.

(b) **External economies of scale**

These are potentially significant to smaller firms who specialise in the **ancillary services** to a larger industry. For example, the development of a large world-wide industry in drilling for oil and natural gas off-shore has led to the creation of many new specialist supplier firms, making drilling rigs and various types of equipment. Thus, a specialist firm may benefit more from the market demand created by a large customer industry than from its own internal economies of scale.

6.7 Diseconomies of scale

Economic theory predicts that there will be **diseconomies of scale** in the long-run costs of a firm, once the firm gets beyond an ideal size. The main reasons for possible diseconomies of scale are the human and behavioural problems of managing a large firm. In a large firm employing many people, with many levels in the hierarchy of management, there may be a number of undesirable effects.

- Communicating information and instructions may become difficult.
- Chains of command may become excessively long.
- Morale and motivation amongst staff may deteriorate.
- Senior management may have difficulty in assimilating all the information they need in sufficient detail to make good quality decisions.

There will not usually be **technical** factors producing diseconomies of scale. The technology of higher volume equipment, on the contrary, is more likely to create further economies of scale.

The implication of diseconomies of scale is that companies should achieve a certain size to benefit fully from scale economies, but should not become too big, when cost controls might slacken and organisational inefficiency is likely to develop.

6.8 Economies of scale in marketing

Economies and diseconomies of scale also apply in relation to the marketing function. You may be tempted to assume that larger companies enjoy all the advantages. They can employ a specialist marketing department with expert knowledge and can afford large advertising and promotions budgets.

However, small businesses have many potential marketing advantages over public limited companies. The following are particularly important advantages.

(a) **Overheads**

Overhead costs may be **lower** as a result of having no headquarters staff overheads, among other costs. These cost savings can be passed on to customers, giving a big advantage in price sensitive markets. This effect is noticeable in the market for small building work.

(b) **Flexibility**

Because there is **less bureaucracy** in a small company, it can **respond more quickly** to changes in the marketing environment. It can therefore exploit market niches before their larger competitors move in.

(c) **Development**

The relative lack of bureaucracy can also facilitate the **development** of **innovative products**, of which a larger company may not have had the courage to pursue.

(d) **Closeness to customers**

Small business owners are generally **closer** to their **customers** and may have better knowledge of the marketing environment than decision makers in large organisations whose knowledge comes through lengthy research processes.

(e) **Personal service**

Small businesses can often claim to offer a **personal service** where each customer is known by name. In some markets this can be a big advantage.

> **Exam tip**
>
> The December 2005 exam asked candidates to compare the *marketing advantages* of a small hairdressing business and a national chain of hair-styling salons. Note the context: see which of the economies and diseconomies of scale would apply to the larger business, given that it is a chain of local salons – within a large corporate network (and nationally-promoted brand).
>
> Always think theoretical *content* through in the *context* presented by different sectors, industries and organisation types!

Chapter Roundup

- **Organisations** achieve results through the division of labour and co-operative efforts which individuals cannot achieve alone.
- Organisations can be analysed by **size, legal form** and **activity**.
- Many **public sector organisations** have the primary goals of providing a service. A secondary goal is the efficiency and effectiveness with which resources are used.
- The boundaries between public and private sectors are altering with **privatisation** and the introduction of **market-based measures**.
- Non-commercial organisations include trade unions, employers' organisations, professional associations, clubs and **charities.**
- Organisations have **goals**. Business organisations' primary goal is to provide a return on money invested. This they do by selling goods and services.
- **Sole traderships** and **partnerships** tend to be small. They have the advantage of privacy and flexibility, but the disadvantages of vulnerability and unlimited liability, except in the case of **limited liability partnerships (LLPs)**.
- **Limited companies** separate, in theory, ownership from control. The main difference between **private** limited companies and **public** limited companies is that the latter can offer their shares to the general public.
- In contrasting different types of organisation
    - the ease of formation
    - the way and ease with which finance is raised
    - size, and hence
    - economies of scale,

  are issues for comparison. Your syllabus requires you to understand the strengths and weaknesses of each type of formation.

PART A   THE ORGANISATION AND ITS ENVIRONMENT

Quick Quiz

1. *Fill in the blank*

    An organisation is a social arrangement for the .... of collective goals.

2. Give three reasons why organisations exist.

3. Which of the following are essential elements of formal organisations?

    A   Authority
    B   Flexibility
    C   Responsibility
    D   Fluid membership

4. Suggest five ways of classifying organisations.

5. Which of the following is not a characteristic of the non-profit making public sector?

    A   Command of resources
    B   Fairness
    C   No financial targets
    D   Equal profits

6. A sole trader benefits from economies of scale.

    True ☐
    False ☐

7. What is the arrangement called where a retail group sells the right to operate under the store name?

8. Which of the following would be possible sources of finance for a sole trader?

    A   Savings
    B   Money from friends
    C   Bank loan
    D   Profits

9. What are 'diseconomies of scale'?

Answers to Quick Quiz

1. Controlled performance

2. Three of
    - Overcoming problems
    - Providing companionship
    - Increasing production
    - Accumulating knowledge
    - Saving time

3. A Authority
   B Responsibility

4. Any five of:
    - Ownership
    - Control
    - Activity
    - Legal structure
    - Objectives
    - Accountability
    - Sources of finance

5. C   Targets may be set even if the body does not exist to make a profit

6. False. Economies of scale benefit large organisations.

7. A franchise

8. All of them

9. Cost inefficiencies arising when a firm grows beyond the optimum size, eg due to structural inefficiencies or slackening cost control.

Action Programme Review

1. Governments have become involved in commerce and taken over companies or industries for a number of reasons including the nature of the business (public utilities such as water), the need to preserve jobs (for example, nationalisation of motor firms), national security (for example, aspects of the defence industry) or technological sensitivity (for example, nuclear power). In the last twenty years, however, many governments have privatised state-run enterprises, in order to inject competition.

2. Public sector organisations run some activities, for example theatres or swimming pools, that exist to make a return. These need to be marketed to potential customers. They will also need marketing skills to cope with competition, for example compulsory competitive tendering or competition with the commercial sector for potential employees.

   However, marketing techniques can also be used in public sector activities that are purely non-profit making. Public sector authorities will need to identify the targets for whom services are being provided, and recognise their needs and desires. These needs and desires will need to be considered in the light of available resources, and the provision of services planned carefully.

   The potential recipients will need to be informed not only that the services are being provided, but also the benefits that they offer. The service provider should not assume that the services will automatically be taken up; if they aren't, it will be a waste of resources providing them. For the same reason, the services will have to be delivered effectively to the beneficiaries, otherwise they may stop using them.

PART A THE ORGANISATION AND ITS ENVIRONMENT

Marketing techniques will also be vital in dealing with others involved in the provision of services. For example, public sector organisations may co-operate with charities in seeking to provide services.

3   At the time of review, significant features of the NSPCC's website were:

   (a)   A welcome page focused on the NSPCC's 'Cruelty to children must stop. FULL STOP.' campaign.

   (b)   A separate Kidszone focused on child users. This area:

      (i)   Again highlights the Full Stop Campaign

      (ii) Provides links into other campaigns

      (iii) Provided advice for children who are bullied and tips for children to keep themselves safe

      (iv) Has various non-serious features including pop star interviews and a promise of 'lots more fun and surprises' on future visits (to increase repeat visits to the site)

   (c)   A home page that:

      (i)   Provides links into the Full stop campaign and other campaigns

      (ii) Provides a rolling summary of what's new

      (iii) Gives links into fundraising and volunteering and how you can help. There is also a section devoted to what media stars are doing for the NSPCC

4   This is quite a tricky question, which Florence had better sort out for her sake and for that of her customers. For example, if suppliers have contracts with Scutari Ltd, the contract is with the company, and Florence is not legally liable for the debts. If their contracts are with Florence, then they are dealing with her personally. Florence has to make a choice. She can:

   (a)   Run her entire business as a sole trader, in which case Scutari Ltd's assets must be transferred to her

   (b)   Run her entire business as a limited company, in which case she would contribute the assets of her business as capital to the company

   (c)   Ensure that the two business are legally distinct in their assets, liabilities, income and expenditure

5   (a)   Large firms attract better quality employees if the employees see better career prospects than in a small firm.

   (b)   Specialisation of labour applies to management, and there are thus managerial economies; the cost per unit of management will fall as output rises.

   (c)   Marketing economies are available, because a firm can make more effective use of advertising, specialist salesmen, and specialised channels of distribution.

   (d)   Large companies are able to devote more resources to research and development (R & D). In an industry where R & D is essential for survival, large companies are more likely to prosper.

   (e)   Large companies find raising finance easier and can often do so more cheaply. Quoted public limited companies have access to the Stock Exchange for new share issues. They are also able to borrow money more readily.

> Now try Questions 1 and 2 at the end of the Study Text

Organisations as systems

Chapter topic list

1. Mission and vision
2. Commercial goals and objectives
3. The systems approach to organisations
4. The contingency approach to organisations
5. Marketing and other functions

Syllabus content

- 1.4 State the meaning and importance of an organisation's mission and explain the nature and significance of the objectives pursued
- 1.5 Identify the internal and external influences on the formulation of objectives and specify the key drivers for organisational change
- 1.6 Explain the nature of open systems and the interface between organisations and their marketing environment
- 1.7 Represent the organisation as an open system responding to changing environmental conditions

PART A   THE ORGANISATION AND ITS ENVIRONMENT

Introduction

In this chapter we first focus on the organisation's mission. The mission of an organisation consists of not just its purpose but also its values, its strategy and its policies.

Within its mission an organisation may have a number of objectives. We focus on these in Section 2, describing the various ways in which objectives can be classified. We give examples of the objectives that are important for many organisations.

We then discuss how organisations view themselves and view their relationships with their environment. This will determine how organisations react to their environment, and in particular respond to changes in their environment. We consider in detail the systems and contingency approaches.

Lastly in this chapter we discuss briefly the role of marketing within an organisation, and in particular how marketing relates to other departments within the organisation.

1 Mission and vision

FAST FORWARD

A **mission** can contain both the organisation's values and its overwhelming commercial imperatives. Mission could be said to include four elements.

- Purpose (why a company exists)
- Strategy (commercial logic)
- Values (basic beliefs and moral principles)
- Policies and standards of behaviour

Key concept

Mission is an organisation's rationale for existing at all and/or its long-term strategic direction and/or its values; its basic function in terms of the products and services the organisation produces for its clients.

Mission and vision give shape and direction to the behaviour and decisions of the organisation and people within it.

(a) **Mission** 'describes the organisation's basic function in society, in terms of the products and services it produces for its clients' (Mintzberg).

(b) **Vision** is 'what we are aiming for'.

Marketing at Work

'The Co-op' (UK grocery chain)

The Co-operative movement is a good example of the role of mission. The Co-operative Wholesale Society and Co-operative Retail Society are business organisations, but their mission is not simply profit.

Rather, being owned by their suppliers/customers rather than external shareholders, they have always, since foundation, had a wider social concern.

The Co-op has been criticised by some analysts on the grounds that it is insufficiently profitable, certainly in comparison with supermarket chains such as Tescos.

The Co-op has explicit social objectives. In some cases it will retain stores which, although too small to be as profitable as a large supermarket, provide an important social function in the communities which host them.

Of course, the Co-op's performance as a retailer can be improved, but judging it on the conventional basis of profitability ignores its social objectives.

1.1 Why have a mission?

In *A Sense of Mission*, Andrew Campbell, Marion Devine and David Young note two alternative ways of looking at mission.

(a) 'The strategy school .... views mission primarily as a **strategic tool**, an intellectual discipline which defines the business's commercial rationale and target market ....'

(b) On the other hand, a mission would be defined as the '**cultural glue** that enables an organisation to function as a collective unity'. In this case, it is a set of **values** rather than a description of ultimate commercial goals.

ELEMENTS OF MISSION	
Purpose	Why the organisation exists • Creation of wealth • Satisfaction of stakeholder needs • Reaching higher goal
Strategy	Provision of commercial logic, defining business and competitive advantages and priorities
Values	Beliefs of people working in the organisation, relating to its culture
Policies and behaviour standards	Exist to convert strategy into everyday performance, eg politeness to customers, speed of answering phone calls

For there to be a strong sense of mission, the elements above must be mutually re-inforcing. Strategy and values unite in policies and standards of behaviour.

Mission fuels success for the following reasons.

(a) **Loyalty and commitment**

Employees who feel a sense of mission will be willing to sacrifice their own interests for the good of the whole. The company, however, has to reciprocate this loyalty.

(b) **Guidance for behaviour**

A sense of mission helps create a work environment where there is a sense of common purpose. In matters of **ethical conflict**, divergencies between organisational values and personal values are hard to resolve if a person's values differ from those of the organisation.

Exam tip

Four marks were available in June 2006 simply for explaining the purpose of a mission statement. Don't neglect points like these that seem 'soft' subjects!

PART A   THE ORGANISATION AND ITS ENVIRONMENT

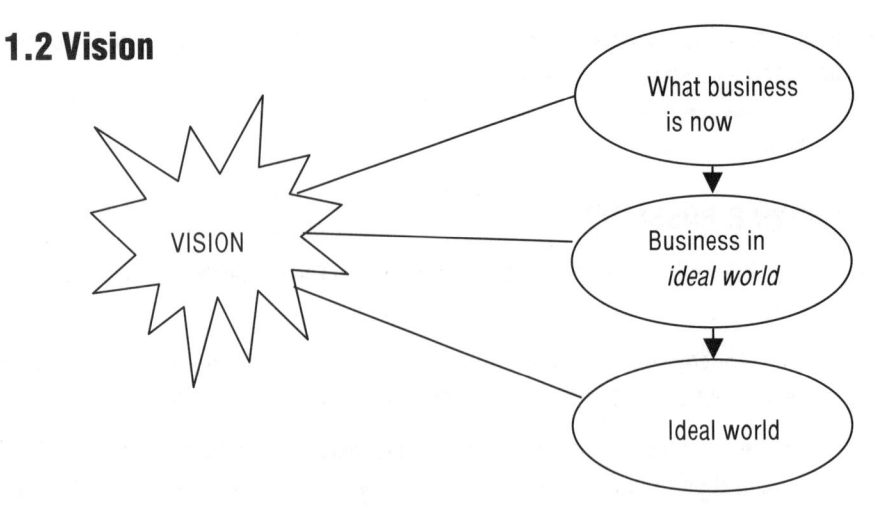

1.2 Vision

A vision gives a general sense of direction to the company, even if there is not too much attention to detail. A vision should be clear. The vision of Apple Computers, in the early days of the PC industry, was to 'democratise the computer'. (Hinterhuber and Popp)

A **vision** is a view of the future state of the organisation or its industry. A **vision statement** may sum it up. For example, the managing director of a personal computer firm might have the 'vision' of 'A computer in every home'.

MISSION AND VISION	
Mission	**Vision**
Here and now	Future
Motivate	Fails to motivate if too vague
Continual	Renewed if achieved
Realities	Unrealistic?
Relevant	Potentially out-of-date

1.3 Mission statements

Mission statements are formal documents, which might be reproduced in a number of places (eg at the front of an organisation's annual report, on publicity material, in the chairman's office, in communal work areas). There is no standard format.

Most mission statements will include the following.

MISSION STATEMENTS	
Identity of persons for whom the organisation exists	Shareholders Customers Community Staff and other employees
Nature of the firm's business	Product it makes or services it provides Markets it produces for
Ways of competing	Reliance on quality, innovation, low prices Commitment to customer care Policy on acquisition versus organic growth Geographical spread of its operations
Principles of business	Commitment to suppliers and staff Social policy eg non-discrimination or ecology Commitments to customers

1.3.1 Characteristics of effective mission statements

According to Guy Kawasaki (*Selling the Dream,* 1991) good mission statements exhibit three qualities.

(a) **Brevity**

Brief and simple mission statements are easy to understand and remember – they are also evidence of clear thinking. For example, the Girl Scouts' mission statement is 'To help a girl reach her highest potential'. It is short, simple, easy to understand and easy to remember.

(b) **Flexibility**

Flexible mission statements can last a long time. For example, 'ensuring an adequate supply of water' is inflexible and confining; it may not survive the next dry season. By contrast, the Macintosh Division's mission statement was: 'To improve the creativity and productivity of people'. It was flexible enough to accommodate a computer and peripheral products such as laser printers, software, books and training.

(c) **Distinctiveness**

Distinctive mission statements differentiate a cause from other organisations with similar missions.

Ideally a strong mission statement is a powerful tool to help enable an organisation to change to become more **market-orientated.** Mission should define the products or services a business offers and therefore its competitive position. It should also define the **competencies** by which the business hopes to prosper, and therefore its **method of competing**.

Marketing at Work

Evaluate the following mission statements against Kawasaki's three criteria.

Glaxo 'is an integrated research-based group of companies whose corporate purpose is to create, discover, develop, manufacture and market throughout the world, safe, effective medicines of the highest quality which will bring benefit to patients through improved longevity and quality of life, and to society through economic value.'

IBM (UK): 'We shall increase the pace of change. Market-driven quality is our aim. It means listening and responding more sensitively to our customers. It means eliminating defects and errors, speeding up all our processes, measuring everything we do against a common standard, and it means involving employees totally in our aims'.

Matsushita: 'The duty of the manufacturer is to serve the foundation of man's happiness by making man's life affluent with an inexpensive and inexhaustible supply of life's necessities.'

Komatsu: 'Encircle Caterpillar.' (*Note.* Caterpillar is a competitor)

Apple Computer: 'Our goal has always been to create the world's friendliest, most understandable, most useable computers – computers that empower the individual ... Our mission is to transform the way people do things by focusing on their experience with our computers. We believe the innovation and creativity of a person's work depends directly on the quality of his or her total experience, not just on the speed of a microprocessor.'

PART A   THE ORGANISATION AND ITS ENVIRONMENT

PROBLEMS WITH MISSION	
Problem	**Comment**
Ignored in practice	The inherent danger of mission is that it will not be implemented.
Public relations	Sometimes, of course, mission is merely for public consumption, not for internal decision making.
'Post hoc'	Mission does not drive the organisation, but what the organisation actually does is assumed to be a mission.
Too general	'Best', 'quality', 'major': is just a wish list.

1.4 Enforcing mission

Mission can be enforced in the following ways.

(a) **Formal imposition**

Powerful persons or groups with power can impose their idea of the mission on others.

(b) **Shared values**

A professional organisation (eg a hospital) might pursue mission as part of the professional ethics of the organisation's members.

(c) **Value system and culture**

The organisation with a strong ideology (eg a religious sect) has a strong sense of mission.

2 Commercial goals and objectives

FAST FORWARD

Objectives might be included in the mission statement, depending on the type of mission statement used, but may be subsidiary to it.

Key concept

Objectives are normally quantified statements of what the organisation actually intends to achieve over a period of time.

Objectives are important for the following reasons.

(a) Objectives **direct the activities** of the organisation towards the fulfilment of the organisation's mission, in theory if not always in practice.

(b) In business organisations, a paramount consideration is **profitability**. The mission of a business, whether this is stated or not, must be to carry on its activities at a profit.

(c) Objectives can also be used as standards **for measuring the performance** of the organisation and departments in it.

2.1 Corporate and unit objectives

FAST FORWARD

Objectives can be corporate and unit, primary and secondary, and long-term and short-term.

Corporate objectives concern the firm as **a whole**, for example:

- Profitability
- Market share
- Growth
- Cash flow
- Return on capital employed
- Risk
- Customer satisfaction
- Quality
- Industrial relations
- Added value
- Earnings per share

Similar objectives can be developed for each **Strategic Business Unit (SBU)**.

Key concept

A **Strategic Business Unit** is a part of the company that for all intents and purposes has its **own distinct** products, markets and assets.

Unit objectives are objectives that are specific to individual units of an organisation.

	EXAMPLES OF OBJECTIVES
Commercial	• Increase number of customers by x% (sales)
	• Increase market share by x% (sales)
	• Derive 5% of revenues each year from new products (sales, research and development)
	• Reduce number of rejects by x% (production)
	• Organise annual appraisals for all staff (human resources)
	• Inform all staff of new regulations (training)
	• Provide monthly reports within x days (management accounting)
Public sector	• Introduce x more places at nursery schools (education)
	• Reduce response times to calls (ambulance, fire service)

2.2 Trade-off between objectives

When there are several key objectives, some might be achieved only at the expense of others. For example, a company's objective of achieving good profits and profit growth might have adverse consequences for the cash flow of the business, or the quality of the firm's products.

There will be a **trade-off** between objectives when strategies are formulated, and a choice will have to be made. For example, there might be a choice between the following two options.

Option A
- 15% sales growth
- 10% profit growth
- £2 million cash outflow
- Reduced product quality
- Reduced customer satisfaction

Option B
- 8% sales growth
- 5% profits growth
- £½ million cash inflow
- Same product quality
- Same customer satisfaction

If the firm chose option B in preference to option A, it would be trading off sales growth and profit growth for better cash flow, product quality and customer satisfaction. The long-term effect of reduced quality has not been considered.

2.3 Long-term and short-term objectives

Objectives may be long-term and short-term. A company that is suffering from a recession in its core industries and making losses in the short term might nevertheless continue to have a long-term objective of achieving a steady growth in earnings or profits. However, in the short term its primary objective might be survival.

2.4 Primary and secondary objectives

Some objectives are more important than others. There is a **primary corporate objective** and other **secondary objectives** which are strategic objectives: these should combine to ensure the achievement of the primary corporate objective.

(a) For example, if a company sets growth in profits as its primary objective, it will then have to develop strategies by which this primary objective can be achieved.

(b) Secondary objectives might then be concerned with sales growth, continual technological innovation, customer service, product quality, efficient resource management (eg labour productivity) or reducing the company's reliance on debt capital etc.

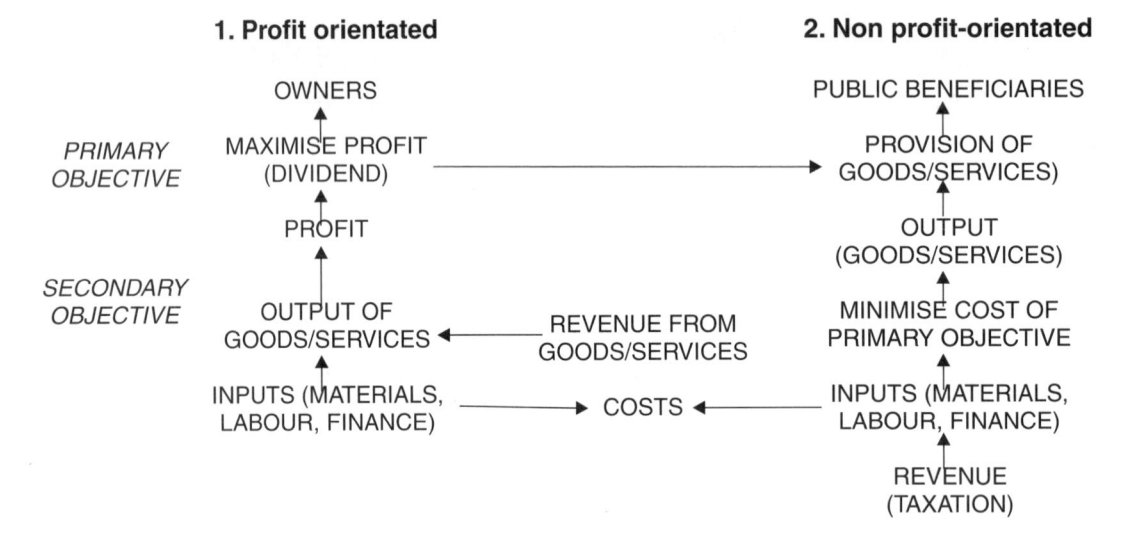

```
                   1. Profit orientated              2. Non profit-orientated

                        OWNERS                         PUBLIC BENEFICIARIES
                          ↑                                    ↑
    PRIMARY        MAXIMISE PROFIT                      PROVISION OF
    OBJECTIVE        (DIVIDEND)        ──────────►    GOODS/SERVICES)
                          ↑                                    ↑
                        PROFIT                              OUTPUT
                          ↑                            (GOODS/SERVICES)
    SECONDARY                                                  ↑
    OBJECTIVE       OUTPUT OF           REVENUE FROM     MINIMISE COST OF
                 GOODS/SERVICES ◄───── GOODS/SERVICES    PRIMARY OBJECTIVE
                          ↑                                    ↑
                 INPUTS (MATERIALS,                     INPUTS (MATERIALS,
                 LABOUR, FINANCE) ─────►  COSTS ◄──     LABOUR, FINANCE)
                                                               ↑
                                                            REVENUE
                                                           (TAXATION)
```

2.5 Alternative primary objectives

The primary objective for a company must be a financial objective based on earning profits, but there are different ways of expressing such an objective in quantitative terms.

2.5.1 Profitability

A company must make profits, but profitability on its own is not satisfactory as an overall long-term corporate objective.

(a) It fails to allow for the size of the **capital investment** required to make the profit. Since capital is often in restricted supply, **profitability** must be measured in terms of the scarce financial resources that a company will have at its disposal.

(b) Shareholders, as a group, should be interested in **maximising profits over time**, not short-term current year profits. In order to maximise profits over time, costs will have to be incurred today in order to generate returns in the future.

Another way of analysing productivity is by **value added**. The primary measure is the difference between revenue and the cost of bought-in materials and services. The value added is distributed to **employees** (as wages), **government** (as taxes), and **shareholders** (as dividends).

2.5.2 Return on capital employed (ROCE) or return on investment (ROI)

Some companies use an accounting ROCE as a prime objective. This measures the profit as a percentage of the investment (capital employed) needed to make the profit.

There are drawbacks in using ROCE.

(a) Capital employed is notoriously suspect as a financial measure.

(b) If ROCE were used, the company would find it difficult to balance short-term results against long-term requirements.

(c) The choice of ROCE as an objective also ignores the **risk of investments**. High risk projects might promise a high return if they succeed, but it may be safer to opt for a project with a lower return but a greater guarantee of success.

Ansoff suggested that return on capital employed should be the overall corporate objective, over the next 3 to 10 years, when forecasts can be made with reasonable accuracy. Beyond this period Ansoff suggested a **variety of long-term objectives** be pursued because they are more easily measurable and contribute towards the overall return.

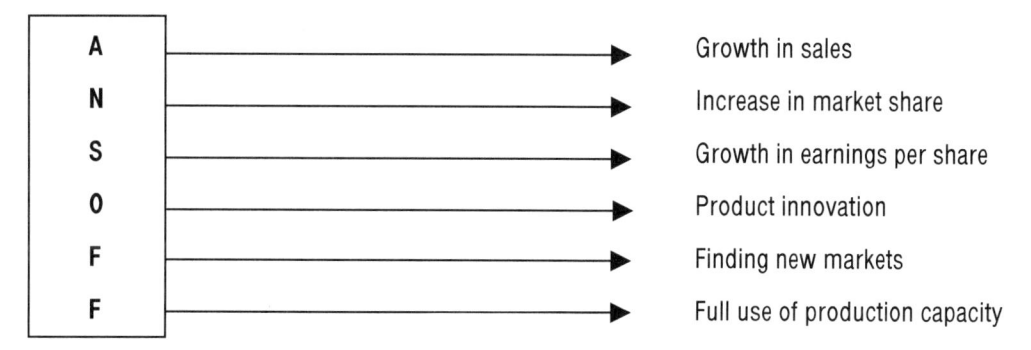

ANSOFF →
- Growth in sales
- Increase in market share
- Growth in earnings per share
- Product innovation
- Finding new markets
- Full use of production capacity

2.5.3 EPS and dividends

Earnings per share or dividend payments are both measures which recognise that a company is owned by its shareholder-investors and the purpose of a company is the provision of a satisfactory return for its owners.

The main disadvantage of using EPS as an objective is that earnings and dividends do not relate shareholder profit or revenue to the amount of money invested by the shareholders. The shareholder is concerned with the size of the **return** he gets, but also with the size of the **investment** he must make to achieve the return.

2.5.4 Survival

Drucker suggested that the prime objective of a company is not simply financial, but is one of survival. He argued that there are five major areas in which to decide objectives for survival.

(a) A company needs to anticipate the **social climate** and **economic policy** in those areas where the company operates and sells. A business must organise its behaviour in such a way as to survive in respect to both.

(b) A business is a **human organisation** and must be designed for joint performance by everyone in it.

(c) Survival also depends on the **supply** of an economic product or service.

(d) A business must **innovate**, because the economy and markets are continually changing.

(e) Inevitably, a business must be **profitable** to survive.

2.5.5 Growth

It is arguable that a company should make growth its prime objective – growth in EPS, growth in profits, growth in ROCE or growth in dividends per share. There are some difficulties, however, in accepting growth as an overall objective.

(a) **Growth of what?** 'Balanced growth' might be applicable in the short term. However, in the long run, some elements must be expected to grow faster than others because of the dynamics of the business environment.

(b) In the long run, growth might lead to **diseconomies of scale** so that inefficiencies will occur and the growth pattern will inevitably stagnate. The idea that a company must grow to survive is no longer widely accepted.

(c) There is little reason why in theory companies should not pay all their earnings as dividends and have **no growth**. A practical consequence of such a policy would be that if no money was reinvested in the business, it would be overtaken by competitors.

(d) Growth is, however, in the interests of management as it provides them with a career!

Growth is likely to be a prime objective for the following types of company.

(a) Smaller companies, since these will usually have a **greater potential** for significant rates of growth.

(b) Larger companies which are seeking to achieve a size which will enable them to **compete** with other multinationals in world markets. Very big companies will probably only achieve significant growth through takeovers or mergers, rather than through internal growth.

2.6 Other objectives and goals

An organisation's leaders should also be formulating objectives for other aspects of their business, so that the strategic plans that are eventually made will conform to these objectives.

Goals for **products and markets** will involve the following type of decisions.

(a) Whether the organisation wants to be the **market leader**, or number two in the market, or whatever

(b) Whether the **product range** needs to be expanded. Whether the organisation relies too heavily on one product or one market

(c) Whether there should be an objective to **shift position** in the market – eg from producing low-cost standard items for the mass market to higher-cost and higher-priced specialist products for individual segments of the market

(d) Whether there should be a broad objective of **modernising** the product range (or more general **innovation**) or **extending** the organisation's markets

Goals for the **organisation structure** are particularly important for growing organisations. When companies get beyond a certain size, the old organisation may cease to be efficient.

In addition, it is now common for organisations to set objectives in qualitative areas such as:

(a) **Innovation** or technology leverage/leadership

(b) **Human resource development** and empowerment

2: ORGANISATIONS AS SYSTEMS

(c) **Ethics** and **corporate social responsibility** in relation to secondary stakeholders: ethical trading, sustainability, use of local suppliers, community investment and so on.

(d) **Environmental responsibility**: 'green' sourcing, product design, production, waste management, etc.

2.7 Influences on objectives

Having established what an organisation's objectives might be, we now need to consider what influences the choice of objectives.

Influences are both internal and external. Internal influences include what the organisation was established to do, its **objects**. The **views and attitudes** of owners and senior managers will be key influences on establishing objectives. The **level of return** they will regard as sufficient and the **degree of risk** that they are prepared to run are particularly important. The level of **financial resources available** will also be a key early influence.

Early **external influences** will include **anyone** who is **interested** in the organisation. Their potential influence must be carefully evaluated, since the business may need to please them. There may however be conflicts between the need to obtain a return for the owners of the business, and the need to please external **stakeholders**.

The **competitive environment** within which the organisation operates will also be a key influence on objectives. It will act as a constraint on the business over certain lengths of time. However, the business must be alert for changes in the environment which will imply changes in objectives, both in terms of **market changes** and **technological changes** that will improve the efficiency of the production process.

To gain a more detailed understanding of the influences on objectives, we need to consider how organisations can be viewed as systems, which is the subject of the next section.

Exam tip

> Exams have asked for comparison of the objective pursued by organisations in different sectors (public, private and voluntary) – as in June 2004 and June 2005. The Case Study question in December 2005 also asked candidates to assess, from the data given, what objectives Microsoft was pursuing: profitability/shareholder value; market share/leadership; innovation; social responsibility. The examiner was disappointed that candidates confused objectives with policies, tactics (eg selling software to other manufacturers) and targets (eg improving anti-virus controls). Get to grips with this terminology!
>
> Exams have also asked about influences on the objectives of a large private sector firm (June 2005) and a national energy provider in a country of your choice (June 2006). We have given a broad outline above – but really, the whole syllabus is about this!

3 The systems approach to organisations

FAST FORWARD

> The **systems approach** analyses organisations in terms of their processes and interactions with their environment.

Key concept

> A **system** is 'an organised or complex whole' or 'an entity which consists of interdependent parts'.

The systems approach to organisation defines the organisation as a type of system.

3.1 The system boundary and the environment

Every system has a **boundary**, which defines what it is. The boundary will be expressed in terms of areas, or constraints that separate it from its environment. For example, a marketing department's boundary can be expressed in terms of who works in it and what work it does.

Anything which is external to a system belongs to the **environment** and not to the system itself. The environment exerts a considerable influence on the behaviour of the system; at the same time the system can rarely do much to control the behaviour of the environment.

Action Programme 1

If you were running a business, what factors in the business's environment might cause you particular concern?

3.2 Open and closed systems

FAST FORWARD

In systems theory, a distinction is made between open and closed systems.

Key concepts

A **closed system** is a system which is isolated from its environment and independent of it, so that no environmental influences affect the behaviour of the system, nor does the system exert any influence on its environment.

An **open system** is a system connected to and interacting with its environment. It takes in influences (or 'energy') from its environment and also influences this environment by its behaviour (it exports energy). An open system is a stable system which is nevertheless continually changing or evolving.

In practice, few systems are entirely closed. Many are **semi-closed**, in that the relationship with the environment is in some degree restricted.

The different types of system are described in the diagram below.

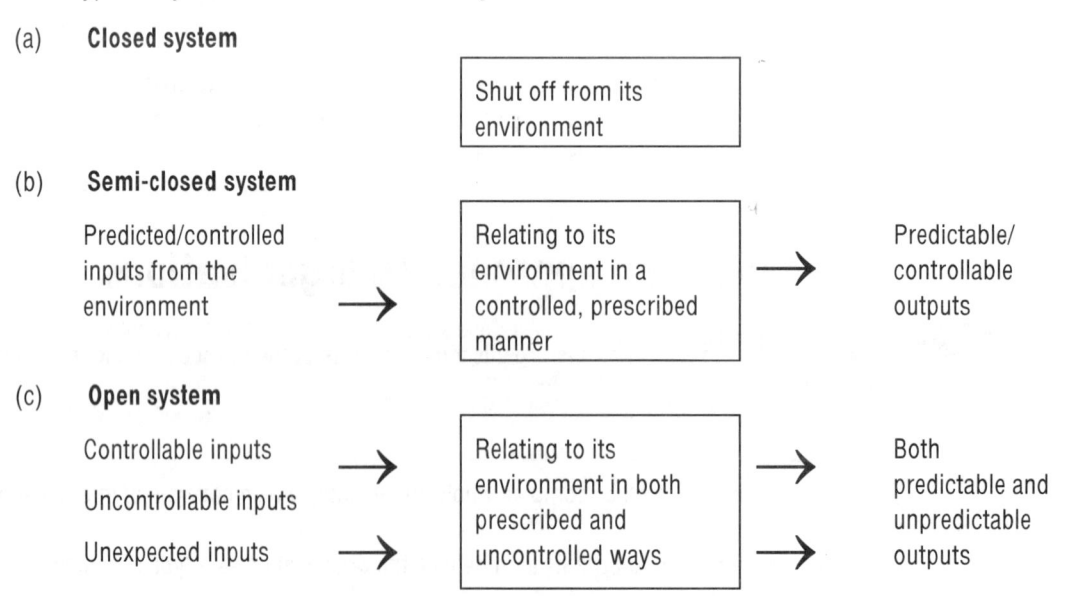

(a) **Closed system**

> Shut off from its environment

(b) **Semi-closed system**

Predicted/controlled inputs from the environment → Relating to its environment in a controlled, prescribed manner → Predictable/controllable outputs

(c) **Open system**

Controllable inputs →
Uncontrollable inputs →
Unexpected inputs →
Relating to its environment in both prescribed and uncontrolled ways → Both predictable and unpredictable outputs

On the other hand, social organisations such as businesses and government departments are by definition **open systems**. Why? All social organisations are made up of human beings.

(a) Human beings participate in any number of social systems (family, friends), of which the work organisation is only one, although it is important.

(b) In most societies, human beings are exposed to a variety of influences from the social environment, such as advertising messages, family attitudes, government demands.

An organisation, or its management, might however try to limit the extent to which these external environmental influences are imported to the organisation's smooth functioning. For example, as we have discussed, organisations like to standardise work for the sake of predictability.

Business systems have some of the operational features of a semi-closed system. The inputs to a nuclear power station are controllable, predictable (uranium), as (we hope!) are its outputs (a steady supply of electricity).

Exam tip

> Open systems are often examined in this paper. The December 2005 exam asked you to compare open-sourcing and closed-sourcing strategies (for making software available) to an open and closed system model: you needed a clear awareness of the elements of an open system in order to make the comparison and earn the marks. The June 2006 exam asked you to explain how a multinational food manufacturer operates as an open system: the examiner explicitly wanted to see discussion of how the organisation interacts with its external environment, as well as an input – conversion – output – feedback model.

3.3 Businesses as systems of transformation

FAST FORWARD

> As an open system, an organisation obtains **inputs** from the environment and **converts** them (through internal processes) into **outputs** to the environment. **Feedback** is obtained which allows further inputs to be adjusted, in order to control the outputs as far as possible.

In order to make profits businesses obtain **inputs** (resources) from the environment and transform them into **outputs** to the environment. **Feedback** information allows future inputs to be adjusted, as a way of controlling outputs as far as possible: if the outputs are not expected, the inputs or conversion processes may need adjustment. Figure 2.1 below illustrates this process.

Figure 2.1: The conversion system

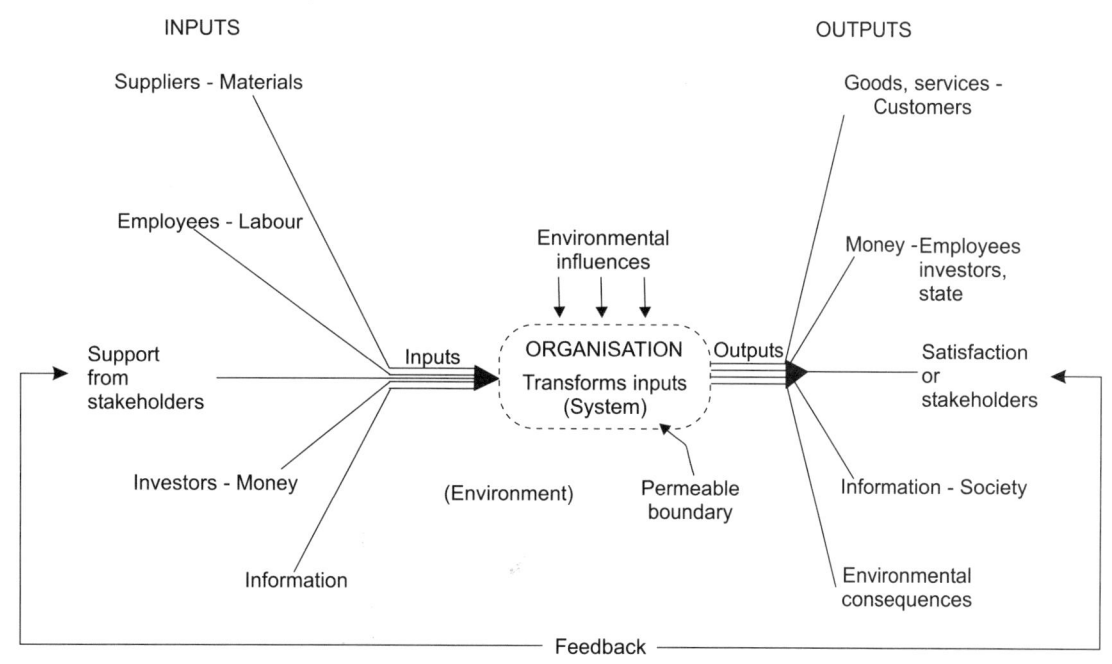

INPUTS
- Suppliers - Materials
- Employees - Labour
- Support from stakeholders
- Investors - Money
- Information

Environmental influences

ORGANISATION
Transforms inputs
(System)

(Environment) Permeable boundary

OUTPUTS
- Goods, services - Customers
- Money - Employees investors, state
- Satisfaction or stakeholders
- Information - Society
- Environmental consequences

Feedback

Inputs

- Materials, components and sub-components
- Labour
- Money
- Information and ideas
- Tangible property

Transformation or conversion processes

- Using people and machinery to make goods such as cars
- The provision of services (eg transport)
- The creation of knowledge to be more efficient

Outputs

- Goods and/or services
- Money (dividends, interest, wages)
- Information
- Environmental consequences of its activities (eg pollution, increased traffic)
- Social consequences of its activities

Sometimes this is known as the process of **adding value**. In other words the process of transformation ensures that the outputs are worth more in the customers' estimation than the inputs.

There are two points to note here.

(a) Customers **purchase value**, which they measure by comparing a firm's products and services with similar offerings by competitors.

(b) The business **creates value** by carrying out its activities either more efficiently than other businesses, or combined in such a way as to provide a unique product or service.

3.4 Stakeholders

> **FAST FORWARD**
>
> **Stakeholders** are individuals and groups who have an interest or 'stake' in the organisation. They represent an important interface between the organisation and its environment.

For businesses, the motive of adding value to please customers in order to make a profit for investors seems clear cut. For many public sector organisations, the issue is not so clear cut, as different stakeholders exercise different degrees of power.

Key concepts

Stakeholders are those people or groups with an interest in the organisation's activities.

Internal stakeholders exist *within* the boundaries of the organisation. They include employees and management.

Connected stakeholders are those outside the organisation, such as suppliers, customers and shareholders, who have a direct interest in the organisation's activities.

External stakeholders include the state, local authorities, the public, pressure groups and so forth.

For many organisations, the principal stakeholders are diffuse. We shall discuss stakeholders in greater detail in Chapter 5.

For now, Figure 2.2 opposite illustrates the various elements of a particular system/organisation and the objectives of the people within it as they confront an internal reorganisation. (It is adapted from *Avison and Fitzgerald : Information System Methodologies*.)

Figure 2.2: Stakeholders in a hospital

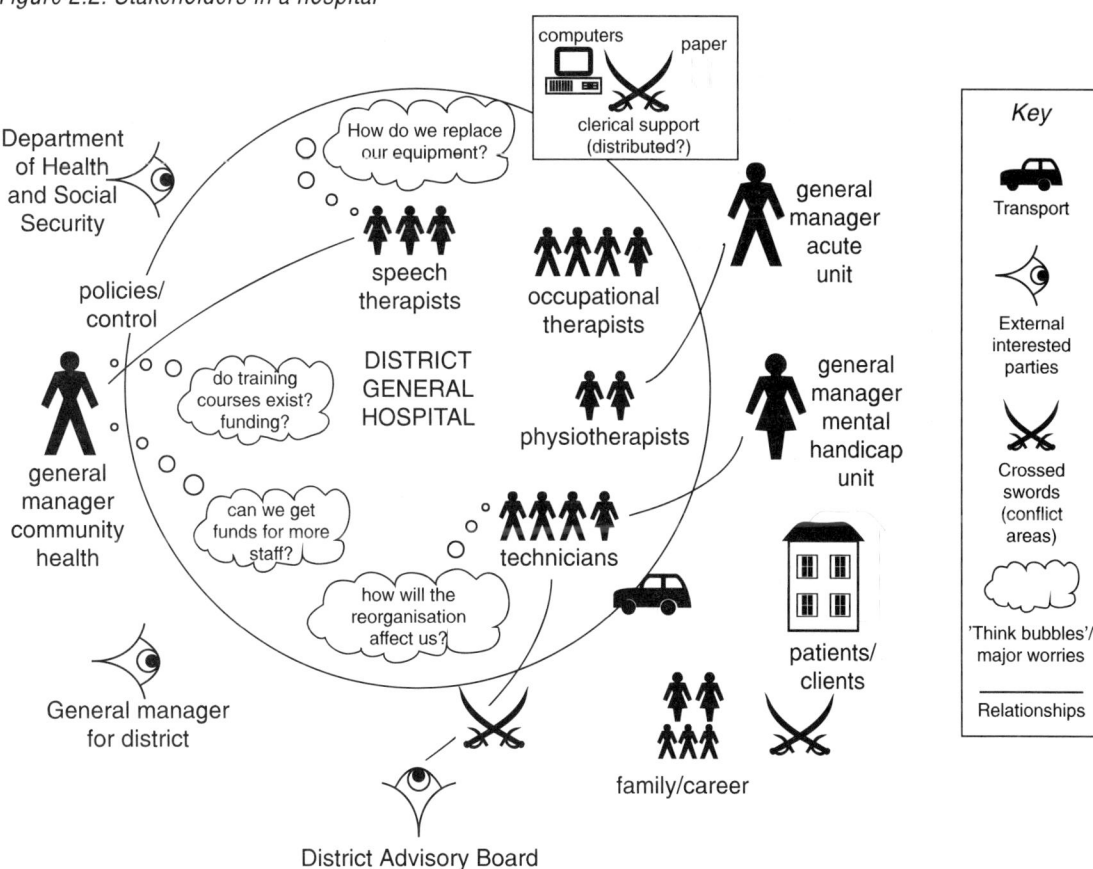

Note how certain objectives can come into conflict, for example the District Advisory Board's wish to re-organise facing opposition from technicians.

3.5 Subsystems

FAST FORWARD

Every system can be broken down into **subsystems**. Separate subsystems interact with each other, and respond to each other by means of communication or observation.

Subsystems may be differentiated from each other by:

- Function
- Space
- Time
- People
- Formality
- Automation

Action Programme 2

Demonstrate how each factor might have a major impact on organisational structure. For example, an organisation structured by function might have a production department, a sales department, an accounts department and a personnel department.

3.6 Adaptation

FAST FORWARD

If a system does not **adapt** and alter its own performance, it risks extinction. A system adapts by acquiring information about its environment and responding appropriately.

PART A   THE ORGANISATION AND ITS ENVIRONMENT

Social systems have to adapt to survive. Businesses, in particular, have to adapt to changes in the legal, political, economic, social and competitive environment.

As the environment changes, a system may react in one of two ways.

(a) It may respond to external changes by making adjustments to its own operations. These changes are **short-term**, **functional** adaptations.

(b) It may also adopt a **long-term** approach, making **structural alterations**.

Action Programme 3

A tobacco company manufacturing cigarettes may become aware of changes in the environment symptomatic of increased health awareness and concern over the dangers of smoking. How might the company survive

(a) In the short term?
(b) In the long term?

3.6.1 Adapting to changes in inputs

Often, a business has to cope with changes in the input resources they consume. Frequently, such changes are **changes in costs**, relative to other costs, or fluctuations in the **availability** of resources (raw materials, skills information).

Marketing at Work

In 1974 the **price of oil** quadrupled, and petrol prices and hence business costs went up. Various responses occurred.

- New oil fields were developed
- Cars were designed that used less petrol
- A number of ways of saving energy were invented
- The search for alternative energies (wind, solar, vegetable fuels) was initiated

Similar pressures are facing the global economy in 2007 with risks to oil supplies and an added awareness of the detrimental environmental effects of fossil fuels (global warming etc).

Other changes to inputs may be more long term, such as a slow increase in wages or a shortage in skills. To maintain competitiveness, firms will try and increase the efficiency with which labour is used, in order to minimise the impact of the cost rise.

3.6.2 Adapting the transformation processes

Many firms have adapted the way they **transform inputs into outputs** to cut costs, and to use resources more efficiently, in the light of competitive pressures. Such changes include:

- Machinery and technology
- The use of information technology
- A change in management structures

Fundamental changes to systems design have been suggested by **business process re-engineering**.

Key concept

> **Business process re-engineering** (BPR), also known as **process innovation** and **core process re-design**, is the introduction of radical changes in business processes to achieve breakthrough results in terms of major gains in levels of performance plus reductions in costs.

The chief BPR tool is a clean sheet of paper. Re-engineers start from the future and work backwards. They are unconstrained by existing methods, people or departments. In effect, they ask, 'If we were a new company, how would we run the place?' Hammer and Champey (initiators of BPR) point out that 'At the heart of re-engineering is the notion of discontinuous thinking – of recognising and breaking away from the outdated rules and fundamental assumptions that underlie operations.'

3.6.3 Adapting outputs

In market economies, businesses are supposed to adapt to changing customer needs, and even to anticipate them. Businesses and all organisations often have to **adapt what they produce**, in order to continue to add value for the customer. Any advertisement stating 'new, improved' is an example. We discuss the factors that cause customer needs to change in later chapters.

3.7 Value of the systems approach

Systems theory can be used to demonstrate how organisations can be managed, and how marketing enhances the organisation.

(a) **Environment**

Systems theory emphasises the impact of **environmental factors** on a system. Customer needs are of particular importance.

(b) **Dynamic factors**

Systems theory emphasises the **dynamic** aspects of organisation and what causes its sub-systems to develop.

(c) **Relationships**

System theory focuses on **inter-relationships** between marketing and other departments, and between the organisation and its environment. It also may demonstrate how other parts of the organisation (**sub-systems**) pursue goals that are in conflict with those of marketing.

(d) **Feedback**

Marketing can give feedback on **outcomes** which enable management to compare them with objectives. Management is less likely to take a simple "A always causes B" approach to marketing.

(e) **Appeal**

Systems theory has **imaginative appeal**. It is possible to draw the analogy between living systems and organisations (the 'organic analogy') and make some assumptions about how organisations are likely to behave on that basis. The analogy provides a framework for thinking about the organisation and designing its structure.

4 The contingency approach to organisations

FAST FORWARD

> The **contingency approach to organisations** holds that there is no universal best structure for them. What is best for an individual business will be dependent upon **contingent factors** (age, size, technology, dispersion, personnel, environment, activities, strategy).

4.1 Influences on organisation structure

Contingency theory holds that there is no universally best organisation structure, but that there could well be a best structure for each individual organisation, which will depend on **contingent factors** such as those below.

(a) **Age**. The older the organisation, the more formalised its behaviour. Work is repeated, so is more easily formalised. Organisation structure reflects the age of the industry's foundation.

(b) **Size**. The larger the organisation the more elaborate and bureaucratic its structure, the larger the average size of the units within it and the more formalised its behaviour (for consistency).

(c) **Technology**. The stronger the technical system, the more formalised the work, and the more **bureaucratic** the structure of the operating core. (We discuss technology below.) The more sophisticated the technology, the more elaborate and professional the support staff will be (eg specialists who understand it).

(d) **Geographical dispersion**. An organisation on a single site will be organised differently from one in which there are several geographically separated units.

(e) **Personnel employed**. Formalisation, bureaucracy might be needed for a large, low-skilled work-force.

(f) The **environment**, which presents constraints and opportunities.

(g) The type of **activities**, which can be organised in different ways: the nature of the market/customer base will dictate the grouping of tasks into functions, sales territories or customer groups, say.

(h) The business **strategy**, since structure should be designed to support business objectives.

(Mnemonic, using words in bold above: AS Ten Green PEAS)

5 Marketing and other functions

5.1 The role of the marketing department

Marketing orientation (as we will see below) is a business philosophy: it is not restricted to the people in the marketing department.

Typically, however, **marketing personnel** are responsible for:

- Researching customers' needs
- Assisting in the design of the product
- Suggesting a suitable pricing strategy
- Promotion: advertising, public relations etc
- Distribution: identifying how the product should be distributed
- Customer service: specifying service levels

These activities also involve other departments. In effect, the marketing department in a marketing orientated firm should:

- Champion the customer in the organisation
- Promote the organisation to the customer

Involvement of other business functions in marketing

Department	Activity
Finance	Credit terms
	Dealing with customers – invoicing payment
Production	Product manufacture; delivery times; quality
Human resources	Customer care training

5.2 Marketing and business orientation

> **FAST FORWARD**
>
> Marketing's role within an organisation will depend upon the organisation's **orientation** (functional, sales or marketing).

The precise role of marketing will depend on the way the business is orientated.

(a) **Functional orientation**

If the business has a **functional** orientation, it will mean it is organised on the basis of **specialist roles**. The production function will be geared to producing products at low cost or on the basis of certain well-defined features. The key functions are likely to be finance and technical/design, and marketing is likely to play only a small role. For businesses to be able to do without marketing, the demand for the product will probably have to exceed supply significantly.

(b) **Sales orientation**

A **sales** orientation involves an emphasis on the activities of **selling and promotion**. Rather than being based on function, this sort of organisation may be based on products, with product managers managing specific products and developing skills in relation to promotion, pricing and distribution. The problem may be, however, that marketing may be merely a support function to sales, with little emphasis being placed on the needs of the customer.

(c) **Marketing orientation**

A **marketing** orientation means the primary purpose is to fulfil the **customer's needs** and so maximise sales in this way rather than maximising sales by focusing on the mechanics of the selling process. The marketing department is obviously a key function in this kind of organisation, but the whole organisation has to be marketing oriented and to work towards the customer's needs. This has certain implications for the way the business is organised.

- Marketing involvement in senior management
- Delegation of decision-making to staff in contact with the customer
- Strong communications and information systems
- An emphasis on customer service in training and assessment

5.3 How to change the organisation's orientation

The marketing function will have a significant role if the organisation is to change towards a marketing orientation. However change may be difficult, as changes in missions and objectives must be reflected in changing the way the entity is organised.

(a) **Departmental differences**

Departmental goals may conflict: for example, research and development's objective to develop new products may be ranged against production's objective of cost limitation.

(b) **Timescale**

Marketing will also be aware that the **timescale** each department perceives as important will differ; the need for a few years' work to break into particular markets will have to be considered against the desire of financial management for maximisation of short-term profits.

(c) **Formality**

Differences in the degree of **formality** of departmental organisations may lead to internal culture clashes: for example, the idea that only certain members of a department are permitted to deal directly with other departments. However, a change in orientation will demand a significant degree of co-operation between departments.

To overcome these problems, leadership will be required from the most senior people within the organisation, and also clear statements of, *and* emphasis upon, the mission and objectives of the organisation. Marketing will have input into these processes and may play a proactive role itself in other ways.

(a) **Providing information**

Marketing can publicise the extent to which the organisation's objectives have translated into better performance in the markets and the problems which have been encountered.

(b) **Facilitating liaison**

For example, marketing can set up a system of departmental contacts, also running projects which involve a number of different departments.

(c) **Undertaking work**

For example, marketing can carry out SWOT analyses (see chapter 16) and provide a sounding board for how proposed changes will be perceived in the market.

(d) **Provision of training**

Training can cover issues such as telephone technique, and the presentation of areas that the customers see in the course of business.

These are all key aspects of a marketing department's **internal marketing**, the way it markets itself to other departments.

> **Exam tip**
>
> The topics discussed in this section are important for exam purposes. You may be asked about the objectives of the marketing department, and how compatible they are (or how they conflict!) with those of the organisation.

Chapter Roundup

- A **mission** can contain both the organisation's values and its overwhelming commercial imperatives. Mission could be said to include four elements.
    - Purpose (why a company exists)
    - Strategy (commercial logic)
    - Values (basic beliefs and moral principles)
    - Policies and standards of behaviour

- **Objectives** might be included in the mission statement, depending on the type of mission statement used, but may be subsidiary to it.

- Objectives can be **corporate** and **unit, primary** and **secondary**, and **long-term** and **short-term.**

- The **systems approach** analyses organisations in terms of their processes and interactions with their environment.

- In systems theory, a distinction is made between open and closed systems.

- As an open system, an organisation obtains **inputs** from the environment and **converts** them (through internal processes) into **outputs** to the environment. **Feedback** is obtained which allows further inputs to be adjusted, in order to control the outputs as far as possible.

- **Stakeholders** are individuals and groups who have an interest or 'stake' in the organisation. They represent an important interface between the organisation and its environment.

- Every system can be broken down into **subsystems**. Separate subsystems interact with each other, and respond to each other by means of communication or observation.

- If a system does not **adapt** and alter its own performance, it risks extinction. A system adapts by acquiring information about its environment and responding appropriately.

- The **contingency approach to organisations** holds that there is no universal best structure for organisations. What is best for an individual business will be dependent upon **contingent factors** (age, size, technology, dispersion, personnel, environment, activities, strategy).

- Marketing's role within an organisation will depend upon the organisation's **orientation** (functional, sales or marketing).

PART A   THE ORGANISATION AND ITS ENVIRONMENT

Quick Quiz

1   Which of the following is not a characteristic of mission?

    A   Rationale for existence
    B   General statement of future aims
    C   Long-term strategic direction
    D   Values

2   What are the four elements of mission?

3   Which of the following would normally be contained in a mission statement?

    A   Nature of the business
    B   Methods of competition
    C   Financial targets
    D   Principles of business

4   Give six examples of corporate objectives.

5   *Fill in the blank*

    .... is an organised or complex whole or an entity that consists of interdependent parts.

6   The outputs from an open system may be both predictable and unpredictable.

    True   ☐
    False   ☐

7   What is the difference between internal and connected stakeholders?

8   A marketing-orientated business emphasises the activities of sales and promotion.

    True   ☐
    False   ☐

Answers to Quick Quiz

1. B   A general statement of future aims is a company's vision.

2.
   - Purposes
   - Strategy
   - Values
   - Behaviour standards

3. A, B and D. C is wrong; a mission statement would not be quantified in this way.

4. Any six of:
   - Profitability
   - Market share
   - Growth
   - Cash flow
   - Return on capital employed
   - Risk
   - Customer satisfaction
   - Quality
   - Industrial relations
   - Added values
   - Earnings per share

5. A system

6. True

7. Internal stakeholders exist within the boundaries of the organisation (employees, managers).

   Connected stakeholders are those outside the organisation who have a direct interest in its affairs (suppliers, customers, shareholders).

8. False. A business with a **sales** orientation emphasises selling and promotion.

PART A   THE ORGANISATION AND ITS ENVIRONMENT

Action Programme Review

1   (a)   The number of competitors in the marketplace and the strategies they adopt
    (b)   The products of competitors; their price and quality
    (c)   The strength of the domestic currency of the organisation's country of operation
    (d)   The structure of company and personal taxation
    (e)   Policies adopted by the government or ruling political body
    (f)   Social attitudes: concern for the natural environment
    (g)   The regulatory and legislative framework within which the company operates

2   (a)   Functional departments might include production, sales, accounts and personnel.

    (b)   Differentiation by space might include the geographical division of a sales function (subsystem) into sales regions (sub-subsystems).

    (c)   A production system might be subdivided into three eight-hour shifts.

    (d)   The hierarchy may consist of senior management, middle management, junior (operational) management and the workforce.

    (e)   There may be a formal management information system and a 'grapevine'.

    (f)   Some systems might be automated (sales order processing, production planning), while others may be 'manual' (public relations, staff appraisal).

3   (a)   In the short term the company may increase production of low tar brands or reduce the price of high tar brands.

    (b)   In the long term it may diversify into sectors that do not face threats from government.

Now try Questions 3 and 4 at the end of the Study Text

The marketing environment and change

Chapter topic list

1. The marketing environment
2. Environmental complexity and dynamism
3. Coping with change
4. Managing change

Syllabus content

- 1.8 Demonstrate the dynamic and complex nature of environmental change and its importance to the development of marketing strategy and planning
- 1.9 Appreciate the potential significance of emerging environmental challenges to effective marketing in the present and future

PART A   THE ORGANISATION AND ITS ENVIRONMENT

Introduction

This chapter provides an introduction to the challenges that anyone involved in marketing is likely to face in the future, and how best to respond to those challenges.

In order to appreciate the impact of what the future may hold, we need to discuss the importance of change, and how best to respond to change. We focus first on the concepts of economic complexity and dynamism, and also turbulence, which provide a guide on how to consider environmental changes.

Change can be very traumatic for certain people and resistance to change may well occur. In Section 4 of the chapter we consider how resistance to change happens.

1 The marketing environment

FAST FORWARD

An organisation must **understand its environment** if it is to exploit changing market conditions and target its market successfully, the essence of a successful marketing strategy.

The **micro environment** includes all factors which impact directly on a firm and its activities in relation to a particular market in which it operates, and also any internal aspects of the organisation which influence the development of a marketing strategy.

The **macro environment** is concerned with broad trends and patterns in society as a whole which may affect all markets, but will be more relevant to some than others. Careful monitoring of the macro environment can enable an organisation to identify opportunities for and threats to its business, and will enable it to adopt a proactive rather than a reactive approach in the action it takes.

The macro environment is large and complex. We shall explore in detail, later in this Text, ways in which **economic** factors, at home and abroad, **social** and **cultural** factors within families and larger groups, and **legal** and **political** considerations, can all affect the marketing of goods and services.

Developments in **technology** are happening at an ever-increasing pace. The rapid appearance of completely new products, such as the digital camera and MP3 player, and the obsolescence of those previously thought essential, such as traditional camera film and the personal cassette player presents a special challenge to marketers. The Internet is also having a profound effect on the way commerce operates.

Marketing will undoubtedly also be increasingly affected by **ecological** and **ethical** issues. In the past there was a tendency to regard business activities as antithetical to 'greenness', but now it is being recognised that the two are complementary, and that one of the key factors in future business success will be the **sustainability** of business activity. This refers to the idea that resources which are used up must be replaced, and that business dealings must support work forces and communities, in order to secure on-going working relationships.

2 Environmental complexity and dynamism

FAST FORWARD

To cope with the varying and changing environment, organisations need to be able to cope with **economic complexity** and **economic dynamism** (the ability of an economy to grow rapidly).

One of the key challenges for open systems is the uncertainty of their external environments. **Environmental uncertainty** can arise from whether the environment is:

(a) **Stable** (changes slowly and predictably) or **dynamic** (changes often, rapidly and unpredictably eg rapid technological innovation, consumer fashion)

(b) **Simple** (relatively few environmental factors influencing what the organisation does) or **complex** (the firm is subject to many influences)

Exam tip

> The December 2006 exam asked you to explain 'the dynamic and complex nature of change' in the mobile phone marketing environment. You were not only expected to know about the market (basing your answer on Nokia or Vodafone, say) but specifically to define and give examples of the nature of complexity and dynamism as features of change.

2.1 Complexity

Key concept

> **Environmental complexity** relates to the uncertainties and variety of factors which impact upon an organisation.

Complexity arises from three factors.

- **Variety** of influences
- **Knowledge** needed
- **Interconnectedness** of influences

2.2 Dynamism

Key concept

> **Environmental dynamism** describes the ability of an economy to grow rapidly and smoothly without the need for intervention.

An economy which has high economic dynamism is likely to be driven by significant powerful forces such as expanding global demand, increased use of information technology or deregulation. A dynamic economy is reflected in a **high annual rate of growth** in national income, which is likely to be related to a rapid growth in households' discretionary incomes.

An assessment of the relative uncertainty of the environment might be called for, and any changes identified. Historical perspectives are useful if the environment is stable, but dynamic environments require a more **future-oriented perspective**, including changing business and marketing strategies to take advantage of dynamic conditions.

Businesses are likely to have to take the following steps to adapt to environments that are complex and dynamic.

(a) **Flexibility in business planning**

This may imply a simpler management structure because of the need for immediate communication of change.

(b) **Awareness of the risks inherent in environmental conditions**

This emphasises the importance of risk analysis and contingency planning being built into future business strategy.

Marketing at Work

Singapore is an example of a **dynamic economy**. Its GDP has grown by an annual rate of about 8% over the past couple of decades, way ahead of the West European average of about 2% pa. Evidence of Singapore's dynamism is seen in the country's rising trade surplus, strong currency and rapidly rising standards of living for its people. As well as being about economic outcomes, economic dynamism can refer to a state of mind in which the people and institutions of a country have a determination to achieve economic growth. The entrepreneurial attitudes of the Chinese community in Singapore have contributed significantly to the country's recent economic success.

Marketers have contributed significantly to Singapore's economic success. The country has a long tradition of deregulation, in which the country's entrepreneurs have had to compete in order to survive against competition. A very good example of marketers' contribution is found in Singapore Airlines which is very market-orientated in the importance which it attaches to understanding and satisfying air travellers' needs. The airline has achieved significant market-led growth and a high level of profits, and has won numerous awards for its high levels of customer service.

Action Programme 1

How complex do you think the situations below are?

(a) A new product has just been introduced to a market segment. It is proving popular. As it is based on a unique technology, barriers to entry are high. The product will not be sold outside this market segment.

(b) A group of scientists has recently been guaranteed, by an EU research sponsoring body, funds for the next ten years to investigate new technologies in the construction industry, such as 'smart materials' (which respond automatically to weather and light conditions). This is a multi-disciplinary project with possible benefits for the construction industry. A number of building firms have also guaranteed funds.

2.3 Turbulence

FAST FORWARD

Turbulence is the degree of instability in the environment. Current causes of turbulence include the political situation in the Middle East and the economic problems in America.

Key concept

Turbulence might be described as the degree of volatility in the environment.

The international business environment is not static, and turbulence can arise from a number of sources.

(a) Changing governments or **political instability**. Other political problems such as terrorism are also sources of turbulence.

(b) There may be massive changes in **regional balances of power**, as a consequence of economic growth.

(c) Exchange rates are less determined by trade than before; instead the capital markets are **global**: 'when New York sneezes, London catches a cold'. The Asian crisis of 1997, in which many Asian currencies and shares fell sharply in value, is an example.

Exam tip

For the exam you must keep in mind, when considering uncertainty and change, how organisations might attempt to cope with it. The December 2004 paper tied this in with SWOT analysis, asking candidates to assess the comparative strengths and weaknesses of a small supermarket and a multinational grocery retailer when faced with environmental change. Most of the Case Study question in December 2005 was devoted to how various organisations could respond to a specific environmental crisis: the SARS virus.

3 Coping with change

> **FAST FORWARD**
>
> **Responding to the changing environment** is a serious, on-going challenge for businesses. Monitoring and planning are essential, as is a readiness to adapt by fundamentally transforming the structure of the organisation. Such uncomfortable change is needed to safeguard the organisation's continuation and growth.

A number of issues need to be addressed if businesses are to cope successfully with a changing environment.

(a) **Environmental intelligence**

Clearly the possession of relevant environmental intelligence is a great help to any business seeking to deal actively with its environment. Businesses need to consider the variety of information sources used, the reliability of what is available and (importantly) the speed at which data is obtained.

(b) **Forecasting change**

We consider the forecasting techniques businesses use in detail in Chapter 16. For now, businesses need to consider a variety of possible options: best and worst case scenarios, as well as the outcome they consider to be most likely. Often they may construct a forecast or a range of forecasts using different assumptions about the rate of change of key factors. Plans made should reflect the outcomes forecast, and also the uncertainties identified during the forecasting process. If uncertainties are significant, plans for dealing with difficulties may be required.

(c) **Organising for change**

A number of commentators have stressed the need for businesses to undergo regular fundamental re-organisations, to be able to cope better with a changing environment. Increasingly decisions will have to be taken away from a centralised head office function and lines of communication simplified, to ensure information is passed quickly to where it is needed.

(d) **Marketing change**

Managers need to consider the internal marketing of change: how change is presented to employees.

Suggested approach	Comment
Tell	The people: clearly, realistically, openly
Sell	The pressures which make change necessary and desirable
	The vision of successful, realistically attainable change
Evolve	The people's attitudes, ideas, capacity to learn new ways
Involve	The people where possible in planning implementation

(e) **Promoting a culture of change**

This implies not just suggesting changes that need to be made because a changing environment is anticipated, but creating a more outward looking organisation which actively seeks new products, markets, processes and ways to improve productivity.

4 Managing change

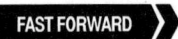

FAST FORWARD

Resistance to change can be due to self-interest, misunderstanding, contradictory assessment or intolerance of change.

4.1 Causes of resistance

Arthur Bedeian cites four common **causes** of resistance to change.

(a) **Self-interest**

If the status quo is perceived to be comfortable, or advantageous to the individual or the group.

(b) **Misunderstanding and distrust**

Opposition can occur if the reasons for, or the nature and consequences of, the change have not been made clear. This aggravates uncertainty and suspicion about the perceived threat. This may well be aggravated by imposition of change without consultation.

(c) **Contradictory assessments**

Different individuals' evaluations of the likely costs and benefits of some change. Resistance arises from individuals' perceptions of the undesirability of change.

(d) **Low tolerance of change itself**

Differences in tolerance of ambiguity, uncertainty etc. This may arise because of bad past experiences of change or because of lack of experience of change.

4.2 Symptoms of resistance

Resistance to change has a number of manifestations.

(a) Symptoms of workforce resistance to change include working-to-rule, absenteeism, go-slows, deliberate errors, sabotage.

(b) Customer resistance to change may be important entry barriers in a market with customers sticking with goods or suppliers that they are used to, or which have served them well in the past.

Action Programme 2

Think of a company you know something about. How has it changed over the past few years in relation to new technology? How might it have to change over the next few years?

4.3 Change management strategies

The following strategies were put forward by *Johnson and Scholes*.

Method	Techniques	Benefits	Drawbacks
Education and communication	- Small group briefings - Newsletters - Management development - Training	Overcomes lack of information	Time consuming Direction of change may be unclear Can't cope with change that opposes vested interests
Participation & involvement	- Small groups - Delegates & representatives	Increases ownership of decisions and change May improve quality of decisions	Time consuming Changes are limited to existing paradigm
Facilitation & support	- One on one counselling - Personal development - Provision of organisational resources	Creates learning Minimises feelings of being left out	No guarantee of valuable outcome Very slow
Negotiation & agreement	- Provision of rewards - Collective bargaining	Retains goodwill Deals with powerful interests	May sacrifice change to need for agreement Agreements may not be adhered to
Manipulation & co-optation	- Influence staff that are positively disposed - Buy-off informal leaders - Provide biased information	Can remove powerful obstacles Creates ambassadors for change Swift	Ethically questionable Becomes like blackmail May eliminate trust
Explicit and implicit coercion	- Threaten staff with penalties - Create sense of fear - Victimise individuals to send message to the rest	Swift Management control direction of change	Ethically questionable May eliminate trust May rebound in future when management are weak

PART A   THE ORGANISATION AND ITS ENVIRONMENT

Chapter Roundup

- An organisation must **understand its environment** if it is to exploit changing market conditions and target its market successfully, the essence of a successful marketing strategy.

- To cope with the varying and changing environment, organisations need to be able to cope with **economic complexity** and **economic dynamism** (the ability of an economy to grow rapidly).

- **Turbulence** is the degree of instability in the environment. Current causes of turbulence include the political situation in the Middle East and the economic problems in America.

- **Responding to the changing environment** is a serious, on-going challenge for businesses. Monitoring and planning are essential, as is a readiness to adapt by fundamentally transforming the structure of the organisation. Such uncomfortable change is needed to safeguard the organisation's continuation and growth.

- **Resistance** to change can be due to self-interest, misunderstanding, contradictory assessment or intolerance of change.

Quick Quiz

1   *Fill in the blanks*

    The marketing environment consists of the .... environment and the............... environment.

2   Define environmental complexity.

3   *Fill in the blank*

    .... describes the ability of the economy to grow rapidly and smoothly without the need for intervention.

4   What steps will businesses have to take to adapt to environments that are complex and dynamic?

5   What is turbulence?

6   What are the four causes of resistance to change described by Bedeian?

7   Which of the following factors influence the degree of complexity in a environment?

    A   Variety of influences
    B   Knowledge needed
    C   Whether the influence are macro or micro
    D   Interconnectedness of influences

8   List the six strategies for change management.

Answers to Quick Quiz

1. Micro and macro

2. Environmental complexity arises from the uncertainties and variety of the factors that impact on an organisation.

3. Environmental dynamism

4. - Flexibility in business planning
   - Awareness of the risks inherent in environmental conditions

5. The degree of volatility in an environment

6. - Self-interest
   - Misunderstanding and distrust
   - Contradictory assessments
   - Low tolerance of change

7. A, B and D

8. Education and communication, participation and involvement, facilitation and support, negotiation and agreement, manipulation and co-optation, explicit and implicit coercion.

Action Programme Review

1. (a) The environment is **simple**, as the product is only being sold in one market. The environment is **dynamic**, as the product is still at the introduction stage and demand might be predicted to increase dramatically.

   (b) The environment is **complex**, but **stable**. The knowledge required is uncertain, but funds are guaranteed for ten years.

2. Your own research.

> Now try Questions 5, 6 and 7 at the end of the Study Text

Part B
The micro-environment

The micro-environment

Chapter topic list

1. Defining the micro-environment
2. Collecting data
3. Environmental scanning
4. Published statistics
5. Bought-in data
6. External databases and the Internet

Syllabus content

- 2.3 Demonstrate an awareness of key internal and external sources of information on the micro-environment

PART B   THE MICRO-ENVIRONMENT

Introduction

The next few chapters of this Text deal with the micro-environment. In these chapters we shall be particularly concerned with how organisations analyse their micro-environment, and who is concerned with what the organisation is doing.

Marketing is about **allocating resources**. For the organisation to get the maximum benefit from its limited resources, it needs to ensure that the goods and services it produces are not wasted. The role of marketing is to **identify** and **anticipate customer needs** and wants so that the operation can use its skills and other resources to satisfy them.

Before we discuss the different elements of an organisation's micro-environment in depth, we shall look briefly at what the micro-environment is, and then discuss how **different information sources** can provide intelligence about the micro-environment.

1 Defining the micro-environment

FAST FORWARD

An organisation's micro-environment consists of itself and its current and potential **customers, suppliers** and **intermediaries**. The competition also has a key influence on the micro-environment.

Key concept

The **micro-environment** comprises all those individuals and organisations that affect the operations of a business on a day-to-day basis.

The following groups are important influences on how successful a business is:

- Customers
- Suppliers
- Intermediaries
- Competitors
- Employees
- Shareholders

We might need to remind ourselves of some of the underlying relationships between an organisation and the other organisations in its environment.

We have already mentioned that a business must generate profits. However, Drucker tells us that in order to generate profits it is necessary to **'create a customer'**.

The **market economy** based on **capitalism** contrasts with the centrally planned economy in which the State controls production, as in Soviet Russia up to the 1980s for example. A feature of market economies is that many firms compete with each other to create a customer. This is a spur to innovation and marketing activities, which *Drucker* holds are the distinguishing characteristics of business organisation.

Figure 4.1: Elements of the micro-environment

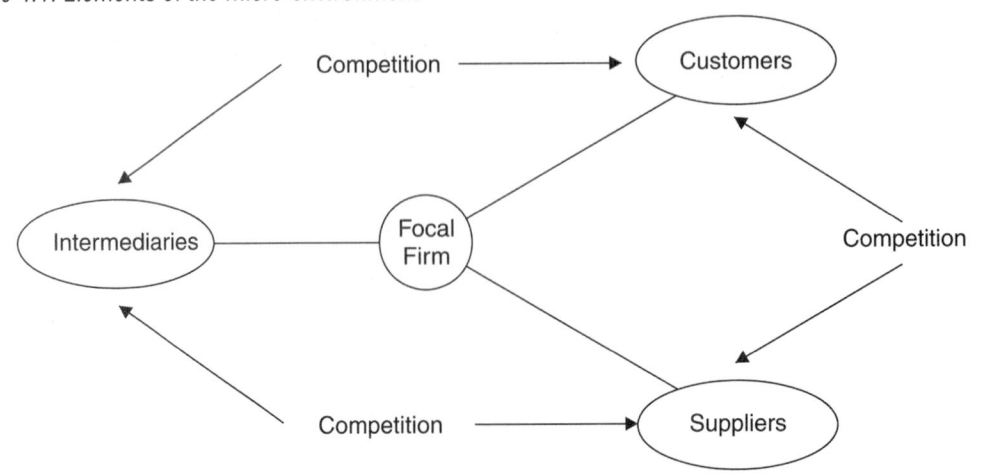

4: THE MICRO-ENVIRONMENT

The diagram shows that the micro-environment comprises not just those firms that an organisation **actually** does business with. It also includes those firms and individuals that an organisation could **potentially** do business with.

Therefore it includes not just our current customers, but potential customers who may currently be served by another organisation. Thus, an important element in understanding the micro-environment is **competition** between organisations.

- To get **customers**
- To obtain **supplies**
- To get access to the best **intermediaries**

In assessing competition, the various factors can be considered under these basic headings.

- **Who are** the **competitors**; how strong are they?
- What are the **characteristics** of the markets they compete in?
- What are the **environmental influences** on the market?
- How can the organisation maintain a **competitive advantage**?

Exam tip

> The examiner is so concerned at inattentive students mixing up the 'micro' and 'macro' environments, that exams now capitalise them as MICRO and MACRO! Pay careful attention to this simple pitfall.

For your *Marketing Environment* examination you need to have an understanding of the factors that affect the relationships between an organisation and its customers, suppliers and intermediaries. You need to know the basic factors that influence demand and supply.

1.1 Demand

Several factors influence the total market demand for a good. One of these factors is obviously its price, but there are other factors too. To help you to appreciate some of these other factors, you need to recognise that households buy not just one good with their money but a whole range of goods and services. The determinants of demand include:

- The **price** of the good
- The **price** of **other goods** (products and services)
- The size of households' **income**
- **Tastes** and **fashion**
- **Expectations**
- The **distribution** of **income** among households

1.1.1 Substitutes and complements

A change in the price of one good will not necessarily change the demand for another good. However, there are goods and services for which the market demand is inter-connected. These inter-related goods are referred to as either **substitutes** or **complements**.

(a) **Substitute goods** are goods that are alternatives to each other, so that an *increase* in the demand for one is likely to cause a *decrease* in the demand for another.

SUBSTITUTES

Coca Cola	V	Pepsi Cola
Tea	V	Coffee
Bus	V	Car
Terrestrial TV	V	Satellite TV

PART B THE MICRO-ENVIRONMENT

In this way the activities of competitors may have a major impact upon the demand for an organisation's products, even if the price and all other features of those products remain unchanged.

(b) **Complements** are goods that tend to be bought and used together, so that an *increase* in the demand for one is likely to cause an *increase* in the demand for the other.

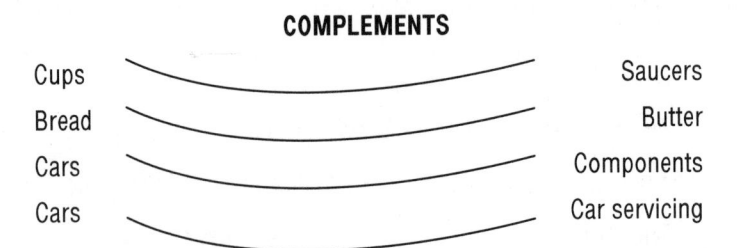

COMPLEMENTS

Cups — Saucers
Bread — Butter
Cars — Components
Cars — Car servicing

Action Programme 1

If the ownership of domestic deep freezers increases, what do you think might happen to the demand for perishable food products?

1.2 Supply

The quantity supplied of a good depends, as you might expect, on prices and costs. More specifically, it depends on the following.

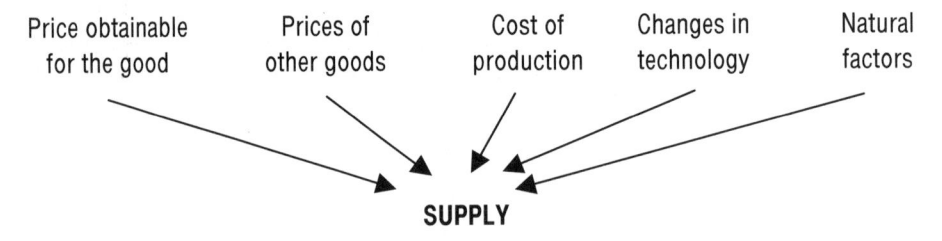

Price obtainable for the good · Prices of other goods · Cost of production · Changes in technology · Natural factors → **SUPPLY**

Exam tip

> Start thinking through how marketing organisations can manipulate supply and demand factors if they need to. The case study question in December 2006, for example, focused on the global issue of water. You were asked to explain why demand might be increasing faster than supply: what demand and supply factors can you identify? (You might immediately think of demand factors such as population growth and lifestyle changes; and supply factors such as drought, ageing infrastructure and so on.) You were also asked how you could *reduce* the demand for water, using regulation, persuasion/education and incentives. We will cover supply/demand calculations later in this text – but resist the temptation to think of them as graphs or equations: they are about an interplay of environmental factors.

1.3 The micro and macro-environments

In Part C of this Study Text we will look at the **macro-environment**. You can distinguish the micro-environment from the macro in terms of the directness of its effects.

(a) The **micro-environment** is about actual and potential transactions between a firm and its environment on a day-to-day basis.

(b) The **macro-environment** is about external forces which have a long-term impact upon the organisation's activities.

2 Collecting data

FAST FORWARD

There are various ways of **collecting data** about an organisation's micro-environment.

In Sections 2 to 5 of this chapter we will discuss how marketing departments can make use of available data.

2.1 Types of data

Data can be classified in various ways.

Key concepts

Primary data are data collected especially for a particular purpose, directly from the relevant source. Primary sources of consumer information, for example, would be the consumers themselves. Primary research is usually '**field research**', involving surveys, interviews, questionnaires, observation or experiments.

Secondary data are data which have already been gathered and assembled for other purposes or general reference. Secondary sources of consumer information would include published statistics and reports on consumer behaviour, books, Internet sites and so on. They are accessed by '**desk research**' which can often be carried out literally from the researcher's desk (given access to appropriate reference sources).

Internal data are data gathered within the organisation as a result of its operations, for example, information.

External data are data gathered from external sources, such as competitors' websites or government publications.

Desk research is the term used to describe the search for available data, usually as initial, exploratory research. Typical desk research activities include:

(a) Making use of **library sources**, such as journals, periodicals and recent academic books.

(b) Accessing the **organisation's information systems** and **records**, for information gathered by another department for a different purpose to the research in hand; internal data would include:

- **Production** data about quantities produced, materials and labour used etc
- Data about **stock**
- Data about **sales volumes**, analysed by sales area, salesman, quantity etc
- Data about **marketing** itself – ie promotion and brand data etc
- All **cost and management accounting data**
- **Financial management data** relating to capital tied up in stocks etc

(c) Tapping into industry internal **on-line databases**

(d) Buying in **data** and **reports prepared externally**, either as primary data for another organisation which is then syndicated, or as secondary data material for all users

Action Programme 2

Can you think of any limitations to desk research?

We shall discuss a systematic approach to developing an environmental information system in Part D of this Study Text. For now we shall list important sources of information that provide further details of the micro-environment of a business.

PART B THE MICRO-ENVIRONMENT

Exam tip

> The June 2006 exam explicitly asked you to identify 'key internal and external sources of information' on the MICRO environment for an organisation of your choice. It would be worth picking an organisation now and trying this as a quick exercise.

3 Environmental scanning

FAST FORWARD

> **Environmental scanning** means keeping one's eyes and ears open to what is going on generally in the market place, especially with respect to competitors, and more widely in the technological, social, economic and political environment.

The result of environmental scanning is **market intelligence**. Its sources are:

- Financial newspapers, especially the *Financial Times* and the *Wall Street Journal*
- General business magazines, such as the *Economist* and *Business Week*
- Trade journals, such as *Campaign*
- Academic journals, such as *Harvard Business Review*
- Attending conferences, exhibitions, courses and trade fairs
- Making use of salesforce feedback
- Developing and making use of a network of personal contacts in the trade
- Watching competitors

Action Programme 3

Here is a small selection of headlines from *The Times* in the UK on a given day.

(a) House prices show signs of slowdown
(b) Checks to make sure gold isn't tarnished
(c) Professions in insurance crisis

In each case, give examples of organisations that should think about the threats and opportunities that these stories indicate?

With regard to watching competitors, a **competitor intelligence system** needs to be set up to cope with a vast amount of data from:

- Financial statements
- Common customers and suppliers
- Inspection of a competitor's products
- The competitor's former employees
- Job advertisements

All this data needs to be compiled (eg clipping services, standard monthly reports on competitors' activities), catalogued for easy access, and analysed (eg summarised, ranked by reliability, extrapolating data from financial reports).

Action Programme 4

What information does your organisation hold on its competitors? How does it obtain that information? What does it use it for?

4 Published statistics

> **FAST FORWARD**
>
> There is a wealth of published statistics which can be used by marketing departments. There are two prime sources – government and non-government.

The government is a major source of economic information and information about industry and population trends. Examples of UK **government publications,** many of which are available free online at **www.statistics.gov.uk**, are as follows.

(a) The *Annual Abstract of Statistics* contains data about manufacturing output, housing, population etc.

(b) The *Digest of UK Energy Statistics*.

(c) *Housing and Construction Statistics.* This is published quarterly.

(d) *Financial Statistics*.

(e) *Economic Trends*.

(f) *Census of Population.* The Office for National Statistics publishes continuous datasets including the *National Food Survey,* the *Household Survey* and the *Family Expenditure Survey*.

(g) *Census of Production* (annual). This has been described as 'one of the most important sources of desk research for industrial marketers'. It provides data about production by firms in each industry in the UK.

(h) *Department of Employment Gazette* (monthly) gives details of employment in the UK.

(i) *British Business*, published weekly by the Department of Trade and Industry, gives data on industrial and commercial trends at home and overseas.

(j) *Business Monitor,* published by the Business Statistics Office, gives detailed information about various industries.

(k) *Social Trends* is published annually.

Official statistics are also published by other government bodies such as the European Union, the United Nations and local authorities.

Non-government sources of information include the following.

(a) Companies and other organisations specialising in the provision of economic and financial data (eg the *Financial Times* Business Information Service, the Data Research Institute, Reuters and the Extel Group)

(b) **Directories and yearbooks**, such as Kompass or Kelly's Directory

(c) **Professional institutions** (eg Chartered Institute of Marketing, Industrial Marketing Research Association, British Institute of Management, Institute of Practitioners in Advertising)

(d) **Specialist libraries**, such as the City Business Library in London, collect published information from a wide variety of sources

(e) **Trade associations**, trade unions and Chambers of Commerce

(f) **Trade journals**

(g) **Commercial organisations** such as banks and TV networks

(h) **Market research agencies**

PART B   THE MICRO-ENVIRONMENT

Action Programme 5

Most industries are served by one or more trade journals which can provide invaluable information on new developments in the industry, articles about competitors' products, details of industry costs and prices and so on.

Find out to what trade journals your organisation subscribes. Look through a number of them and note the type of information they contain and assess how that information may be used by both you and other members of your organisation.

5 Bought-in data

The sources of data we have looked at so far have generally been free because they are in the public domain. Inexpensiveness is an advantage which can be offset by the fact that the information is unspecific and needs considerable analysis before being useable.

A middle step between adapting secondary data and commissioning research is the purchase of data collected by market research companies or business publishing houses. The data tend to be expensive but less costly than research.

There are a great many commercial sources of secondary data, and a number of guides to these sources are available.

- *The Blue Book* (ONS National Income and Expenditure)
- *Guide to Official Statistics*, The Stationery Office
- *Compendium of Marketing Information Sources*, Euromonitor
- *Market Search*

Commonly used sources of data on particular industries and markets include:

- Key Note Publications
- Mintel publications
- *Market Research GB*, Euromonitor

Exam tip | Lack of knowledge of information sources is a very common weakness in exam scripts.

Marketing at Work

Country factfile: Malaysia

Socio-economic indicators

	Unit	2004	2005	2006
Population aged 65+	'000	1,074.50	1,106.47	1,140.82
Annual disposable income	$US million	64,225.21	68,129.90	69,261.94
Consumer expenditure	$US million	45,040.37	47,951.41	49,438.32
New registrations of passenger cars	'000	406.50		
Consumer expenditure on food	$US million	9,415.8	10,210.4	10,666.0
Internet users	'000	10,108.70	10,769.48	11,255.46
Soft drink market	Million litres	937	970	1,012

Source

International Marketing Data and Statistics 2006
World Consumer lifestyles Databook
Consumer Asia 2006
World Consumer Spending 2005-2006
Bank Negara Malaysia (Central Bank of Malaysia)   (www.bnm.gov.my)
Jabatan Perangkaan Malaysia (Department of Statistics)   (www.statistics.gov.my)

www.euromonitor.com

6 External databases and the Internet

6.1 Sources of information

FAST FORWARD

> As well as the **paper-based** sources of information, financial newspapers, business magazines, trade and academic journals and government-produced statistics, organisations can also use **computer databases** and the **Internet**.

Key concepts

> A **database** is a collection of structured data. Any item of data can be used as the subject for enquiry.
>
> A **real-time system** is a system where data is continually received and processed so that updating of data on the system is continuous and almost instantaneous.
>
> An **online system** is a system that can be accessed by telephone at locations that are remote from the main computer.

The continual updating of real-time systems is of course their major advantage from the marketer's viewpoint. Up-to-date information about competitors and the general micro-environment is readily available.

Exam tip

> Marks were available in the June 2005 exam for noting the role of real-time on-line information as part of an environmental information system, alongside other elements – discussed later in this text – such as market research, environmental audits and trade sources.

6.2 External databases

An organisation can obtain data from an **external database** operated by another organisation.

6.2.1 Online databases

Most external databases are online databases, which are very large computer files of information, supplied by **database providers** and managed by **host** companies. Access to such databases is open to anyone prepared to pay, and who is equipped with a personal computer plus a modem (to provide a phone link to the database) and communication software. Most databases can be accessed around the clock.

Providers of **database information** include the following.

- Directory publishers such as Kompass
- Market research publishers such as Mintel, Key Note and Frost & Sullivan
- Producers of statistical data, including the UK government and Eurostat
- Reuters Business Briefing
- FT Profile

PART B   THE MICRO-ENVIRONMENT

As well as making information available, online searches can be considerably more time-efficient than searches of paper-based material. The structure of the database enables the user to access data quickly and to able to specify what data is required (for example, information about a specific competitor), rather than having to look through considerable amounts of paper-based data for little reward.

6.3 The Internet

Key concept

> The **Internet** is a world-wide network of powerful computers and telecommunications systems.

Internet usage has expanded considerably over the last few years with improved access and decreased cost.

Most companies of any size now have a site on the Internet available for access by customers or indeed competitors. A site is a collection of screens on the Internet providing information in text or graphic form.

The Internet is discussed in detail in Chapter 13. For now, simply note its value as a research tool! (You should be familiar with this already, as a lay skill for marketers.)

Chapter Roundup

- An organisation's micro-environment consists of itself and its current and potential **customers, suppliers** and **intermediaries**. The competition also has a key influence on the micro-environment.
- There are various ways of **collecting data** about an organisation's micro-environment.
- **Environmental scanning** means keeping one's eyes and ears open to what is going on generally in the market place, especially with respect to competitors, and more widely in the technological, social, economic and political environment.
- There is a wealth of **published statistics** which can be used by marketing departments. There are two prime sources – government and non-government.
- As well as the **paper-based** sources of information, financial newspapers, business magazines, trade and academic journals and government-produced statistics, organisations can also use **computer databases** and the **Internet**.

Quick Quiz

1   Define the micro-environment.

2   Who are the key constituents of the micro-environment?

3   If the demand for a good goes up, the demand for a complement good will normally go down.

　　True　☐
　　False　☐

4   Match the following types of data with the description given.

　　(a)   Primary data
　　(b)   Secondary data
　　(c)   Internal data
　　(d)   External data

        (1)   Data gathered for general reference
        (2)   Data gathered from within the organisation
        (3)   Data gathered directly for a particular purpose
        (4)   Data gathered from sources maintained by others

5   *Fill in the blank*

    A database is a collection of .... data.

6   A system where data is continually received and processed so that updating of the data on the system is continuous and is almost instantaneous is called a:

    A   Direct-update system
    B   Online system
    C   Real-time system
    D   Instant-update system

7   How else might competitors compete, other than over customers?

8   Give three examples of techniques that might be used in field research.

Answers to Quick Quiz

1   The micro-environment comprises all those individuals and organisations that affect the operations of a business on a day-to-day basis

2   - Customers
    - Suppliers
    - Intermediaries
    - Competitors
    - Employees
    - Shareholders

3   False. The demand for complements tends to rise or fall together.

4   (a)   (3)
    (b)   (1)
    (c)   (2)
    (d)   (4)

5   Structured

6   C   Real time system

7   Competitors may also compete to obtain supplies and gain access to the best intermediaries

8   Any three of:
    - Surveys
    - Interviews
    - Questionnaires
    - Observation
    - Experiments

PART B THE MICRO-ENVIRONMENT

Action Programme Review

1   (a)   Domestic deep freezers and perishable products are complements because people buy deep freezers to store perishable products.

    (b)   Perishable products are supplied either as fresh produce (for example, fresh meat and fresh vegetables) or as frozen produce, which can be kept for a short time in a refrigerator but for longer in a freezer. The demand for frozen produce will rise (the demand curve will move to the right), while the demand for fresh produce will fall (the demand curve will move to the left).

    (c)   Wider ownership of deep freezers is likely to increase bulk buying of perishable products. Suppliers can save some packaging costs, and can therefore offer lower prices for bulk purchases.

2   The limitations of desk research are as follows.

    (a)   The data gathered is by definition not specific to the matter under analysis. It was gathered and prepared for another purpose and so is unlikely to be ideal.

    (b)   Because it was gathered for another purpose, the data are likely to require a fair amount of adaptation and analysis before they can be used.

    (c)   The data gathered are historical and may be some time out-of-date.

3   (a)   Property development companies, builders, mortgage providers, mortgage advisers, estate agents

    (b)   Gold and silver producers and buyers

    (c)   Accountants, solicitors, surveyors, insurance companies, insurance brokers, clients of professionals

    It is a good idea to get into the habit of playing this game whenever you read a newspaper. One day you will spot a golden opportunity for your organisation that all competitors will miss.

4   Own research.

5   Own research.

Now try Question 8 at the end of the Study Text

5

Stakeholders

Chapter topic list

1. The stakeholders of organisations
2. Internal stakeholders
3. Connected stakeholders
4. External stakeholders
5. The importance of stakeholders

Syllabus content

- 2.1 Describe the external and internal stakeholders that constitute the micro-environment within which organisations operate and their importance to the marketing process
- 2.2 Explain the nature of the interactions between the organisation and its various stakeholders

PART B   THE MICRO-ENVIRONMENT

Introduction

In this chapter we discuss the importance of those interested parties that can have an impact upon, and are affected by, an organisation's activities. These are its **stakeholders.**

We stressed in Chapter 4 the need for active analysis of the micro-environment, and obviously stakeholder analysis is a vital part of this. Businesses need to understand:

- The **relative importance** of each stakeholder
- Their **actual** or **possible impact** upon the business
- Whether their **impact** is potentially positive, negative or neither
- The **interests** of each stakeholder group
- The **relationships** with each group of stakeholders
- How the business's **actions** affect stakeholders
- How the organisation and its marketing department should **respond to stakeholder concerns**

Action Programme 1

Give four examples of an organisation's stakeholders.

Exam tip — Be prepared to be asked about the stakeholders of a variety of organisations, not just businesses.

1 The stakeholders of organisations

FAST FORWARD

Stakeholder groups can exert influence on strategy. The greater the power of a stakeholder group, the greater its influence will be.

Each stakeholder group has different expectations and objectives, and the objectives of the various groups may conflict.

Very generally, a stakeholder can be understood as anyone who is affected by the decisions made by an organisation.

Figure 5.1 below illustrates the types of stakeholders an organisation might have, as mentioned in Chapter 2.

Figure 5.1: Organisational stakeholders

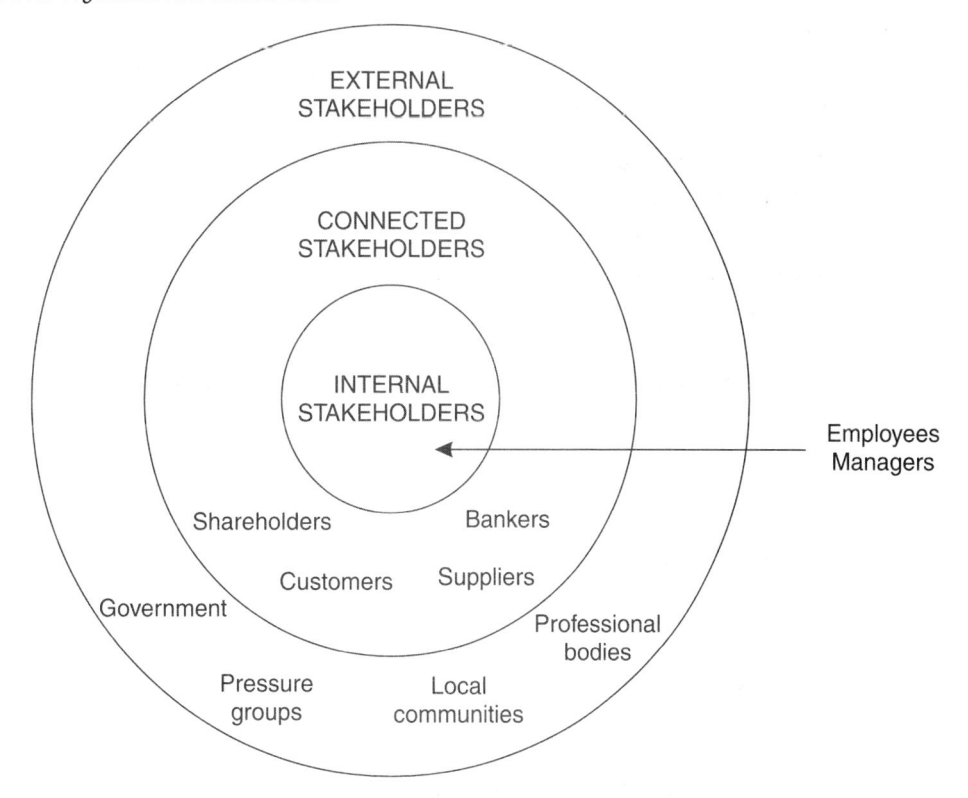

1.1 How important are stakeholder relationships?

There are two approaches to stakeholder theory for profit-orientated business organisations.

Strong view	Weak view
Each stakeholder in the business has a legitimate claim on management attention. Management's job is to balance stakeholder demands.	Satisfying stakeholders such as customers *is* a good thing – but only because it enables the business to satisfy its primary purpose, the long-term growth in owner wealth.

Although stakeholder management is an increasing fashionable discipline, there are problems with the strong stakeholder view.

(a) Managers who are accountable to everyone are, in fact, accountable to no-one.

(b) Managers decide on the balance between different stakeholders – they will favour their own interests.

(c) It confuses a stakeholder's interest in a firm with a person's citizenship of a state.

(d) People have interests, but this does not give them rights.

1.1.1 Conflict of stakeholder interests

Not all stakeholder demands can be legitimately balanced. A relationship in which **conflict between stakeholder interests** can be dramatic is that between managers and shareholders. The relationship can run into trouble when:

(a) Managers focus on maintaining the corporation as a vehicle for their managerial skills.

(b) The shareholders wish to see radical changes to enhance their dividend stream and increase the value of their shares.

The conflict in this case can be seriously detrimental to the company's stability.

Shareholders may force resignations and divestments of businesses, while managers may seek to preserve their empire and provide growth at the same time by undertaking risky policies.

Similar conflicts of interest may occur between shareholders (focus on profitability) and customers (desire for affordable price, quality) and/or society (desire for investment in environmental protection, secure employment etc).

1.2 Stakeholder management

In practice an organisation's management may, consciously or unconsciously, do the following.

- **Identify who** their stakeholders are
- **Identify** their **respective importance**
- **Identify** their **power** (see below)
- **Assess how the business affects stakeholders**, and vice versa business
- **Identify stakeholders' interests**

How stakeholders relate to the management of the company depends very much on what type of stakeholder they are and on the level in the management hierarchy at which they are able to apply pressure. Clearly a company's management will respond differently to the demands of, say, its shareholders and the community at large.

The way in which the relationship between company and stakeholders is conducted is equally a function of the character of the relationship, the parties' **relative bargaining strength** and the philosophy underlying each party's objectives. This can be shown by means of a spectrum as follows (Figure 5.2).

Figure 5.2: Stakeholders' bargaining strength

Company's conduct of relationship	Command/ dictated by company	Consultation and consideration of stakeholders' views	Negotiation	Participation and acceptance of stakeholders' views	Democratic voting by stakeholders	Command/ dictated by stakeholders

Weak ← Stakeholders' bargaining strength → Strong

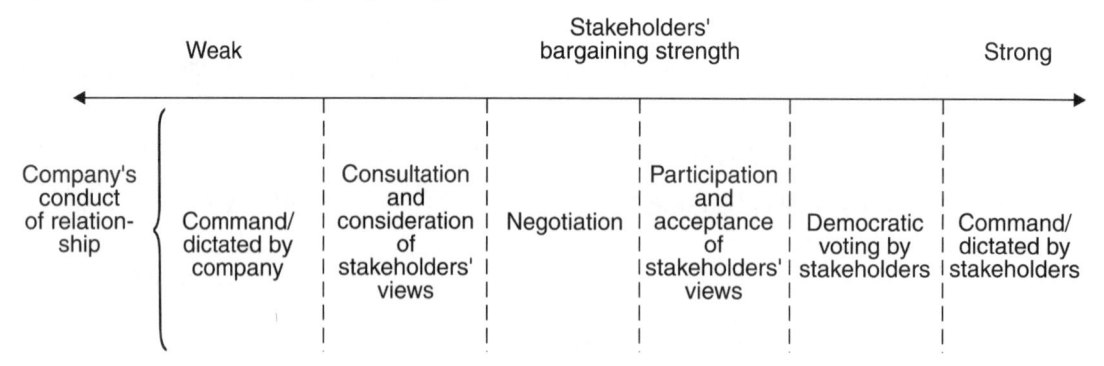

1.3 Stakeholder mapping

Mendelow classifies stakeholders on a matrix (Figure 5.3) whose axes are **power held** and **likelihood of showing an interest** in the organisation's activities. These factors will help define the type of relationship the organisation should seek with its stakeholders.

Figure 5.3: Mendelow's power/interest matrix

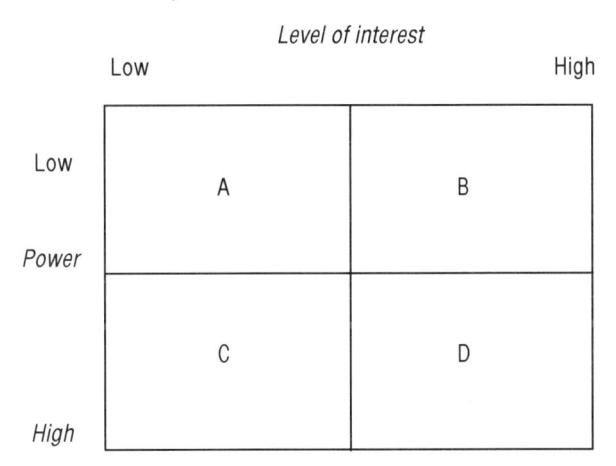

	Level of interest Low	Level of interest High
Low Power	A	B
High Power	C	D

(a) **Key players** are found in segment D: strategy must be **acceptable** to them, at least. An example would be a major customer.

(b) Stakeholders in segment C must be treated with care because of their power. While often passive, they are capable of moving to segment D if their interest is aroused. They should, therefore be **kept satisfied**. Large institutional shareholders might fall into segment C.

(c) Stakeholders in segment B do not have great ability to influence strategy, but their views can be important in influencing more powerful stakeholders, perhaps by lobbying. They should therefore be **kept informed.** Community representatives and charities might fall into segment B.

(d) Minimal effort is expended on segment A.

Stakeholder mapping is used to assess the significance of stakeholders. This in turn has implications for the organisation.

(a) The framework of corporate governance and the direction and control of the business should recognise **stakeholders' levels** of **interest** and **power**.

(b) Companies may try to **reposition** certain stakeholders and discourage others from repositioning themselves, depending on their attitudes.

(c) Key **blockers** and **facilitators** of change must be identified.

Stakeholder mapping can also be used to establish **political priorities**. A map of the current position can be compared with a map of a desired future state. This will indicate critical shifts that must be pursued.

2 Internal stakeholders

> **FAST FORWARD**
>
> **Management and employees**, the key internal stakeholders, have a close, personal, interest in the organisation's continuation, growth, expectations and goals.

Because employees and management (which includes the chairman and the board of directors) are so intimately connected with the company, their objectives are likely to have a strong and immediate influence on how it is run. Management and employees, key internal stakeholders, are interested in the following issues.

PART B THE MICRO-ENVIRONMENT

(a) **Organisation's continuation and growth**

The organisation is a place where management and employees spend a great deal of their time and energy. It pays them. Management and employees have a special interest in the organisation's continued existence.

(b) **Expectation and goals**

Managers and employees have certain **individual expectations** and goals which, it is hoped, can be harnessed, in part at least, to the goals of the organisation. These include security of income, interesting work and skills and career development.

2.1 Employee expectations

The interests and expectations of internal stakeholders vary between cultures and change over time. In Japan, for example, a 'job for life' has until recently been accepted as a responsibility which organisations have held towards their workers. In the UK, employees are increasingly coming to expect short-term employment contracts, but expectations are rising in respect of such issues as work-life balance, flexible working (to support working parents) and so on.

Companies often face a dilemma in reconciling the needs of internal stakeholders with marketing needs. Providing crèche facilities for workers may satisfy the former but will it put the company at a price disadvantage in the market place?

On the other hand, satisfying the needs of internal stakeholders may actually help the marketing effort. Many enlightened work policies secure greater **commitment and loyalty** from workers. If the workforce is demotivated, a number of adverse consequences are possible.

- Low productivity
- High staff turnover leading to recruitment and training costs
- Increased militancy
- Presentation of a poor image to the customer, no 'happy smiling faces'

Many organisations are now practising what is called **internal marketing**. This applies the principles of marketing to employees as though they are internal customers. As with all external marketing, employers need to consider the diverse range of needs that employees seek to satisfy at work, and aim to meet them. Communication of a company's values are a key part of internal marketing.

Marketing at Work

United Biscuits' statement of responsibility to its employees:

'To achieve the dynamic morale and team spirit based on mutual confidence without which a business cannot be successful, people have to be cared for during their working lives and in retirement. In return we expect from all our staff loyalty and commitment to the company. We respect the rights and innate worth of the individual. In addition to being financially rewarding, working life should provide as much job satisfaction as possible. The company encourages all employees to be trained and developed to achieve their full potential.

United Biscuits takes a responsible attitude towards employment legislation and codes of practice, union activities and communications with staff. We place the highest priority on promoting and preserving the health and safety of employees. Employees, for their part, have a clear duty to take every reasonable precaution to avoid injury to themselves, their colleagues and members of the public.'

2.2 The Board of Directors: co-ordinating internal and some connected stakeholders

At the top of the chain of command in any organisation is a body of people with decision-making powers. A local council, a board of trustees or a board of directors all have powers delegated to them by another body – the voting population, the settlor and beneficiaries and the shareholders in each case respectively. The quality of this body's decisions is therefore subject to review, but for practical purposes a board should 'run' the organisation.

In many UK companies, the Board provides both functions with **executive directors** who run the business, and **non-executive directors** who are supposed to keep watch on the shareholders' behalf. So, in theory, the board is an institution combining internal and connected stakeholders. If it is not to be a rubber stamp for executive management, it must include non-executive directors with real influence.

3 Connected stakeholders

FAST FORWARD

> **Connected stakeholders** have an interest in an organisation in so far as its continuation and profitability affects their own business or returns. For consumers, another category of connected stakeholder, their interest lies in their experience of dealing with the organisation, on a material and possibly even moral level.

3.1 Shareholders

Shareholders look for a **return** on their **investment**, whether in the short or long term. As shareholders own the business, this is a commercial organisation's prime objective (at least in the UK). Some shareholders are concerned with a corporation's ethical performance, hence the growth of investment funds designed to avoid certain companies.

Shareholder involvement, particularly institutional shareholder involvement, has been encouraged by the recent interest in **corporate governance** in many countries. Other reasons, particularly large remuneration for directors, have led to increased shareholder pressure. The most potent weapon shareholders have is to sell their shares, as the falling share prices that will result may encourage a takeover bid.

Exam tip

> Marks were available in the December 2005 exam for distinguishing between 'stakeholders' and 'shareholders'. The examiner is serious about testing potential pitfalls and confusing in terms like this. Make sure you know the difference between stakeholders and shareholders – and between public sector organisations and public limited companies, to cite another common example. If nothing else, this will help you to read exam questions accurately!

3.2 Bankers

Bankers and other financiers are also interested in a firm's overall condition, but from the point of view of the security of any loan they make. A bank is keen to minimise the risk of interest not being paid, or of its security being poor.

If financiers are unhappy, they can limit or withdraw credit facilities, and thus leave a business with insufficient funds to fulfil its objectives.

3.3 Suppliers

Suppliers will expect to be paid and will be interested in future business.

If the relationship with suppliers deteriorates because of a poor payment record, suppliers can limit or withdraw credit and charge higher rates of interest. They can also reduce their level of **service,** or even switch to supplying competitors.

Major suppliers will often be key stakeholders, particularly in businesses where material costs and quality are significant. Supplier co-operation is also important if organisations are trying to improve their management of assets by keeping stock levels to a minimum; they will need to rely on suppliers for reliability of delivery.

The position of suppliers will depend on the level of competition they themselves face. If supply arrangements appear to be complicated or are often disrupted, organisations may consider taking these arrangements in-house.

3.4 Distributors

The main interest of distributors are for reliable supply, improvements in quality and support on marketing. Distributors can stock competing brands and can delay payments for goods received.

Problems with distribution arrangements can also threaten sales.

As with suppliers, most businesses are seeking to **develop relationships** with their distributors. Not only does this assist businesses' asset management, distributors can enhance the product by the ways in which they sell it, and the after-sales service. They can also provide important **market intelligence**.

3.5 Consumers

Consumers have increasingly high expectations of the goods and services they buy, both from the private and public sectors. These include not just low costs, but value for money, quality and service support.

In theory, if consumers are not happy with their purchases, they will take their business elsewhere next time. The consumer is thus sovereign and if suppliers do not cater for their complex set of needs and expectations, they will lose business. With increasingly competitive markets, consumers are able to exercise increasing levels of power over companies as individuals.

More sophisticated analysis of consumer behaviour has also enhanced the importance of consumers. Dissatisfied customers are more likely to make their views known than satisfied customers. Moreover businesses now believe that normally the costs of retaining existing customers are significantly less than those of obtaining new customers. The implications of this will be discussed many times during your CIM studies.

Consumers are increasingly evaluating goods and services not just on the basis of how they will perhaps satisfy their immediate material needs, but also how they will satisfy their **deeper moral needs**. For example, a shopper may prefer one brand of baked beans not for its taste but because the manufacturer supports a good cause of which the consumer approves. Marketing managers must be alert to the ever-changing social concerns of buyers and seek to accommodate these within their marketing mix.

Organisations can respond to consumer concerns by having systems in place for dealing with customer comments and criticisms.

(a) **Customer panels** (focus groups) or visits to customers

(b) A written **customer services policy** (a customer charter)

(c) Giving **staff** in contact with customers the authority to deal with complaints or problems

(d) **Formal procedures** for dealing with customer complaints including staff dedicated to responding to comments or criticisms

3.5.1 Limitations of consumer power

It is, however, true that in a number of markets consumers do not have complete sovereignty over suppliers.

(a) **Lack of competition**

In many markets, competition is very limited and consumers cannot realistically take their business elsewhere. Even if there are large numbers of competitors, there may be little differentiation between products in respect of the moral concerns of consumers.

(b) **Limited knowledge**

Consumer sovereignty may also be limited by the limited knowledge that consumers have of a product. How many people are capable of fully evaluating the tangible qualities of DVD players (let alone the moral and social credentials of their manufacturers)?

(c) **Unfair contracts**

Consumers have been subject to unfair contracts, as they do not have the resources to evaluate properly the choices put to them. For example, a consumer is often not in a position to judge the safety of one product as opposed to another.

(d) **Redress**

In the past, it has not always been easy for consumers to get redress. A large company is better able to absorb the costs of a legal action than an individual consumer.

In short, consumerism (the consumer rights movement) arose because in many FMCG (fast-moving consumer goods) industries, the bargaining power of the consumer is low.

Because of the limitations of consumer sovereignty described above, a number of means are available for the protection of consumers' wider interests. We shall discuss these in later chapters of this Text.

4 External stakeholders

> **FAST FORWARD**
>
> **External stakeholder groups** – the government, local authorities, pressure groups, the community at large, professional bodies – are likely to have quite diverse objectives and have a varying ability to ensure that the company meets them.

External stakeholder groups include:

(a) The **government** which has an interest in tax revenue, compliance with legislation and required development.

(b) **Local authorities** which are also interested, because companies can bring local employment and affect the local environment (eg by increasing road traffic).

(c) **Professional bodies** are interested to ensure that members who work for companies comply with professional ethics and standards.

(d) **Pressure groups** deal with a variety of issues.

Marketing at Work

Increasingly the **stakeholders of charities** are being given the rights to be consulted, and trustees must report on contacts with stakeholders. Recently the Charity Commission in the UK emphasised that trustees must state whether they have consulted stakeholders (major funders, members, beneficiaries and donors) about payments to trustees, and must also disclose the results of the consultation.

Many charities are of course proactive in communicating with stakeholders and have made efforts to explore a number of channels of communication. The anxiety disorder charity No Panic, for example, runs its support and recovery groups by teleconferencing.

Action Programme 2

A key document in communication with stakeholders is a charity's annual report. What do you think are the key elements in a charity's annual report?

4.1 The government as a stakeholder

The government at local and national level is a very important stakeholder and, **in theory**, reflects the values of the people which it represents. Consider the following examples of the reasons why government bodies take an interest in the activities of commercial organisations.

(a) The **spending patterns** of companies on capital equipment can have significant macroeconomic effects.

(b) Government often looks to private companies to relieve it of **responsibilities**, eg in respect of the employment of disabled people.

(c) A profitable business sector results in greater **tax collection potential** for governments.

4.2 Society as a stakeholder

The actions of organisations can affect the core social values of a culture. Consider the following examples.

(a) Does **advertising** of luxury goods create a greater sense of alienation by poorer members of society who will never be able to afford them?

(b) Does the use of **foreign languages** (eg American terms in England; English in France) threaten the cultural identity of a nation?

(c) Do **newspapers** have a duty to represent the interests and views of all sections of society?

Pressure groups are often the interface between an organisation and the community, since they have a higher degree of interest in the issues and impacts. This may be a problem for the organisation (if pressure groups lobby against them or organise boycotts of their brands), but it may also be a source of marketing advantage (for example, by co-opting support from the group; getting products endorsed; using experts in marketing messages; gathering feedback information and ideas; showing willingness to engage in socially responsible dialogue; putting social responsibility higher on the corporate agenda; and perhaps influencing governing policies and standards which might suit the organisation but *not* its competitors!). We discuss pressure groups in detail in Chapter 6.

Marketing at Work

Look out for examples of:

- Organisations or brands which are **opposed by interest or pressure groups**. Examples include the targeting of canned tuna brands by environmental groups, and lobbying for controls on the advertisement of 'junk' foods due to concerns over childhood obesity.

- Organisations or brands which are **supported or endorsed by interest or pressure groups**. Examples include the Heart Foundation 'Tick' on healthy foods; ethical brand listings and awards; the endorsement of animal-friendly or child-friendly products and so on.

(Check out the 'Top Ethical Brands' list published by the Medinge Group: www.medinge.com.)

Strategies for dealing with different external stakeholders will vary. Businesses may find it easier to negotiate with an external stakeholder who has a number of interests than it would be to negotiate with one whose interest is only one issue. Local stakeholders may be best dealt with by local management, whereas stakeholders with national or international concerns may be best dealt with on a business-wide or even industry-wide basis.

Action Programme 3

Stakeholders can also be split up into primary and secondary stakeholders. What do you suppose would be the differences between the two groups?

5 The importance of stakeholders

FAST FORWARD

Organisations must identify the relative importance of the different classes of stakeholders. This means considering the degree of **power** stakeholders have, and their degree of **interest** in the organisation.

We have discussed in this chapter the pressures that stakeholders can exert. Organisations must thus identify the relative importance of the different classes of stakeholders. This means considering the degree of **power** stakeholders have, and their degree of **interest** in the organisation.

Once this analysis has been undertaken, organisations have to decide how best to deal with stakeholder concerns.

5.1 Responding to stakeholder power

As we have seen, **shareholders** can influence and constrain the management of a company at a number of different levels. When deciding on the company's objectives, management actions will be directed to maximise long term owner value.

However in order to fulfil the company's mission and maximise long-term owner value, management activities will be influenced to a greater or lesser extent by *other* stakeholders.

(a) **Customers' demands** will dictate decisions for investment in new products, development of existing ones and setting-up of new outlets. They will also affect the standards adopted for quality control. The extent to which they can be enticed away by competitors' products will affect the planned advertising spend.

PART B   THE MICRO-ENVIRONMENT

(b) **Suppliers' and distributors' demands** will affect the timing and amount of production.

(c) **Employees' attitudes and objectives** will greatly affect the organisation and co-ordination required to put production plans into effect. Construction of departments and work groups, job design, workflow and the amount of training undertaken will all be matters in which management will have to take employees' views into account.

(d) **Legislation, regulations and the community at large**. At the planning level, management discretion can be constrained both by legal requirements designed to protect the community as a whole and the potential consequences of popular dissatisfaction.

Exam tip

> In the exam you may be asked to identify the most important stakeholder interests for your own or another organisation, including a charity (June 2003), or a government agency (December 2006), or commercial concerns in a variety of markets (June and December 2005). Questions may focus on the conflicting interests of different stakeholders (June 2004, June 2006), or on particular strategies: the December 2004 paper asked about the key stakeholders to be consulted when a company is considering diversification. Get used to thinking about who the stakeholders are in any industry or sector you encounter!

Action Programme 4

You now have a chance to put Mendelow's classification (see above) into practice. Select an organisation, think what stakeholders are interested in it and assess their relative power and interest. Justify your measurements of power and interest.

Chapter Roundup

- **Stakeholder groups** can exert influence on strategy. The greater the power of a stakeholder group, the greater its influence will be.

  Each stakeholder group has different expectations and objectives, and the objectives of the various groups may conflict.

- **Management and employees**, the key internal stakeholders, have a close, personal, interest in the organisation's continuation, growth, expectations and goals.

- **Connected stakeholders** have an interest in an organisation in so far as its continuation and profitability affects their own business or returns. For consumers, another category of connected stakeholder, their interest lies in their experience of dealing with the organisation, on a material and, even possibly, moral level.

- **External stakeholder groups** – the government, local authorities, pressure groups, the community at large, professional bodies – are likely to have quite diverse objectives and have a varying ability to ensure that the company meets them.

- Organisations must identify the relative importance of the different classes of stakeholders. This means considering the degree of **power** stakeholders have, and their degree of **interest** in the organisation.

Quick Quiz

1. Give five examples of connected stakeholders.
2. Match the descriptions with the letters in Mendelow's grid.

	Level of Interest	
	Low	High
Power Low	A	B
Power High	C	D

- Keep informed
- Keep satisfied
- Need minimal effort
- Must find strategy acceptable

3. What is the most powerful weapon shareholders have in their dealings with the company?
4. *Fill in the blank*

   A .... is a written customer services policy.

5. What is the strong view of stakeholder theory for profit-centred organisations?
6. What is the weak view of stakeholder theory for profit-centred organisations?
7. What is internal marketing?

   A   The marketing department
   B   The principles of marketing to employees as if they were customers
   C   The promotion of the interests of internal stakeholders
   D   The activities of the staff shop

8. What are the main requirements of distributors as connected stakeholders?

Answers to Quick Quiz

1.
   - Shareholders
   - Bankers
   - Customers
   - Suppliers
   - Distributors

2.
   A   Need minimal effort
   B   Keep informed
   C   Keep satisfied
   D   Must find strategy acceptable

3. The right to sell their shares and hence possibly cause share prices to fall.

4. A customer charter.

5. Each stakeholder in the business has a legitimate claim on management attention. Management's job is to balance stakeholder demands.

6. Satisfying stakeholders such as the customer is good only because it enables the business to satisfy its primary purpose, long-term growth in owner wealth.

PART B THE MICRO-ENVIRONMENT

7 B The principles of marketing to employees as if they were customers.

8
- Reliable supply
- Quality improvements
- Support in marketing

Action Programme Review

1 In a sense we are all stakeholders, but more specific examples are shown in the diagram in Section 1 of this chapter.

2 Ian Mathieson, a partner in the Chartered Accountants Pannell Kerr Foster, highlighted the following elements as being important in a good annual report:

- The trustees' report should explain the charity's strategy, policies and performance, demonstrating how resources are used, outlining successes and setbacks and giving a balanced message. The report should also set out the planning processes and organisational structure, and indicate the charity's plans for the future.

- A key policy which the report should highlight is the charity's risk management policy. Being able to demonstrate a sound risk management policy and its links to other key policies can appeal to potential donors.

- Mathieson points out that although stakeholders expect to see innovative and informative annual reports, charities shouldn't be looking to spend large sums on glossy publications. Good means of demonstrating what the charity does include case studies, comments from stakeholders and users, and statistics presented in a reader-friendly way (through charts and graphs).

There is no single ideal report as charities differ significantly in the work they do. 'All charities are unique and have a different message to communicate.' However, readers of the report who haven't been actively involved should be able to understand from the annual reports what charities have achieved.

3 **Primary stakeholders** are stakeholders who participate in the organisation's primary activities. For organisations producing goods or services, primary stakeholders would include employees, customers and suppliers.

Secondary stakeholders are those individuals and groups who do not participate in the primary activities. They are however affected by the organisation's secondary impacts and involvements – those over and above its primary activity of producing goods or services for consumption. Examples of secondary stakeholders include local communities, pressure groups, the media, government and general public.

4 Criteria which you might have considered:

(a) Who the members of each group of stakeholders are

(b) How much power they can exercise over the organisation

(c) What claims the individuals have on the organisation

(d) How significant the concerns of individuals are and the extent to which the concerns are being addressed

> Now try Question 9 at the end of the Study Text

6

Pressure groups

Chapter topic list

1 Pressure groups
2 Consumer groups

Syllabus content

- 2.4 Explain the significance of the range of pressure groups interested in the organisation and their potential impacts
- 2.5 Specify the role of marketing in managing these pressure groups

PART B THE MICRO-ENVIRONMENT

Introduction

> Society has expectations of business organisations, in particular that they behave in a socially responsible way.
>
> Balancing the needs for **social responsibility** with the need to make profit for shareholders can be a difficult problem to reconcile. Although the organisation has pressures from external financial stakeholders to maximise sales and profits, other external stakeholders have different ends in mind.
>
> We therefore discuss in the rest of the chapter those outside influences that are concerned with what they see as an organisation's social duties. We give examples of pressure groups and then discuss in detail the role of consumer pressure groups. We then move on to consider the issues of environmentalism and market failure, and show how organisations may be influenced by pressures arising from these issues.

1 Pressure groups

FAST FORWARD

> The members of **pressure groups** are people who have come together either because they come from a similar area of society with common interests, or because they wish to promote an issue or cause.

Key concept

> A **pressure group** is a group of people who have got together to promote a particular cause. An alternative name is a cause group. The term is also used to mean any interest group.

Stakeholders may be unable to exercise any power over an organisation, whether as consumers, employees or members of the public at large. In these circumstances, individuals may seek to influence an organisation by joining a **pressure group**.

Exam tip

> Pressure groups are of more importance in some sectors than others, but they often feature in the *Marketing Environment* exam. Questions will often focus on the impact of pressure groups on organisations, eg a chemical company (June 2004) or the airline industry in relation to global warming (June 2006), or a government department or agency of your choice (December 2006). In June 2005, candidates were asked to discuss how a pressure group could be used positively, for marketing advantage. The examiner has expressed frustration that candidates seem unable to distinguish pressure groups from regulatory bodies: these are not considered valid examples – so don't use them!

Interest and pressure groups arise from two causes.

- The failure of parliamentary representatives to air important concerns
- The inevitable fact that different groups in society have different interests

1.1 Types of pressure group

Pressure groups have an interest in matters of public policy, but do not aspire to control the machinery of government. There are many thousands of groups ranging from major umbrella groups to small purely local groups, often established for a specific purpose.

(a) **Cause** groups (or **promotional** groups) promote a distinct cause or issue (eg CND, Greenpeace, Howard League for Penal Reform).

(b) **Interest groups** (or **defensive** or **sectional** groups) defend the wide interests of groups in society such as mineworkers (NUM), business firms (CBI) or consumers.

Action Programme 1

Compare the websites of a cause and interest group of your choice. Are there major differences in areas such as the information they give about themselves, the press coverage quoted of their activities, items of special interest such as specially-commissioned surveys, and any products they offer?

Some of these groups have other activities than trying to influence government and might regard political activity as only one of their many roles. Some of the major charities, such as Oxfam, do good work and also try to influence government policy. A group can have one of two sorts of relationship with government.

(a) **Insider groups** are regularly consulted by government as a matter of routine in areas of policy. In fact, some insider groups *expect* to be consulted. Note that insider groups do not necessarily support the government of the day. The British Medical Association, for example, although not always supporting government policy on the NHS, is still regularly consulted.

(b) **Outsider groups** do not have a direct link to government. Some of their activities are to promote interest in their cause outside government (eg in the media) so that the issue is raised in the public arena and to gain credibility in the eyes of the public and recognition of their importance by the government, so that their pronouncements are taken seriously.

1.2 The role of pressure groups

The role of pressure groups is controversial.

(a) Some argue that the existence of a pressure group means that power is diffused widely, and that they are an informal check on ever-increasing power of the state. They also help protect minorities.

(b) Others argue that some pressure groups (eg business interests) are far more influential than others (eg some supporters of rail transport believe that 'the road lobby' has undue influence on UK transport policy) and that this is anti-democratic.

(c) In the US some people argue that lobbying by the National Rifle Association against firearm restrictions has impeded gun control legislation, which might have helped reduce the US's high murder rate.

Action Programme 2

There has been increased concern with the costs caused by traffic congestion in large cities. Some, like Singapore, have responded by *road pricing*. Drivers are charged for using certain roads at certain times. Think of as many interested parties (including government institutions) as you can who would favour or oppose such a move.

Pressure groups may either encourage or try to discourage a policy.

Marketing at Work

Examples of two **contrasting pressure groups** in Britain are the Countryside Alliance and the Hunt Saboteurs Association. The main press focus on the Countryside Alliance has been on its opposition to the ban on hunting. As well as marches, the Association also tried to increase understanding and support for hunting with dogs by campaigns and information packs. The Alliance also investigated legal challenges to any proposed ban on hunting, including challenges under human rights legislation and problems over contract law.

PART B THE MICRO-ENVIRONMENT

Over time the Alliance's remit widened, to cover 'the real rural agenda'. This included other country sports, such as angling and fishing. As well as campaigns, the Alliance provided members with advice on recent legislation and practical skills, for example shotgun technique courses.

Wider rural concerns of the Alliance include the production of food; the concern is that smaller businesses are being edged out due to inappropriate regulations and failure by businesses and consumers to buy local products. '(We) believe that food production in Britain does not need special exemptions or subsidies. It needs sensible regulation and an ability to compete in the marketplace. Consumers who demand higher standards, in terms of food safety, environmental protection and animal welfare must be willing to pay for the true cost of this food production.'

The Hunt Saboteurs Association's website is rather more narrowly-focused. It is designed to arouse strong reactions from users by including graphic pictures of animal suffering. It also includes quotes allegedly made by leading huntsmen that do not portray them in a good light. Apart from these the site is focused on sabotage operations, covering not just hunts, but also dealing with traps and snares and angling. The main support service offered is legal advice, with details of how saboteurs have fared when charged with offences under public order legislation, and also contact details should saboteurs find themselves in difficulty.

Action Programme 3

See if you can find your own examples of two opposing pressure groups, and compare and contrast the techniques they use.

The Sunday trading issue was an interesting example, as a number of different interest groups combined in a campaign for a mutual objective.

1.3 Economic pressure groups

The main pressure groups reflecting economic interests are as follows.

(a) **Businesses**: Employers' organisations. These can be supplemented by smaller, more specified trade associations in particular industries, which gang together to promote common interests (eg newspapers to oppose tax on the press).

(b) **Professional associations** are groups of people who do the same type of job or use similar skills, such as accountants and doctors. Professional associations are generally involved in setting standards of skill and enforcing adherence to good practice (for example, through disciplinary schemes) on the part of members.

(c) **Trade unions** are similar to professional associations, in that they represent people who work.

(d) **Consumers' associations** represent people as consumers, in other words, campaigning for the interests of consumers on issues such as product pricing, safety and quality. Consumer associations have campaigned for labelling on food, for example.

1.4 How to influence government

FAST FORWARD Pressure groups **influence government** in a number of ways, depending on whether they are insiders or outsiders.

1.4.1 Insiders

Pressure groups can influence national governments in various ways.

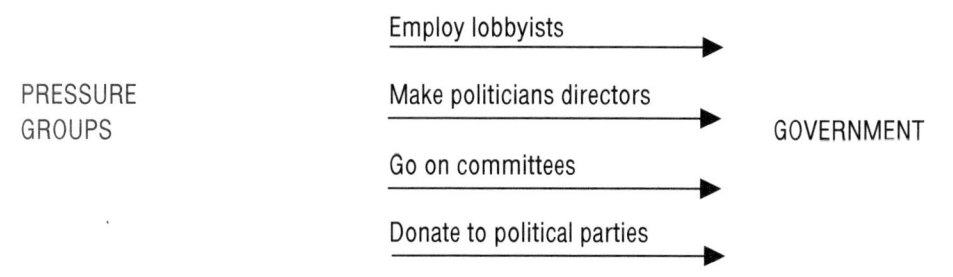

```
                    Employ lobbyists         →
    PRESSURE        Make politicians directors →
    GROUPS                                            GOVERNMENT
                    Go on committees         →
                    Donate to political parties →
```

The UK government has itself issued details on how to influence government – in this case the EU. Of particular importance is the need to influence the decision making processes of the European Commission. EU regulations, for practical purposes, take priority over national law. They are arrived at after a great deal of negotiation, and for this reason alone, are difficult to change. It is therefore much better to influence the **drafting process** of new regulations than to try and get them changed once they have been implemented.

1.4.2 Outsiders

Some interest groups can act as both insiders *and* outsiders. When not walking up and down the corridors of power, members of an interest group can do the following to influence government policy.

(a) They can try and influence public opinion and the legislative agenda by **advertising**. The RSPCA advertised (unsuccessfully) for a dog registration scheme in the UK. This was more than just an appeal for donations: the advertising was specifically designed to change government policy.

(b) Few organisations can afford expensive press advertising. However there are other ways of getting publicity: demonstrations, petitions, direct action and public relations.

These methods may or may not have a direct impact. If the action is public, ministers might not wish to be seen to lose face by submitting. However, they can create a climate of opinion to which politicians can later respond. The adoption of *environmental* issues by politicians is the result of many years of campaigning by pressure groups.

1.5 Marketing implications of pressure groups

Many of the tactics used against governments can be used against businesses (eg feeding stories to the media, marches and so on).

Some pressure groups are unremittingly hostile to certain businesses, and their aim is to extinguish them altogether. For example, businesses exporting veal calves have faced pressure group hostility. In such cases, all businesses can do, other than rely on the law, is exercise important public relations issues. The nuclear power industry, for example, is very well placed to exploit, in advertisements, public concern about global warming and environmental pollution.

Other pressure groups have more restricted aims, and may be amenable to negotiation. A firm might see considerable PR benefit from this as well as advice.

A firm has a number of basic responses.

- Ignore the pressure group
- Deal with the pressure group, and take some of its ideas on board
- Employ a pro-active public relations and advertising policy
- Sue for libel – but McDonald's, for example, has found that this can be a public relations disaster

PART B   THE MICRO-ENVIRONMENT

The firm's response will be conditioned by:

(a) The **number of interests of the pressure groups**

A multi-interest pressure group may be more open to negotiation than a single-issue pressure group, but expertise in a variety of fields may be needed for effective negotiation with a multi-issue group.

(b) **Nature of the interests**

An economic pressure group will be concerned with tangible economic benefits; a social or environmental group with less tangible benefits, which may be difficult to measure.

(c) **Implications of continuing conflict**

If conflict drags on or escalates, the firm may suffer public relations or economic damage.

2 Consumer groups

> **FAST FORWARD**
>
> **Consumer groups** represent consumers' interests. They exist to ensure that products give good value. They promote safeguards for consumers against unethical business practice.

Key concept

> **Consumerism** is a term used to describe the increased importance and power of consumers. It includes the increasingly organised consumer groups, and the recognition by producers that consumer satisfaction is the key to long-term profitability.

2.1 Basic consumer rights

Consumerism is an attempt to even up the relationship between individual consumers and large powerful corporations. The basis of consumerism is often taken to be President Kennedy's Consumer Bill of Rights which highlighted four basic rights.

2.1.1 The right to safety

The right that a product be **safe to use** is covered by **legislation** in many countries. The main problem is that research may reveal that there are, in fact, specific risks to consumers in using certain products that were at one time thought to be safe, for example cigarettes. The future may also reveal damage to the wider environment, for example the effect of leaded petrol on the earth's atmosphere.

2.1.2 The right to be informed

This means that **instructions** on products should be sufficient, and there should be **clear labelling** of the ingredients that should be used in foodstuffs. This right also covers information about **purchase terms** (excessive small print could be called unfair.) It places an obligation on advertisers to make sure that adverts for products are factually correct and are not misleading.

2.1.3 The right to choose

In theory this should encourage **competition**, although where there is competition, marketers will be trying to influence consumer choice. Therefore the right to choose could be seen as less important provided customers are fully informed; however the right to choose might also be interpreted as the right to choose without being unduly pressurised, thus discouraging unsolicited marketing and pressurised selling.

2.1.4 The right to be heard

An alternative description might be the right to give **feedback**, particularly the right to make complaints and know that those complaints will be quickly and fairly answered.

2.2 Fair trading

A large number of countries have officers or departments who have the authority to promote fair trading and competition, and act against restrictive practices. Their roles might include:

(a) Various functions in relation to monopolies, mergers, restrictive practices and uncompetitive practices

(b) Review of the carrying on of the commercial supply to consumers of goods and services

(c) Issuing licences

(d) Collation of evidence of harmful practices which may adversely affect the interests of consumers

(e) Taking action against persons who persist in conduct detrimental to the consumer

(f) Encouraging relevant associations to prepare codes of practice

2.3 Consequences of consumer protection legislation

Consumer protection legislation might appear to be an onerous burden on businesses. Product standards act as additional guidelines.

Although managers might complain about the extra costs there are a number of wider issues to be considered.

(a) Does consumer protection legislation **impede business performance**?

(b) Does consumer protection legislation put business at a **competitive disadvantage** from overseas competitors?

Such costs are very hard to quantify but there are a number of salient features which might be noted, which limit the competitive impact of such legislation.

(a) **Overseas competitors in the domestic market**

Products sold in the local market are subject to local law. The fact that they are imported does not exempt them from consumer protection legislation in the UK. Overseas producers may be at a disadvantage, being less familiar with the UK market and practice. At the very least, there is no obvious gain.

(b) **Domestic businesses in overseas markets**

Domestic businesses are subject to the laws regarding consumer protection prevalent in the overseas markets.

There might indeed be burdens, but they are shared equally.

If the effect of consumer protection legislation enhances business's **best practice**, then overall, there may even be a benefit. After all, the USA, where the consumer movement first started, was the birthplace of consumerism. Germany, whose export performance is generally impressive, has had some of the most exacting product quality regulations in Europe.

2.4 Self-regulation

The use of law to regulate the relationship between buyers and sellers can often seem like a case of using a sledgehammer to crack a nut. Instead, many organisations regulate their dealings by **voluntary codes of conduct**.

A voluntary code of conduct is a statement by an organisation of the standards by which it seeks to do business. Codes are usually developed by a trade association and individual members incorporate the code into the dealings they have with their customers.

Voluntary codes usually include a mechanism for **resolving disputes** through arbitration.

Many countries have bodies promoting advertising standards. In Germany, for example, the *Zentrale zur Bekämpfung unlauteren Wettbewerbs e.V.* deals with issues of misleading advertising and unfair competition, whilst the Deutscher Werberat deals with issues of taste and decency. The European Advertising Alliance brings together national advertising self-regulatory organisations ('SROs') and organisations representing the advertising industry in Europe.

Possible sanctions that these bodies might employ include:

(a) **Published disapproval**

The organisations publish reports which detail public complaints and decisions in respect of the complaint.

(b) **Media recommendations**

The organisations will have power to recommend to media owners that certain advertisements or advertisers should not be accepted on their books.

2.5 Consumer protection organisations

As well as government bodies, there are voluntary associations.

Marketing at Work

The **Consumers' Association of Canada (CAC)** is an independent, not-for-profit, volunteer-based, charitable organisation. Its mandate is to inform and educate consumers on marketplace issues, to advocate for consumers with government and industry, and work with government and industry to solve marketplace problems.

CAC focuses its work in the areas of food, health, trade, standards, financial services, communications industries and other marketplace issues as they emerge.

Recent projects of the CAC have included the Food Tips project where the CAC worked together with key partners in the food, literacy, and health sectors. The Food Tips were written in plain language to help consumers with lower literacy skills to shop smart and eat well.

CAC has also been collaborating with a number of health care and health professional associations to design and test a set of symbols that could replace standard instructions that are found on containers of medication.

Some industries may have panels of individuals appointed to represent consumer interests. This is particularly true of **utilities** such as public transport.

There are also a number of private groups which aim to protect consumer interests in various ways.

(a) Campaigners for the maintenance and improvement in the **quality of specific products**, for example campaigners promoting real ale (cask beer) over keg beer

(b) Groups lobbying for **legal changes** to protect the public, for example anti-smoking groups

(c) **Relatives/friends of disaster victims** lobbying for changes to prevent future disasters

Action Programme 4

Consumerism has been called 'the shame of marketing' (Drucker). Why might this be so – or not?

Marketing at Work

Sometimes, consumer sovereignty and protection organisations fail to protect the wider interests of consumers. In these circumstances, consumers sometimes turn to pressure groups. These are a few examples in which consumers have been successful in **applying pressure** to seek changes in business practices.

(a) Consumers began boycotting Shell filling stations in large numbers, leading the company to reverse its policy on a controversial environmental subject concerning the disposal of an oil drilling platform.

(b) Pressure was applied to change the Nestlé company's practice of exploiting the market for processed milk in developing countries.

Similar campaigns have targeted Nike (alleged exploitation of overseas garment-trade workers) and McDonalds (alleged contribution to obesity and related illnesses). Keep your eyes open!

Developments such as the Citizens' Charter aim to specify precisely the levels of service that consumers of **public sector services** can expect. The aim is to make providers of public services more responsive to what users demand.

(a) Note that some users or consumers of public services may not be in a position to pay for them directly (eg the dependent elderly). As consumers, their needs should be specified.

(b) It may not be possible for consumers to find an alternative supplier of utility services.

2.6 Impact on marketing

Organisations need to understand how consumer groups can influence the industry environment. Working with consumer groups can have significant advantages, even the **positive endorsement** of products by the groups (as suggested in chapter 5). A failure to respond to concerns can lead to **boycotts** not just of the products concerned, but also all other products sold by the organisation. Animal welfare groups have targeted organisations' whole product ranges rather than just those products which have been tested on animals, for example.

Marketing at Work

Alcoholic versions of soft drinks – so-called 'alcopops' – caused considerable controversy, particularly because the products seem to be directed mainly at young people.

As reported in *Marketing Business*, the need for tighter controls over the marketing of alcopops led to action by the drinks industry itself. A code of practice was introduced by The Portman Group, an organisation founded by the major UK drinks producers to promote sensible drinking and to reduce misuse of alcohol.

PART B   THE MICRO-ENVIRONMENT

The code of practice complements and is consistent with all other relevant self-regulatory codes, and it helps to control the industry without the burden of new legislation. The provisions of the code are wide-ranging and cover the naming, packaging and merchandising of drinks.

An example of its operation could be seen in the marketing of Carlsberg-Tetley's 'Thickhead' drink, which was held by The Portman Group to be in breach of industry guidelines, and a 'serious misjudgement'. Carlsberg-Tetley responded by agreeing to change the label.

Chapter Roundup

- The members of **pressure groups** are people who have come together either because they come from a similar area of society with common interests, or because they wish to promote an issue or cause.
- Pressure groups: *influence government* in a number of ways, depending on whether they are insiders or outsiders.
- **Consumer groups** represent consumers' interests. They exist to ensure that products give good value. They promote safeguards for consumers against unethical business practice.

Quick Quiz

1   Match the type of pressure group with the description.

   (1)   Cause group   (a)   Promotes wide issues
   (2)   Interest group (b)   Promotes a specific issue

2   Give three examples of ways in which pressure groups can influence government.

3   What are the four steps that the UK government has recommended be used to influence European Union decision-making?

4   Which of the following method would be least likely to be used by an outsider pressure group to influence government policy?

   A   Advertising
   B   Petitions
   C   Demonstrations
   D   Serving on government committees

5   What is consumerism?

6   Which of the following rights were part of US President Kennedy's Bill of Consumer Rights?

   A   Safety
   B   Choice
   C   Information
   D   Hearing

7   What are the main methods used by advertising standard bodies to enforce their views?

6: PRESSURE GROUPS

Answers to Quick Quiz

1. (1) (b)
   (2) (a)

2. Any three of:
   - Employing lobbyists
   - Making politicians directors
   - Going on committees
   - Donating to political parties

3. - Get in early
   - Work with others
   - Think European
   - Be prepared

4. D   Serving on government committees would imply the group was an insider pressure group

5. A description of the increased importance and power of consumers

6. All of them

7. - Publishing disapproval of conduct
   - Making recommendations that certain advertisers or advertisements should not be accepted

Action Programme Review

1. Your own research.

2. Here are some possible suggestions. (Please note that the list below does not claim to represent the policies and practices, whether stated or informal, of any of the organisations mentioned.)

   Possibly for
   - Emergency services (lower congestion means fast trips to fires etc)
   - Local authorities of congested areas (eg City of Cambridge)
   - Environmental groups (eg Friends of the Earth) who wish to reduce pollution
   - Public transport organisations
   - Tax raising authorities
   - Technology companies (for design contracts)

   Possibly against
   - Motorists' associations (eg AA and RAC)
   - The car industry generally
   - Petrol companies (reduced motoring means fewer sales)
   - Many individual motorists
   - Residents associations worried about traffic being diverted
   - Civil liberties organisations (as people's movements might be tracked)

3. Your own research.

4. The marketing concept deals with the identification of customer needs and their satisfaction at a profit. Consumerism arose in reaction to poor quality, unethical marketing and pricing strategies, and sharp practice. If these did not exist, consumer groups would not be necessary.

   That said, magazines like *Which?* provide a valuable service in spreading information, in that they rigorously analyse the *product* and *price* elements of the marketing mix.

   Furthermore, the individual consumer is powerless in the face of a large corporation. Only by pooling their interests can consumers get effective redress against bad business practice.

> Now try Question 10 at the end of the Study Text

PART B THE MICRO-ENVIRONMENT

The industry environment

Chapter topic list

1. Competition for customers
2. Industry structure and competitive behaviour
3. Regulation of competition
4. Monitoring competitors

Syllabus content

- 2.6 Explain the importance of monitoring competitors and industries and how the organisation assesses their strategic and marketing implications
- 2.7 Examine the impact of competition policies on the organisation and its marketing environment

PART B   THE MICRO-ENVIRONMENT

Introduction

In this chapter on the micro environment we discuss the influences on an industry within which the organisation operates, and in particular the impact of competition.

We start off by discussing how competition works. Michael Porter described five basic **competitive forces** which apply in most situations. We then go on to discuss how much the competitive environment can depend on the industry and market structure.

It is one of an organisation's social responsibilities to compete fairly – however aggressively. National governments and the EU have attempted to **regulate anti-competitive** practices that appear to be contrary to the public interest, and we discuss what these practices are, and how regulation works, in section 4 of this chapter.

Lastly we consider how an organisation might respond to the competitive environment it faces, both in **analysing competitors** and **formulating its own strategy**. The strategic issues introduced here will be developed in much more detail in your studies for later CIM papers.

1 Competition for customers

FAST FORWARD

Porter suggests that there are five basic **competitive forces** which influence the state of competition in an industry and can be used as the outline for a **structural analysis** of an industry.

- Threat of new entrants
- The threat of substitute products and services
- The bargaining power of customers
- The bargaining power of suppliers
- The rivalry amongst current competitors

Are the people who buy our products customers with a choice, or are they captive?

Any organisation wishing to expand or move into a market must consider whether the market is growing or has the capacity to grow. For example, the UK market for mineral water was more or less established by Perrier in the 1980s. As public doubts about the quality of the water supply increased, a number of other bottled waters were offered for sale (eg Malvern) together with own-brands, created by supermarkets.

The characteristics of the market also need to be investigated. *Michael Porter (Competitive Strategy)* makes a distinction between two groups of characteristics.

(a) **Environmental factors** characterise the nature of competition in one industry compared with another – for example, in the chemicals industry compared with the clothing retail industry. They make one industry as a whole potentially more profitable than another.

(b) Factors that characterise the **nature of competition** within a particular industry. These relate to the competitive strategies that individual firms might select.

1.1 Competitive forces

Porter suggests that there are five basic competitive forces which influence the state of competition in an industry and can be used as the outline for a **structural analysis** of an industry: Figure 7.1.

Key concept

Competitive forces are 'the structural determinants of the intensity of competition' which collectively determine the profit (ie long-run return on capital) potential of the industry as a whole.

7: THE INDUSTRY ENVIRONMENT

Competitive force analysis indicates the likely **size of profits**, and the long-term prospects, in particular the **degree of future competition**. It thus provides a basis for developing future strategy.

PORTER'S COMPETITIVE FORCES (THE FIVE FORCES MODEL)	
The **threat** of new **entrants** to the industry	
The **threat** of **substitute products** or services	
The **bargaining power** of **customers**	
The **bargaining power** of **suppliers**	
The **rivalry** amongst current competitors in the industry	

Figure 7.1: Five competitive forces

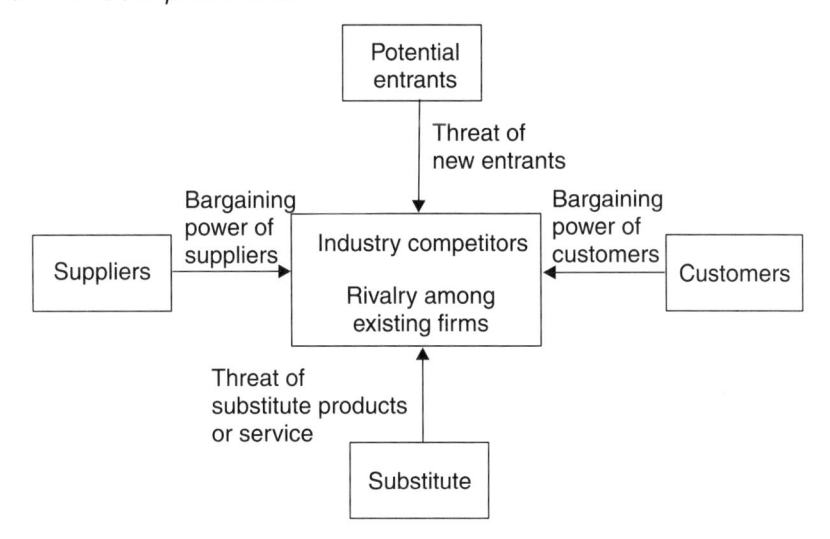

Adapted from *Porter (Competitive Strategy)*

We will look at each of the forces in turn.

1.2 The threat of new entrants

A new entrant into an industry will bring extra capacity. The new entrant will have to make an **investment** to break into the market, and will want to obtain a certain market share. The strength of the threat from new entrants is likely to vary from industry to industry, depending on two factors.

(a) **Strength of the barriers to entry**

The stronger the barriers, the less likely entry is.

(b) **Response of existing competitors to the new entrant**

If a new prospective entrant thinks that firms which are already in the industry would respond to a new competitor by reducing their prices and starting a price war, the new entrant would be more likely to think twice before deciding to make its entry into the market.

Key concept

Barriers to entry are the factors which make it difficult for a new entrant to gain a foothold in an industry.

Barriers to entry can be categorised as follows: Figure 7.2.

Figure 7.2: Barriers to entry

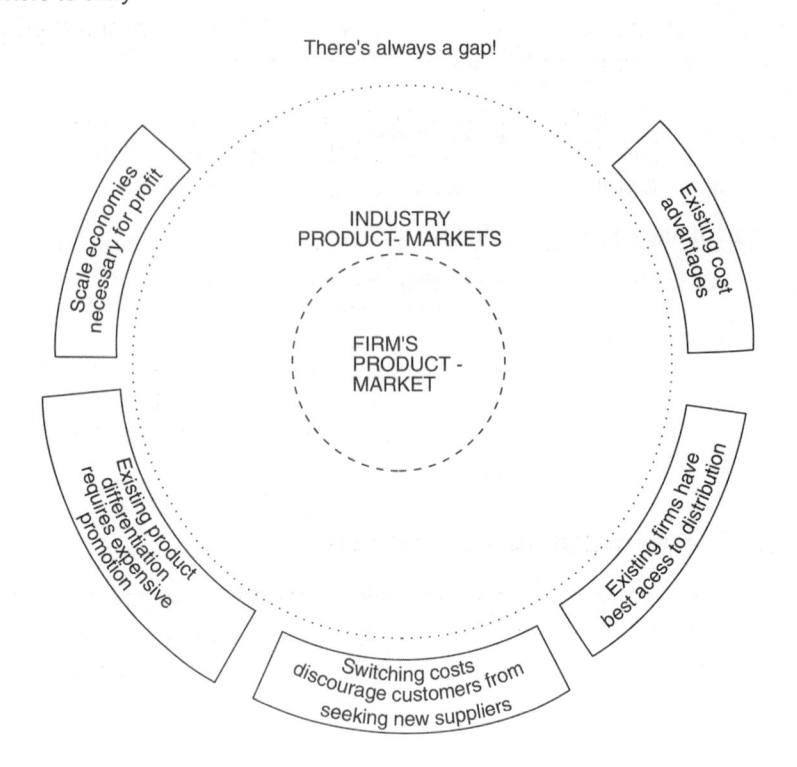

There's always a gap!

- Scale economies necessary for profit
- Existing cost advantages
- Existing firms have best access to distribution
- Switching costs discourage customers from seeking new suppliers
- Existing product differentiation requires expensive promotion

INDUSTRY PRODUCT-MARKETS

FIRM'S PRODUCT-MARKET

1.2.1 Economies of scale

High fixed costs (ie costs that do not rise as output volume increases) imply a **high breakeven point** (number of units sold to cover fixed costs). Profit might depend on the ability to achieve a high volume of sales. If significant economies can be obtained by producing above certain volumes of output, existing firms in the industry will have a big cost advantage over a new entrant.

1.2.2 Product differentiation

Existing firms in an industry may have built up a good brand image and strong customer loyalty over a long period of time, through advertising, product quality and so on.

Moreover a firm might develop a **variety of brands** to 'crowd out' the competition. This creates a barrier to entry, because new entrants would have to spend heavily to overcome the existing brand loyalties and to build up a brand image of their own. These high 'start-up' losses might deter would-be competitors, given that the chances of eventual success in the new market might be fairly slim anyway.

1.2.3 Capital requirements

The amount of capital that a new entrant needs to invest varies from one industry to another. In some industries, for example, capital requirements are low, whereas in other industries, a substantial investment might be required. When capital requirements are high, the barrier against new entrants will be strong, particularly when the investment would possibly be high-risk.

Investment in Information and Communication Technology (ICT) may be a further example. On the other hand ICT can be used to leap over certain entry barriers. An example is the use of telephone banking, which may obviate the need to establish a branch network.

1.2.4 Switching costs

Switching costs are the costs that a customer would have to incur by switching from one supplier's products to another's. The costs are not just financial: **time** and **inconvenience** are costs in this context. The consequences of a switch might include the following.

- Buying **new ancillary equipment** compatible with the equipment of the new supplier
- Loss of the existing supplier's **after-sales service**
- Risk that the new supplier will be **less reliable** than the existing supplier

When customers think that switching costs would be high, there would be a strong barrier to entry against new competitors in the industry. Shared information and administrative systems may also tie customers and suppliers into the same distribution channel.

Switching costs also apply to retailers and distributors as well as to consumers. It might cost a consumer nothing to switch from buying one brand of frozen peas or one make of car to buying another, but the potential costs for the **retailer** or **distributor** might be high. How reliable will the new supplier be in providing fresh stock on demand?

1.2.5 Access to distribution channels

Distribution channels are the means by which a manufacturer's products reach the end-buyer. In some industries new distribution channels are difficult to establish, and existing distribution channels hard to gain access to. This is a universal complaint of Western countries trying to export to Japan.

Marketing at Work

Food products in the UK are largely sold through **supermarket chains**, and it can be difficult for a new producer to get supermarket organisations to agree to stock the product. In Australia, major supermarket chains are launching 'own brand' products, to the exclusion of many traditional brands.

As retailers become more powerful, they are placing more and more demands on food producers: failure to comply can mean exclusion from the channel of distribution.

1.2.6 Cost advantages of existing producers, independent of economies of scale

Barriers to entry may exist when existing firms in an industry have certain cost advantages over new entrants which are nothing to do with economies of scale. These would include the following.

(a) **Patent rights**; these, however, expire after a certain time, but this time does give the firm a breathing space

(b) **Experience** and **know-how** (eg cost benefits obtained through the learning curve factor)

(c) **Government subsidies**

(d) **Access** to **sources** of raw materials on favourable terms, such as a long-term low-price supply contract

Entry barriers are not static.

(a) They can be **raised** by a number of measures, such as maximising early sales demand to increase the cumulative volume needed to be profitable. A firm can increase the perception of risk.

(b) Entry barriers might be **lowered** by changes in the environment, in particular by cost-reducing technological changes, which a new entrant can invest in straightaway, and so compete more effectively against established firms in the industry. New entrants might be able to identify novel distribution channels for products or services.

PART B THE MICRO-ENVIRONMENT

Exam tip

> A whole range of topics on the competitive environment was tested in the December 2005 exam. Using the case study of Microsoft, falling foul of regulation and opposition because of its aggressive – and occasionally ruled unfair – competitive tactics, the examiner asked for an explanation of: monopoly power, unfair competition, barriers to entry and patents/copyrights, and their impact on software marketing. Think each of these issues through, as you read on…

1.3 The threat from substitute products

The products or services that are produced in one industry are likely to have substitutes that are produced by another industry. Substitutes offer different ways of meeting the same customer need.

For example, you may need to go to Paris from London. Crossing the English channel, railway travel is a substitute for flying or going by car-ferry. Note that they are different ways of meeting the same need. (The ferry companies compete with each other, but they are not substitute products. They offer the same type of service.)

When firms in an industry are faced with threats from substitute products they are likely to find that demand for their products is relatively **sensitive to price**. A significant threat is any improvement in the price-performance characteristics of these substitutes.

Marketing at Work

An example of **substitute products** is provided by the metals industry. For many years 'tin cans' were made out of steel: however, aluminium, which is thinner and lighter, has replaced it in many applications.

In response to this, the steel industry has developed new alloys of steel, which it hopes will enable it to fight back in this significant market.

1.4 The bargaining power of customers

Customers want better quality products and services at a lower price. If they succeed in getting what they want, they will force down the profitability of suppliers in the industry. The profitability of an industry is therefore dependent on the strength of the bargaining power of its customers, which is dependent upon a number of factors.

CUSTOMER BARGAINING POWER	
Purchases are substantial % of sales	Customer will be in a strong position
Purchases are high % of total purchases by customer	Customer will be a weaker position if most of purchases come from one supplier or industry
Level of switching costs	IT can raise switching costs in cash terms and operational inconvenience
Nature of products	Suppliers may increase bargaining power by creating a strong brand which customers feel obliged to have
Level of profits	Customers making low profits need low cost suppliers
Takeover threat	Possibility that customers may take over sources of supply if supplier charges too much

CUSTOMER BARGAINING POWER	
Knowledge of customers	Level of awareness customers have, or the skills of their purchasing staff
Product quality	If quality is important, customers are less likely to be price-sensitive, and industry might be more profitable

1.5 The bargaining power of suppliers

Just as customers can influence the profitability of an industry by exerting pressure for higher quality products or lower prices, so too can suppliers influence profitability by exerting pressure for higher prices.

The ability of suppliers to get higher prices depends on the following factors.

- **One or two dominant suppliers** to the industry may be able to charge monopoly prices.
- The suppliers may be **threatened** by new entrants, or by substitute products.
- The suppliers may have **other customers** outside the industry, and do not rely on the industry for the majority of their sales.
- The **suppliers' products** may be vital to the customers' business.
- The supplier may produce a **differentiated product** which reduces the number of acceptable substitutes.
- **Switching costs** for buyers may be high.

1.6 Rivalry amongst current competitors in the industry

The intensity of competitive rivalry within an industry will affect the profitability of the industry as a whole. Competitive actions might take the form of price competition, advertising battles, sales promotion campaigns, introducing new products for the market, improving after-sales service or providing guarantees or warranties.

The intensity of competition will depend on the following factors.

- **Whether there is a large number of equally balanced competitors**. Industries with a large number of firms are likely to be very competitive. When the industry is dominated by a small number of large firms, competition is likely to be less intense, or is restricted.
- **The rate of growth in the industry**. When firms are all benefiting from growth in total demand, their rivalry will be less intense. Rivalry will be greater when firms are competing for a greater market share in a total market where growth is slow or stagnant, especially where the costs of leaving the market are high.
- **Whether fixed costs are high**. If fixed costs are high, and variable costs are a relatively small proportion of the selling price, firms will often compete on price, and sell at prices above marginal cost, even though this will mean a failure to cover fixed costs and make an adequate return in the longer run. In the short run any contribution towards covering fixed costs is better than none at all.
- **Ease of switching**. Whether buyers can switch easily from one supplier to another will influence competition. Easy switching will encourage suppliers to compete (eg Coke and Pepsi): this is common in FMCG markets.
- **Capacity and unit costs**. A supplier might need to achieve a substantial increase in output capacity in order to obtain reductions in unit costs, eg by acquiring labour-saving equipment.

- **The difficulty that competitors may have in guessing each other's intentions**. When one firm is not sure what another is up to, it may well respond to the uncertainty by formulating a more competitive strategy.
- **High strategic stakes**. If a firm has put a lot of capital and effort into achieving certain targets and has made success in the industry a prime strategic objective, the firm will be likely to act very competitively in order to ensure that its targets are achieved. Japanese firms allegedly place market share as a high strategic objective, and will act keenly to achieve it.

1.7 Exit barriers

Just as there are barriers to entry into an industry, so too are there barriers to exit which make it difficult for an existing supplier to leave the industry.

INDUSTRY

Firm

| EXIT BARRIERS | Fixed assets with low break-up value | Cost of Redundancy Payments | Effect on rest of group | Reluctance of managers | Government pressures |

EXIT

Exam tip

Porter's 'five forces' model is a useful tool for analysing the competitive environment faced by an organisation. In June 2004, the subject was the road haulage industry. Beware, though: the examiner has complained that candidates use the model because they know it – regardless of whether it is the *right* model to use in addressing the question!

1.8 Competitive strategies – a summary

FAST FORWARD

There are three basic competitive strategies: **cost leadership**, **differentiation** and **focus**.

Competitive advantage or **competitive edge** is anything which gives one organisation an edge over its rivals in the products it sells or the services it offers. Much of the competitive advantage which an organisation might hope to achieve, however, is provided by the nature/quality/price of its products.

(a) One company's products might have a definite edge over its rivals' because it is better in **quality**, or cheaper in **price**.

(b) Where rival products are much alike (eg petrol, many processed foods etc) competitive advantage may be sought by creating a superior **brand image** and making the product **seem different** and more desirable than a rival producer's similar product.

The type of competitive strategy which a firm adopts will depend on the competitive strategies adopted by rivals and will have implications for product design and quality, pricing and advertising. The following have been identified as the main generic strategies.

7: THE INDUSTRY ENVIRONMENT

(a) **Cost leadership strategy**

This seeks to achieve the position of lowest-cost producer in the industry as a *whole*. By producing at the lowest cost, the manufacturer can compete on price with every other producer in the industry, and earn the highest unit profits.

(b) **Differentiation strategy**

This is based on the assumption that competitive advantage can be gained through particular characteristics of a firm's products or brands. The customer is prepared to pay more for this distinguishing characteristic.

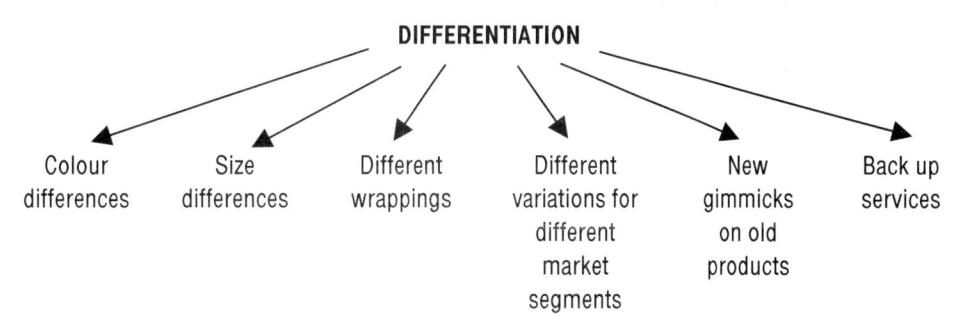

```
                          DIFFERENTIATION
        ┌──────┬──────┬──────┼──────┬──────┐
        ▼      ▼      ▼      ▼      ▼      ▼
     Colour  Size  Different Different  New    Back up
  differences differences wrappings variations gimmicks services
                              for      on old
                           different  products
                            market
                           segments
```

Differentiation can take place in other ways. Businesses can be flexible as to the means of payment they allow (credit terms, smartcards etc), for example.

(c) **Focus strategy**

This is where a firm concentrates its attention on one or more particular **segments or niches** of the market, and does not try to serve the entire market with a single product. The firm will focus on a particular type of buyer or geographical area.

Drawbacks to a focus strategy include the following:

The market segment might **not be big enough** to provide the firm with a profitable basis for its operations.

The segment's needs may eventually become **less distinct** from the main markets.

Competitors can move into the chosen segment (as the Japanese have done into the luxury car market previously dominated by BMW and Mercedes).

1.8.1 ICT support for competitive strategy

Examples of how information and communications technology can support each of these strategies are shown in the following table.

Strategy	How ICT can support the strategy
Cost-leadership	By facilitating reductions in cost levels, for example by reducing the number of administration staff required.
	Allowing better resource utilisation, for example by providing accurate stock information allowing lower buffer inventories to be held.
	Using ICT to support just-in-time and advanced manufacturing systems.
Differentiation	Differentiation can be suggested by ICT, perhaps in the product itself or in the way it is marketed.
	Publishing and music are examples with the move from physical products (books, CDs) to electronic (downloads, CD ROM, MP3).
Focus	ICT may enable a more customised or specialised product/service to be produced.
	ICT also facilitates the collection of sales and customer information that identifies targetable market segments.

PART B THE MICRO-ENVIRONMENT

2 Industry structure and competitive behaviour

FAST FORWARD

The **nature of competition** differs in different industries.

- **Fragmented industries** are characterised by a large number of small firms.
- **Concentrated industries** are characterised by a small number of large firms.
- **Emerging industries** are characterised by greater uncertainty.

Although the five competitive forces are at work in any industry, the balance of power between the different competitors in an industry can vary.

(a) An industry might be populated by a number of **small scale competitors**. An example in the UK is hairdressing: there are few large 'chains' of hairdressers; most hairdressing salons are independent.

(b) On the other hand an industry might be **dominated** by a small number of large competitors: for example, major supermarkets or mining operations.

(c) There may be a **combination**: a few leading companies may dominate the market, but smaller ones might exist as well. The fast-food industry in many countries features major chains such as McDonalds as well as independent outlets (for example, fish and chip shops and kebab shops).

2.1 Fragmented industries

Key concept

A **fragmented industry**, according to Porter, is 'populated by a large number of small and medium-sized companies.' Moreover, a fragmented industry is characterised by 'the absence of market leaders with the power to shape industry events.'

This corresponds to market structure known as perfect competition.

Key concept

Perfect competition is a situation where there is

- a large number of firms,
- each with a very small share of the market,
- producing a homogeneous product,
- firms and consumers possessing perfect information, and
- free entry to, and exit from, the industry.

Perfect competition acts as a useful theoretical benchmark against which we can:

(a) **Judge or predict** what firms might do in markets where **competition** shows some or most of the **characteristics of being perfect**

(b) **Contrast the behaviour** of firms in markets that are imperfect

2.1.1 Characteristics of perfect competition

In a fragmented industry:

- There is a **large number** of **buyers** and **sellers** in the market.
- **Individual firms** are 'price takers', unable to influence the market price individually.
- **Producers** and **consumers** act **rationally** and have the same information.
- The **product** is **homogeneous**: one unit of the product is the same as any other unit.
- There is **free entry** into and exit of firms out of the market.
- There are **no transport** or **information gathering** costs.

Action Programme 1

Think about the market for a particular product – say, motor cars. To what extent is this market 'perfect'?

2.1.2 Reasons for fragmentation

Industries may become fragmented if:

- **Barriers to entry** are low: it is easy to set up in business.
- There are few **economies of scale** to be had by a large firm.
- Small scale businesses may be more **flexible** in coping with erratic demand.
- A large firm in a fragmented industry **cannot use its size** when dealing with suppliers.
- Being too large might lead to **higher overhead costs**.
- **Local image** and **reputation** are important.
- The **market** itself might be fragmented, as buyers can have a variety of different tastes.
- **Government** can forbid concentration.
- If **standards** are enforced locally, this can encourage fragmentation.

A fragmented industry can be consolidated into one with fewer companies as follows.

(a) **Technology may change**.

(b) **New standard product**

A standard product might be preferred to the previous custom-made variety for a number of reasons. Fast food chains such as McDonalds or Spud-u-like offer a consistent standard, and customers might welcome this lowering of the risk of disappointment.

(c) **Separate cause of fragmentation and deal with it**

Many big publishing companies have a large number of smaller **imprints**, with their own characteristics. (The BPP Holdings plc group, in addition to offering training, publishes a number of different imprints which serve different markets in different ways.)

(d) **Consolidation**

Some industries **consolidate naturally** as they age.

Long-run equilibrium will occur in the industry when there are no more firms entering or leaving the industry because no new firm thinks it could earn profits by entering and no existing firm thinks it could do better by leaving. In the **long run**, equilibrium will occur when the **revenue from selling an extra unit equals its cost and its price.**

2.2 Concentrated industries

Key concept

A concentrated industry is dominated by a small number of large firms, which are able to exercise a significant influence over the market as a whole.

This corresponds to the market structure known as oligopoly.

Key concept

An **oligopoly** is a market dominated by a few suppliers.

The essence of oligopoly is that **firms' production decisions are interdependent**. One firm cannot set price and output without considering how its rivals' response will affect its own profits. How an oligopolist will actually set his output and price depends on what assumption firms make about their competitors' behaviour.

2.2.1 Reasons for concentration

An industry may be concentrated if:

- It is cheaper to **produce in bulk** (ie where there are economies of scale).
- The amounts of money needed to stay in the business are **large**.
- **Entry barriers** are high: in other words it is hard to set up in business.
- The service does not depend uniquely on the **skills** of a particular individual.
- A large firm can benefit from an **integrated distribution network**.
- **Customers' needs** are fairly standard in the market.
- There are **economies of scale** in marketing distribution, purchasing etc.
- The company has **proprietary product technology**.

The importance of industry concentration is that there is nearly always a **'market leader'** who can significantly influence:

- The way business is done
- Relationships with sources of supply
- Distribution
- Pricing

Marketing at Work

Competition can be intensive in concentrated markets. Witness the **aggressive competition** in the 'Cola wars'. In 2006, the battleground was the FIFA World Cup.

'At the moment, it looks likely Pepsi will be left out in the cold as action hots up at the soccer World Cup starting in June 2006 in Germany – at least in India, Pakistan, Nepal, Bangladesh and Sri Lanka. Coca-Cola India is an associate sponsor of ESPN-Star, the broadest rights holder for this geographical spread. Coca-Cola Inc, on the other hand, has the in-stadia rights for the cup. The two tie-ups have been used by Coke to put Pepsi and is constellation of brand ambassadors, who include David Beckham, Ronaldinho, Thierry Henry, Roberto Carlos and Raul Gonzales, in the advertising equivalent of the bench. Thus, Pepsi is likely to be kept out of not only the TV advertising spots, but also in-stadia advertising. For good measure, Coke has also tied up with Adidas, the official sponsor of the World Cup, to distribute soccer memorabilia through promotions and contests.'

B&T (Australia), 12 May 2006

2.2.2 Price leadership and price wars in concentrated industries

Key concept

A **cartel** is an association of suppliers formed for the purpose of co-operating on the fixing of variables such as price or output levels.

A **price cartel** or **price ring** is created when a group of oligopoly firms combine to agree on a price at which they will sell their product to the market.

Each oligopoly firm could increase its profits if all the big firms in the market charge the same price as a monopolist would, and split the output between them. This is known as **collusion**, which can either be tacit or openly admitted. Such collusion is illegal in Europe and the USA.

The success of a price cartel will depend on:

(a) Whether it **consists** of **most or all** of the **producers** of the product.

(b) Whether or not there are **close substitutes** for the product. For example, a price cartel by taxi drivers might lead to a shift in demand for transport services to buses, cars and trains.

7: THE INDUSTRY ENVIRONMENT

(c) The **ease** with which **supply** can be **regulated**.

(d) The **price elasticity** of **demand** for the product. An attempt to raise prices might result in such a large a fall in demand that the total income of producers also falls.

(e) Whether **producers** can **agree** on their individual shares of the total restricted supply to the market. This is often the greatest difficulty of all.

Exam tip

> Eight marks were available in the June 2005 exam for using examples to compare the competitive environment of a fragmented and a concentrated industry. Another twelve marks were available for suggesting why businesses might want to monitor their competitors, in a concentrated industry – and how they might go about it (we will cover these areas later – but try and come up with an answer now, using your common sense…). In December 2006, you were asked to analyse 'the nature of competition' in the mobile phone market and suggest one strategic response. The examiner expected you to recognise this as a concentrated market or oligopoly, dominated by two or three firms (despite the number of different phones on offer!)

2.3 The monopoly market

Monopoly is the opposite of perfect competition.

Key concept

> In a **monopoly**, there is only one firm, the sole producer of a good which has no closely competing substitutes.

In monopoly the firm can earn **supernormal profits** in the long run as well as in the short run, because there are **barriers to entry** which prevent rivals entering the market. Much of the thrust of competitive policy in recent decades has been to open monopolistic markets to competition.

2.3.1 Price discrimination

Key concept

> The term **price discrimination** refers to a situation in which a firm sells the 'same' product at different prices in different markets.

Action Programme 2

Have you come across price discrimination in practice?

When?

Three basic conditions are necessary for price discrimination to be effective and profitable.

(a) The seller must be able to **control the supply** of the product. Clearly, this will apply under monopoly conditions. The monopoly seller has control over the quantity of the product offered to a particular buyer.

(b) The seller must be able to **prevent** the **resale** of the good by one buyer to another.

Services are less easily resold than goods while transportation costs, tariff barriers or import quotas may separate classes of buyers geographically and thus make price discrimination possible.

(c) There must be **significant differences** in the willingness to pay among the different classes of buyers.

PART B   THE MICRO-ENVIRONMENT

2.4 Emerging industries

Key concept

> An **emerging industry** is a new, or re-formed, industry. It can be created by technological innovation, changes in costs, social and economic changes.

Examples, of new, new-ish and emerging industries include the following.

- Electronic publishing (ie 'books' transferred to CD-ROM), interactive television and electronic music (ie. I-pod)
- Waste recycling (in some countries)
- Virtual reality applications (eg virtual 'fitting rooms' for clothing mail-order firms)

The problems with emerging industries include the following.

- The **technology** is uncertain.
- **Customer requirements** are not known.
- New industries start with **high costs**, but these fall eventually.
- **Newly formed companies** are in a good position to get into the industry.
- Consumers need to be **informed** about what the industry can offer in order to be interested in new products or services.
- Some new industries receive **subsidies**.
- **Early barriers to entry** include technology, access to materials, problems obtaining funds.

In an emerging market, even the approach to competitors differs. Licensing can encourage competition. This helps build the market, and in any case, it is rarely feasible to maintain a monopoly in the long run. In the 1950s, for example, Pilkington licensed its revolutionary glass making technology to its competitors.

3 Regulation of competition

FAST FORWARD

> The object of UK **competition law** is to protect the public interest by ensuring that the beneficial effects of competition can be exercised. In the UK, it is regulated by the **Office of Fair Trading** and the **Competition Commission**. The objects of the competition legislation are to protect the **public interest** and regulate **anti-competitive practices**.

The government, through legislation, can significantly influence the nature of relationships between a firm and members of its micro environment. Legislation can be used, for example, to control the price at which goals or services are sold to customers, or to allow a supplier access to a market from which economic and technical barriers had previously excluded it.

3.1 UK law and regulation

A good example of competition regulation is the UK's **Competition Act 1998**. The Act prohibits:

(a) Certain agreements or concerted practices which have as their object or effect the **prevention, restriction** or **distortion** of **competition** within the United Kingdom

(b) The **abuse** of a **dominant position** in a market if it may affect trade within the United Kingdom

The **Director General of Fair Trading** enforces these provisions; he can give directions for bringing any infringement to an end and impose penalties of up to 10% of turnover.

7: THE INDUSTRY ENVIRONMENT

The Competition Act also established the **Competition Commission**. The Commission has two aspects to its work:

(a) Preparation of **reports**

(b) The **appeals tribunal** which will hear appeals against decisions made under the prohibition provisions of the Competition Act 1998

Investigations carried out by the Competition Commission have included:

(a) Possible monopoly in the supply of prescription-only veterinary medicine
(b) The level of termination charges made to other operators by mobile phone companies
(c) The level of charges levied at the three biggest London airports by BAA plc

The **Enterprise Act 2002** introduced criminal sanctions for operating a cartel, with a maximum penalty of five years in prison for those found guilty of dishonestly operating deliberate agreements to fix prices, share markets, limit production and rig bids.

Marketing at Work

A good example of a situation where a **merger** was allowed to proceed with safeguards in place was the merger of the two largest companies involved in the UK's ITV television network, Carlton Communications and Granada. In its report in October 2003 the Competition Commission accepted the companies' views that the merger would remove dysfunctionality in the ITV network. The Commission believed that the merger would benefit viewers, through better programme quality and choice, and independent producers. Provided safeguards operated effectively, advertisers would also benefit through a stronger, more competitive, ITV.

The Commission was particularly concerned about the impact on the remaining small ITV companies. In response Carlton and Granada agreed a package of safeguards proposed by the ITC. The merged company would also give the other regional licensees the option to roll over existing airtime sales contracts.

3.2 EU competition law

Anticompetitive practices which affect only the trader within one member state of the European Union (EU) are subject only to national legislation. However, where such practices may affect free trade between member states, the EU rules on competition come into force. EU rules prohibit 'all agreements between undertakings, decisions by associations of undertakings and concerted practices which may affect trade between member states and which have as their object or effect the prevention, restriction or distortion of competition within the common market'.

Mergers, for example, must be notified to the Commission when:

(a) All the undertakings concerned achieve combined aggregate worldwide sales revenue of more than 2.5 billion euros.

(b) In each of at least three Member States, combined aggregate sales of more than 100 million euros.

(c) In each of these three Member States, at least two of the firms concerned should exceed 25 million euros in sales.

(d) Each of at least two of the companies concerned boast aggregate EU-wide sales of more than 100 million euros.

PART B   THE MICRO-ENVIRONMENT

3.2.1 Quotas

Member states of the EU are prevented from restricting competition by the fact that any form of **quota** is strictly controlled. A quota is a restriction which limits the import, export or through-transit of goods by reference to quantity or value.

3.2.2 Article 81 of the EC Treaty: anti-competitive agreements

This prohibits all agreements between businesses, decisions of associations of businesses and concerted practices which affect trade between members and **prevent, restrict or distort** competition. Any such agreement or decision shall be void. There then follows a list of activities of particular concern eg fixing prices, limiting production, sharing markets, discriminatory conditions of trading.

Any agreement may be 'justified' (subject to certain conditions) and the prohibition declared to be inapplicable if it contributes to **improving production** or **distribution** or promotes **technical or economic** progress, while allowing consumers a fair share of the resulting benefit.

3.2.3 Article 82 of the EC Treaty: abuse of monopoly position

Any **abuse** by one or more businesses of a dominant position within the common market or in a substantial part of it shall be prohibited as incompatible with the common market so far as it affects free trade between member states; the list of particular abuses is similar to that set out in Article 85. Where a group of inter-related companies is involved, their conduct jointly may infringe Article 86.

A business will enjoy a **dominant position** where it has power to hinder the maintenance of effective competition on the relevant market by allowing it to behave independently of its competitors and customers and ultimately of consumers. A dominant position itself is not reprehensible – only an *abuse* of it is an infringement.

Marketing at Work

Software giant Microsoft has been found guilty of abusing its monopoly power over the Netscape web browser under US anti-trust legislation; and of exploiting its dominant Windows platform unfairly, by the European Commission. (This was the subject of the December 2005 case study: a reminder to keep an eye on the quality press!)

3.3 Competition in the USA

The USA has some of the strongest laws on competition in the industrialised world, reflecting the practice in the USA of resolving many conflicts in court.

In the past they have been used against companies such as Microsoft and AT&T, the monopoly telephone supplier. During the 1980s AT&T lost its hold over local calls, as seven regional telephone companies were set up under court supervision. AT&T became the long distance supplier and faced more competition in that field.

However, Congress subsequently modified the law to allow local companies and long-distance operators to compete with each other. The result has been the consolidation of the industry into three giant telecoms operations.

Critics of the US approach claim that in many fields government intervention is irrelevant, as technology changes too quickly. In addition, laws have not been enforced consistently over time, but only when political fashion has dictated.

Other criticisms of competition legislation include its failure to take into account social needs other than competition, for example the preservation of employment. In addition, the attempts by domestic firms to compete abroad may be undermined by fierce competition at home. Firms may not be able to obtain the returns they need for activities such as innovation and research and development, which will improve their prospects overseas.

3.4 Regulations governing specific industries

In many countries regulators are given significant authority over specific industries. Utilities are one common example; their supply is a necessity for daily life, and their providers may hold a national or regional monopoly.

In practice, the regulators of these industries do have considerable power.

(a) They can specify a minimum **level of services**.

(b) They can **limit the increases in prices** the companies can charge their customers. For example, a utility might only be allowed to increase prices by the retail price index less a percentage. This is to encourage efficiency.

(c) They can **encourage greater competition** in the industry by adjudicating over uncompetitive practices, referring the issue to the competition authorities, or restructuring the industry.

3.5 Other government influences on competition in an industry

As a buyer, controller and supplier in a mixed economy, the government can bring considerable pressure to bear on competition within an industry.

(a) The government can influence the **timing and extent of structural changes** within an industry. Direct influence can take the form of 'full-blown regulation of such key variables as entry to the industry, competitive practices or profitability' (Porter).

(b) Governments can influence an **industry's structure** in indirect ways, such as the imposition of minimum product quality and testing standards.

(c) Governments might impose **competition policies** which keep an industry fragmented, and prevent the concentration of too much market share in the hands of one or two producers.

(d) In some industries, governments regulate the adoption of **new products**. In the pharmaceuticals industry new drugs or medicines must undergo stringent testing and obtain government approval before they can be marketed.

(e) **Subsidies** from the government to firms in an industry can take the form of cash grants, tax incentives or other incentives (eg rent-free government factories).

(f) Government policy can affect the position of products in one industry with respect to the position of **substitute products**. More stringent safety regulations on one type of product, say, might weaken its competitive position against substitute products.

Exam tip

A question on competition policies was crucial to success in the compulsory case study section of the December 2005 exam. The examiner was disappointed that candidates seemed unaware that his phrase 'competition policies' referred to legislation and regulations governing the actions or intent of monopolies and cartels - *not* to the policies organisations use to compete. This is clear from the syllabus – and the examiner warns all candidates to make themselves familiar with key syllabus terms!

PART B   THE MICRO-ENVIRONMENT

4 Monitoring competitors

FAST FORWARD

> **Competitor analysis** involves analysing **competitors' goals, assumptions** about the industry and their position in it, current **strategies** and likely **responses.**

The purpose of analysing competitors is to try and assess what they will do. This will enable the organisation to respond accordingly. Competitive advantage is about **relative** competitive position. Competitors are sometimes used as benchmarks.

We discussed in Chapter 4 the sources that can be used to obtain information about competitors. The increased importance of information technology means that organisations have to consider carefully how they should monitor competitors and what they are aiming to achieve.

4.1 Competitor analysis

Key aspects of competitor analysis include the following:

- What are the competitor's future goals?
- What **assumptions** does the competitor hold about the industry and its place in it?
- Is the competitor **competing on price**?
- Is the competitor **offering a different product**?
- Is the competitor **concentrating on one set of customers**?
- What are the competitor's **capabilities** (ie its strengths and weaknesses)?

We will look briefly at each of these in turn.

4.1.1 Future goals

Useful information about the competitor's goals may include the following:

- What are the business's **stated financial goals**?
- What **trade-offs** are made between long-term and short-term objectives?
- What is the competitor's **attitude to risk**?
- Do **managerial beliefs** (eg that the firm should be a market leader) affect its goals?
- **Structure**: for example, do marketing staff have more power than finance staff?
- What **incentive systems** are in place?
- What are the **managers** like? Are they united? Do they have a favourite strategy?
- To what extent does the business **cross-subsidise** others in the group?
- What is the purpose of the business: to raise money for the group?

4.1.2 Assumptions

Other questions relate to each competitor's **assumptions** (accurate or otherwise) about:

- Itself and its position in the industry
- The industry as a whole (eg does the competitor consider the industry is in decline?)

Assumptions:

- Indicate the way in which the competitor might react
- Explain **biases or blind spots** in how the competitor's managers see the environment

Useful information about competitor assumptions may include the following:

- What are the competitor's perceptions of its **relative position** (in terms of cost, product quality) in the industry?
- Is there a particularly strong **'emotional' bond** with particular products and markets?

- Are there **cultural or regional differences** that influence the actions of managers?
- What does the competitor believe about the **future demand** for the industry?
- Does the competitor accept the industry's **'conventional wisdom'**?
- In addition a **career analysis** of key managers can be informative. An accountant in charge is likely to have different priorities from a marketer.

4.1.3 Current strategy

Analysing the competitor's current strategy covers:

- Products
- Distribution
- Marketing and selling
- Operations
- Research and engineering
- Prices
- Overall costs
- Financial strengths
- Organisation
- General managerial skills
- Managerial ability
- Stakeholder relationships

4.1.4 Capabilities

Analysis should identify the competitor's:

- Core or distinctive strengths
- Ability to expand in a particular market

4.1.5 Other information

Information might include:

- Market share
- Sales volumes and margins
- Discounts
- Major changes in the internal environment (eg boardroom disputes)
- New product development plans
- Relationships with stakeholders, or potential relationships (eg exclusive rights)

4.2 Competitor response profiles

All the above information may be combined in a **competitor response profile**. This indicates:

- The **competitor's vulnerability** to environmental forces, competitors' actions etc
- The **'battleground'**, eg potential opportunity to invade a competitor's position in a low-priority product range

4.3 Competitor information systems

Development of a successful CIS needs to follow six steps.

Step 1	**Decide** what **information** is **required**
Step 2	**Design appropriate data capture systems** and collect the data
Step 3	**Analyse** and evaluate the **data**
Step 4	**Communicate** the resulting information
Step 5	**Incorporate** the information and conclusions reached **into strategy**
Step 6	**Feedback** results so that the information system may be refined

PART B THE MICRO-ENVIRONMENT

Action Programme 3

What problems can you identify for a marketer seeking to gather competitor data?

Chapter Roundup

- Porter suggests that there are five basic **competitive forces** which influence the state of competition in an industry and can be used as the outline for a **structural analysis** of an industry.
    - Threat of new entrants
    - The threat of substitute products and services
    - The bargaining power of customers
    - The bargaining power of suppliers
    - The rivalry amongst current competitors

- There are three basic competitive strategies: **cost leadership**, **differentiation** and **focus**.

- **The nature of competition** differs in different industries.
    - **Fragmented industries** are characterised by a large number of small firms.
    - **Concentrated industries** are characterised by a small number of large firms.
    - **Emerging industries** are characterised by greater uncertainty.

- The object of UK **competition law** is to protect the public interest by ensuring that the beneficial effects of competition can be exercised. In the UK, it is regulated by the **Office of Fair Trading** and the **Competition Commission**. The objects of the competition legislation are to protect the **public interest** and regulate **anti-competitive practices**.

- Organisations can adopt various competitive strategies
    - **Cost leadership** (being the lowest cost producer within an industry)
    - **Differentiation** (emphasising the **particular characteristics** of a firm's products or brands)
    - **Focus strategy** (concentrating on niches, either **products** or **market segments**)

- **Competitor analysis** involves analysing **competitors' goals, assumptions** about the industry and their position in it, current **strategies** and likely **responses.**

Quick Quiz

1   List Porter's five competitive forces.

2   Give five examples of barriers to entry.

3   Fill in the blank.

    A .... strategy is based on the assumption that competitive advantage can be gained through particular characteristics of a firm's products of brands.

4   Which of the following is not a competitive strategy?

    A   Cost leadership
    B   Price promotion
    C   Differentiation
    D   Focus

5   Fill in the blank.

    A .... industry is populated by a large number of small and medium-sized companies.

6   Oligopoly is a market where there is a large number of firms, each with a small share of the market.

    True   ☐
    False   ☐

7   What is a cartel?

8   Give six aspects of competitor analysis.

Answers to Quick Quiz

1   - Threat of new entrants
    - Threat of substitute products
    - Bargaining power of customers
    - Bargaining power of suppliers
    - Rivalry amongst current competitors

2   Any five of
    - Economies of scale
    - Product differentiation
    - Switching costs
    - Capital requirements
    - Access to distribution channels
    - Other cost advantages

3   Differentiation

4   B   Price promotion

5   Fragmented

6   False. The description is of perfect competition. Oligopoly is a market dominated by a few suppliers.

7   An association of suppliers that fixes prices or output levels.

8   - Future goals
    - Assumptions
    - Competition on price
    - Differentiation of product
    - Concentration on certain customers
    - Capabilities

PART B THE MICRO-ENVIRONMENT

Action Programme Review

1. (a) There is a huge number of buyers, and many sellers too. For any given model of car, a particular dealer is likely to be a price taker.

   (b) Communication is generally good. Product features are well known and list prices are freely available. Discount levels too are widely commented on, in the press and by word of mouth.

   (c) Consumers don't always act rationally. A car which appeals to a buyer's self-image, or snobbishness, may command a higher price than another apparently similar model.

   (d) The product is very far from homogeneous.

   (e) Entry to the market is not easy, whether we are talking about manufacturers of motor cars (very high start-up costs), or dealers.

   (f) Transport costs are *not* absent. On the contrary, significant geographical price differentiation is possible because of the high transport costs involved.

2. You might have thought of:

   (a) Telephone calls (different prices for peak and off-peak calls)
   (b) Rail travel (there are many different tickets you can buy for an identical journey)
   (c) Package holidays (more expensive during school holidays)

3. There are practical and ethical difficulties in gathering competitor data. Although much useful data and information will be available from accessible sources (as outlined in Chapter 4):

   (a) The most valuable competitive information (eg re future plans, new product designs) will be sensitive and confidential.

   (b) Primary data may be difficult to gather, since some sources may have obligations (contractual or loyalty-based) to the competitor, and be reluctant to disclose information.

   (c) There are ethical issues in trying to gather data which may be to the detriment of the competitor. Industrial espionage is clearly unethical (and illegal), but there may be 'grey' areas such as gathering data from employees, suppliers or customers of the competitor. (It would be unethical to do this under false pretences, for example, by claiming to be a market researcher or trade journalist.)

Now try Questions 11 and 12 at the end of the Study Text

Part C
The macro-environment

The macro-environment

Chapter topic list

1. Defining the macro-environment
2. Macro-environmental factors
3. The environmental set
4. Sources of environmental information
5. Information on the UK economy
6. Information on international markets

Syllabus content

- 3.1 Appreciate the importance of the macro-environment to the marketing process
- 3.2 Awareness of key sources of information on the macro-environment

PART C   THE MACRO-ENVIRONMENT

Introduction

In this chapter we introduce the concept of the macro-environment. The macroenvironment consists of the general forces which are impacting, or will be impacting, upon a company's micro-environment.

Clearly the number of possible factors that could have an impact upon an organisation is quite daunting. We therefore start off by providing a general framework for analysis of the environment. We shall discuss each of the most significant factors briefly here, and in more detail in the succeeding chapters.

As with the micro-environment, it is important for an organisation to know about the possible sources of information it can use. We discuss in general terms the sources of information about macro-factors, and then go into more detail about how information on the UK economy and world markets can be obtained.

1 Defining the macro-environment

FAST FORWARD

The **macro-environment** comprises all those organisations and individuals with which a business unit interacts, whether directly or indirectly.

Key concept

The **macro-environment** is concerned with general forces in the environment which may one day affect a company in its micro-environment.

To illustrate the contrast between the micro and macro-environments, customers and potential customers are real individuals existing in a company's micro-environment. However, demographic change is one of those more abstract phenomena in a company's macro-environment which won't directly affect the company's customers today, but may do at some time in the future.

However, sometimes there is overlap. For example, government bodies feature prominently in most organisations' micro-environment (eg as customers; as tax collector). But government bodies also create legislation which indirectly affects the environment in which a business operates.

Exam tip

Make sure that you can distinguish clearly between the micro and macro-environments. Such related clusters of terms are a clear exam pitfall, and the examiner has emphasised that marks will not be awarded for answers on the 'wrong' environment!

An organisation can easily monitor its micro-environment, but it can be quite critical that it also adequately monitors its macro-environment. **Macro-environmental analysis** involves:

- **Identifying** the key factors in the environment
- **Forecasting** what is likely to happen to each of the factors in the future
- **Responding** to environmental change

1.1 Factors in the environment

FAST FORWARD

There are a variety of ways of classifying the **factors** in the **macro environment**. The PEST, SLEPT or PESTLE model is the most popular framework.

There are any number of models for describing **general** environmental factors. One in common use in the UK is SLEPT, which stands for:

- Social-cultural
- Legal
- Economic
- Political
- Technical (or Technological)

SLEPT analysis is widely used in the UK for discussion of the general environment, so we shall use this framework.

The most basic variation of SLEPT is PEST:

- Political/legal
- Economic
- Social
- Technical/Technological

A more extensive version, STEEPLE, gives equal prominence to **environmental** and **ethical** issues.

Exam tip

> You may be asked to apply one or more of the SLEPT factors to a specific industry or to an organisation of your choice.. You may also be asked about specific external environmental factors (eg in December 2004, new government; economic cycle; new competitor; digital TV) and how it would affect their chosen organisation. SLEPT might also be a convenient framework to use if you are asked, more generally, to evaluate environmental factors, changes or challenges. But – as with other models – take care to use it only when relevant: the examiner has recently emphasised that a question on a macro environment does not necessarily mean that an analysis of SLEPT factors is required, or that it should be the main focus of an answer.

In addition, the natural environment is seen by many people as becoming an increasingly important element of organisations' macro-environment. 'Environmentalism' is a concept which does not divide neatly into 'micro' and 'macro' environmental elements.

1.2 Other classifications

Richard Daft (*Organisation Theory and Design*) proposed an alternative arrangement of ten 'sectors' in the environment, in no particular order, as follows.

- Financial resources sector
- Industry sector
- Government sector
- Human resources sector
- Technology sector
- Market sector
- Economic conditions sector
- Socio-cultural sector
- International sector
- Raw materials sector

You might like to remember these using the mnemonic: FIGHT ME SIR.

2 Macro-environmental factors

FAST FORWARD

> Before answering any question on the macro-environment, you should think about the possible relevance of the following.
>
> - **Economic change** at a regional, national or international level (eg trade developments)
> - The **political environment** and government influence
> - **Social and cultural changes** (eg changing attitudes, demographics)
> - The **law** and changes in the law
> - **Technological developments**
> - **Environmental** (green) and **ethical** issues and pressures

PART C   THE MACRO-ENVIRONMENT

2.1 Social change and social trends

Social change involves changes in the nature, attitudes and habits of society. Social changes are continually happening, and trends can be identified, for example in:

(a) **Rising standards of living**

These may result in wider ownership of consumer and luxury goods, which have implications for those industries.

(b) **Society's attitude to business**

Increasing social obligations and responsibilities are being heaped on to companies in many countries, not least with respect to ethical conduct (towards customers, employees etc).

Jones classified the social factors in a slightly different way, as follows.

(a) **Underlying factors**

These include population trends; education policy and the educational standards of the workforce; and attitudes to acquiring skills.

(b) **People at work**

The labour market, trade unions and work attitudes are all important. In these areas organisations are at the mercy of legislation and political pressures.

(c) **Individuals and society**

This category of social factors includes challenges to the existing social order, involvement by junior employees in decisions taken within their organisation, the social responsibility of employers to their employees, income and wealth distribution, and spending patterns.

The various factors can be summarised as follows: Figure 8.1.

Figure 8.1: The social environment

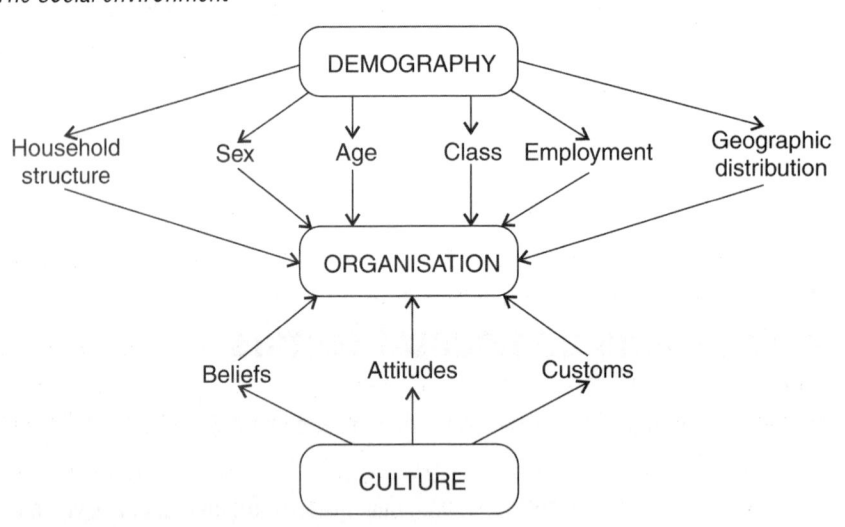

```
                    DEMOGRAPHY
         ↙    ↙    ↓    ↓    ↘    ↘
   Household  Sex  Age  Class  Employment  Geographic
   structure                                distribution
         ↘    ↘    ↓    ↓    ↙    ↙
                   ORGANISATION
         ↖    ↖    ↑    ↗    ↗
              Beliefs Attitudes Customs
                   ↑    ↑    ↑
                     CULTURE
```

2.1.1 Demography

One of the most important social changes is that related to population numbers and composition. Demography is the study of population and population trends.

2.1.2 Cultural changes

Each society has a certain culture (its own attitudes and ways of doing things). Within each society, there are many culture groups. Examples are as follows.

- Ethnic and racial cultures
- Religious cultures
- Classes
- The way business is conducted in each country

Marketing at Work

Cultural change might have to be planned for. An example is suggested by Japan. Since World War II, Japanese employees have been famed for their work ethic. The company came first. Holidays would be sacrificed for extra work and people rarely changed jobs. This cultural ethic was helpful in reconstructing Japan after the devastation of war.

However, Japan's growing prosperity has meant that the work ethic is declining as the new generation wants more leisure time and so on. People are less averse to changing jobs. Japanese companies might be able to plan for this change by forcing employees to take holidays or investing in leisure businesses.

We discuss the socio-cultural environment further in Chapter 9.

2.2 The political and legal environments

Many economic forecasts ignore the implications of a **change in government policy**, irrespective of whether or not there is a change of government. This limits their value.

(a) At **national level**, politics is significant as the political process includes **legislation**.

(b) Politics at **international level** also has a direct bearing on organisations. European Union **directives** affect all countries in the EU.

(c) The **government and supra-national institutions** control much of the economy. The government is the nation's largest supplier, employer, customer and investor. The slightest shift in political emphasis can decimate a particular market almost overnight (for example, aerospace and defence).

(d) For a variety of reasons, nations want to have **national champions** in particular industries. The shipping and airline industries have been particularly affected by the desire and insistence of many countries to have their own fleets.

Political change complicates the task of predicting future influences, and planning to meet them. Some political changes cannot easily be planned for.

Marketing managers must be constantly aware of the **legal implications** of their actions. The amount of law affecting marketers, both directly and indirectly, is increasing in most countries. Here are some examples of the ways in which a marketing manager needs to be aware of the law.

- **Customers** are gaining more rights in their dealings with a supplier.
- Similarly, **employees** are gaining more rights.
- **Advertisers** are increasingly restricted in the claims they can make.
- Governments in most countries have passed laws against **anti-competitive** practices.
- The law is often resorted to in **disputes** between manufacturers and their distributors.

As well as the law, there is an increasing amount of quasi-law which affects marketers. This is based on voluntary codes which do not normally have the full sanction of legal punishment, but companies find it in their interest to abide by them.

We discuss the political and legal environments further in Chapter 11.

2.3 The economic environment

The state of the economy affects all organisations, both commercial and non-commercial. The rate of growth in the economy is a measure of the overall change in demand for goods and services. Growth is an indication of increases in demand. For example, an increase in Gross National Product per head of the population might result in a greater demand for:

- Private cars and less demand for public transport
- Domestic consumer goods, such as dishwashers and compact disc players
- Services (eg restaurant meals or holidays abroad)

OTHER ECONOMIC INFLUENCES	
Regional or national level	The rate of inflation
	Unemployment and the availability of manpower with appropriate skills
	Interest rates and availability of credit
	The balance of trade and foreign exchange rates
	Taxation levels and incentives
	Government subsidies
	Public expenditure (and public sector procurement policies)
Rate of inflation, unemployment and so on.	Comparative growth rates, inflation rates, interest rates and wage rates in other countries
	The extent of protectionist measures against imports
	Freedom of capital movement between different countries
	The development of international economic communities, such as the European Union, and the prospects of international trade agreements between countries
	The levels of corporate and personal taxation in different countries
	Relative exchange rates
	Economic agreements

The state of the economy or more often the forecast state of the economy will influence the planning process for organisations which operate within it.

(a) In times of **boom** and increased demand and consumption, the overall planning problem will be to identify the demand.

(b) Conversely, in times of **recession**, the emphasis will be on cost-effectiveness, continuing profitability, survival and competition.

Economists can contribute to the strategic planning process with economic forecasts and information about economic trends.

Marketing at Work

Economic, political and legal factors: Russian retail

'Continuing **growth** of constant value incomes, a GDP increase and a reduction in unemployment boosted consumer economic confidence in Russia. In addition, the active construction of residential and commercial buildings and a gradual decrease of interest rates for consumer credit are making Russian consumers more confident about their future in general. Demand for consumer goods in this market continues to increase faster compared to the developed countries of Western Europe.

'The current legislative environment is favourable for the development of most retail channels in Russia. However local government authorities have helped to decrease the number of unorganised outdoor markets, stalls and kiosks without proper registration. Local government policies are instead directed towards the construction of modern retail and entertainment centres in place of old-fashioned outdoor markets. Big multiple retailers can meanwhile easily establish good relationships with government authorities, which help them to develop rapidly in Russia.

'Russian consumers still spend the biggest share of their total incomes on food. In 2004, 46% of total income was spent on food and beverages. This factor **constrains** the development of non-grocery retailers. However, with continuing constant value income growth, non-grocery retailers have a high potential for further increases.

'Consumer credit has been introduced to the big independent and chained non-grocery retailers, which has helped to increase non-grocery retailers' sales significantly. However, credit rates are still too high in Russia.

'Small independent retailers also face problems with local government authorities concerning outlet locations. Local government authorities can forbid the opening of a new retail outlet by denying planning permission.'

Nicholas, '*Russian Retailing*', Euromonitor, 27 February 2007

2.4 The natural environment

Physical environmental conditions are important for organisations in the following ways (in addition to obvious factors like earthquakes and the weather and pressure groups).

(a) The physical environment is a source of **resource inputs**. Managing physical resources successfully (eg oil companies, mining companies) is a good source of profits. If resources are scarce or valuable, this is doubly important.

(b) The physical environment presents threats and opportunities to organisations. Proximity to road and rail links can be a reason for siting a warehouse in a particular area, for example. Natural disasters can destroy commodities (eg crops) or disrupt supply. Governments can make regulations about some of the organisation's environmental interactions, for example pollution and waste control.

We discuss the natural environment further in Chapter 12.

2.5 The technical environment

Technological change is rapid, and organisations must adapt themselves to it.

Organisations that operate in an environment where the pace of technological change is very fast must be flexible enough to adapt to change quickly and must plan for change and innovation, perhaps by spending heavily on research and development. We discuss the technical environment in more detail in Chapter 13.

PART C   THE MACRO-ENVIRONMENT

2.6 Total environment: summary

The various factors in the total environment can be seen in overview as follows: Figure 8.2.

Figure 8.2: The total environment

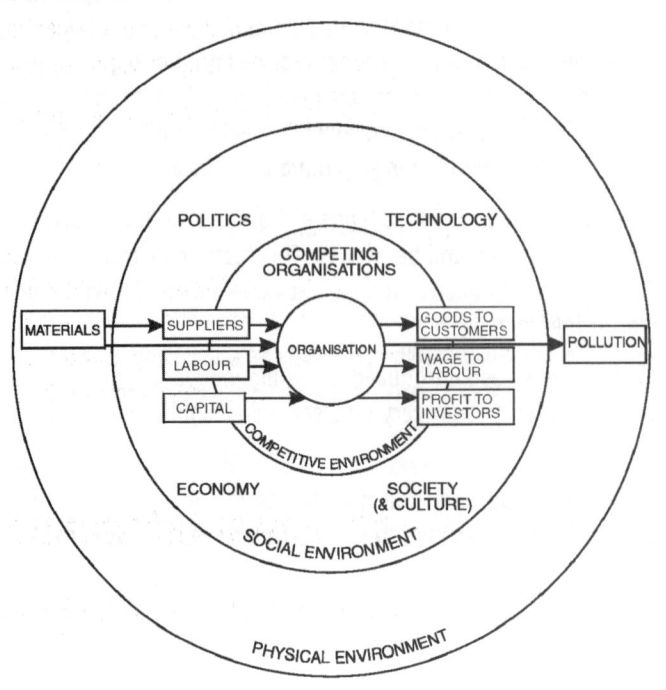

[Diagram: Concentric circles showing the total environment. Outer ring: PHYSICAL ENVIRONMENT. Next: SOCIAL ENVIRONMENT, with POLITICS, TECHNOLOGY, ECONOMY, SOCIETY (& CULTURE). Inner ring: COMPETITIVE ENVIRONMENT with COMPETING ORGANISATIONS. Centre: ORGANISATION, with inputs MATERIALS → SUPPLIERS, LABOUR, CAPITAL, and outputs GOODS TO CUSTOMERS, WAGE TO LABOUR, PROFIT TO INVESTORS → POLLUTION.]

Action Programme 1

Carry out a macroenvironmental analysis on your employer or another organisation you know well, taking into account the SLEPT factors and also the natural environment. You'll find that marketing personnel are a good source of information; after all, they have to find out what customers are after.

3 The environmental set

FAST FORWARD

A business's **environmental set** may change in nature and importance and includes:

- General economic conditions
- Local conditions
- Social trends
- Government policy

Key concept

A firm's **environmental set** includes those factors in the environment which affect it but over which it has limited control.

A feature of a public house's environmental set, for example, might include at any one time:

- **General economic conditions** (can people afford to go out drinking?)
- **Local conditions** (eg the closure of a nearby business might reduce the numbers of regular customers)

132

- **Social trends** (leading to a cut in the number of drinkers)
- **Government policy** (to raise money by taxing alcohol)

Set elements can change over time.

A factor may be a critical factor in the environmental set of one organisation, but irrelevant to another (eg the state of the economy may be critical to an estate agency, but almost irrelevant to an undertaker).

An organisation should consider how each of the key macroenvironmental factors which make up its environmental set are likely to affect it.

3.1 Opportunities and threats

In terms of SWOT analysis (Strengths/Weaknesses/Opportunities/Threats), an external appraisal of the environment identifies **profit-making opportunities** which can be exploited by the company's strengths. It also anticipates **environmental threats** (such as a declining economy, competitors' actions, government legislation or industrial unrest) against which the company must protect itself. (**SWOT analysis** is covered in Chapter 16.)

4 Sources of environmental information

> **FAST FORWARD**
>
> There are a number of **statistical sources** on the UK and international economy which businesses should scan.

Part D of this Study Text will discuss in some detail the process of marketing research. For now we list some sources of information about the macroenvironment that may be helpful background in the next few chapters. These include newspaper, trade journals, government publications and databases.

4.1 Environmental scanning

It is easy to be overwhelmed by the volume of environmental information on offer, and the variety of data that must be used. The temptation to ignore these factors completely might be understandable especially as managers are more concerned with short-term issues relating to immediate production.

However, some sort of scanning of environmental information sources is essential. In a large company, this can be done by the **strategic planning department**, if there is one. In a small company, everybody involved might keep an eye open for relevant environmental changes.

Managers can easily read about a topic in the paper. However it is not always easy to ensure that relevant environmental information is acted upon, especially if it is not something that requires an immediate reaction.

One way of ensuring that wider environmental issues are not overlooked is a type of **scanning exercise**. At regular intervals, an individual deputised to the task reports to managers on developments in the firm's environment.

Organisations should look **routinely** and **continuously** to obtain macro-environmental data. With developments in information technology (for example, the development of Mintel online services and McCarthy CD ROM databases), increasing volumes of information are becoming available. Competitive advantage will go to companies who not only collect such data, but are able to *process* it and make appropriate responses.

4.2 Environmental data

McNamee lists various areas of environmental information that ought to be included in a database for strategic planners. These are briefly described below.

4.2.1 Economic data

Economic data includes details of past growth and predictions of future growth in GDP and disposable income, the pattern of interest rates, predictions of the rate of inflation, unemployment levels and tax rates, developments in international trade etc. This is used to discern future demand and spending patterns.

Industry data including sales volume, product facilities and technological changes will also be important.

4.2.2 Political data

Political data (on what influence the government is having on the industry) comes from the mainstream media, unless the firm has inside knowledge and contacts in the government. One of the advantages of lobbying is not only to influence government but to get an early indication of policy.

4.2.3 Legal data

What are the likely implications of recent legislation, what legislation is likely to be introduced in the future, and what implications would this have? Legal data also comes mainly from the mainstream media. In addition, there are specialist publications indicating the significance of recent case law. Other firms specialise in certain types of information.

4.2.4 Social data

What are the changing habits, attitudes, cultures and educational standards of the population as a whole, and customers in particular? Social data comes from an enormous variety of sources. Governmental publications may be helpful. Surveys conducted by market researchers are also a useful source, although not publicly accessible.

4.2.5 Natural environment data

Data about the resources available to businesses is important, but businesses also need to consider how concerns about the natural environment may act as present constraints or future limitations. Knowledge about the activities and campaigns of pressure groups can be important. There is overlap with the political environment, as businesses will need to gauge how the government is responding to green concerns.

4.2.6 Technological data

Information on general technological development is widely available in the general and technical press. Technological developments specific to particular industries (electronics, bio-tech and so on) may be monitored through industry journals, specialist conferences, R&D consultancies and trade sources. Information on proprietary technology may be protected (particularly during the development phase): competitor activity should be monitored in ethical ways, to anticipate research and development breakthrough.

4.3 Public databases

You can now access large volumes of generally available information through databases held by public bodies. A variety of such services are available.

(a) Some newspapers offer computerised access to old editions, with search facilities looking for information on particular companies or issues.

(b) A variety of public databases are also available for inspection.

(c) Some databases have been designed specifically for marketing users such as ACORN (demographic data).

5 Information on the UK economy

5.1 UK statistical sources

Here, we summarise important sources of statistical information on the UK economy, on the UK in a European context and on the UK in a world context. Similar sources are available for other countries.

The **Office for National Statistics** website **www.statistics.gov.uk** provides an initial starting point and covers a range of official statistics. (Most of the statistical sources below are available free from the ONS website as PDF files. A quick way to reach them is to search (for example, for *Regional Trends*) at www.google.co.uk, specifying 'pages from the UK'.)

UK STATISTICAL SOURCES	
Annual Abstract of Statistics	Major annual statistics of government departments under eighteen headings, generally over a ten-year period up to the previous calendar year.
Bank of England Quarterly Bulletin	Statistics on assets and liabilities of banks and building societies and on the money supply, government debt, exchange rates and interest rates.
Business Monitor	Summary statistics on the annual Census of Production, with a two to three-year time lag.
Business Ratio Reports	Annual analyses of accounting ratios for 12,000 leading companies.
Economic Trends	Tables and charts showing trends in the UK economy.
Labour Market Trends	Data on the labour market, including earnings and retail prices.
Financial Statistics	Financial data for the latest month or quarter. Includes financial accounts for the various sectors of the economy.
Monthly Digest of Statistics	Monthly data on output of a wide range of industries. Statistics on components of national income and expenditure, demography, the labour market and various social issues.
National Income and Expenditure	Also called 'The Blue Book'. The most comprehensive source of data on national income, output and expenditure and their components.
Regional Trends	Detailed regional data including economic, social and demographic indices, based on the UK Standard Planning Regions.
Social Trends	Detailed data on household wealth, income and expenditure, and demographic and social trends.
United Kingdom Balance of Payments	Also called 'The Pink Book'. The prime source of data on the balance of payments broken down into its various components.

5.2 Other information

Other useful sources of information and articles on the economy include bank reviews and the National Institute Economic Review. The NIER comments on the state of the UK economy and the world economy. It provides useful comparisons between the UK and competitors, for example regarding labour costs, productivity and education.

5.3 Interpretation of statistical sources

Naturally, statistics need to be interpreted cautiously. Many sources are not published until they are out of date, although the internet has made publication faster for many statistics. Some statistics may be of doubtful reliability. The uses made of statistical data by governments in the management of the economy and by businesses in marketing and planning are considered in the next chapter.

6 Information on international markets

Companies can obtain considerable help and advice in their attempts to research foreign markets. Informal contacts may be made with a variety of organisations including the following.

- Overseas agents and distributors
- Banks
- Trade and professional organisations
- Government departments
- Foreign embassies and consulates
- Academic institutions

6.1 UK in a European context

Among the statistical sources on Europe, the following publications are of particular interest.

Economic Survey of Europe	This annual publication presents data by individual country and also by geographical groupings, including the Eastern bloc. Identifies and analyses trends in industry, investment, consumer spending, national output and trade.
European Economy	This is published three times a year, together with a statistical supplement giving annual economic indicators, by the Commission of the EU. An annual report on the economic situation within the EU is included in each November issue.
Eurostat	The Statistical Offices of the European Communities provide annual publications giving major economic indices and these are available from The Stationery Office under the heading **Eurostat**.

6.2 UK in a world context

Statistical sources relating to worldwide economic issues include the following.

World Economic Outlook (IMF)	Provides and analyses short and medium-term projections for individual countries. Includes discussion of key policy issues.
UN Statistical Yearbook	Includes a wide variety of indices.
World Economic Survey (United Nations)	Analyses fluctuations in various world economic indicators. Covers problems and prospects for developed and developing economies and the international trade outlooks.
Monthly Digest of Statistics	Includes regular statistical series, plus special statistics compiled on specific issues. Areas covered include demography, earnings, prices, human resources and production.

Others commonly consulted sources on international markets are listed below.

(a) The **Bank of England** and the major UK banks have published booklets on trade prospects for various countries.

(b) The major 'serious' **newspapers** produce periodic surveys on various countries.

(c) The **Economist Intelligence Unit** produces reports on various industries, countries and long term developments.

(d) Most **major trade associations** and **Chambers of Commerce** hold data on trade fairs, visits and market intelligence for various countries.

(e) There are numerous **trade directories** for overseas markets including Kompass, Dun and Bradstreet, Kluwer and Croner.

(f) The **EU** and **OECD** produce numerous reports on trade statistics and prospects for member countries.

(g) The **Department of Trade and Industry** and the Overseas Trade Services provide many publications, statistical summaries and intelligence reports.

(h) The **Confederation of British Industry** produces a monthly report on foreign markets.

(i) Many Anglo-foreign **Chambers of Commerce** and major Chambers of Commerce based in foreign countries provide regular market reports.

(j) The **Office for National Statistics** produces regular data on international trade.

(k) Many **reference libraries** subscribe to syndicated market research and abstract services including Emerald, Key Note, Mintel and Euromonitor.

Among the more commonly available and used data sources are the following.

- Guide to Official Statistics
- Monthly Digest of Statistics
- Overseas Trade Statistics

Various international bodies including the United Nations, the European Union, the European Coal and Steel Community, the Organisation for Economic Co-operation and Development and the International Monetary Fund also produce publications.

PART C   THE MACRO-ENVIRONMENT

Action Programme 2

As you progress through your CIM studies, it will be very helpful to have information about countries with different marketing environments. We recommend that you have files on three contrasting countries. Collect background data on your chosen countries, watch out for relevant news items and review key political, social, economic and technological developments.

[*Key skill for Marketers: Using ICT and the Internet*]

Exam tip

The marking guide for the June 2003 paper emphasised 'The syllabus gives equal weight to all the various macro-environments and examiners should recognise that a detailed knowledge of one is no longer required. Emphasis should be on the significance of the environment and its implications for marketers'. In the December 2005 exam, for example, 20 marks were available for assessing any *one* challenge presented by any *two* macro-environments (social, natural, technical or economic) of an insurance company, and formulating marketing action plans to overcome those challenges. The 2006 exams focused their case study questions on broad environmental issues such as global warming and globalisation.

Chapter Roundup

- The **macro-environment** comprises all those organisations and individuals with which a business unit interacts, whether directly or indirectly.

- There are a variety of ways of classifying the factors in the **macro-environment**. (The PEST, SLEPT or PESTLE model is the most popular framework).

- Before answering a question on the macro-environment, you should think about the possible relevance of the following.

    - **Economic change** at a regional, national or international level (eg trade developments)
    - The **political environment** and government influence
    - **Social and cultural changes** (eg changing attitudes)
    - The **law** and changes in the law
    - Changes in the size and make-up of the **population**
    - **Technological change**

- A business's **environmental set** may change in nature and importance and includes:

    - General economic conditions
    - Local conditions
    - Social trends
    - Government policy

- There are a number of **statistical sources** on the UK and international economy which businesses should scan.

8: THE MACRO-ENVIRONMENT

Quick Quiz

1 Define the macro-environment.

2 What does the acronym SLEPT stand for?

3 What does the acronym FIGHT ME SIR stand for?

4 Give four examples of demographic factors that may impact upon an organisation.

5 *Fill in the blank*

   .... includes those factors in the environment that affect a firm but over which it has limited control.

6 Give three examples of sources of information about international markets.

7 What are the main economic influences affecting a business at a regional or national level?

8 Which of the following types of law might impact upon a business?

   A   Criminal
   B   Tort
   C   Contract
   D   Health and safety
   E   Consumer protection
   F   Employment

Answers to Quick Quiz

1 The macro-environment is concerned with general forces in the environment which may one day affect a company in its micro-environment.

2 Socio-cultural
  Legal
  Economic
  Political
  Technological

3 Financial resources sector
  Industry sector
  Government sector
  Human resources sector
  Technology sector
  Market sector
  Economic conditions sector
  Socio-cultural sector
  International sector
  Raw materials sector

4 Any four of:
   - Household structure
   - Sex
   - Age
   - Class
   - Employment
   - Geographical distribution

139

PART C   THE MACRO-ENVIRONMENT

5   The environmental set

6   • Overseas agents
    • Banks
    • Trade and professional organisations
    • Government and department
    • Foreign embassies and consultants
    • Academic institutions

7   • The rate of inflation
    • Unemployment and the availability of labour
    • Interest rates and availability of credit
    • Balance of trade and foreign exchange rates
    • Taxation levels and incentives
    • Government subsidies
    • Public expenditure

8   All of them

Action Programme Review

1   Did you remember to prioritise the factors? Which are the most important?

2   Your own research.

Now try Question 13 at the end of the Study Text

The social and cultural environments

Chapter topic list

1. Demography
2. The demographic profile of the UK
3. Demography and human resources
4. Demography and product markets
5. Social structure
6. Culture
7. Lifestyle and health

Syllabus content

- 3.3 Explain the social, demographic and cultural environments, and in general terms, their influence on and implications for marketing

PART C   THE MACRO-ENVIRONMENT

Introduction

In this chapter we describe how social and cultural factors can influence marketing.

A key influence on the social environment is what is happening to population. We therefore start by discussing **demography**, the study of population. This involves studying a population's rate of growth or decline, its geographical and social distribution and its age structure (ie the proportion of young, middle aged and elderly people in the population).

You should realise that demographic developments not only affect the pattern of demand, but also the availability of resources to meet that demand. In section 4 of this chapter we describe how organisations can respond to the strains on available labour resources caused by demographic change.

We then move on to discuss **social class**. Social class is fundamentally an economic issue, with cultural connotations. We shall discuss how social class is reflected in income and buying decisions.

Lastly in this chapter we consider **culture**, the system of beliefs, values and behaviour in a group of people. The acquisition of culture, language and so on is referred to as socialisation. Values learnt can affect consumer behaviour in a number of different ways.

All of these factors are important in analysing and segmenting markets.

Exam tip

A widely drawn question on the Specimen Paper asked for a discussion of the marketing implications of three social or lifestyle changes. The 40 mark question on the December 2004 paper was entirely devoted to discussions of population and how it affects the marketing environment. The June 2006 exam asked you to identify changes in the 'SOCIAL environment' (the examiner is getting increasingly explicit in making the topic key words clear) and their impact on consumer demand for a worldwide tour operator.

1 Demography

FAST FORWARD

Demography is the study of population and population trends. It is relevant to businesses, as long-range trends in the population affect the demand for goods and services and the supply of labour.

Key concept

Demography is an 'analysis of statistics on birth and death rates, age structures of populations, ethnic groups within communities etc' (Bennett, *Dictionary of personnel and human resources management*).

The **purposes** of studying population and trends within it are as follows.

- People create a **demand** for goods and services.
- **Economic growth** should exceed population growth for enhanced standards of living.
- Population is a source of **labour**, one of the factors of production.
- Population creates demands on the **physical environment** and its resources.
- The structure of the population has implications for how markets are **segmented**.

1.1 Population size

There is some argument that a country has an optimum population size. Why might a country's population size be important?

(a) **Importing of labour**

If a population is too small, the country will have to import labour to exploit its resources or provide services. A population below a certain size might make it hard to achieve economies of scale.

(b) **Demand for resources**

A population that is too large might create excessive demand on food and resources and more demand for educational resources, housing and public services than the state or the private sector are able to supply.

(c) **Supply of labour**

Population size might determine supply of labour in relation to other factors of production (eg land, capital).

1.2 Causes and measurement of changes in the rate of population growth

> **FAST FORWARD**
>
> **Population size** can affect overall economic activity and the exploitation of natural resources. The **rate of population change** also affects government investment decisions and infrastructural plans.

What might be most important is the **rate of change** in population size. Note that countries with large populations may have a slow rate of population growth. In the 20th century, the population of European countries increased significantly. However, as a proportion of global population, it has decreased, as the populations of countries in Asia and Latin America, for example, have grown much faster.

Changes in the rate of population growth are caused by the following factors.

- Changes in the **birth rate**, or fertility rate. The birth rate can fluctuate sharply in the short run, with temporary 'baby booms' and falls in the rate of new births
- Changes in the **death rate** or mortality rate
- **Emigration** and/or immigration

Key concept

The **Rate of Natural Increase in population** (RNI) is the birth rate minus the death rate.

The long-term **growth in the world's population** has been due mainly to the reduction in the death rate. In earlier times, the world's population growth was lower because although the birth rate was high, so too was the death rate. Improved medicine and medical practice has reduced loss of life through disease and the death of new-born children and of mothers in childbirth.

The reasons for population growth or decline are cultural, technological and economic. The higher rate of population growth in less developed countries compared with developed countries has arisen due to a high birth rate, as well as a declining death rate. This has led to what is known as exponential growth, whereby population growth is increasingly rapid.

Population increase can put immense stress on infrastructure (eg water, sewage), but also provides a labour force. It is projected that by 2025, with anticipated migration, over 60% of the world's population will be living in urban areas. Failure to meet the aspirations of the population can lead to political unrest. Economic growth and encouragement of people to have fewer children (if they are no longer needed as an insurance policy for the future) become political priorities.

PART C   THE MACRO-ENVIRONMENT

| FEATURES OF GROWING AND FALLING POPULATIONS ||
Growing populations	Falling populations
Fast economic growth required	More productive techniques needed to maintain output
Overcrowding	Difficult to achieve economies of scale
More resources for capital investment required	Greater burden on young
Increased market stimulating investment	Changing consumption patterns
Labour mobility	

Governments can indirectly influence population size by:

- **Subsidising children** (eg through child allowances, flexible working policies)
- **Publicising birth control**, and offering cheap provision of it

Population size will be generally a more important factor than income per head for companies seeking to develop in worldwide markets for **essentials** or **low-cost products**.

1.3 Age structure and distribution

FAST FORWARD

Many industrialised countries are **ageing societies**. In other words, whilst the population is still growing in absolute terms, this is because people are living longer: a greater proportion of the population is elderly. (These trends tend to fluctuate, as the result of the working through of 'baby booms' and so on.)

Exam tip

This topic was worth 10 out of the 40 marks available for compulsory Question 1 on the December 2004 paper.

In our discussion of population growth we mentioned the **age structure** of the population. The effect of greater life expectancy is that a larger proportion of the population will be senior citizens (say 65 years or over) and unlikely to be working.

(a) A country with an expanding population will have larger proportions of children and old people, and lower proportions of people of working age.

(b) A country with a declining population will eventually have a large proportion of old people and reducing proportions of people of other ages.

The **working population** must create a country's economic wealth. With more people at retirement age, and also more young children, the proportion of the population which is working will be lower, and the proportion which is non-working and dependent on the working population will be higher.

From a **demand perspective**, the following are typical implications for marketing of an ageing population.

(a) Holiday tour companies may find increased demand for cruise holidays relative to demand for family beach holidays.

(b) Durability may replace fashionability as key design attributes.

(c) Distribution systems may favour home delivery at the expense of large out-of-town stores, if people are unable or unwilling to drive.

(d) 'Grey'/mature-age market segments may be increasingly targeted with products and marketing messages.

9: THE SOCIAL AND CULTURAL ENVIRONMENTS

Marketers should not overlook the **supply implications** of an ageing population.

- If a company has relied on a young work force, will these continue to be available?
- If so, at what price?
- Should the company consider recruiting older people instead? Age discrimination in the workplace has been outlawed in the UK by the Employment Equality (Age) Regulations 2006.

Marketing at Work

In the UK, Saga is a very good example of a company that is **focused on the mature population**. Saga is exclusively for people who are 50 or over and provides a range of services specifically designed for them. Initially Saga specialised in holidays outside peak season, but has now branched out into publishing, insurance, home shopping, financial services and radio stations.

Saga holidays are a mix of holidays to popular destinations and some less obvious places; the company runs a number of holidays to Latin America, for example. Many holidays focus on particular interests, for example opera, heritage and gardens. The company also runs holidays for singles. The Saga magazine has articles on a wide range of subjects, ranging from First World War survivors to students at Oxford University who are grandparents, and also the ten sexiest women over 50.

Saga is increasingly trying to target its campaigns, and increase cross-selling to customers, as well as considering customer acquisition and retention. Customised mailing appealing to the right person at the right time can be used to cut mailing costs and also improve mailing results.

1.4 Geographic distribution

> **FAST FORWARD**
>
> Demography also deals with the effect of **concentration** and **location** of the population.

In terms of the **location** of the population, a country may suffer the problems of overpopulation in some areas and underpopulation in others.

Action Programme 1

The (fictitious) Republic of Guarana in Latin America is undergoing a number of major changes. Now a democracy, it has re-established links with Western providers of capital, who are investing in the country, to extract its unique resource of Vrillium. In particular, large numbers of Vrillium mines have been opened in the San Serif valley. This comprises about 10% of the country's land area and is the site of Guarana's elegant capital Bosanova. This new economic activity is welcome. The mines and related industries will spur rapid economic growth. Bosanova has a population of 50,000. 80% of Guarana's population are peasant farmers. The prices of their crops on world markets have plummeted and the government of Guarana is alarmed at the growing rural poverty, especially as the population is increasing and agriculture is primitive and inefficient. The government has little money to invest in the countryside.

What consequences do you think the developments will have for Guarana?

Demography also deals with the effect of **concentration** and **dispersal** of population in particular areas. Industrialisation has traditionally meant a shift from the countryside to the towns, or **urbanisation**. In some countries people are moving away from big cities to suburbs or smaller towns (**devolution**) and are commuting elsewhere to work.

PART C   THE MACRO-ENVIRONMENT

1.5 Gender

Sex is important in population studies. The work roles played by males and females in different societies vary, even within the industrial world. In different societies, women and men have distinct purchasing and social powers.

1.6 Ethnicity

Only a few societies are homogeneous, with populations of one culture and ethnic background. Japan is an example, although the population includes descendants of Koreans. On the other hand, societies in Western Europe and the USA have populations drawn from a variety of different ethnic backgrounds.

Ethnicity is interesting to demographers, insofar as it acts as a marker for other social factors. The local authority of an area with a population drawn from a variety of ethnic backgrounds will have to take note in its education provision, if, say, English is not widely spoken.

1.7 Problems with evidence

Businesses need to be aware of the **limitations of the statistics** that they use. National income averages may mask differences that are significant from the marketer's viewpoint: for example, the existence of fast-growing, high-income sectors of the population. Marketers also need to be aware of the definitions used: the number of people classified as middle-class could significantly differ depending on whether middle-class is defined as people owning a refrigerator or owning a television, say.

Exam tip

> In the exam you may be asked how demographic changes affect specific types of business. Think through each of the changes or factors discussed above: what sorts of business might they particularly affect?

2 The demographic profile of the UK

In this section we use the example of the UK to show how demographic change may have implications for marketing activity.

2.1 Collecting the figures

Many important facts about a country's demographic profile are collected by government to aid planning. Every ten years, the UK government conducts a **census**. Originally this was undertaken as a population count alone, but recently additional information about the population has been requested.

The UK government publishes various statistics every year, as a result of its various data collection exercises. Two examples are the **Annual Abstract of Statistics** and **Social Trends**. Both contain population data, although **Social Trends** goes into more detail about people's habits. Summary Census information can also be viewed at **www.statistics.gov.uk**. Some data comparisons from the past and projections into the future are given below.

2.2 Population size

The population of the UK as a whole grew significantly during the last century, but this growth has begun to level off.

Population of the United Kingdom

	2021 projected '000s	2001 '000s	1991 '000s	1901 '000s	% change 1901–2001
England & Wales	55,527	52,042	51,100	32,528	60
Scotland	4,993	5,062	5,107	4,472	13
Northern Ireland	1,724	1,685	1,601	1,237	36
United Kingdom	62,244	58,789	57,808	38,237	54

2.3 Gender distribution

There is a slightly greater number of women than men in the UK population. Women generally have a longer life expectancy than men, and there are more males below the age of 65 than females.

2.4 Age structure

The age structure of the population is of particular concern to planners and business organisations. In 1961, 12% of the population were 65 or over. This is expected to rise to 24% by 2031.

It can be seen that, while the working population is fairly constant as a percentage, there is a shift in the relative proportion of elderly and young dependants. This shift is important for the following reasons.

(a) Elderly dependants have **different needs** (for long-term health provision, for example) to dependant children whose needs are for education and so on. Planners must take this into account when allocating resources for social provision.

(b) The elderly, as a **market segment**, are likely to be increasingly important.

(c) The decline in the number of young people will mean that organisations might have to change their **recruitment policies** or **production methods**. There will be fewer young people, and more competition for them.

Action Programme 2

Choose an organisation, and describe how recent changes in the number of young people in the population will impact upon its marketing activities.

2.5 Ethnicity

Ethnic minorities form around 5% of the UK's population, although about half the UK's ethnic minority population lives in London and the South-East (comprising 9% of the population there as opposed to 1% in the North). *Social Trends* reports that ethnic minority populations are younger (around one in three under 16 as opposed to one in five otherwise) than the average population.

PART C   THE MACRO-ENVIRONMENT

2.6 Regional distribution

As well as changes in aggregate population numbers, there are changes in where people choose to live and work. These differences can have a significant influence on social provision (eg schools, hospitals) and infrastructure (eg roads).

Over the last twenty years or so there has been a shift from cities and built-up areas to non-metropolitan regions.

Some of these trends may reverse over the next few years. There is pressure from government on local authorities in South-East England to build more homes, and create new or greatly expanded towns. There is also pressure to build on 'brown field' sites (sites of previous development) in cities.

2.7 Family

Demographic information is also used to map the social units in which people live (eg family size). Some trends in the UK are as follows.

(a) More and more people **live alone**, with one-person households accounting for 30% (6.5 million) of all households in 2001 (compared to 12% in 1961). This fact was marked in some advertising for a bank's mortgage service. Instead of featuring couples buying a house, it featured an individual buying a flat.

(b) Almost 30% of households in England and Wales contain **dependent children** and one in nine have children under five years old.

(c) 9.6% of households in England and Wales are **lone-parent** and over 90% of these are headed by a woman. Two thirds of lone-parent households have dependent children and the remaining third contain only grown up children.

3 Demography and human resources

FAST FORWARD

The characteristics of the population are also changing, with an increasingly qualified and skilled **labour force**. The job for human resources managers is to tap the labour market in the most effective way.

Demographic influences have a long-term influence on an organisation's supply of human resources, and hence its policies of **human resources management** (HRM). This section uses the example of the UK.

3.1 Demography and the labour force

In many countries, **women** are increasing their participation in the labour force. The increasing participation of women is related to:

(a) An increase in the availability of part-time jobs
(b) Male unemployment arising from the decline of traditional heavy industries
(c) The growth of the service sector
(d) An increase in the average age at which women have children
(d) Deliberate policy to ensure equality of opportunity

The HRM implications of long-term demographic changes can easily be overwhelmed by fluctuations in the business cycle. In the UK recession in the 1990s, 'the easing of the labour market for IT specialists, accountants and other specialisms was very marked' (Connock, *HR Vision*). To ignore demographics and other long-term trends in HR planning, however, is an example of short-termism.

Organisations must also consider **education trends** such as the proportion of school leavers going into higher education. This will impact upon the base of potential recruits with the right qualifications. Any other changes, such as a decline in engineering and technology graduates, should also be considered carefully.

Population trends and trends in education are thus the crucial influences on the supply of labour. However, it is often asserted, even in times of high unemployment, that there is a **skills shortage**. This probably means that there is not **the right mix** of skills on supply to satisfy the demand in particular skill (or geographic) areas.

3.2 Coping with demographic and education trends

Stephen Connock suggests six steps by which organisations can cope with these demographic and educational trends. In effect this is a form of segmentation.

Step 1.   **Establish** the **labour market** the organisation is in (eg young people, part-time workers)

Step 2.   **Discover** the **organisation's catchment areas** (ie location of potential recruits)

Step 3.   **Discern** the **supply side trends** in the catchment area labour force (eg how many school leavers are expected? What is the rate of growth/decline of local population?)

Step 4.   **Examine education trends** in the area

Step 5.   **Assess** the **demand** from **other employers** for the skills you need

Step 6.   Assess whether some of your demand can be satisfied by a **supply from other sources**

Organisations will need proper 'resourcing strategies' to make sure their demand for labour is properly met.

Older workers are one possible 'new' labour market. This was a feature of the mid-1980s, when some companies in the retail sector targeted older workers (over-40s and over-45s) because of their:

- Skills and experience
- High regard for customer service
- Stabilising influence on younger staff
- Contribution to better staff retention rates

Women returners are also being facilitated in returning to work (after child-rearing) by the need for independent income and family friendly HR policies such as career break schemes, flexible working and child care facilities.

4 Demography and product markets

FAST FORWARD

Businesses must monitor changes in demographic profile in order to exploit new **segment opportunities** or protect themselves against shrinking markets. The **family life cycle model** is a classic use of demography in marketing.

4.1 General demographic opportunities and threats

Businesses must remain aware of the changes in demographic profile. Some changes are predictable, others less so.

(a)   A **baby boom** will result in increased demand for infant and children's goods, while the ageing population will support age segmentation to the 'grey' market.

(b)   The **consequences of earlier baby booms** will result in many people reaching their peak earning potential at the same time.

(c) **Changes in government policy** may have a sufficient impact on the geographical distribution of the population, including pressures to build in certain areas and on certain types of land.

(d) **Changes** in **working patterns** are likely to affect both the workforce employed (more women, more part-time workers) and a wide variety of goods and services: for example, financial services with flexible payment plans, because of decreased security in the labour market.

Marketing at Work

A recent report illustrated the marketing threats and opportunities of demographic change.

- Falling birth rates in Western Europe have caused a sharp decline in sales of nappies.
- As the consumer base shrinks, manufacturers are increasing the pace of innovation to defend market share eg added features for convenience and comfort.
- Marketers have also increased segmentation for specific usages (eg swimming pants and night nappies) to increase sales.
- The ageing population, however, is presenting new marketing opportunities in the area of incontinence products. In order to exploit this market, producers are focusing on issues of discretion (in packaging and distribution, for example).

Euromonitor, 21 March 2007

4.2 The family life cycle model

An example of a use of demography in marketing is **family life cycle** (FLC). This is a summary of demographic variables.

```
      Age
+     Marital status
+     Career status
+     Whether have children
      Family life cycle
```

The family life cycle model attempts to identify the various stages through which households progress. Particular products and services can be targeted at people who occupy specific stages in the life cycle of families. The following provides a broad outline, but remember that in modern society there are many family forms.

(a) **Single adulthood**

Individuals may have high disposable income; although they are at a low point on the career ladder, they will have few financial commitments. They will be able to indulge in activities such as attending concerts or dining out. With no family responsibilities, there may be little planning for the future.

(b) **Young married couples with no children**

Again this is a prosperous period with two incomes and no costs of children. They may have the income to afford luxury purchases such as overseas holidays or fashionable clothing. However, there may be more concern about the future, for example taking out mortgages or pensions.

(c) **Married couple with dependent children**

Disposal income may fall as children consume resources of money and also time, thus leaving less time for other lifestyle activities.

(d) **Empty nesters**

These middle-aged people whose children have grown up and left home are the marketer's holy grail. Having no responsibilities and with mortgages paid off, they are seen as a wealthy market.

Marketing at Work

A survey published in 2001 by Andersen Consulting and Online Insight, *Beyond the Blur: Correcting the Vision of Internet Brands* suggested that many **e-marketing initiatives** were ill-aimed. Marketers 'were looking in the mirror instead of at their target audience.'

The survey suggested that many companies could achieve much better returns if they concentrated on consumers aged 35 or older who comprise about 10% of the population but who comprise 70% of online purchasers.

The best ways to reach this public were to:

(a) Provide a satisfying experience for the customers rather than bombarding them with heavy, unfocused advertising

(b) Recognise that different customers had different needs, and therefore move websites away from the 'one size fits all' category

Action Programme 3

What do the findings of this survey suggest about the best approach to targeting older consumers?

5 Social structure

FAST FORWARD

The **social structure** of the population can be analysed in a number of ways, on the basis that there is a correlation in the activities of certain groups. Class is not always easy to define but there are significant differences in income, education and wealth in different segments of the population.

Exam tip

Part of the 40-mark Question 1 on the June 2004 paper concerned the marketing opportunities afforded by a prospering middle class. The context of the question was the emerging market of China, but the principles outlined here would still apply, with some modifications for the specific cultural aspects of China (such as its one child policy). Remember that any question in this area will not test theory alone – you will invariably need to consider specific marketing implications.

A society is a large agglomeration of people, deployed in a variety of complex social relationships. The term **social structure** can be used to describe these relationships.

PART C THE MACRO-ENVIRONMENT

To say that a society has a social structure implies that it can be aggregated into groups:

(a) Whose members share certain things in common

(b) Which, more importantly, have relationships of superiority or inferiority in relation to, or influence over, other groups

Action Programme 4

Here is a quotation from *The Wealth of Nations* by Adam Smith.

'... the common wages of labour depends upon the contract made between those two parties [workmen and master] whose interests are by no means the same. The workmen desire to get as much, the masters to give as little as possible... We rarely hear, it has been said, of the combinations [trade unions] of masters, though frequently of those of the workmen... Masters are always and everywhere in a sort of tacit, but constant and uniform combination not to raise the wages of labour above their actual rate ... [and] ... sometimes enter into particular combinations to sink the wages of labour even below this rate. These are always conducted with the utmost silence and secrecy ... Such combinations, however, are frequently resisted by a contrary defensive combination of workmen ... They are desperate, and act with the folly and extravagance of desperate men who must either starve or frighten their masters into immediate compliance.'

What can you tell about the social structure of the society outlined in the quotation?

5.1 Measures of social class

Key concept

Class is a term used in many different contexts in the UK.

(a) **Subjective** definitions of class relate to the way in which people consider themselves.

(b) **Objective** measures of social class consist of selected demographic (mainly socio-economic) variables: income, education and occupation are the most common.

In practice, class strata or divisions are commonly derived from the specific demographic factors of **wealth/income** (economic resources), **educational attainment**, and **occupational status**.

Social groups are most commonly divided into strata or **classes**, with each class sharing a common level of **status**.

Shared values, attitudes and behaviour are characteristics of a social class, as distinct from those of a higher or lower class: research has been able to relate consumption behaviour to class standing. Social classes can be used as the basis of market segmentation.

Social grade definitions vary.

(a) There are two-category schemes, such as the following.

Producers of goods and services	Managers and organisers
Blue-collar	White collar
Lower-class/working class	Middle class

(b) Five or six category schemes include the National Readership Survey (formerly JICNAR) and the Registrar General's Scale.

Registrar General's Social Classes	NRS Social grades	Social status	Characteristics of occupation
I	A	Upper middle class	Higher managerial/professional eg lawyers, directors
II	B	Middle class	Intermediate managerial/administrative/ professional eg teachers, managers, computer operators, sales managers
III (i) non-manual	C$_1$	Lower middle class	Supervisory, clerical, junior managerial/ administrative/professional eg foremen, shop assistants
(ii) manual	C$_2$	Skilled working class	Skilled manual labour eg electricians, mechanics
IV	D	Working class	Semi-skilled manual labour eg machine operators
V			Unskilled manual labour eg cleaning, waiting tables, assembly
	E	Lowest level of subsistence	State pensioners, widows (no other earner), casual workers

(c) Some definitions also add a seventh stratum: upper class, consisting of the aristocracy (titled landowners) and the very wealthy (through ownership or investment). This stratum undoubtedly still exists in the UK, and this 1% of the adult population is reckoned to own around one quarter of the wealth of Britain!

5.1.1 Using social class data

'Social class' should be used in marketing planning with caution, for the following reasons.

(a) **Definition**

It is not exactly or consistently defined in terms of specific economic, influence or educational characteristics (such as would be most useful to a marketer).

(b) **Social changes mobilier**

Social mobility may make it difficult to use the concept in a meaningful way. People commonly perceive themselves to be in a different class to that in which they are objectively classified, and/or may aspire to membership of a higher class.

(c) **Dual income families**

Conventional gradings take into consideration the occupation of the head of the household, but with dual-income families, fluctuating family/household patterns, the mobility of labour and changes in employment circumstances (eg redundancy or insolvency), this may give a rather misleading picture.

More sophisticated measures of socio-economic and group membership have been devised. Housing type and ownership are particularly important methods of segmentation for many types of good. The use of this method is made much easier by the major categorisation scheme for all housing types in the UK, known as ACORN (A Classification Of Residential Neighbourhoods), which enables precise target marketing based on housing type to be conducted by suppliers.

5.2 Educational attainment

In many industrialised countries, it is likely that more and more people will achieve some form of educational or work-related qualification.

There is a definite correlation between academic attainments and occupational status (and related income measures).

5.3 Socio-economic position, income and wealth

Action Programme 5

'Comparing people's income is a simple matter. All you need to do is compare income after direct tax and social security contributions to see how well off people are.'

What's wrong with this statement?

The exercise above indicates some of the problems collecting and presenting data relating to wealth and living standards: there are wide variations in original income (wages, pensions), disposable income (after tax and other contributions) and final income (after essential educational and health expenses).

5.4 Buying patterns

Buying behaviour is an important aspect of marketing. Many factors influence the buying decisions of individuals and households. Demography and the class structure are relevant in that they can be both behavioural determinants and inhibitors.

(a) **Behavioural determinants**

These encourage people to buy a product or service. The individual's personality, culture, social class, and the importance of the purchase decision (eg a necessity such as food or water, or a luxury) can predispose a person to purchase something.

(b) **Inhibitors**

These are factors, such as the individual's income, which will make the person less likely to purchase something.

Socio-economic status can be related to buying patterns in a number of ways, both in the amount people **have to spend** and **what they spend it on**. It affects both the **quantity** of **goods** and **services supplied**, and the **proportion** of their **income** that **households spend** on goods and services.

Exam tip

The June 2004 paper contained a question on the social and cultural environment in the context of jewellery marketing. Think about the factors in a jewellery purchase: fashion styles, cultural differences, aspiration value, income/cost considerations, symbolic value (eg wedding and engagement rings) and so on.

9: THE SOCIAL AND CULTURAL ENVIRONMENTS

6 Culture

FAST FORWARD

Culture is a concept which denotes the beliefs, values, rituals, artefacts and habitual ways of behaving which are shared by a group of people (nation, region, class, organisation etc).

Key concept

Culture is 'the sum total of the beliefs, knowledge, attitudes of mind and customs to which people are exposed in their social conditioning'. Through contact with a particular culture, individuals learn a language, acquire values and learn habits of behaviour and thought.

6.1 Elements of culture

As suggested by our definition above, culture embraces the following aspects of social life.

(a) **Beliefs and values**

Beliefs are what we feel to be the case on the basis of objective and subjective information (eg people can believe the world is round or flat – some beliefs are truer than others). Values are beliefs which are enduring, general and accepted as a guide to culturally appropriate behaviour. They shape attitudes and so create tendencies for individuals and societies to behave in certain ways.

(b) **Customs**

Customs are modes of behaviour which represent culturally accepted ways of behaving in response to given situations. There are various types of social behavioural norms. Keith Williams (*Behavioural aspects of marketing*) identifies four.

EXAMPLES OF CUSTOMS	
Folkways	Appropriate patterns of behaviour; violations are noticed but not severely punished
Conventions	Accustomed or habitual standards of behaviour such as social etiquette
Mores	Significant social norms (eg monogamy) and taboos (eg against incest)
Laws	Formal recognition of mores considered necessary in interests of society, with penalties against violation

(c) **Artefacts**

Culture embraces all the physical tools designed by human beings for their physical and psychological well-being. Works of art, technology, products, buildings etc are all physical manifestations of social existence. Some of these physical objects may be **symbolic** of other things. A logo stands for the company, for example.

(d) **Rituals**

A ritual is a type of activity which takes on symbolic meaning, consisting of a fixed sequence of behaviour repeated over time. Ritualised behaviour tends to be public, elaborate, formal and ceremonial – like religious services, marriage ceremonies, court procedures, even sporting events.

6.2 Communicating culture

The learning and sharing of culture is made possible by **language** (both written and spoken, verbal *and* non-verbal).

Symbols are an important aspect of language and culture. Each symbol may carry a number of different meanings and associations for different people. The advertiser using slang words or pictorial images must take care that they are valid for the people he wants to reach – and up-to-date.

Some consumer researchers talk about the **transfer of cultural meaning** at different stages of the marketing process: Figure 9.1. The culturally constituted world produces products which are invested with cultural meaning or significance by advertising and fashion or, indeed, consumers.

Figure 9.1: Transfer of cultural meaning

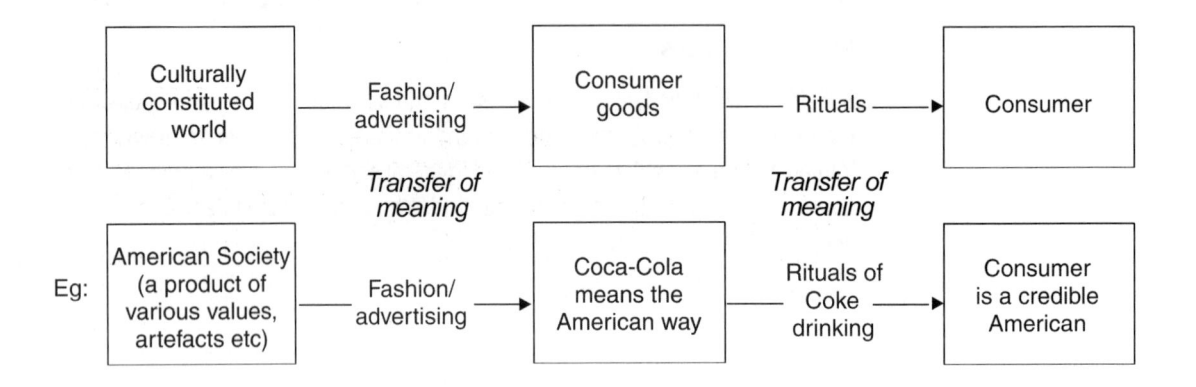

```
Culturally          Fashion/       Consumer                      
constituted   ───▶  advertising ─▶ goods    ─── Rituals ───▶  Consumer
world                                                                 
                    Transfer of                   Transfer of
                    meaning                       meaning

       American Society                                          Consumer
Eg:    (a product of    Fashion/    Coca-Cola     Rituals of     is a credible
       various values,  advertising means the     Coke           American
       artefacts etc)              American way   drinking
```

6.3 Uses of cultural analysis

Knowledge of the culture of a society is clearly of value to businesses in a number of ways.

(a) Marketers can **adapt their products and appeals** accordingly, and be fairly sure of a sizeable market (or a well-targeted market segment). Perhaps more importantly, they can avoid cultural 'gaffes' which alienate international or ethnic markets.

(b) Marketers can also plan to participate in the **teaching process** that creates culture. Mass media advertising, in particular, is an important agent by which cultural meanings are attached to products, people and situations.

(c) Managers may need to tackle **cultural differences** for cross-cultural or international management and team working.

Cultural differences (Figure 9.2) are a major challenge for a marketing organisation moving into an international or globalised market, as we will see in the next chapter.

Figure 9.2: Elements of cultural difference

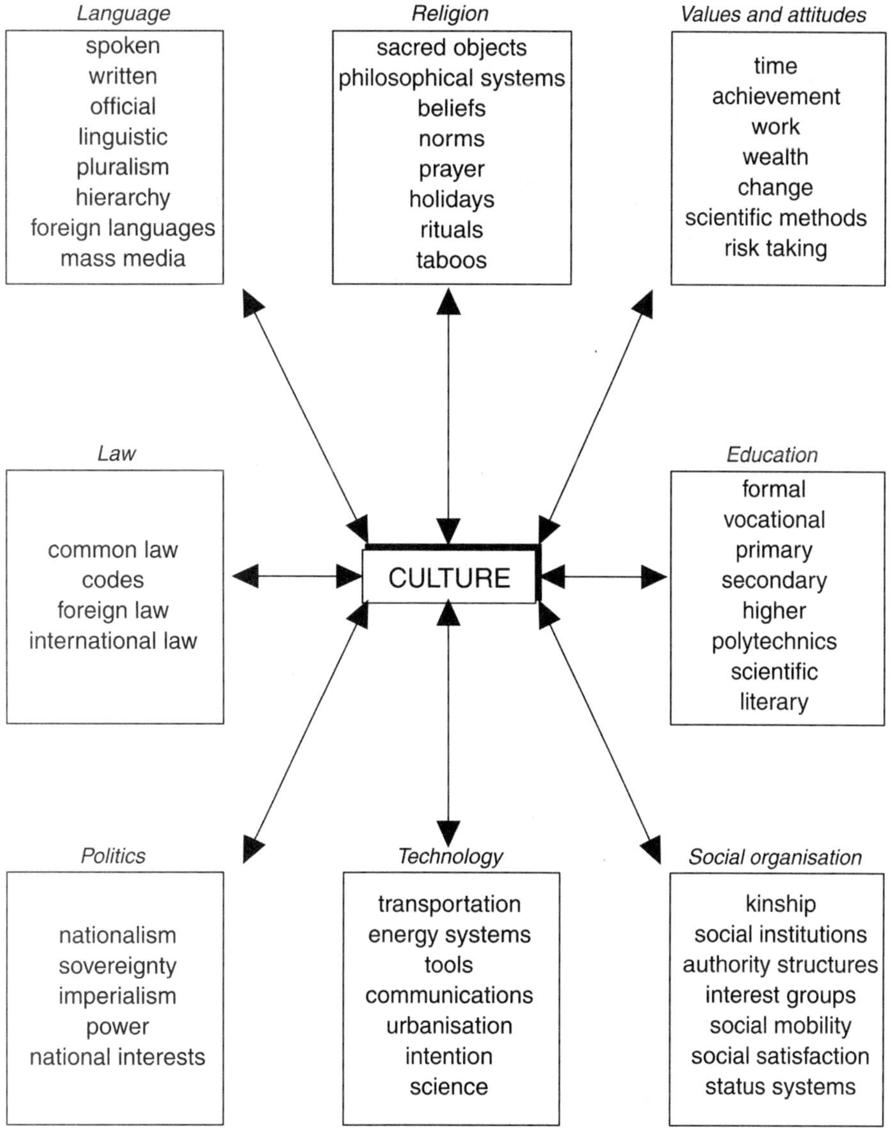

Language
- spoken
- written
- official
- linguistic
- pluralism
- hierarchy
- foreign languages
- mass media

Religion
- sacred objects
- philosophical systems
- beliefs
- norms
- prayer
- holidays
- rituals
- taboos

Values and attitudes
- time
- achievement
- work
- wealth
- change
- scientific methods
- risk taking

Law
- common law
- codes
- foreign law
- international law

CULTURE

Education
- formal
- vocational
- primary
- secondary
- higher
- polytechnics
- scientific
- literary

Politics
- nationalism
- sovereignty
- imperialism
- power
- national interests

Technology
- transportation
- energy systems
- tools
- communications
- urbanisation
- intention
- science

Social organisation
- kinship
- social institutions
- authority structures
- interest groups
- social mobility
- social satisfaction
- status systems

Action Programme 6

Schiffman & Kanuk (*Consumer Behaviour*) gives the following summary of American core values and their relevance to why people are motivated to buy products or services. Consider how far they are applicable to *your* social culture.

Value	General features	Relevance to consumer behaviour
Achievement and success	Hard work is good; success flows from hard work	Acts as a justification for acquisition of goods ('You deserve it')
Activity	Keeping busy is healthy and natural	Stimulates interest in products that are time-savers and enhance leisure time
Efficiency and practicality	Admiration of things that solve problems (eg save time and effort)	Stimulates purchase of products that function well and save time

Value	General features	Relevance to consumer behaviour
Progress	People can improve themselves; tomorrow should be better than today	Stimulates desire for new products that fulfil unsatisfied needs, ready acceptance of products that claim to be 'new' or 'improved'.
Material comfort	'The good life'	Fosters acceptance of convenience and luxury products that make life more comfortable and enjoyable.
Individualism	Being oneself (eg self-reliance, self-interest, self-esteem)	Stimulates acceptance of customised or unique products that enable a person to 'express his or her own personality'.
Freedom	Freedom of choice	Fosters interest in wide product lines and differentiated products.
External conformity	Uniformity of observable behaviour; desire for acceptance	Stimulates interest in products that are used or owned by others in the same social group.
Humanitarianism	Caring for others, particularly the underdog	Stimulates patronage of firms that compete with market leaders.
Youthfulness	A state of mind that stresses being young at heart and a youthful appearance	Stimulates acceptance of products that provide the illusion of maintaining or fostering youthfulness.

6.4 Sub-culture groups (segments)

Culture in a society can be divided into **subcultures** reflecting social differences.

(a) **Class**

People from different social classes might have different values reflecting their position in society. These values might relate to attitudes to work, or the value of education. Different classes might dress differently.

(b) **Ethnic background**

Social Trends makes a distinction between **white** ethnic groups and all others (although within the white group, there are also many ethnic minorities). Even though most people from minority ethnic backgrounds may have been born in the home country, they can still be considered a distinct cultural group.

(c) **Religion**

Religion and ethnicity are related in that most Muslims in the UK, for example, come from Pakistan, Bangladesh or Africa. Values and lifestyles are affected by religions (the prohibition of eating certain kinds of food, for example): religious beliefs are protected by UK law (eg. the Employment Equality Regulations 2003, which outlaw discrimination and harassment in the workplace).

(d) **Geography or region**

Even in such a small country as England, there are distinct regional differences. Speech accents most noticeably differ, but there are also perceived variations in personality, life style, eating and drinking habits between the North and South, or the South West and South East – and even between West and East London! Some regions, such as Yorkshire, have a particularly strong self-image and loyalty to local products.

(e) **Age**

Age subcultures vary according to the period in which individuals were socialised to an extent, because of the great shifts in social values and customs in this century. Age subcultures also vary through each individual's life. Each individual progresses through the **'teen'** or **'youth'** (14-24 year old) **subcultures**, which are the most strongly bonded and identifiable groups. The elderly are another **distinct subculture**.

(f) **Sex**

There are some subcultures related to sex. Some products, for example, are targeted directly to women or to men. The homosexual community, also, might be considered a subculture in its own right.

(g) **Work**

Different organisations have different corporate cultures, in that the shared values of one workplace may be different from another.

The exclusivity of subcultures should not be exaggerated, since each consumer is simultaneously a member of many subcultural segments.

Action Programme 7

(a) Find at least one example of marketing targeted at a segment of each of the above subcultures.

(b) Visit shops or look through magazines that are not targeted at the subcultures into which you happen to fit. Make a note of the differences you see.

7 Lifestyle and health

FAST FORWARD

Lifestyle is the way in which people live in terms of attitudes, preferences, interests and aspirations.

Key concept

Lifestyle is distinctive ways of living adopted by particular communities or sub-sections of society.

7.1 Lifestyle classifications

Lifestyle is a manifestation of a number of behavioural factors, such as motivation, personality and culture. When the numbers of people sharing lifestyle characteristics are quantified, marketers can **target products** and promotions to the identified segment.

Exam tip

Four marks were available in the case study question in December 2006 simply for defining and describing the key characteristics of 'lifestyle changes'. (The phrase came up in the scenario as one cause of increasing demand for water supply.) In this context, lifestyle simply means 'how people live': taking more showers and baths, for example, or using more washing machines and dishwashers.

PART C   THE MACRO-ENVIRONMENT

The **green movement** has become part of many lifestyle segments. Companies segment some market clients according to whether they are 'pale' or 'dark' green in their attitude to the environment and therefore how significant environmentally friendly product attributes will be to the purchasing decision.

Lifestyle segmentation seeks to classify people according to their **values, opinions, personality characteristics, interests and so on.** The relevance of this concept is bound up in its ability to introduce various new dimensions to existing customer information. These include customers' disposition towards savings, investment and the use of credit, general attitude to money, leisure and other key influences.

Lifestyle segmentation attempts to discover the particular unique life style patterns of customers, which will give an **insight into their preferences** for various products and services. Strategists who use this segmentation tool will be better able to direct their marketing energies to meet the future needs of these identified groups.

Marketing at Work

An advertising campaign for the restaurant chain **TGI Fridays** contrasted the excitement of TGIs compared with a more sedate environment.

Different types of food are offered, the waiting staff are younger, and the bar staff perform juggling acts when making cocktails.

7.2 Health issues

There have been significant changes in the UK in attitudes to diet and health. Most obvious has been a decrease in smoking, concern about obesity (particularly in children) and increased interest in alternative and complementary medicines and exercise.

In addition there has been an increase in vegetarianism, and 'green consumerism'. This includes a concern with 'organic food' now found in many supermarkets. The increased consumption of poultry is caused, not so much by concern with health, but more by its relative fall in price resulting from battery farming techniques. Sugar has been replaced by artificial sweeteners.

Marketing at Work

Fruit drinks such as Snapple began to compete with other soft drinks such as Coca-Cola, which faced a loss in market share as a result of a **change in consumer tastes** and consumer awareness of issues such as childhood obesity.

Coca-Cola revamped its marketing, and also introduced the *Fruitopia* brand to compete with the rival fruit drinks. In 2007, it also acquired a leading Mexican fruit juice firm (Jugos del Valle) to give it a strong presence in the Latin American juice market.

Sport is a health issue, but has a wider significance in that the 'provision of sporting and recreational facilities has been recognised by the police, probation officers and social workers as being beneficial in reducing crime, particularly in the inner cities' *(Social Trends)*.

The impact of health on businesses is as follows.

(a) Increasing market for **sports-related goods** (even though, as in the case with training shoes, sporting goods might be purchased as fashion accessories).

(b) Increasing concern with **employee health** and the effect of ill-health on productivity. Some employers provide gyms and physical recreation facilities. Others offer counselling programmes to employees who are alcohol abusers.

(c) The developing of **new food products and brands** with certain characteristics (eg for 'healthy eating'). Some supermarket chains have Healthy Eating programmes.

Marketing at Work

'The place with nothing' has been suggested as an advertising slogan for the Philippines' new luxury resort. The resort is devoted to **health and relaxation** and offers yoga, blood-cell analysis, and massage and cleansing regimes. Many cottages have their own gardens, but there are a number of places in the communal grounds where visitors can relax quietly. The resort claims that its restaurant is the only restaurant in the world devoted to raw food, although guests who are tired of it have the option of the local McDonald's down the road.

The resort has won an international reputation despite having 'no televisions, no telephones, no refrigerators in the rooms, no all-you-can-eat seafood buffet, no smoking and absolutely no nightlife.' It seems to appeal in particular to tired and stressed city dwellers seeking calm.

Far Eastern Economic Review

Chapter Roundup

- **Demography** is the study of population and population trends. It is relevant to businesses as long-range trends in the population affect the demand for goods and services and the supply of labour.

- **Population size** can affect overall economic activity and the exploitation of natural resources. The **rate of population change** also affects government investment decisions and infrastructural plans.

- Many industrialised countries are **ageing societies**. In other words, whilst the population is still growing in absolute terms, this is because people are living longer: a greater proportion of the population is elderly. (These trends tend to fluctuate, as the result of the working through of 'baby booms' and so on.)

- Demography also deals with the effect of **concentration** and **location** of the population.

- The characteristics of the population are also changing, with an increasingly qualified and skilled **labour force**. The job for human resources managers is to tap the labour market in the most effective way.

- Businesses must monitor changes in demographic profile in order to exploit new **segment opportunities** or protect themselves against shrinking markets. The **family life cycle model** is a classic use of demography in marketing.

- The **social structure** of the population can be analysed in a number of ways, on the basis that there is a correlation in the activities of certain groups. Class is not always easy to define but there are significant differences in income, education and wealth in different segments of the population.

- **Culture** is a concept which denotes the beliefs, values, rituals, artefacts and habitual ways of behaving which are shared by a group of people (nation, region, class, organisation etc).

- **Lifestyle** is the way in which people live in terms of attitudes, preferences, interests and applications.

PART C   THE MACRO-ENVIRONMENT

Quick Quiz

1   The Rate of Natural Increase in population = ?

2   Which of the following is not a feature of a growing population?

    A   Overcrowding
    B   Labour mobility
    C   Difficulties in achieving economies of scale
    D   Requirement for fast economic growth

3   *Fill in the blank*

    .... is the sum total of the beliefs, knowledge, attitudes of mind and customs to which people are exposed in their social conditioning.

4   Give five examples of subcultures.

5   *Fill in the blank*

    ....refers to distinctive ways of living adopted by particular communities

6   Give three examples of objective measure of class.

7   What is an 'empty nester'?

8   Which of the following are lifestyle categories?

    A   Upwardly mobile and ambitious
    B   Hedonistic preference
    C   Affluent grey
    D   Intermediate non-manual

Answers to Quick Quiz

1   Birth rate minus death rate

2   C   Difficulties in achieving economies of scale is a characteristic of a declining population

3   Culture

4   Any five of:

    - Class
    - Ethnic background
    - Religion
    - Geography
    - Age
    - Sex
    - Work

5   Lifestyle

6   - Income
    - Education
    - Occupation

7   Middle-aged person whose children have grown up and left home

8   A and B. These categories are simply aspects of a person's views and aspirations. C and D are objective categories which could be used as social classes.

Action Programme Review

1 Here is one possible answer. The existence of the new wealth will encourage:

   (a) Mass urbanisation
   (b) Potential rural depopulation

   as the new industries will encourage peasants to move in from the land in the hope of a better life. Bosanova's resources will become more and more strained. At the same time it is possible that, without parallel increases in agricultural efficiency, the ageing rural workforce, who cannot move, will become less productive.

2 Your own research.

3 You need to consider not just age but also the life experiences of the ageing population. For instance, many people now in their early or middle fifties benefited from the expansion in higher education in the 1960s, and marketers have to take these increased education levels into account. Overall fitness levels may also have increased with the result that older consumers may be more interested in 'adventure holidays than recliner chairs'.

   The article in the *Financial Times* that covered the survey suggested the following steps.

   (a) Carefully acknowledging age without drawing too much attention to it
   (b) Not automatically using the opposite advertising messages to those used in the 'yoof' market
   (c) Taking into account how older consumers see and wish to portray themselves; sales of toiletries, cosmetics and clothing have increased significantly among the over-50s

4 There are two groups distinct from, but connected with, each other: masters and workmen, with masters in a position of superiority when it comes to wealth and power. This position is held in relation to the workmen. You are also told that the relationship between the two groups is *necessarily* antagonistic (traditionally held to be a Marxist view). Many would dispute this and would say that it is in the interest of both groups to co-operate. The example shows that a society can have groups who have relationships with each other, without necessarily having the same interests.

5 Unfortunately the issue is not that simple. Firstly, there is indirect taxation, particularly VAT. Households on different incomes are more or less exposed to this. Secondly, there is the issue of mortgage interest relief, which is not available to people renting their accommodation. Thirdly, there are additional social benefits such as education. It is hard to combine all these factors together.

6 Your own research.

7 Your own research.

Now try Questions 14 and 15 at the end of the Study Text

PART C THE MACRO-ENVIRONMENT

The economic and international environments

Chapter topic list

1. Economic policy objectives
2. National income
3. Economic growth, unemployment and inflation
4. The business cycle
5. Fiscal and monetary policies
6. The international environment

Syllabus content

- 3.4 Explain the economic and international environments and, in general terms, their influence on and implications for marketing

PART C   THE MACRO-ENVIRONMENT

Introduction

In this chapter we consider various aspects of the economic environment which organisations face.

We firstly describe certain key aspects of economies, including in Section 4 the business cycle, which is a key influence on economic policy. In Section 5 we briefly discuss how governments go about managing the economy.

The other aspect of this chapter is the **international environment**. Even firms based in and selling solely in domestic economies will face competition from imports. Moreover government policies designed to affect the exchange rate and the balance of payments can have other economic consequences as we shall see in Section 6 of the chapter.

1 Economic policy objectives

FAST FORWARD

The primary aim of economic policy is to provide a **stable economic framework** from which sustainable growth can be achieved. Other objectives include control of inflation and unemployment and balancing trade.

Before we discuss the most important aspects of an economy's performance, and the various ways in which governments attempt to control the economy, we shall start off by briefly discussing the main **aims** of economic policy. The following sections should be read with these aims in mind.

Among the aims of a government's economic policy may be the following.

(a) **To achieve sustainable growth in national income per head of the population**

Growth implies an increase in national income in real terms. The idea of sustainable growth implies that the fluctuations of the business cycle are avoided and that output grows on a steady upward trend. This is the most important goal.

(b) **To control price inflation**

This has become a central objective of economic policy in many countries in recent years.

(c) **To achieve full employment**

Full employment does not mean that everyone who wants a job has one all the time, but it does mean that unemployment levels are low, and involuntary unemployment is short-term.

(d) **To achieve a balance between exports and imports**

The wealth of a country relative to others, a country's creditworthiness as a borrower, and the goodwill between countries in international relations might all depend on the achievement of an external balance over time. Deficits in external trade, with imports exceeding exports, might also be damaging for the prospects of economic growth.

1.1 The changing emphasis of economic policy

The emphasis on different policy objectives has changed in line with political, social and economic events. The objective of **full employment** was central to policy in developed countries following the Second World War. Later, other macro economic objectives came to the fore. Explicit policy commitments have been made by governments at different times in different countries to the objectives of **low inflation, balance of payments equilibrium** and **sustainable development** of the economy.

Sustainable development describes a pattern of growth at a local or a national level which is stable over the long term and is unlikely to be a victim of its own success. Sustainability implies that there will always be **sufficient natural, financial** and **human resources** available to meet future growth. Sustainable

10: THE ECONOMIC AND INTERNATIONAL ENVIRONMENTS

development has been particularly used to describe growth which does not destroy the natural resources which are vital to further production.

To try to achieve its intermediate and overall objectives, a government will use a number of different policy tools or policy instruments.

These policy tools are not mutually exclusive and a government might adopt a mix of policies to achieve its economic objectives. As will become clearer when we look at different policy objectives, conflict may arise between different objectives, meaning that choices have to be made.

Exam tip

> A Specimen Paper question covered government economic objectives, indicators of their success and the marketing implications of an objective.

2 National income

FAST FORWARD

> There are various ways of defining **national income**; one way is to say that it equals the sum of expenditure (consumption + investment + government) *plus* exports *minus* imports.

Three key measures of economic activity are:

- National income
- Gross national product (GNP)
- Gross domestic product (GDP)

2.1 National income

Key concept

> UK **national income** is 'the sum of all incomes of residents in the UK which arise as a result of economic activity, from the production of goods and services. Such incomes, which include rent, employment income and profit, are known as **factor incomes** because they are earned by the so-called factors of production: land, labour and capital'. *(Office for National Statistics (ONS))*

National income is also called **net national product**.

The terms 'income' and 'product' are just two different aspects of the same circular flow of income. The term 'net' means 'after deducting an amount for capital consumption or depreciation of fixed assets' from the gross figure.

2.2 Gross domestic product (GDP)

National income is largely derived from economic activity within the country itself. Domestic economic activity is referred to as total **domestic income** or **domestic product**. It is measured gross.

Key concept

> **Gross domestic product (GDP)** refers in the UK to the total value of income/production from economic activity within the UK.

Exam tip

> Part of Question 1 in December 2004 asked candidates to define GDP, and assess its impact upon the marketing environment.

167

PART C   THE MACRO-ENVIRONMENT

2.3 Gross national product (GNP)

'Some national income arises from overseas investments while some of the income generated within the UK is earned by non-residents. The difference between these items is **net property income from abroad**.' (ONS).

Key concept

> Gross national income or gross national product (GNP) is the gross domestic product (GDP) plus the net property income from abroad – or after subtracting the net property income from abroad, if it is a negative value.

2.4 The relationship between GDP, GNP and national income

The relationship between GDP, GNP and national income is therefore as follows.

	GDP
plus	Net property income from abroad
equals	GNP
minus	Capital consumption
equals	National income (net)

Action Programme 1

Which of the following may cause an increase in national income?

(a) A rise in exports
(b) An increase in saving
(c) A fall in consumer spending

2.5 Measuring national income

Total spending in a given economy consists of consumption spending, government spending, investment spending, plus spending by foreigners on our goods and services *minus* spending by us on foreign goods and services. This is often symbolised as $C + I + G - S - T + (X - M)$ (the circular flow of national income: Figure 10.1) where:

- C = consumption expenditure
- I = investment expenditure
- G = government expenditure
- S = savings
- T = taxation
- X = expenditure on our exports by foreigners
- M = expenditure by us on imports

10: THE ECONOMIC AND INTERNATIONAL ENVIRONMENTS

Figure 10.1: The circular flow of national income

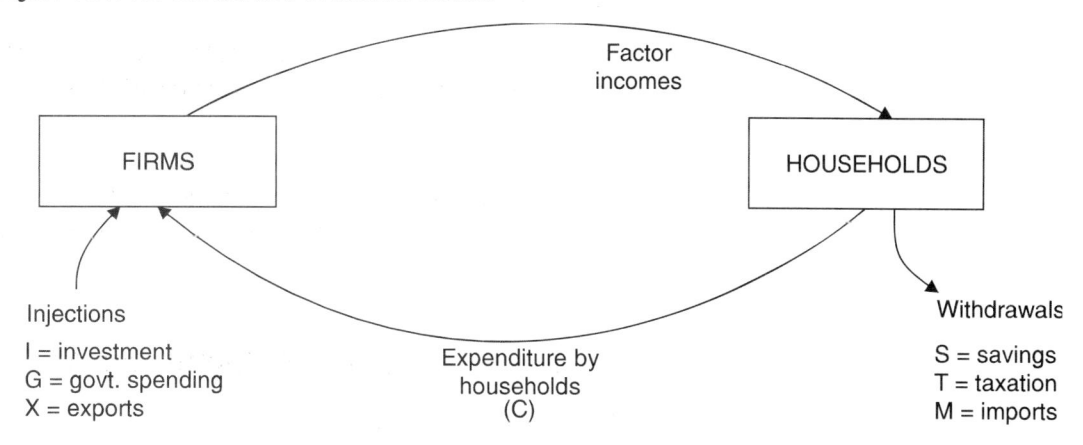

```
                    Factor
                    incomes
         ┌──────────────────────────┐
         │                          ↓
    ┌─────────┐                ┌──────────┐
    │  FIRMS  │                │HOUSEHOLDS│
    └─────────┘                └──────────┘
      ↑   ↑                          │
      │   └──────────────────────────┘
      │         Expenditure by
  Injections    households              Withdrawals
                    (C)
  I = investment                        S = savings
  G = govt. spending                    T = taxation
  X = exports                           M = imports
```

If a government is planning its economic policy, and wishes to increase the country's GDP and GNP, it might wish to turn its attention to any of these items, ie:

- Trying to increase consumer spending, C
- Trying to increase private investment, I
- Deciding to increase government spending, G and/or I
- Trying to improve the balance of payments on overseas trade, (X – M)

Although technically national income has a particular definition, generally you will find all these measures (GDP, GNP and NI) loosely referred to as 'national income'.

Calculating the national income serves several purposes:

- **Measuring** the **standard** of **living** in a country (national income per head)
- **Comparing** the **wealth** of different countries
- Measuring the **change** in **national wealth** and the standard of living
- Ascertaining **long-term trends**
- Assisting central government in its **economic planning**

2.5.1 National income and inflation

Inflation is a particular problem in using national income as a measure of national wealth. Price inflation increases the **money value** of national income.

We should be careful not to interpret this as meaning that there is more economic activity going on in our economy. All that has happened is that the prices of the things we are measuring have increased. To see if there has been any *real* change in the level of activity we must deduct any influence due to inflation.

2.5.2 Problems with making comparisons

When evaluating international marketing opportunities, national income figures can be useful to the marketer. It is therefore important to appreciate the factors to consider when analysing comparative data.

The national income figures say nothing about the **distribution of income** in the country: what segments of the population have high or low incomes.

When comparing countries there is also the problem of **converting** national income calculated in one currency to that of another. This is not necessarily as straightforward as it sounds and may make conclusions about such comparisons difficult to reach.

Simpler and more direct comparisons are sometimes used for making international comparisons. One way of doing this is to select a **number of products** which are widely in demand. Examples might be television sets and motor cars. Measurements can then be obtained of:

PART C   THE MACRO-ENVIRONMENT

- The average number of cars or TV sets per household or per head of the population
- How long it takes an average worker to earn enough in wages to buy a car or a TV set

However, this kind of comparison is also problematic, since cars and televisions (to take our examples above) are of limited use or value to some people and in some cultures.

William Nordhaus and James Tobin proposed a **'measure of economic welfare'** (MEW) to give more useful comparisons of people's welfare. The MEW adjusts GNP for various items.

(a) Items **added** are allowances for **leisure** and **non-marketed goods**, for public amenities such as roads, and for private durable goods such as jewellery and furniture.

(b) Items **subtracted** are expenditure on **'regrettables'** such as defence and commuting, various **'disamenities'** such as pollution, and an allowance for the benefits of education, since these arise later in enhanced labour earnings.

(c) To ensure that a **per capita** figure is arrived at, further deductions are made to reflect the extra capital and current output required to meet any increase in population.

2.6 The level of investment in the economy

The total or aggregate amount of investment spending in a national economy is a sign of the strength of the economy. New investment will increase output and so national income. A change in the level of investment spending is a major reason for the upswings and downswings in economic activity which we call business cycles.

2.6.1 Private sector investments

Private sector investment will come from retained profits, new issues of shares, or borrowing. However, in an economic recession profits might be low, and investors might lack confidence in a recovery, so that new shares issues are impossible on a large scale.

2.6.2 Public sector investment

Public sector investment might be financed by higher taxation, or by an increased deficit between government income and expenditure: that is, a higher **public sector borrowing requirement (PSBR)**.

(a) Public sector spending should have socially valuable 'spin-off' effects, such as improved roads, sewers and public buildings.

(b) However, a high PSBR, meaning large government borrowings, might force up **interest rates** in the capital markets and 'crowd out' private sector investment, by making it too expensive for firms to borrow and invest profitably.

3 Economic growth, unemployment and inflation

3.1 Economic growth

FAST FORWARD

Economic growth may be measured by increases in the real gross national product (GNP) per head of the population.

Key concepts

Actual economic growth is the annual percentage increase in national output. **Potential economic growth** is the rate at which the economy would grow if all resources (eg people and machinery) were utilised.

3.1.1 Actual growth

Actual growth in the long run is determined by two factors.

- Potential output
- Aggregate demand: the total spent on domestic goods and services

3.1.2 Potential growth

The causes of growth in potential output are the determinants of the **capacity of the economy** (the supply side) rather than actual spending (the demand side).

There may be increases in the quantity or quality of domestic **resources** available such as the discovery of new natural resources, change in the size of the working population and invention of new technology and methods.

Increases in the **productivity of resources** may result from technological progress, changed labour practices, or effective distribution infrastructure. In addition, there may be access to externally provided and/or inward investment, to boost economic activity.

3.2 Factors needed for sustained economic growth

Sustained economic growth depends heavily on an adequate level of new investment, which will be undertaken if there are expectations of future growth in demand.

3.2.1 Natural resources

The rate of extraction of natural resources will impose a limit on the rate of growth. Production which uses up a country's natural resources, such as oil, coal and other minerals, depletes the stock of available resources; it is therefore in a sense **disinvestment**.

3.2.2 Technological progress

Technological progress is a very important source of faster economic growth.

- The same amounts of the factors of production can produce a higher output.
- New products will be developed, thus adding to output growth.

There can also be technical progress in the labour force. If workers are better educated and trained they will be able to produce more.

(If technological progress is labour saving, however, **unemployment** will rise unless there is either a simultaneous expansion of demand or a reduction in hours worked by each person. In this case there is no productivity increase associated with the technological progress.)

3.3 External trade influences on economic growth

An improvement in the **terms of trade** (the quantity of imports that can be bought in exchange for a given quantity of exports) means that more imports can be bought, or a given volume of exports will earn higher profits. This will boost investment and hence growth. Note that a country's terms of trade are not the same thing as the exchange rate of its currency. The terms of trade are about the prices of the goods concerned, which can move because of changes in supply and demand as well as because of exchange rate movements.

Exam tip

> The June 2005 exam made 7 marks available for explaining any three factors that determine the economic growth rate of an economy (using Hong Kong as an example). A further 3 marks was available for identifying three sources of information you could use to monitor growth. In December 2006, you were asked to define and describe the key characteristics of 'economic growth': the examiner emphasised that growth does not necessarily equate to 'economic development', but needed precise definition in GNP terms.

PART C   THE MACRO-ENVIRONMENT

The rate of growth of the rest of the world is important for an economy that has a large foreign trade sector. If trading partners have slow growth, the amount of exports a country can sell to them will grow only slowly. This limits the country's own opportunities for investment and growth.

3.4 Advantages and disadvantages of economic growth

Economic growth should mean that the population as a whole will be able to raise its **standard of living** in material terms, and that there should also be an improvement in **economic welfare.** A country with economic growth is more easily able to provide a welfare state service without creating intolerable tax burdens on the community.

There are potential disadvantages to growth, however.

(a) Growth implies faster use of natural resources. Without growth, these resources would last longer.

(b) Much economic activity tends to create **pollution**, such as acid rain and nuclear waste. It leads to emissions which threaten to produce disruptive climatic changes through an increase in the greenhouse effect. It results in more roads, cultivated farmland, new and larger towns, and less unspoilt countryside.

(c) There is a danger that some sections of the population, unable to adapt to the demands for new skills and more training, will not find jobs in the developing economy.

Action Programme 2

Which of the factors listed above have contributed most to your own company's economic growth over the last few years? Have there been any significant problems with growth?

3.5 Unemployment

RESULTS OF UNEMPLOYMENT	
Loss of output	Unemployed labour is not producing anything, and therefore total national income is less than it could be.
Loss of human capital	Unemployed labour will gradually lose their skills through lack of practice.
Increasing inequalities in income	The unemployed poor become poorer.
Social costs	Unemployment can result in personal suffering and distress, and possibly increases in crime.

Unemployment may be classified into categories.

(a) **Frictional unemployment**

Frictional unemployment occurs where there is a shortage of a given type of worker in one region, but a surplus of the same type in another (for example, clerical staff may be plentiful in Wales but in short supply in London). In general, it takes time to match prospective employees with employers, and individuals will be unemployed during the search period for a new job.

(b) **Seasonal unemployment**

This occurs in certain industries, for example building, tourism and farming, where the demand for labour fluctuates in seasonal patterns throughout the year.

(c) **Structural unemployment**

This occurs where long-term changes in the conditions of an industry occur.

(d) **Technological unemployment**

This is a form of structural unemployment, which occurs when new technologies are introduced.

(e) **Cyclical or demand-deficient unemployment**

Domestic and foreign trade go through cycles of boom, decline, recession, recovery, then boom again, and so on. During recovery and boom years, the demand for output and jobs is high, and unemployment is low. During decline and recession years, the demand for output and jobs falls, and unemployment rises to a high level.

A government can try **to create jobs** or **reduce unemployment** by:

- Spending more money directly on jobs (for example, hiring more civil servants)
- Encouraging growth in the 'private sector' of the economy
- Encouraging training in job skills

Action Programme 3

Is unemployment a bad thing for businesses?

3.6 Inflation

An economic policy objective which now has a central place in the policy approaches of the governments of many developed countries is that of **stable prices**. Why is a high rate of price inflation harmful and undesirable?

RESULTS OF INFLATION	
Redistribution of income and wealth	Those with economic power may gain at expense of the weak, particularly those on fixed incomes
Balance of payments	If the rate of inflation is higher than in trading partners, exports become relatively expensive, imports relatively cheap and balance of trade and employment will suffer
Uncertainty in value of money	Resource allocation and decision-making are harder and businesses may defer long-term decisions
Resource costs of changing prices	Substantial labour time is spent on planning and implementing price changes, and customers have to spend more time making price comparisons

3.6.1 Types of inflation

Demand-pull inflation occurs when the economy is buoyant and there is a high aggregate demand which is in excess of the economy's ability to supply.

(a) Because aggregate demand exceeds supply, prices rise.

(b) Since supply needs to be raised to meet the higher demand, demand for factors of production will increase, and so factor rewards (wages, interest rates, and so on) will also rise.

(c) Since aggregate demand exceeds the output capability of the economy, demand-pull inflation can only exist when unemployment is low.

Cost-push inflation occurs where the costs of factors of production rise, regardless of whether or not they are in short supply. This appears to be particularly the case with wages: workers anticipate inflation rates and demand wage increases to compensate, thus initiating a wage-price spiral. Interest rate rises can also add to the rate of inflation, because mortgage costs will rise.

Import cost-push inflation occurs when the cost of essential imports rise, regardless of whether or not they are in short supply.

A further problem is that once the rate of inflation has begun to increase, **expectational inflation** may occur. This means that, regardless of whether the factors that have caused inflation are still persistent or not, inflation will be expected. To protect future income, wages and prices will be raised by the expected amount of future inflation. This can lead to the vicious circle known as the **wage-price spiral**, in which inflation becomes a relatively permanent feature because of people's expectations that it will occur.

3.6.2 Control of inflation: various approaches

The best way of controlling inflation will depend on the causes of it. In practice, it may be difficult to know which cause is most significant. The table below sets out various policies designed to control inflation.

ANTI-INFLATION POLICIES	
Perceived cause of inflation	**Policy to control inflation**
Demand-pull	Take steps to reduce demand in the economy, perhaps by • higher taxation, to cut consumer spending • lower government expenditure (and lower government borrowing to finance its expenditure) • higher interest rates
Cost-push	Take steps to reduce production costs and price rises • de-regulate labour markets • encourage greater productivity in industry • apply controls over wage and price rises (prices and incomes policy)
Import cost-push	Take steps to reduce the quantities or the price of imports. Such a policy might involve trying to achieve either an appreciation or depreciation of the domestic currency
Growth of the money supply	Take steps to try to reduce the rate of money supply growth, perhaps by • cutting the Public Sector Borrowing Requirement • funding the PSBR by borrowing from the non-bank private sector • trying to control or reduce bank lending • trying to achieve a balance of trade surplus • maintaining interest rates at a level that might deter money supply growth
Perceived cause of inflation	**Policy to control inflation**
Expectations of inflation	Pursue clear policies which indicate the government's determination to reduce the rate of inflation

4 The business cycle

FAST FORWARD

The periodic rise and fall of trading activity over a number of years is known as the **business cycle** or **trade cycle**.

Key concept

The business cycle is the periodic fluctuation of levels of economic activity, for example output and employment.

The **business cycle** (or **trade cycle**) is the continual sequence of rapid growth in national income, followed by a slow-down in growth and then a fall in national income. A sustained fall in national income is an **economic recession**. After the recession comes growth again, and when this has reached a peak, the cycle turns into recession once more.

The understanding of business cycles can be crucial in many sectors, especially the capital goods sector, as investment in capital goods represents an expensive anticipation of future rewards.

Exam tip

The December 2005 exam set a 20-mark question on business cycles in the construction industry and plant (machinery) hire sectors. Turning points in the cycle represent major changes in demand, to which companies must respond: the scale of investment and lead times for planning mean that responses must be planned in advance. This was the essence of parts (a) and (b) of the question.

4.1 Phases of the business cycle

Four main phases of the business cycle can be distinguished.

	THE BUSINESS CYCLE
Depression	Heavy unemployment
	Low consumer demand
	Over-capacity (unused capacity) in production
	Prices stable, or even falling
	Business profits low
	Business confidence in the future low
Recovery	Investment picks up
	Employment rises
	Consumer spending rises
	Profits rise
	Business confidence grows
	Prices stable, or slowly rising
Boom	Consumer spending rising fast
	Output capacity reached: labour shortages occur
	Output can only be increased by new labour-saving investment
	Investment spending high
	Increases in demand now stimulate price rises
	Business profits high

PART C THE MACRO-ENVIRONMENT

THE BUSINESS CYCLE	
Recession	Consumption falls off
	Many investments suddenly become unprofitable and new investment falls
	Production falls
	Employment falls
	Profits fall. Some businesses fail
	Recession can turn into severe depression

Recession tends to occur quickly, while recovery is typically a slower process. Figure 10.2 can be used to help explain how this is so.

Figure 10.2: Business cycle

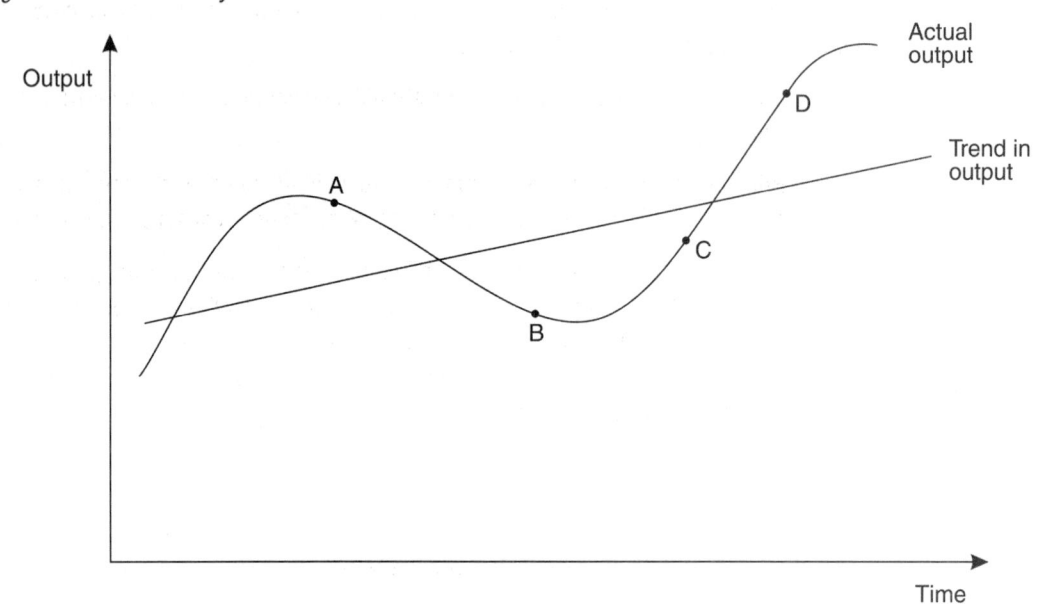

At point A the economy is **entering a recession**. In the recession phase, consumer demand falls and many investment projects already undertaken begin to look unprofitable. Eventually, in the absence of any stimulus to aggregate demand, a period of full **depression** sets in and the economy will reach point B.

Recovery can be slow to begin because of the effect of recession on levels of confidence. It can take some time for confidence to return, and initial moves towards expansion of activity are likely to be tentative.

At point C the economy has reached the **recovery phase** of the cycle. Once begun, the phase of recovery is likely to quicken as confidence returns.

As recovery proceeds, the output level climbs above its trend path, reaching point D, which is the **boom phase** of the cycle.

Exam tip

> The diagram above can be used to describe the business cycle (briefly) – but don't forget to address the particular requirements of a question: diagrams on their own do not impress the examiner!

4.2 Consequences of the business cycle

Wide fluctuations in levels of economic activity may be damaging to the overall economic well-being of society. The inflation and speculation which accompanies boom periods may be inequitable in their impact on different sections of the population, while the bottom of the trade cycle may bring high unemployment. Governments generally seek to stabilise the economic system, trying to avoid the distortions of a widely fluctuating trade cycle, for example by maintaining a stable level of prices.

Forecasting the pattern of the business cycle is very difficult in practice. The cycle is affected by such things as oil prices and international political stability, all of which are themselves difficult to predict.

Businesses must identify those measures which tend to give **advance warning** of movements in the business cycle such as **leading indicators** (a combined measure including share prices, house building and interest rates) and **trend measures**, which can be extrapolated (perhaps using moving averages). Other forecasting techniques include: **scenario modelling** and the **Delphi method**: using questionnaires to elicit opinions from individual experts, and then analysing and combining responses to develop a group response. (This is a variation on simpler forms of **expert opinion**, since it refines responses from multiple sources without the potential biases arising from interpersonal group discussions.)

4.3 Responding to the business cycle

Marketers may need to adopt a different marketing mix, and adapt HR and other resourcing decisions, to suit each stage of the cycle – lead times for planning will emphasise the importance of forecasting and anticipating turning points in the cycle. For example:

- Investment/stock control decisions should be tailored to the anticipated level of demand and activity.

- Price/promotion adjustments may have to be made to stimulate demand and retain sales during recessionary phases – and to capitalise on boom phases by profit-taking.

- Recruitment may need to be suspended in advance of recessionary phases, to allow the workforce to be reduced by natural wastage. More effectively, in highly cyclical industries, companies should develop a numerically and functionally flexible workforce (eg a core-periphery model), so that fluctuations in demand can be absorbed by deployment of short-contract or outsourced labour.

Action Programme 4

(a) Compare the ability of large and small businesses to:
  (i) Survive recessions
  (ii) Benefit from booms

(b) How important is the feel good factor in marketing?

5 Fiscal and monetary policies

FAST FORWARD

A government must decide how it intends to raise tax revenues, from direct or indirect taxes, and in what proportions tax revenues will be raised from each source. **Fiscal policy** provides a method of managing aggregate demand in the economy.

5.1 Fiscal policy

Key concepts

Fiscal policy is government policy on taxation, public borrowing and public spending.

Direct taxation is taxation of incomes.

Indirect taxation is taxation of products and services, for example value added tax (UK) or goods and services tax (Australia).

PART C THE MACRO-ENVIRONMENT

Fiscal policy leads to action by the government to spend money, or to collect money in taxes, with the purpose of influencing the condition of the national economy.

A government might intervene in the economy by:

(a) **Spending more money** and financing this expenditure by borrowing

(b) **Collecting more in taxes** without increasing spending

(c) **Collecting more in taxes** in order to **increase spending**, thus diverting income from one part of the economy to another.

Fiscal policy is concerned with government spending and taxation.

If **government spending** is increased, expenditure in the economy will rise and so national income will rise.

If **government taxation** is increased, expenditure and national income will fall. A government might deliberately raise taxation to take inflationary pressures out of the economy.

Fiscal policy can also be used to reduce unemployment and provide jobs, for example through:

- More government spending on capital projects
- Government-funded training schemes
- Taxation of companies on the basis of the numbers and pay levels of employees.

5.1.1 Marketing implications of fiscal policy

Marketers are interested in fiscal policy for a number of reasons.

(a) The **overall level of taxation** affects the level of aggregate demand in the economy.

(b) **Taxation of specific groups** may affect the spending power of particular market segments.

(c) **Taxation of specific products** may have a serious impact on a specialised business. Whisky manufacturers are lobbying for a reduction in indirect taxes, for example.

(d) There is **uncertainty** about the time lag between the implementation of economic policies and their effect. For example, the speed with which tax cuts affect consumer spending will depend upon consumer confidence.

(e) If policy objectives are set at the same time each year, there is scope for **lobbying** for favourable tax treatment of certain types of product.

Action Programme 5

The burden of an indirect tax must either be borne by the producer or passed on by the producer to consumers. If a producer passes on the whole of the burden, what does that tell you about the demand for his product?

5.2 Monetary policy

FAST FORWARD

Monetary and **fiscal policy** should be used in conjunction with each other.

The reality of economic management tends to be complex.

- The behaviour of economic agents (consumers, producers and others) may be **unpredictable** and **unstable**.
- There are often **time lags or delays** between policy actions and their effects.

Key concept

> **Monetary policy** is the regulation of the economy through control of the monetary system by operating on such variables as the money supply, the level of interest rates and the conditions for availability of credit.

Monetary policy can be used as a means towards achieving the ultimate economic objectives for inflation, the balance of trade, full employment and real economic growth.

To achieve these ultimate objectives of economic policy, the authorities will set intermediate objectives for monetary policy.

```
                          Intermediate              Ultimate
                           objectives              objective
   ┌──────────┐          ┌──────────────┐        ┌──────────────┐
   │ MONETARY │          │MONETARY POLICY│       │   ECONOMIC   │
   │  POLICY  │  ──────▶ │   TARGETS    │ ─────▶ │POLICY TARGETS│
   │          │          │              │        │AND OBJECTIVES│
   └──────────┘          └──────────────┘        └──────────────┘
```

In the UK, the ultimate objective of monetary policy in recent years has been principally to **reduce** the **rate of inflation** and to reduce it to a sustainable low level. The intermediate objectives of monetary policy have related to the level of interest rates, growth in the money supply, and the exchange rate for sterling.

5.2.1 Marketing effects of monetary policies

Marketers should be clear about how targets and indicators will impact on their marketing efforts.

(a) What do targets for **interest rates** mean for new house sales? What do indicators of actual interest rates imply for the success that government is having in implementing its policy?

(b) What does movement in the **exchange rate** mean for the competitiveness of exporters?

(c) What do targets and indicators of **Gross Domestic Product** imply for aggregate demand in the economy?

(d) What is the **time lag** between changes in interest rates and their impact upon the domestic economy?

5.3 Supply side economic policies

Key concept

> **Supply side economics** is an approach to economic policy making which advocates measures to improve the supply of goods and services (eg through deregulation) rather than measures to affect aggregate demand.

Supply side economists argue that by putting resources to work an economy will automatically generate the additional incomes necessary to purchase the higher outputs: that is, **supply creates its own demand**.

The main propositions which characterise supply side economics are as follows.

(a) The predominant long-term influence upon **output, prices and employment** are the conditions of aggregate supply.

(b) Left to itself, the **free market** will automatically generate the highest level of national income and employment available to the economy.

(c) **Inflexibility** in the labour market through the existence of trade unions and other restrictive practices retain wages at uncompetitively high levels. This creates unemployment and restricts aggregate supply.

(d) The rates of **direct taxation** have a major influence upon aggregate supply through their effects upon the incentive to work.

(e) **Government** only has a limited role in the economic system. Demand management can only influence output and employment 'artificially' in the short-run, whilst in the long-run creating inflation and hampering growth.

There are a number of steps governments can take to improve supply flexibility in the labour market.

- Privatisation of state monopolies, allowing for price competition
- Abolition of restrictions on wages and other regulations limiting competitiveness
- Limitations on the power of trade unions
- Removal of distortions in the tax and benefit systems
- Encouragement of training, labour mobility and innovation

Certain recent and proposed changes (for example the minimum wage, fairness at work and limitations on working hours) have allegedly reduced flexibility within the economies of European Union countries.

5.3.1 Marketing effects of supply side policies

For marketers, an emphasis on supply side economics brings opportunities and problems.

(a) Opportunities are made available to firms to reduce their input prices (eg lower labour and telephone costs).

(b) On the other hand, liberalisation of markets has put many companies under great pressure to reduce their own costs.

Action Programme 6

(a) Draw up a checklist of key economic indicators and detail the sources of information you would use.

(b) Use these indicators to analyse the current economic situation in your country.

6 The international environment

FAST FORWARD

The **international marketer** always operates in a wider economic context, and part of that context relates to trade and funds flows arising out of the general economic relationships between the exporting countries and other countries.

6.1 Advantages of international trade

FAST FORWARD

The principle of **comparative advantage** suggests that countries with a comparative cost advantage in producing particular goods should partly or completely specialise in producing those goods.

International trade:

- Enables countries to **specialise**
- Serves as a means of **developing political links** with other countries
- **Increases competition** and possibly efficiency of production
- **Creates larger markets**, with the potential for economies of scale in production

6.1.1 Comparative advantage

Comparative advantage is important in international trade.

Key concept

> **Comparative advantage** is the principle that economic agents are best employed in activities which they carry out relatively better than other activities.

(a) A country normally exports goods which it can **produce most efficiently**, that is, at lowest cost relative to other countries, and it normally imports goods in which other countries are relatively more efficient. This is called the principle of comparative advantage.

(b) When countries exchange goods on the basis of **comparative advantage**, they all gain. The source of the gain is that worked output is larger when each country specialises in goods it can produce most efficiently.

6.1.2 Other advantages

Free international trade makes it possible to enjoy the benefits suggested by the principle of comparative advantage. However, there are other advantages to the countries of the world in encouraging free international trade.

(a) **Raw materials**

Some countries have raw materials surplus to their needs and others have a deficit. A country with a surplus (for example, of oil) can take advantage of its resources to export them. A country with a deficit of raw materials must either import them or accept restrictions on its economic prosperity and standard of living.

(b) **Competition**

International trade increases competition amongst suppliers in the world's markets. Greater competition reduces the likelihood of a market for a good in a country being dominated by a monopolist. The greater competition will force firms to be competitive.

(c) **Bigger markets**

International trade creates larger markets for a firm's output, and so some firms can benefit from economies of scale, expand from limited domestic markets or spread their risks by engaging in export activities. **Economies of scale** improve the efficiency of the use of resources, reduce the output costs and also increase the likelihood of output being sold to the consumer at lower prices.

(d) **Political factors**

There are political advantages associated with international trade because the development of trading links provides a foundation for closer economic and political links. An example of closer links based on trade is the European Union and its development of a Single Market in Europe.

(e) **Consumers**

From the consumer's point of view, international trade should provide greater choice, **lower prices** and better quality products all resulting from increased competition.

Exam tip

> Eight marks were available in the June 2005 exam for making a case for the continued expansion of international trade – despite threats such as the SARS virus, political instabilities and risk vulnerability. Similarly, the December 2006 exam asked you to explain why opening up international trade might be more beneficial for a developing country than debt relief. The broader challenges and strategies of globalisation are discussed in Chapter 14.

PART C   THE MACRO-ENVIRONMENT

6.2 Trading blocks

Countries in various regions have entered into closer economic arrangements such as NAFTA (USA, Canada, Mexico), the EU, Mercosur (Brazil, Argentina, Uruguay, Paraguay, Bolivia and Chile.)

However, there are limits to trading blocks.

(a) **Free movement of capital** between the world's major financial centres has increased over recent years.

(b) Trade on a **global scale** is becoming **liberalised**, as discussed below, with the removal or reduction of protective tariffs and quotas.

(c) Some of the world's markets offering the greatest potential for growth (eg India and China) are not part of a trading bloc.

(d) **New technology**, such as the Internet, makes it harder to police trade barriers in some areas.

6.3 International trade liberalisation: the WTO

Key concept

Trade liberalisation is the removal or reduction of tariffs and quotas to facilitate international trade, and the negotiation of trade agreements to support global competition.

Since 1945, the major industrial nations, and now developing countries also, have sought to increase trade. The fall of communism and the failure of state control of trade have added to the pressure for free trade.

The WTO (World Trade Organisation) was formed in 1995 as successor to the former General Agreement on Tariffs and Trade (GATT).

(a) Membership of the WTO requires adherence to certain conditions regarding competition in the home market.

(b) Membership rules are slightly less onerous for 'developing countries', which can maintain some protectionist measures, although this is a matter of dispute.

Where trade has been liberalised, the boundaries between domestic and international economies/markets are relatively open to flows in both direction – as shown in Figure 10.3. Note that:

(a) In times of increasing free trade, firms (unless they have overwhelming competitive advantages in their national markets) can expect incoming competition. That said, the possibility of competing abroad is also available.

(b) Investment flows can also go two ways. A firm can attract investment from overseas institutions. Competing firms from overseas can receive investments from domestic institutions.

(c) The barrier between the domestic environment and the international environment is relatively permeable, depending on the product and the openness of the market for the product or the economy.

10: THE ECONOMIC AND INTERNATIONAL ENVIRONMENTS

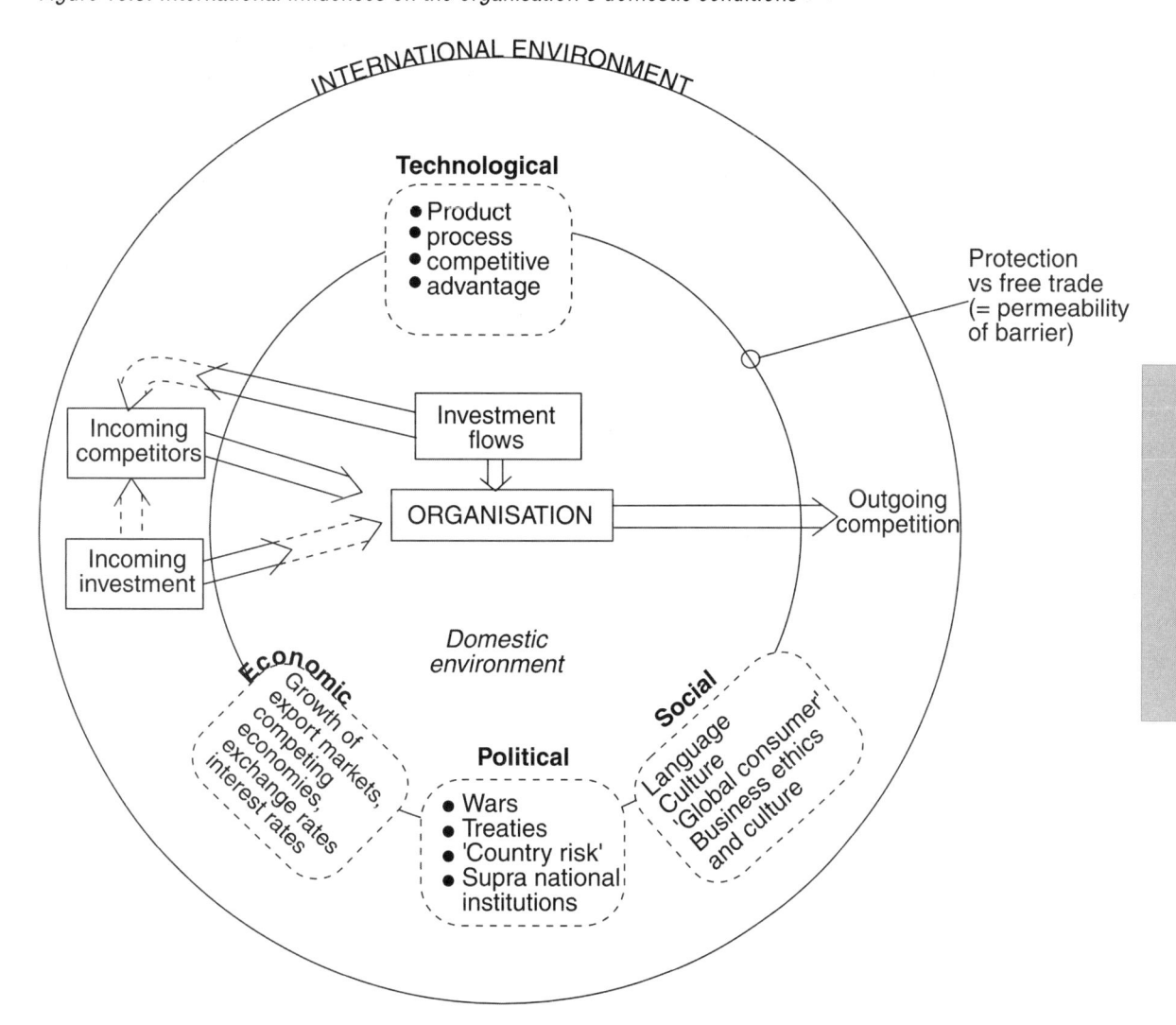

Figure 10.3: International influences on the organisation's domestic conditions

6.4 Exchange rates

Key concept

Exchange rate is the price of a currency expressed in terms of another currency.

The exchange rate between two currencies is determined by the interaction of demand and supply conditions. Demand and supply of a particular country's currency are derived from the country's balance of payments position.

(a) If it is a **surplus** country, where

Value of exports		Value of imports
+ capital inflows	*is greater than*	+ capital outflows

then demand for the currency, relative to supply, will be rising. The foreign exchange markets will therefore tend to quote the currency at a **higher exchange rate**.

(b) If it is a **deficit** country, the supply of its currency will be *rising* relative to demand for it, and so the forex markets will tend to quote the currency at a **lower exchange rate**.

6.4.1 Floating exchange rates

Key concept

Floating exchange rates are exchange rates which are allowed to fluctuate according to demand and supply conditions in the foreign exchange markets.

A **fixed exchange rate** system is theoretically possible but not often found in practice.

Floating exchange rates are at the opposite end of the spectrum to fixed rates. At this extreme, exchange rates are completely left to the free play of demand and supply market forces, and there is no official financing at all. The ruling exchange rate is, therefore, at equilibrium by definition.

In practice, governments seek to combine the advantages of exchange rate **stability** with **flexibility** and to avoid the disadvantages of both rigidly fixed exchange rates and free floating. **Managed** (or dirty) **floating** refers to a system whereby exchange rates are allowed to float, but from time-to-time the authorities will intervene in the foreign exchange market:

- To use their official reserves of foreign currencies to buy their own domestic currency
- To sell their domestic currency to buy more foreign currency for the official reserves

Movements in exchange rates can create **risks** for importers and exporters, for example where prices are agreed in advance in a foreign currency. While exchange rates remain volatile, international trading companies can do a number of things to reduce their risk of suffering losses on foreign exchange transactions, including the following.

(a) Many companies buy currencies **forward** at a fixed and known price.

(b) **Dealing in a hard currency** may lessen the risks attached to volatile currencies.

(c) **Operations can be managed** so that the proportion of sales in one currency are matched by an equal proportion of purchases in that currency.

(d) The marketing and sales department can insist on **invoicing in the domestic currency**. This means that the customer bears all the foreign exchange risk, however this may be an unacceptable arrangement. Furthermore there is the risk that sales will be adversely affected by high prices, reducing demand.

(e) **Activities can be outsourced** to the local market. Firms which have invested made efforts to obtain many of their inputs, subject to quality limits, from local suppliers. Promotional activities can also be sourced locally.

(f) Marketers can try and **aim at price-insensitive segments** in the market. For example, many German car marques such as Mercedes have been marketed in the US on the basis of quality and exclusivity. This is a type of strategy based on differentiation focus.

6.5 The balance of payments

Key concept

The **balance of payments** is the statistical accounting record of all of a country's external transactions in a given period.

Because of the principle of comparative advantage, international trade can be beneficial to all countries that take part in it. However, it can present countries with balance of payments problems arising from a persistent **mismatch in the flows of exports and imports**, resulting in surpluses or deficits in the value of goods and services exchanged.

Problems with **deficits** include the following.

(a) **Effect on growth**

Since a trade deficit represents a leakage of income from the national economy, there is a danger that economic growth diminishes unless internally generated growth can compensate for this.

(b) **Exchange rates**

A persistent trade deficit is likely to put downward pressure on the exchange rate as confidence in the currency is weakened and as demand for it, relative to other currencies in general, falls.

(c) **Domestic consequences**

A depreciating exchange rate will mean that the price of imports in domestic terms will be rising, putting pressure on domestic inflation with consequent knock-on effects for wage demands and unemployment.

Problems can emerge with persistent **surpluses**.

(a) **Overheating**

A trade surplus represents an injection into the national economy which may result in an overheating of the economy if domestic production is already at full capacity. Overheating will tend to reflect itself in upward pressure on prices as total demand for goods (domestic and foreign) exceeds total domestic supply.

(b) **Exchange rates**

Surpluses are likely to put upward pressure on the exchange rate which will push up the price of exported goods in foreign countries. This gives rise to the possibility that the surplus will decline.

6.5.1 Government measures to restore balance

Where trade is out of balance, governments can take a number of measures to restore the balance.

(a) **Transport restrictions**

Governments can discourage imports through **quotas**, controls or taxes (although this would doubtless lead to retaliatory action). Some argue that the imposition of product standards testing is a form of control. It might be illegal under EU rules or other treaty obligations (eg WTO).

(b) **Giving support to exporters**

This may take a number of forms such as export monopolies or subsidies (eg under the EU Common Agricultural Policy), or business. Export credit insurance reduces the risk, and hence the return that might have to be earned. Export subsidies enable producers to export at low prices – although detractors of globalisation argue that this simply allows rich country producers to 'dump' their excess production on world markets at low prices, undermining local producers.

(c) **Devaluing the currency**

Devaluation makes exports cheaper and increases their value.

PART C THE MACRO-ENVIRONMENT

    (d) **General fiscal and monetary policy**

        Economic policy can reduce the overall level of activity in the economy. While (a), (b) and (c) are **expenditure switching** policies, which transfer resources and expenditure away from imports and towards domestic products, this is an **expenditure reducing** policy.

    (e) **Arising interest rates**

        This will increase the value of the currency, to make imports cheaper.

    (f) **Supply side measures**

        In the long term, supply side measures can encourage exports.

6.5.2 Marketing implications

Naturally, marketers should be alert to the problems as well as opportunities which such measures pose.

    (a) **Unpredictable impacts**

        As with other economic policies the magnitude and timing effects of a change in policy may be uncertain, and affected by confidence factors not just in domestic but also in foreign markets.

    (b) **Effect on exporters**

        Recent British experience suggests that an increase in the exchange rate may do more damage to exporters than an equal decrease would help them. This may emphasise the need for measures to be taken quickly to counter the effect of an increase in exchange rate, for example a cut in prices or increased marketing activity. Export subsidies are very rare, but it is common for governments to promote exports in other ways.

    (c) **Effect on costs**

        Import quotas/tariffs raise prices of material inputs. This increases costs of production, and hence the price that has to be charged to earn a profit. It might also stimulate domestic manufacturers to start up production (**import substitution**).

Marketing at Work

Although motivated by the desire to combat terrorism, Australia's prime minister, John Howard, has been attempting to **improve trading relationships** with America on the back of his support for the war against Iraq.

However many critics have accused Howard of seeking to develop the wrong markets, claiming that good economic relations with Asia are much more important for the Australian economy. Former Prime minister, Paul Keating, argues that America will benefit far more from Australian sectors such as the media being open to American conglomerates than Australia's export trade will benefit from access to US markets.

Statistics appear to support Keating's view; trade with Asia accounts for around 60% of Australia's overseas trade, trade with the USA only around 10%. Australian companies have however been unwilling to make significant investments in Asia, deterred by legal problems, corruption and the threat of terrorism. However companies that have invested in more developed markets have often struggled to achieve satisfactory returns. Australia may also be vulnerable if trading relations between China and other Asian countries improve, leading to Australian businesses competing on less advantageous terms.

Far Eastern Economic Review, 5 June 2003

Action Programme 7

Choose a country that is a significant trading partner of your own country, and obtain information about its key economic indicators from relevant websites. From this information, and from relevant recent press coverage, assess how that country's economic prospects are likely to impact upon your own country's trade with it.

[Key skill for Marketers: Using ICT and the Internet]

Action Programme 8

A balance of payments crisis in your country has made policy action inevitable. You have been delegated the task of preparing a two-page submission to the responsible government minister on the case for and against expenditure switching, and expenditure reducing policies, making clear the impacts of each for domestic and international marketers.

Chapter Roundup

- The primary aim of economic policy is to provide a **stable economic framework** from which sustainable growth can be achieved. Other objectives include control of inflation and unemployment and balancing trade.

- There are various ways of defining **national income**; one way is to say that it equals the sum of expenditure (consumption + investment + government) *plus* exports *minus* imports.

- **Economic growth** may be measured by increases in the real gross national product (GNP) per head of the population.

- The periodic rise and fall of trading activity over a number of years is known as the **business cycle** or **trade cycle**.

- A government must decide how it intends to raise **tax revenues**, from direct or indirect taxes, and in what proportions tax revenues will be raised from each source. **Fiscal policy** provides a method of managing aggregate demand in the economy.

- **Monetary** and **fiscal policy** should be used in conjunction with each other.

    The reality of economic management tends to be complex.

    - The behaviour of economic agents (consumers, producers and others) may be **unpredictable** and **unstable**.

    - There are often **time lags or delays** between policy actions and their effects.

- The **international marketer** always operates in a wider economic context, and part of that context relates to trade and funds flows arising out of the general economic relationships between the exporting countries and other countries.

- The principle of **comparative advantage** suggests that countries with a comparative cost advantage in producing particular goods should partly or completely specialise in producing those goods.

PART C THE MACRO-ENVIRONMENT

Quick Quiz

1 Give four examples of aims of economic policy.

2 Which of the following would not lead to an increase in a country's national income?

   A   Increase in consumer spending
   B   Increase in imports
   C   Increase in private investment
   D   Increase in government expenditure

3 Match the following classifications of unemployment to the reasons given for them arising.

   (a) Frictional
   (b) Seasonal
   (c) Structural
   (d) Technological
   (e) Cyclical

   (1) Introduction of more advanced production processes
   (2) Demand differs at different times of the year
   (3) Occurs during decline and recession years
   (4) Long-term changes in industry conditions
   (5) Regional shortages and surpluses

4 What is the difference between demand-pull and cost-push inflation?

5 What are the four phases of the business cycle?

6 Competitive advantage is the principle that economic agents are best employed in activities that they carry out relatively better than other activities.

   True ☐
   False ☐

7 Give four examples of factors influencing the level of a country's exchange rate.

Answers to Quick Quiz

1
   - Achieving sustainable growth
   - Controlling inflation
   - Achieving full employment
   - Achieving a balance of payment equilibrium

2 B Increase in imports

3 (a) (5)
   (b) (2)
   (c) (4)
   (d) (1)
   (e) (3)

4 Demand-pull inflation occurs because of an excess demand which factors of production cannot supply. Cost-push inflation occurs when the costs of factors of production increase irrespective of demand levels.

5
   - Depression
   - Recovery
   - Boom
   - Recession

10: THE ECONOMIC AND INTERNATIONAL ENVIRONMENTS

6 False. The definition given is of comparative advantage.

7 Any four of:
- Balance of payments position
- Comparative inflation rates
- Comparative interest rates
- Speculation
- Government policy

Action Programme Review

1 Only (a). Both (b) and (c) are reductions in national income.

2 Your own research.

3 Various arguments have been advanced to suggest high unemployment can provide benefits for businesses. The threat of unemployment, it is suggested, limits wage rises, means that there is a greater pool of people to recruit from, and means that workers are likely to work longer hours and be more acquiescent.

However, there are also some substantial downsides. In many sectors uncertainty, caused by the threat of unemployment, hits demand and thus hits sales. Additionally evidence suggests that where redundancies have occurred, the remaining employees often are not grateful to be kept in work, nor motivated to work harder, but are unsettled, and spend time looking for new jobs themselves because of the deterioration in atmosphere and the feeling that they will be next to be made redundant. If a culture is created where people expect to change jobs regularly, staff who make the move first may well be those with the most marketable skills whom businesses can least afford to lose.

An example quoted in the *Financial Times* in April 2001 of a company where staff and general cost reduction caused major problems was Marks & Spencer. To fulfil market expectations during the 1990s, staff numbers were limited or reduced, store enhancements were restricted, and relationships with suppliers squeezed. As a result, earnings matched market expectations for a while but eventually: 'Customers started to notice that value for money was not quite as good as it could have been. That you had to wait to get the attention of a sales assistant. That the shops were dowdy and so was the some of the merchandise. These impressions accumulated. Gradually the positive Marks and Spencer anecdotes were replaced by negative ones. Suddenly the company's reputation fell off a cliff. And so did its profits.'

4 (a) (i) A recessionary stage in the business cycle implies that the key indicators of economic activity are showing lower levels of activity. Lower spending by consumers results in lower spending by firms, which in turn leads to depressed prices for the goods and services provided by individuals and firms.

Large firms are able to manage periods of recession successfully in a number of ways. If they are large and diversified, they may be able to shift resources away from areas of contraction towards those of growth (eg some export markets may continue to grow despite a recession in the domestic market). Larger firms may also have the financial strength to see them through a recession until the level of economic activity picks up. This may be lacking with the smaller firm. Furthermore, large well-resourced firms may be able to exploit a recession by investing in new equipment while prices are low. New capacity would then be ready for when an upturn in demand occurred. Finally, large firms may be in a strong position to require their suppliers to bear part of the burden of a recession, for example by requiring them to extend their credit period or to reduce their selling prices.

The main advantage which small firms have over their larger competitors is flexibility. Small firms often operate with equipment which is older and less capital intensive. With lower fixed costs, running at below full capacity can be less of a problem than for a larger capital intensive firm.

(ii) Much of what was said above can also be said about large and small firms' abilities to benefit from boom conditions.

Larger firms may have the capital resources which allow them rapidly to exploit a growing market. They may also be in a better position to collect information which will identify for them where, when and how sectors of the economy are booming. Large firms are often able to keep large stockpiles of goods which are built up during a recession and which can be made available to cater for a sudden boom in the economy.

The principal advantage of small firms is again their flexibility. There may be fewer bureaucratic delays in recruiting new staff and investing in new capacity when an upturn in demand seems imminent.

(b) The business cycle measures what is actually happening to levels of economic activity. It is also important to understand individuals' and companies' confidence and expectations of economic prosperity – the so-called feel good factor. There is evidence that private and company buyers postpone many capital purchases when they are unsure about the ability to support financially such investments in the future. Hence many marketers seek to understand how people feel about the future as an indicator of future demand for their products.

5 Demand for the product must presumably be changed little by an increase in prices, at least in the opinion of the producer. Otherwise he would fear to pass on the tax burden by increasing his prices as this would lead to a fall in revenue.

6 Your own research.

7 Your own research.

8 The country is facing a balance of payments crisis as a result of imports exceeding exports.

Two alternative methods of alleviating the crisis are considered here: switching government spending between expenditure headings; and reducing government expenditure in total. The pros and cons of each approach are considered below.

Expenditure switching policies would involve government switching expenditure between sectors, for example between the household and company sectors. It may decide to switch spending away from sectors which consume resources (for example, welfare benefits) to sectors which generate resources (for example, expenditure on essential infrastructure).

Benefits

(i) Total government expenditure is not cut, and so negative multiplier effects are minimised.

(ii) Positive multiplier benefits may result from directing resources to sectors with a high multiplier effect.

(iii) The government may invest in industries which can produce goods to substitute for imports.

(iv) Investment in infrastructure may lower firms' costs, thereby improving exports.

Disadvantages

(i) The policy may not address a fundamental problem of a government spending beyond its resources.

(ii) There is no guarantee that investment in new production facilities will help to reduce imports, or help to increase exports.

(iii) The process may take a long time to have any effects.

With *expenditure reducing policies*, the government cuts its total expenditure.

Benefits

(i) The international financial community may see spending reductions as a sign of good economic management, thereby strengthening the exchange rate.

(ii) Government interest costs to service its debt are reduced.

(iii) The government will have less need to borrow on international money markets.

(iv) The deflationary effects of cutting expenditure may be to cut total consumption, including consumption of exports.

Disadvantages

(i) Expenditure cuts cause social costs to rise.

(ii) Expenditure on vital infrastructure may be cut, thereby preventing firms' production costs from falling.

(iii) A deflationary effect could cut government tax revenues, makings its borrowing requirement even greater.

> Now try Questions 16 and 17 at the end of the Study Text

PART C THE MACRO-ENVIRONMENT

The political and legal environment

Chapter topic list

1. The state and the public sector
2. State influences over economic activity
3. Influencing government policy
4. Principles of business law
5. Data protection and intellectual property
6. Employment law
7. Marketing and the legal environment

Syllabus content

- 3.5 Explain the political and legislative environments, and in general terms, their influence on and implications for marketing

PART C   THE MACRO-ENVIRONMENT

Introduction

In this chapter we discuss the influence of the political and legal environment on marketing.

Firstly we discuss the role of the state and state influences over economic activity, and various influences on what policies are adopted by the state, particularly focusing on the roles of political parties.

The second part of this chapter deals with certain important aspects of the legal environment. Marketing managers need to be aware of the law for a variety of reasons.

(a) Customers are gaining more rights in their dealings with a supplier.

(b) Similarly, employees – a major cost to most businesses – are gaining more rights, affecting the marketing department's ability to be flexible and to keep costs down.

(c) There are restrictions on the techniques and claims that can be used to promote products (eg. untrue or offensive advertising; unsolicited direct marketing; disclosure of customer data and so on).

(d) Governments in most countries have passed laws to prevent companies developing anti-competitive practices.

(e) Certain types of legislation, for example on health and safety, can impose significant costs on businesses but can also mean that the barriers to entry in the industry are high.

(f) The law is often resorted to in disputes between manufacturers and their distributors.

(g) Increased regulation can help certain businesses: for example, in the area of trademarks or patent protection.

1 The state and the public sector

FAST FORWARD

The state contains a variety of institutions serving a number of purposes. The relationships between the state and other areas of the public sector are characterised by varying degrees of **regulation and control**.

The modern state, in other words the institutions of government, has a large number of historical and philosophical antecedents. Some key features of the modern state are as follows.

(a) It has complete sovereignty in a defined territory, unless it cedes some of this sovereignty.

(b) It has legislative and coercive powers.

(c) It can raise taxation and distribute the proceeds.

(d) In theory, it is supposed to be above sectional interests.

(e) The state's actual autonomy is limited.

   (i) The effects of **international economic trends** are often out of its control.

   (ii) The authority of the state is often delegated to **supra-national institutions** like the European Union (EU) or is constrained by treaty.

1.1 Growth of the public sector

Various reasons have been given for the growth of the public sector and public spending.

(a) The impact of **industrialisation** and **urbanisation**, leading to pressures for increased government intervention in the economy and society

(b) **Demographic pressures**, particularly the substantial increase in the proportion of old people, who place major demands on social service of all kinds

(c) **Electoral pressures**, as parties compete for public support by promising better services

(d) Pressures from **public sector bureaucrats** and **professionals** to maintain and expand services

(e) **Pressures** from **clients**, users and associated pressure groups to improve services

(f) The **welfare state**, with guaranteed benefits, was designed for a society in which most people had paid employment, not one with high levels of unemployment

Critics suggest that there are in-built tendencies in the public sector towards the proliferation of **bureaucracy** and increased **public spending**, because of the absence of the discipline of the market: public sector policy and regulation is now addressing these issues in the UK with efficiency and cost-reduction targets, compulsory competitive tendering for contracts and so on.

The size of the public sector has been the subject of considerable political and ideological controversy.

1.2 Privatisation

> **FAST FORWARD**
>
> The **role of regulation** has changed in recent years. Some formerly-run government activities are now in the private sector. Regulation has decreased in some areas, but increased in others.

Over the last 30 years, however, various areas of the public sector (eg water, gas, electricity, telecommunications) have been delivered to the private sector in a process of **privatisation**. Reductions in public sector borrowing and expenditure resulting from privatisation have financed tax cuts in various countries. Privatisation has also been held to encourage competition, but criticism has been levelled in some cases as public utilities were sold off as private monopolies.

Action Programme 1

Which publicly provided services have you used up until now? What benefits do you think:

(a) You have gained from using them?
(b) You will have gained in 40 years time?
(c) Your neighbour gains from using them?

2 State influences over economic activity

> **FAST FORWARD**
>
> **State intervention** in economic activity is justified by the need to ensure equity and to correct market failures arising from imperfect completion, imperfect information, externalities and public goods.

The state influences activity through:

- Its taxation and interest policies
- Public spending on goods and services
- Regulation

The rationale for state intervention as a whole has two main elements:

(a) **Equity**

An equitable distribution of resources is one which is regarded as fair.

PART C   THE MACRO-ENVIRONMENT

(b) **Market failure**

We have already seen how state action can be used against imperfect competition and externalities.

2.1 State influences over organisations

> **FAST FORWARD**
>
> **Government influences business** indirectly through its conduct of economic policy affecting investment and demand, and directly through company law, corporation tax and indirect taxes. The government can also be a major buyer from, or supplier to, particular industries.

Government economic policy affects organisations in the following ways. The variety of influences are outlined in Figure 11.1.

Figure 11.1: Government policy influences

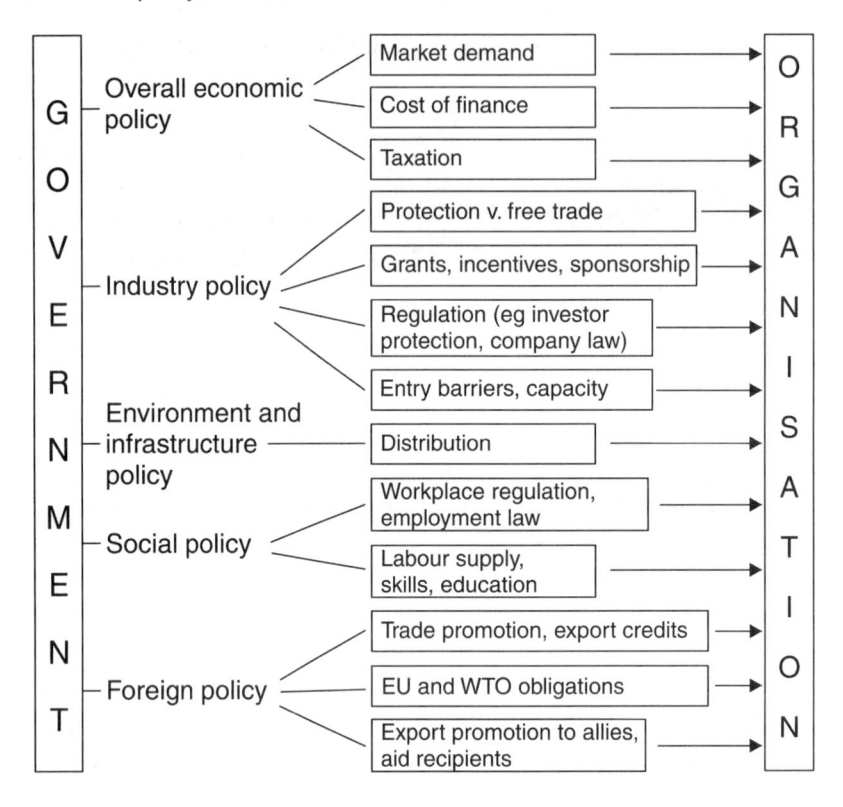

```
                         ┌─ Market demand ─────────────→
         Overall economic│
  G      policy         ─┼─ Cost of finance ───────────→   O
  O                      │                                 R
  V                      └─ Taxation ──────────────────→   G
  E                      ┌─ Protection v. free trade ──→   A
  R                      │                                 N
  N      Industry policy─┼─ Grants, incentives, sponsorship→ I
  M                      │                                 S
  E                      └─ Regulation (eg investor         A
  N                         protection, company law) ───→  T
  T      Environment and ┌─ Entry barriers, capacity ──→   I
         infrastructure ─┤                                 O
         policy          └─ Distribution ──────────────→   N
                         ┌─ Workplace regulation,
         Social policy ──┤   employment law ────────────→
                         └─ Labour supply,
                             skills, education ─────────→
                         ┌─ Trade promotion, export credits→
         Foreign policy ─┼─ EU and WTO obligations ────→
                         └─ Export promotion to allies,
                             aid recipients ────────────→
```

Action Programme 2

List the ways in which the policies of government and local government have affected your employer:

(a) Directly
(b) Indirectly in the past year

3 Influencing government policy

> **FAST FORWARD**
>
> **Politics** is about compromise and so, although governments can influence business, so businesses or industries can be a powerful shaper in political decision-making.

Government policy is determined by a variety of factors:

- Past decisions
- Existing resources and projected future resources
- Promises made to the electorate

The apparatus of government is headed by ministers who, unlike the civil servants advising them, are elected, and whose jobs as ministers can be terminated every so often by the electorate.

3.1 Political parties and interest groups

Key concept

A **political party** is an organisation whose members:

(a) have some shared values or interests

(b) have shared views as to how society should be run

(c) are prepared to work together to ensure that they achieve control over policy making and the apparatus of government

Political parties determine what the government will do (eg raise indirect taxes as opposed to income tax), and are important, but not the only, players in the process by which policy is developed. A political party aims to take over the whole of government, and to be in charge of a variety of public policy areas from crime prevention to arts sponsorship. It is this **universality of ambition** that distinguishes a political party from a special interest group.

Key concept

An **interest group** represents the various points of view on a number of issues held by defined social groupings.

An **interest group** would like to influence the government. It represents people who share certain objectives. A **pressure group** promotes particular issues. In practice, this distinction is hard to maintain.

3.2 Media and lobbyists

Professional **lobbyists** also apply external pressure to the political system. Many trade associations, for example, employ lobbyists to get their message across to influential members of the government.

The **media** are also a source of pressure on governments. In many countries, the opposition of powerful media can be sufficient to force a government to change its policies.

However, the power of the media can be a matter of debate. It is sometimes argued that newspapers are a declining influence, and that most people get their news from television. Television news is required to be balanced in the UK. There is no doubt that the ability to perform well on TV is an essential political skill. Politicians and the government often react to media pressure (eg over directors' pay).

Political parties in democracies have become much more adept in their use of **advertising** and **public relations**. Public relations is now a vital part of the normal political routine, with spin doctors employed to give events a gloss favourable to the party.

3.3 Political parties and business

Although political parties have universal ambitions, this does not mean that they are immune to sectional interests. In the reasonably near past, it was relatively easy to identify the relationship between political parties and interest groups. Socialist and labour parties represented the organised working class, and others represented business and capital.

PART C   THE MACRO-ENVIRONMENT

The relationship between a party's philosophy and its attitudes to business is no longer a simple one. In part, this is because a new consensus seems to have emerged on the value of market-based policies.

(a) **Work place regulation** is supported, in most of Europe, by parties of both left and right.

(b) **Free trade** promotes competition, but many pro-business governments do not wish to see *their* businesses affected. Some EU governments have, in the past, been hostile to Japanese investment in the UK. However, the single European market is designed to promote competition.

3.4 Policies and decision-making

In the UK the party in power gives some sort of direction to government policy and state activity. This political direction, in the UK at least, is exercised much in the manner of the captain on the bridge of a large ship.

(a) Many things will go on as they have before and the political masters will do little to interfere with them (eg the rule that in the UK cars are driven on the left).

(b) Even when a government does wish to change policy, there are usually **extensive consultations** with experts in the Civil Service, interest groups and so on.

(c) Some policies have a **long time scale**, and implementing them is a slow and cumbersome exercise, like turning round a ship.

Politics is also about **compromise**, arising out of negotiation with different interest groups, and so political decision-making on a national scale cannot really be compared to the decision-making framework in a business. This is because governments do not exist to make a profit.

4 Principles of business law

FAST FORWARD

The amount of **law affecting marketers**, both directly and indirectly, is increasing in most countries.

In this section, we are going to start by describing the basic **types of law** that affect marketers. We will look at more specific applications later.

The legal environment consists of **legislation** (made by act of parliament), **case law** (precedents developed by the courts) and **quasi-laws**, such as government-sponsored codes of conduct and rules developed by trade associations. European Union countries also face an increasing body of legislation from the European Commission.

Exam tip

When dealing with questions about legislation, try to think what the legislation is trying to achieve. At a simple level, of course, legislation lays down what is permitted and prohibited for individuals and businesses. There may also be other, more specific, aims including enforcement of fair dealing, settlement of disputes, and balancing the interests of the consumer or business against the wider interests of society. The December 2005 exam offered 20 marks for notes and examples on any three from a range of aspects of the legal environment: the impacts of legal regulation on business (positive and negative); consumer protection; the role of government. You also had an opportunity to discuss the significance of intellectual property law in the compulsory case study question. The examiner was disappointed by the low level of knowledge of legal aspects – and hinted that future (compulsory) questions might be set on this area, to reinforce the point! You have been warned...

4.1 Contract law

FAST FORWARD

Under the UK law of contract, a valid **contract** is a legally binding agreement, formed by the mutual consent of two parties. The three essential elements of a contract are **offer** and **acceptance**, **consideration** and intention to enter into **legal relations**.

One of the most important areas of law for business is the law of contract. The discussion that follows is based on the common law of the UK.

Key concept

A **contract** is a legally binding agreement that defines a relationship between two parties.

4.1.1 The essentials of a contract

The courts will usually look for the evidence of three elements in any contract before they will be prepared to uphold that contract or award a remedy.

(a) The parties must have an **intention** to **create a legally binding relationship** between themselves.

(b) There is an agreement made by **offer** and **acceptance**.

(c) There is a **bargain** by which the obligations assumed by each party are supported by **consideration** (value) given by the other.

A party is said to be in **breach of contract** where, without lawful excuse, he does not perform his contractual obligations precisely.

A party has a number of **remedies** when the other party is in breach of contract, including damages (compensation for loss caused by the breach).

4.1.2 The terms of the contract

FAST FORWARD

As a general rule, the parties to a contract may include in the agreement whatever terms they choose. This is the principle of **freedom of contract**, which the law seeks to protect. However, certain contractual terms are **regulated by statute**, particularly where the parties are of unequal bargaining strength.

As a general principle the parties may by their offer and acceptance include in their contract whatever terms they prefer. But the law may modify these **express terms** in various ways.

(a) The terms must be sufficiently **complete** and **precise** to produce an agreement which can be binding. If they are vague there may be no contract.

(b) To be enforceable, terms must be valid. You can't make a contract top perform illegal activities, say, or with terms which are contrary to law (eg consumer or employee rights).

4.1.3 Court interventions

There has been strong criticism of the use of **exclusion** (or exemption) clauses in contracts. In those conditions the seller may try to exclude or limit his **liability** for failure to perform as promised, for breach of contract or for negligence — or he may try to offer a 'guarantee' which in fact reduces the buyer's rights.

Courts have sought to protect the consumer from the harsher effects of exclusion clauses in two ways.

(a) An exclusion clause must be properly incorporated into a contract to have legal effect.
(b) Exclusion clauses are interpreted strictly; this may prevent the application of the clause.

4.1.4 Statutory intervention

The Unfair Contract Terms Act (UCTA) 1977 in the UK applies to clauses excluding or limiting liability in contract or tort and is a good example of how governments in various countries have tried to legislate.

The Act uses two techniques for controlling exclusion clauses – some types of clauses are **void**, whereas others are subject to a **test of reasonableness**. The main provisions of the Act are as follows.

Main provisions	
Exclusion of liability for negligence	A person cannot, by reference to any contract term, restrict his liability for death or personal injury resulting from negligence.
	In the case of other loss or damage, a person cannot restrict his liability for negligence unless the term is reasonable.
Standard term contracts and consumer contracts	The person who imposes the standard term, or who deals with the consumer, cannot unless the term is reasonable:
	(i) restrict liability for his own breach or fundamental breach; or
	(ii) claim to be entitled to render substantially different performance or no performance at all.
Unreasonable indemnity clauses	A clause whereby one party undertakes to indemnify the other for liability incurred in the other's performance of the contract is void if the party giving the indemnity is a consumer, unless it is reasonable.
Guarantee of consumer goods	The terms of a 'guarantee' of goods cannot exclude or restrict liability for loss or damage caused by defects of the goods.
Sale and supply of goods	Any contract for the sale or hire purchase of goods cannot exclude the implied condition that the seller has a right to sell or transfer ownership of the goods.
Misrepresentation	Any attempt to exclude liability for misrepresentation must satisfy a test of reasonableness.

Action Programme 3

Do you remember the essential elements of a contract?

4.2 The law of tort

A **tort** is a wrong done by one person to another, though it is not necessarily a crime. The law of tort can affect all dealings an organisation has with others, and not just those with whom it has a contractual relationship.

If a person suffers personal injury or damage to property by a defective product he may be able to recover **damages** for **negligence** from the manufacturer under the common law of tort.

To succeed in an action for negligence the plaintiff must prove three things, that:

(a) The defendant owed him (the plaintiff) a **duty of care**.

(b) There was a **breach** of that duty by the defendant.

(c) As a foreseeable consequence the plaintiff suffered **injury, damage** or (in some cases) **financial loss** (although pure loss of profits cannot be recovered).

4.2.1 Duty of care and product liability

The law of negligence applies in **product liability** cases where physical injury or damage results from failure to take proper precautions. However, if there is a reasonable opportunity of avoiding the injury by intermediate inspection or by routine precautions, there is no duty to a plaintiff who could have avoided it by these means.

A company may therefore owe a duty of care, including a duty to avoid injury, to all users and others who come into contact with its products. For example, a toy company selling a dangerous toy may be in breach of a duty of care not only to people who buy its toys, but also to anyone who eventually uses them.

A further area in which the duty of care has been developing is the duty of care owed by **retailers** to customers. Several retailers in various countries, McDonald's being the best-known example, have been sued for selling hot drinks which customers have subsequently spilled and thereby scalded themselves. As a result, businesses have posted warnings on the cups or on the machines that vend the drinks.

4.3 The law of agency

FAST FORWARD

Within the environment of a firm, **agency law** is particularly important in governing the liability of a firm in relation to the actions of its employees and intermediaries.

Organisations frequently use other individuals or organisations to perform functions on their behalf. Within the environment of a firm, agency law is particularly important in governing the liability of a firm in relation to the actions of its employees and intermediaries. The former is often referred to as a **principal**, the latter as **agents**.

Key concept

An **agent** is a person authorised to act for another (the principal) and bring that other person into legal relations with a third party.

The relationship of principal and agent is usually created by mutual consent. The consent (with one exception) need not be formal nor expressed in a written document. It is usually an **express agreement**, even if it is created in an informal manner.

4.3.1 Advertising and 'agencies'

Although businesses involved in handling advertising for customers are commonly known as **advertising agencies**, this is not the case in reality. In fact they are principals in their own right. They are solely liable to the media owners (eg newspapers, TV) for payment for advertising space. If the agency becomes insolvent, the media owners cannot seek payment from the customer whose products were being advertised. If the advertiser becomes insolvent, the agency must still pay the media owners.

When an agent agrees to perform services for his principal for reward there is a contract between them. Even if the agent undertakes his duties without reward he has obligations to his principal. The term **fiduciary duty** is often used. The agent owes to his principal a duty not to put himself in a situation where his own interests conflict with those of the principal.

5 Data protection and intellectual property

FAST FORWARD

Data protection legislation protects the rights of individuals about whom personal data is held by organisations (data users).

5.1 The Data Protection Act

Especially with the advent of computer records systems, fears have arisen with regard to:

- access to personal information by unauthorised parties
- the likelihood that an individual could be harmed by the existence of data which was inaccurate, misleading or sensitive (eg medical details)
- the possibility that personal information could be used for purposes other than those for which it was requested and disclosed.

The Data Protection Act 1998 (and the related Employment Practices Code) address these concerns. The legislation is an attempt to protect:

- **individuals** (not corporate bodies)
- in regard to the gathering, storage and use of **personal data** (information about a living individual, including facts and expressions of opinion)
- which are **processed** (mechanically or manually) so that records can be systematically used to access data about the individual
- by **data controllers**: organisations or individuals who control the contents and use of files of personal data.

Data controllers and computer bureaux have to register with the Data Protection Commissioner. They must limit their use of personal data to the uses registered, and must abide by Data Protection Principles.

DATA PROTECTION PRINCIPLES

(1) The information to be contained in personal data shall be obtained, and personal data shall be processed, fairly and lawfully. (In particular, information must not be obtained by deception.)

(2) Personal data shall be held only for one or more specified (registered) and lawful purposes.

(3) Personal data shall be adequate, relevant and not excessive in relations to its purpose or purposes.

(4) Personal data shall be accurate and, where necessary, kept up to date. ('Accurate' means correct and not misleading as to any matter of *fact*. An *opinion* cannot be challenged.)

(5) Personal data shall not be kept for longer than is necessary for its purpose or purposes.

(6) An individual shall be entitled:

    (i) to be informed by any data controller whether he/she holds personal data of which that individual is the subject

    (ii) to be informed of the purpose or purposes for which personal data is held

    (iii) to have access to any such data held by a data controller and

    (iv) where appropriate, to have such data corrected or erased.

(7) Appropriate security measures shall be taken against unauthorised access to, or alteration, disclosure or destruction of, personal data and against accidental loss or destruction of personal data. The prime responsibility for creating and putting into practice a security policy rests with the data controller.

(8) Data may not be exported outside the European Economic Area, except to countries where the rights of data subjects can be adequately protected.

5.1.1 Benefits of improved data protection

The Information Commissioner (www.informationcommissioner.gov.uk) suggests that following the Employment Practices DP Code will not only help employers to comply with the Data Protection Act, but will:

- Increase trust in the workplace: there will be transparency about information held on individuals, thus helping to create an open atmosphere where workers have trust and confidence in employment practices.

- Encourage good housekeeping: following the Code encourages organisations to dispose of out-of-date information, freeing up both physical and computerised filing systems and making valuable information easier to find.

- Protect organisations from legal action: adhering to the Code will help employers to protect themselves from challenges against their data protection practices.

- Encourage workers to treat customers' personal data with respect: the Code is intended to be consistent with other legislation such as the Human Rights Act 1998 and the Regulation of Investigatory Powers Act 2000 (RIPA).

- Assist global businesses to adopt policies and practices which are consistent with similar legislation in other countries.

- Help to prevent the illicit use of information by workers: informing them of the principles of data protection should discourage them from misusing information held by the organisation.

Action Programme 4

Are the following examples permissible under the Data Protection Act, or not?

(a) You demand your right to access any personal data held by HM Revenue and Customs on your tax affairs.

(b) Your personnel file contains an appraisal report by your supervisor which states: 'In my opinion, [your name] appears to display a negative attitude towards supervision, which may account for recent disciplinary proceedings'. You do not, in fact, have a negative attitude towards supervision: the disciplinary proceedings were caused by factors outside your control. You demand compensation for loss caused to you (since you were not promoted, as expected, following this appraisal) as a result of this inaccurate data.

(c) You discover that your employee record contains a mention of a conviction for drink-driving – which you have never had. You had wondered why you were always refused access to the pool car at work. You claim compensation for the loss caused as a result of this inaccurate data, and ask for it to be wiped from the file.

(d) The Accounts Manager has compiled a recruitment file on a candidate for the position of his assistant. He hired an investigation agency to access her bank records (without her knowledge) in an effort to vet her character and circumstances, in the interest of the firm's security. The report is held on your database.

[Key skill for Marketers: Applying business law]

5.2 Intellectual property protection

> **FAST FORWARD**
>
> **Intellectual property legislation** gives protection to a creator/innovator (individual or business) against the unauthorised copying, misuse or exploitation of their work/ideas.

In most countries it is deemed to be in the public interest that *ideas* in general should be allowed to be exploited. However the law has developed to provide protection to certain specific categories of industrial and intellectual property.

Patent	Monopoly right to exploit an invention for a stated period of time
Trademark	Distinctive word, name or other mark used to indicate a connection in the course of trade between goods and services and their owner
Copyright	Protection for authors, artists, composers etc from being deprived of their rewards by unauthorised copying of their works

Generally, unlike patents and trademarks, copyright does not require registration but comes into effect automatically when a work is created.

Action Programme 5

Give examples of what you would think would be registrable trademarks.

5.2.1 Copyright

The basic idea of copyright is that an individual can assert his or her rights to use and exploit works which (s)he has created – and to prevent others from doing so – for a certain period (usually 70 years).

The Copyright, Designs and Patents Act 1988 covers:

- original literary works (books, stories, poems, song lyrics, articles, letters)
- dramatic and musical works
- artistic works (paintings, drawing, designs, photographs, sculptures)
- sound recordings, films, broadcasts and cable programmes
- computer programs.

Copyright protection covers **the form of an idea** – not ideas themselves. For example, if you go on a course and pick up some new ideas from the lecturer about organising your work, the lecturer cannot sue you for repeating those ideas to your colleagues. However, if the lecturer publishes those ideas in book form, the written version is protected by copyright and cannot be copied or transmitted without permission from the copyright owner.

Unlike patents, there is no need to register copyright with any third party agency: if there is a likelihood that other people will try to exploit your work, it is usual to mark it with the international **copyright symbol**: ©. If you see this symbol on a document, it means that the owners (usually the author or a publisher to whom copyright has been assigned) assert certain rights over the work: if you want to copy, transmit or otherwise use the work, you need their written permission.

Certain uses of material (eg the copying of a few pages for **research** or **private study**) are permissable within the principles of 'fair dealing'. It would not be considered fair to make a copy of a *whole* book or article for wide circulation.

Marketing at Work

A current 'hot' issue in copyright protection is **video sharing** on internet sites featuring **user-generated content**, such as YouTube and MySpace.

In March 2007, it was announced that video distributors Viacom were suing YouTube for compensation and removal of its content from the video sharing site. If Viacom wins the US court battle (watch the news!), there could be massive implications for user-generated content and viral marketing. These were the same issues that eventually destroyed music-sharing site, Napster: because the site facilitated the uploading and downloading of copyrighted material without any filtering or restrictions, it was ruled to be 'authorising infringement'.

Action Programme 6

(a) Does your organisation belong to a copyright licensing scheme? (If so, see if you can gain access to the relevant information pack and familiarise yourself with the requirements of the scheme.)

(b) Do you regularly photocopy or otherwise reproduce materials written or designed by other people or organisations? What should you do about this?

(c) What documents do you regularly handle that are (or possibly should be) marked with a copyright symbol and details?

[*Key skill for Marketers: Applying business law*]

5.3 Privacy

Most customers, and consumers in general, are by now aware that when they supply their names and addresses they will be used in various ways. Most would accept that the details will be kept on file or in a mailing list, and many would expect to be sent information about goods and services by the same company. They may, however, be irritated to find that their details have been passed on to other companies, or that they are on a list for frequent or wide-ranging promotional information.

Direct marketers in most countries must now state clearly, when inviting customers or respondents to provide name and address details, the use to which the details will be put. It is also common to offer an opt-out from details being re-used or passed on.

Legislation and regulation exists to protect consumers from misuse of personal details held on computer, unsolicited mail and invasion of privacy.

(a) There are now stringent **trading practices and regulations** in the direct mail industry, administered by the Direct Mail Services Standards Board (DMSSB) and Mail Order Protection Scheme (for display advertisements in national newspapers that ask for money in advance).

(b) **The Mailing Preference Service** allows customers to state whether they would – and more often, would not – be willing to receive direct mail on a range of specific areas. Similar 'Do not call' registers are kept in the USA and Australia (as of May 2006), for telemarketing.

(c) The UK **Privacy and Electronic Communication Regulations 2003** require proactive acceptance (opt in) to receive electronic direct mail communications (such as e-mail newsletters or offers).

Write to the Mailing Preference Service and ask to be put on the mailing list for business services, whatever product or industry sector you work in, or anything else that interests you. See how many direct marketers there are out there – and how accurate their mailing list labels and general targeting are!

The extent of regulation (and/or voluntary self-regulation) of direct marketing activity is a 'hot issue' worldwide: you may like to follow the debates (about spam control, use of contact information, 'Do not call' registers and so on) in the quality and marketing press.

6 Employment law

FAST FORWARD

Employment law covers a variety of issues in the relationship between employers and employees, including employment protection, health and safety and equal opportunities.

You are unlikely to require detailed knowledge of employment law – but remember that this is also a key area of interrelationship between the external and internal environments of an organisation. In the UK, legislation covers areas such as:

(a) **Health and safety**. There are detailed requirements for risk assessment, protection (duties of employers and employees), training and consultation, reporting of accidents, minimum requirements for working conditions and so on.

(b) **Employment protection**. This covers issues of job or employment security: notice of termination of contract; rules for fair and unfair dismissal; the conduct of redundancies and compensation for redundant workers; protection of contracts in a transfer of undertakings (TUPE); and so on.

(c) **Equal opportunities and diversity**. Discrimination in relation to recruitment, selection, access to training and promotion, access to benefits (and so on) is prohibited on grounds of sex, race, disability and (most recently) age. Under equal pay legislation, women and men must be paid equally for 'work of equal value'.

(d) **Pay and conditions:** eg minimum wage, working hours, rights of temporary workers.

(e) **Industrial relations:** rights of employees to engage in trade union activities; rights to consultation and participation in decision-making; rights and constraints on industrial action (strikes); and so on.

Marketing at Work

What's New in Marketing (May 2007) highlighted the lingering 'ageism' of the marketing profession, in the wake of UK age discrimination legislation and the CIM's White Paper on ageism.

- Ageism forces marketers to follow a rigid career path: brand manager by mid-20s, marketing director by 40 – or stagnation.

- Graduate recruitment schemes are closed to those past their mid-20s. (Conversely, many young marketers are passed over for promotion as 'too young'.)

- There is a lingering perception that 'the young have a monopoly on dynamism and creativity', and that it is only the young who are comfortable and adept in the cyber-marketing environment.

'As the baby boomer generation ages, the average age of our consumers is increasing. It will therefore be essential for marketing departments to reflect this shift and take notice of those who speak the language of these customers.'

7 Marketing and the legal environment

FAST FORWARD

> Marketers must monitor the political environment and be sensitive to the movement of political agendas. They must be aware of how shifts in policy will impact directly on their business.

The political and legal environment can affect businesses in many ways. At the most basic level governments seek to provide **stability**, and a lack of stability will seriously jeopardise the business environment, with external parties not willing to invest in, or do business with, countries where the government is unstable or there is significant political violence.

As far as more specific policies are concerned, we discussed above how policy in many areas only changes slowly over time. Industries and organisations must, however, be alert for likely changes in policy. Marketers must be political realists and understand politicians' hidden agendas which may be quite different to their stated objectives. They must also be aware of the **wider implications** of policy shifts. Although John Major's Citizen's Charter was ridiculed in some quarters, it helped draw more attention to the importance of consumer interests in the UK.

Businesses also need to consider the impact of changes in how powers are **devolved** outside central government. In America state legislatures have been described as 'the forum for the ideas of the nation'. Directly elected mayors also wield considerable power in major cities.

Businesses need to be aware of the wider social consequences of **legislative changes** and how they affect issues that are discussed in other chapters in this book. For example, legislation against sexual discrimination has had an impact on the opportunities women are offered, and through its effect on their working lives has had wider impacts on their lifestyle choices.

Exam tip

> Question 1 in December 2003 asked about the impact of changes in the legal environment on the food industry. In June 2004, the context was the relatively underdeveloped regulatory regime in China.

7.1 Voluntary regulation

One aspect of minimising problems from governmental intervention is social and commercial good **citizenship**, complying with **best practice** and being responsive to **ethical concerns**. Often what is considered good practice at present is likely to acquire some regulatory force in the future, so proactive organisations are only pre-empting measures. They may also be responding proactively to a genuine environment threat or opportunity (eg by voluntarily reducing waste emissions or seeking fuel efficiencies). Voluntary regulation often allows businesses to adopt more cost-effective and realistic approaches than may be imposed on them. In addition, compliance with voluntary codes, particularly those relating to best practice or relations with consumers, can be marketed positively, enhancing the organisation's image.

Marketing at Work

- In the UK, **junk food ads** are banned from being shown during programmes aimed at kids aged four to nine. From 1 January 2008, the restrictions will be extended to TV shows aimed at children up to 15, as well as any TV shows watched by a large number of kids.
- A May 2007 online survey showed that 89% of respondents in Australia would support similar restrictions (rather than voluntary self-regulation) in Australia.
- In April 2007, the Malaysian advertising industry moved towards self-regulation of fast-food advertising by presenting a proposed framework to government, including a cap on ads targeting children under the age of 10.

PART C THE MACRO-ENVIRONMENT

Some governments are more 'interventionist' than others: the UK government has historically preferred non-intervention and encouraged voluntary self-regulation. However, under EU influence, previously unregulated areas have come under regulation: one recent example is the outlawing of age discrimination, which used to be subject to self-regulation. This is partly because voluntary codes of practice are only 'recommendations' and cannot be effectively enforced if organisations choose to ignore them.

Exam tip

> The June 2006 exam required you to define voluntary regulations (in relation to carbon dioxide emissions) and highlight their benefits and drawbacks.

7.2 Drivers for compliance

Businesses that fail to comply with the law run the risk of **legal penalties** and accompanying **bad publicity**. Companies may also be forced into legal action to counter claims of allegedly bad practice that is not actually illegal; as the McDonald's case demonstrates, even a victory in such an action cannot prevent much bad publicity.

Of course compliance with legislation may involve **extra costs**, including the extra procedures and investment necessary to conform to safety standards, staff training costs and legal costs. However, these costs may also act as a **significant barrier to entry**, benefiting companies that are already in the industry.

The issues of legal standards and costs have very significant implications for companies that trade internationally. Companies that meet a strict set of standards in one country may face accusations of hypocrisy if their practices are laxer elsewhere. Ultimately higher costs of compliance, as well as costs of labour, may mean that companies relocate to countries where costs and regulatory burdens are lower.

Companies may wish to take all possible steps to **avoid** the bad publicity resulting from a court action. This includes implementing systems to make sure that the company keeps abreast of changes in the law and staff are kept fully informed. Internal procedures may be designed to minimise the risks from legal action, for example human resource policies that minimise the chances of the company suffering an adverse judgement in a case brought by a disgruntled ex-employee. Contracts may be drawn up requiring **binding arbitration** in the case of disputes. Ultimately, businesses may prefer the costs of settling cases **out of court**, rather than the direct and indirect consequences of court action.

7.3 An active approach

FAST FORWARD

> Businesses must be aware of the priorities of central and local government, and can influence policy by **lobbying** and **feedback**.

As well as **compliance**, businesses also need to consider how they can actively **influence policy**. Influence may be by the industry or an individual business.

(a) **Initial influence**

Industry influence is perhaps most important during the early stages of legislation when as we have seen legislation may be built upon good practice. Industry concerns may also be an important influence upon the fiscal policy.

(b) **Comments**

Later in the legislative programme, when more specific proposals have been published businesses affected directly by the legislation may be given the chance to comment in detail.

11: THE POLITICAL AND LEGAL ENVIRONMENTS

(c) **Lobbying**

Whilst legislation is going through legislature, members may be lobbied, although we have seen above that lobbying of this sort has had much bad publicity in certain countries because of the cash for question scandals.

(d) **Enforcement**

When the legislation is in place, governments may require the help of businesses to enforce it. In any event governments regularly seek feedback on legislation through formal bodies such as Deregulation Taskforces or more informally.

Exam tip

In the exam, you may wish to answer questions in the light of your own country's legislation. You will need to understand how your own country's legislation deals with the issues that we have discussed.

Action Programme 7

Which laws have most impact on your day-to-day work?

PART C   THE MACRO-ENVIRONMENT

Chapter Roundup

- **The state** contains a variety of institutions serving a number of purposes. The relationships between the state and other areas of the public sector are characterised by varying degrees of **regulation and control**.

- The **role of regulation** has changed in recent years. Some formerly-run government activities are now in the private sector. Regulation has decreased in some areas, but increased in others.

- **State intervention** in economic activity is justified by the need to ensure equity and to correct market failures arising from imperfect completion, imperfect information, externalities and public goods.

- **Government influences business** indirectly through its conduct of economic policy affecting investment and demand, and directly through company law, corporation tax and indirect taxes. The government can also be a major buyer from, or supplier to, particular industries.

- **Politics** is about compromise and so, although governments can influence business, so businesses or industries can be a powerful shaper in political decision-making.

- The amount of **law affecting marketers**, both directly and indirectly, is increasing in most countries.

- Under the UK law of contract, a valid **contract** is a legally binding agreement, formed by the mutual consent of two parties. The three essential elements of a contract are **offer** and **acceptance**, **consideration** and intention to enter into **legal relations**.

- As a general rule, the parties to a contract may include in the agreement whatever terms they choose. This is the principle of **freedom of contract**, which the law seeks to protect. However, certain contractual terms are **regulated by statute**, particularly where the parties are of unequal bargaining strength.

- A **tort** is a wrong done by one person to another, though it is not necessarily a crime. The law of tort can affect all dealings which an organisation has with others, and not just those with whom it has a contractual relationship.

- Within the environment of a firm, **agency law** is particularly important in governing the liability of a firm in relation to the actions of its employees and intermediaries.

- **Data protection** legislation requires data users to register with the Data Protection Registrar.

- **Trade descriptions** legislation protects the rights of individuals about whom personal data is held by organisations (data users).

- **Intellectual property** legislation gives protection to a creator/innovator (individual or business) against the unauthorised copying, misuse or exploitation of their work/ideas.

- Marketers must monitor the political environment and be sensitive to the movement of political agendas. They must be aware of how shifts in policy will impact directly on their business.

- Businesses must be aware of the priorities of central and local government, and can influence policy by **lobbying** and **feedback**.

Quick Quiz

1. *Fill in the blank*

   .... represents the various points of view on a number of issues held by defined social groupings.

2. Give five reasons for the growth of the public sector and public spending.

3. How does government social policy impact upon an organisation?

4. Which of the following is not an essential element of a contract?

   A   Intention to create legal relations
   B   Offer and acceptance
   C   Quantum meruit
   D   Bargain for consideration

5. What branch of law is concerned with breaches of the duty of care leading to injury?

6. Which of the following are remedies for breach of contract?

   A   Damages
   B   Specific performance
   C   Force majeure
   D   Decision
   E   Reasonable indemnity

7. A commercial agent is a self-employed intermediary who has continuing authority to negotiate the sale or purchase of goods on behalf of his principal.

   True ☐
   False ☐

8. Name two pieces of legislation aimed at protecting consumer data and privacy.

9. Name four areas of legislation/regulation of the relationship between employers and employees.

Answers to Quick Quiz

1. An interest group

2. Any five of:
   - Consequences of industrialisation
   - Consequences of urbanisation
   - Demographic pressures
   - Electoral pressures
   - Pressure from those employed in public sector
   - Pressures from users and interest groups
   - Consequences of welfare state

3. Through its impact on:
   - Workplace regulation
   - Employment law
   - Labour supply
   - Skills
   - Education

PART C   THE MACRO-ENVIRONMENT

4   C   Quantum meruit is a remedy against breach of contract.

5   Tort

6   A, B and D

7   True

8   Data Protection Act 1998, Privacy and Electronic Communication Regulations 2003

9   Health and safety, employment protection, equal opportunities, pay and conditions, industrial relations

Action Programme Review

1   *Hint.* Consider education, street lighting, health, policing, roads.

   You pay taxes *now* to fund current benefits for yourself and others, in the hope that other people will do the same for you in future. Other people's taxes may well have paid the salaries of your teachers, for example. Your taxes pay the salaries of other people's teachers now.

2   Your own research.

3   There are three essential elements of a contract. An agreement must be reached as a result of an offer and acceptance. The agreement must contain an element of value, known as consideration (although a gratuitous promise is binding if made by deed). The parties to the agreement must intend to create legal relations.

4   (a)   No: this is an exemption from the 'subject access' provisions
    (b)   No: an opinion cannot be challenged on these grounds
    (c)   Yes: this is your right
    (d)   No: data must be obtained 'fairly and lawfully'

5   (a)   *Devices* (eg the Mercedes three-pointed star).
    (b)   *Names* (eg 'Esso').
    (c)   *Words* known or invented (eg 'Crest'; 'Kodak').
    (d)   *Letters* (eg 'BPP').
    (e)   *Numerals* (eg '4711').
    (f)   *Smells* (which computers can now depict graphically to establish their uniqueness).
    (g)   *Colour combinations,* although a trade mark is usually registered for use in any colour.
    (h)   *Sounds*, such as the cavalry charge jingle of the Direct Line red telephone on wheels.
    (i)   Some *three-dimensional figures*, such as the Rolls Royce *Spirit of Ecstasy* silver lady.
    (j)   *Three-dimensional shapes*, such as the traditional glass Coca-Cola bottle.

6   Your own research.

7   Your own research.

Now try Questions 18 and 19 at the end of the Study Text

The natural environment

Chapter topic list
1. Environmental issues
2. Green marketing

Syllabus content
- 3.6 Explain the natural environment and, in general terms, its influence on and implications for marketing

PART C   THE MACRO-ENVIRONMENT

Introduction

Issues relating to the natural environment have already had a considerable impact on marketing policies and this influence is expected to increase in the future. In the past there has been a tendency to regard marketing, and business activities in general, as incompatible with 'green' principles, but it is now recognised that the two can be complementary.

In this chapter we highlight the concerns about the natural environment that have become important over the last few years. We show how pressures from environmental groups have impacted upon businesses, and also show how green issues have linked in with the concepts of social responsibility, sustainability and externalities.

We go on to consider how green issues have affected marketing practice, and how 'green' marketing might differ from conventional marketing.

1 Environmental issues

FAST FORWARD

Environmental issues have become more important over the last 10-20 years, with the emergence of the green movement and green economics.

1.1 Public concern

Much of the concern about companies' social responsibilities focuses on their attitude towards environmental concerns of the public. The environment has come to people's attention for a number of reasons.

(a) The entry into decision-making or political roles of the generation which grew up in the 1960s, where ecological issues became aired for the first time, has affected the political climate.

(b) The growth in prosperity after World War II has encouraged people to feel that **quality of life**, as opposed to material production and consumption, is no longer a luxury.

(c) **Expansion of media coverage** (eg of famines) and wider discussion of long-term environmental trends (eg the impact of global warming on the weather) has fuelled public anxiety. This has been particularly true in relation to third world issues such as rain forest destruction and drought.

(d) Some **notable disasters** (eg Chernobyl, oil slicks caused by the Exxon Valdez accident and the Gulf War) have aroused public attention.

(e) **Greater scientific knowledge** is available about the effect of productive activity on the environment. For example, it has only recently been possible to measure the hole in the ozone layer and assess its causes.

(f) **Longer-term cultural shifts** against the ideals of science and rationality have encouraged the idealisation of a 'natural' way of life. (Appeals to nature are common in advertising.)

It is possible to identify several ways in which the public concern with environmental issues will impinge on business.

- Consumer demand for products which appear to be **environmentally friendly**
- Demand for **less pollution** from industry
- **Greater regulation** by government
- Demand that businesses be charged with the **external cost** of their activities
- Possible requirements to conduct **ecological** (or environmental) **audits**

12: THE NATURAL ENVIRONMENT

- Opportunities to develop products and technologies which are **ecologically friendly** (eg vegetable fuel sources)

Marketing at Work

The increase in the use of recycled and **recyclable packaging materials** over recent years is an example of business recognising its responsibilities toward resource sustainability. The material usually carries a statement declaring it is or can be recycled. This demonstrates that organisations recognise that being considered a relatively 'green' organisation is advantageous to them.

Action Programme 1

In recent years 'green' issues have come into considerable prominence. How have such issues affected the way in which products are marketed?

1.2 The green movement

FAST FORWARD

Environmental issues will have direct and indirect impacts on both marketing practices and on businesses in a more general sense.

Key concept

The **green movement** is concerned with the way the human race interacts with and effects the environment. A major focus of this is concern about the damage to nature and living things which has come about as a consequence of exploitation of natural resources.

A major concern is with the study of **ecology** (the systems of plant and animal life, and the relationships between them). Major environmental themes include the following.

- The ecology is a web of complex interconnected living systems.
- Everything, including pollution, goes somewhere into this system.
- The balance of nature reflects a natural wisdom which is benign.
- All exploitation of nature will ultimately have a cost.

1.3 Which environmental issues will impact upon businesses?

Marketing at Work

Acid rain was linked to large-scale damage to forests throughout northern Europe, and acidification of water supplies and fish-bearing lakes and rivers. However, it has not been possible to establish direct responsibility, and so Swedish foresters and Finnish farmers have not been able to claim from British industrialists or Russian power stations.

The impacts on the environment led to political pressures to constrain the effects of industrial production.

However, it is now clear that there is no link at all between UK industry emissions and Scandinavian forest blight.

A similar controversy currently rages about the role of industrial carbon dioxide emissions in **climate change**, membership of the Kyoto Protocol and the extent to which regulation is required in this area.

PART C   THE MACRO-ENVIRONMENT

Action Programme 2

Can you think of some examples of environmental issues which have caused concern in recent years? Was any of the concern actually justified?

1.4 Green pressures on business

Pressure for better environmental performance is coming from many quarters. **Consumers** are demanding a better environmental performance from companies. In recent surveys, it has been demonstrated that around three-quarters of the population are applying environmental criteria in many purchase considerations.

Green pressure groups have increased their influence dramatically since the late 1980s. Membership of the 13 largest green groups in the UK has grown to over 5 million. Groups have typically exerted pressure through three main types of activity.

Activity	Comment
Information based	Gathering and providing information, mounting political lobbies and publicity campaigns.
Direct action	Varying from peaceful protests and the usually legal activities of organisations such as Greenpeace, through to the terrorism of more extreme organisations.
Partnership and consultancy	Groups work with businesses to pool resources and help them improve environmental performance (eg the farming consultancy of the RSPB).

Employees are increasing pressure on the businesses in which they work – partly for their own safety and partly to improve the public image of the company.

Environmental legislation and regulations are growing. Pressure from the green-influenced vote has led to mainstream political parties taking these issues into their programmes. Most western countries now have laws to cover land-use planning, smoke emissions, water pollution and the destruction of animals and natural habitats.

The **media** has played a part in spreading awareness of environmental issues. Large scale disasters and issues such as global warming have become common themes for newspaper and television features.

Environmental risk screening and **environmental impact research** has become increasingly important. Companies have become responsible for the environmental impact of their operations. As a consequence, many are now checking out the environmental, as well as the business and financial, profile of enterprises in which they wish to invest, or with which they wish to do business. Climate change, for example, has been recognised as a source of:

(a) Regulation/compliance risk (eg where a company may be subject to emissions regulation or buildings compliance).

(b) Physical risk (eg impact on property/insurance costs).

(c) Business risk (including exposure to reputation and brand value).

Marketing at Work

The news and marketing press is full of examples of 'green' branding and industry response to green pressures. Keep an eye out yourself: here's just a small sample:

- Leading detergent manufacturers (such as Proctor & Gamble and Unilever) are attempting to raise their green credentials – and profits – by developing environmentally friendly laundry products. (*Euromonitor*, 8 March 2007)

- The Virgin Group announced in 2006 that it would apportion 100% of all its transport related profits over three years into an enterprise called Virgin Fuels, to research renewable energy sources and bio-fuels. This is partly in response to pressures on the airline industry to reduce carbon dioxide emissions – but it also earned Virgin 'Top ethical brand' status.

- Organic food and drink sales have been steadily increasing in the light of public concern over genetically modified foods, toxicity in foods, mad cow disease and so on. Mintel predicts 72% growth by 2010. (*What's New in Marketing, May 2007*)

- The Toyota Pirus, the first gas-electric hybrid vehicle gained initial recognition through celebrity endorsement, but is also on the 'Top Ten Ethical Brands' list for 2006. (www.medinge.com)

- General Electric, America's biggest corporation, has set a mission of 'defining the cutting edge in cleaner power and environmental technology'. It has promised by 2010 to double its research spending on cleaner technologies; to double its sales of environment-friendly products; and to reduce its emission of greenhouse gases by 1%.

Exam tip

The compulsory case study questions in both 2006 exams focused on environmental issues: corporate response to global warming (June) and challenges of global water shortages (December). You didn't need detailed technical knowledge – but you did need a good general awareness of issues and their potential impacts on marketing.

1.5 Social responsibility and sustainability

FAST FORWARD

Corporate social responsibility (CSR) is based on the moral and ethical duties of businesses to the societies with which they interact, and on the business benefits of ethical and sustainable practices (especially given the high profile of such concerns).

Social responsibility is based on two ideas.

(a) **The moral and ethical responsibilities of businesses**

Businesses must work within a society on which they depend for continued existence. While businesses control many of the resources available to society, the majority of the population actually contribute to the production of wealth, and natural justice demands that they share in its benefits. Society should not be asked to solve and pay for those problems which businesses cause, without help from those businesses. Businesses and business people are also socially prominent, and must be seen to be taking a lead in addressing the problems of society.

(b) **The benefits to business of 'enlightened self-interest'**

In the long term, a business's concern over the possible damage which may result from its activities will safeguard the interests of the business itself. In the short term, responsibility is good for the image of the company, and its ability to recruit and retain staff: increasingly, it is also a positive branding tool – or way of avoiding negative PR.

Opponents of these ideas argue that social responsibility is not part of a company's remit, since it should only be concerned to protect the interests of its shareholders.

A company's responsibility to society involves the following elements.

- Economic responsibilities
- Legal responsibilities
- Ethical responsibilities (eg product safety, labelling)
- Discretionary responsibilities (eg corporate donations to charity)

The degree of morality and legality involved in the social responsibilities of a company may take a number of different forms.

	Moral	Immoral
Legal	Body Shop	Arms sales?
Illegal	Whistle blowing?	Drugs

Many modern companies are publishing the terms under which they choose to operate as a **code of ethics**, although this may well be published under different titles (such as a code of conduct, principles of conduct, guidelines, operating principles, company objectives or a staff handbook).

Marketing at Work

Charity Oxfam suffered a public relations crisis in 2005 when it was revealed that the overseas manufacturer of its 'Make Poverty History' wristbands was, in fact, exploiting its labour force in appalling conditions. With the increase in outsourcing to developing nations, a number of key brands have either positively positioned themselves as **ethical sourcers** (eg. The Body Shop) or taken steps to counter allegations of unethical employment practices (eg. Nike.)

Key concept

Sustainability involves developing strategies so that the company only uses resources at a rate which allows them to be replenished (in order to ensure that they will continue to be available). At the same time emissions of waste are confined to levels which do not exceed the capacity of the environment to absorb them. In relation to the development of the world's resources, policies based on sustainability seek to:

- Pursue equity in the distribution of resources
- Maintain the integrity of the world's ecosystems
- Increase the capacity of human populations for self-reliance

1.6 Market failure

FAST FORWARD

A distinction can be made between **private costs/benefits** and **social costs/benefits**: social costs, in particular, are not always taken into account by the market mechanism, and become **externalities**.

Market failure occurs when a free market mechanism fails to produce the optimum allocation of resources. Market failure arises in several ways, but we will look at some key factors:

- **Divergence** between private costs and social costs (externalities)
- The **existence of public goods**
- The need to consider **non-market goals**, such as 'social justice'

1.6.1 Social costs and private costs

In a free market, suppliers and households make their output and buying decisions for their own private benefit, and these decisions determine how the economy's scarce resources will be allocated to production and consumption. **Private costs** and **private benefits** therefore determine what goods are made and bought in a free market.

Key concepts

(a) **Private cost** measures the cost **to the firm** of the resources it uses to produce a good.

(b) **Social cost** (externality) measures the cost **to society as a whole** of the resources that a firm uses.

(c) **Private benefit** measures the benefit obtained directly by a supplier or by a consumer.

(d) **Social benefit** measures the total benefit obtained, both directly by a supplier or a consumer, and indirectly (at no extra cost), to other suppliers or consumers.

When private benefit is not the same as social benefit, or when private cost is not the same as social cost, an allocation of resources which reflects private costs and benefits only may not be socially acceptable.

An example of a situation where **private and social costs differed** would be where a firm produces a good, and during the production process, pollution occurs.

(a) The private cost to the firm is the cost of the resources needed to make the good.

(b) The social cost consists of the private cost *plus* the additional disadvantage suffered by other members of society.

An example of a situation where **private benefit and social benefit differed** would be where customers at a café in a piazza benefit from the entertainment provided by professional musicians, who are hired by the café.

(a) The customers of the café are paying for the service, in the prices they pay, and they obtain a private benefit from it.

(b) At the same time, other people in the piazza, who are not customers of the café, might stop and listen to the music. They will obtain a benefit, but at no extra cost to themselves. They are **free riders**, taking advantage of the service without contributing to its cost.

(c) The social benefit from the musicians' service is greater than the private benefit to the café's customers.

1.6.2 Externalities

Key concept

Externality is the name given to a difference between the private and the social costs, or benefits, arising from an activity.

Less formally, an externality is a cost or benefit **which the market mechanism fails to take into account**. One activity might produce both harmful and beneficial externalities.

Action Programme 3

Much Wapping is a small town where a municipal swimming pool and sports centre has just been built by a private firm. Which of the following is an external benefit of the project?

(a) The increased trade for local shops
(b) The increased traffic in the neighbourhood
(c) The increased profits for the sports firm
(d) The increased building on previously open land

PART C   THE MACRO-ENVIRONMENT

1.6.3 Public goods

Key concept

> A **public good** is a good whose benefits cannot be restricted to particular customers. Consumption of a good is non-rivalrous, meaning that consumption by one person does not deprive others of the good.

Some goods, by their very nature, involve so much spillover of externalities that they are difficult to provide except as **public goods** whose production is organised by the government.

The consumption of public goods by one individual or group does not significantly reduce the amount available for others. Furthermore, it is often difficult or impossible to exclude anyone from its benefits, once the good has been provided.

Defence and the machinery of justice are perhaps the most obvious examples of public goods. It is not practicable (or desirable) for individuals to buy their own defence or legal systems.

1.6.4 Merit goods and demerit goods

The existence of market failure and of externalities suggests that government must intervene to improve the allocation of resources. Another possible reason for intervention is to increase the consumption of what are termed **merit goods**. Such goods are considered to be worth providing in greater volume than would be purchased in a free market, because higher consumption is in the long-term public interest. Education is one of the chief examples of a merit good.

On the other hand, many governments want to see *less* consumption of certain **demerit goods**, such as tobacco or junk food.

1.6.5 Pollution policy

FAST FORWARD

> **Pollution** is a major or social cost or externality, and has been extensively legislated and controlled in recent years.

One area often discussed in relation to externalities is that of pollution, for example from exhaust gas emissions or the dumping of waste. If polluters take little or no account of their actions on others, this generally results in the output of polluting industries being greater than is optimal.

If polluters were forced to pay, say, a **tax** for any externalities they impose on society, producers would almost certainly change their production techniques so as to minimise pollution. Consumers would choose to consume less of those goods which cause pollution.

Many industrialised countries have also imposed environmental legislation. Companies might have to face a variety of measures designed to deal with the pollution.

(a) **Government fees**

German chemical companies face a charge on each tonne of hazardous waste disposed of, a levy on carbon dioxide emissions, and a charge on sold waste in landfill. This can add significantly to operating costs.

(b) **Government regulations**

Fines might be imposed for persistent breach of pollution guidelines, and pollution might be monitored by government inspectors.

(c) **Tradeable permits**

One means of regulating pollution is the tradeable pollution permit. Every year, the state issues pollution permits to each company for a certain price. A total number of permits are allocated each year, representing the total amount of emissions permitted. These permits can be sold. Therefore, it might be cheaper for a company to reduce its pollution than do nothing, as the cost could be recouped by the revenue gained by selling the permit.

INCREASED REGULATION

- Change production ahead of legislation
- Switch to products combating threats of externalities
- Relocate business to lower regulation country

An example of a product which has had increased sales because of publicity about externalities is sun-tan lotion. The damaging effect of CFCs on the ozone layer led to increased concern about sunlight-induced skin cancer. Lotions are now marketed on the basis of how much protection against radiation they give.

1.7 Environmental management systems

> **FAST FORWARD**
>
> Emphasis is moving away from 'end of pipe' pollution control to **preventing problems at source**. Faced with growing legislation and public pressure, companies have begun to develop new standards themselves, called **environmental management systems**.

By the early 1990s, it was clear that, for many major companies, environmental protection had become a key strategic issue. The 1990s saw a flood of environmental legislation relating to the following issues.

- Product standards
- Plant design standards
- Waste reduction and recycling
- Civil liability for environmental damage
- Environmental impact studies
- Packaging
- Eco-labelling

1.7.1 Potential benefits of environmental management systems

Some of the benefits of environmental management include:

- Reduced insurance premiums
- Easier conformance with environmental legislation
- Reduced fines for infringing regulations
- Cost savings through more efficient resource use
- Improved public relations
- Reduced likelihood of environmental accidents
- Increased staff motivation
- Improved ability to attract and retain staff   (*Grayson, 1992*)

More and more large companies, particularly consumer goods producers, have given a board member responsibility for the environment, and have produced an environmental policy statement. The following statement was produced by the Yamaha Corporation of America.

> **Environmental commitment policy**
>
> Earth exists not only for those of us who currently live on it, but also for our descendants. We must live in a way that will ensure a future for our children. It is, therefore, our duty to protect our valuable environment so that all living creatures can continue to live on this planet.
>
> Yamaha's objective is to contribute to the enhancement of the quality of life around the world and through various activities including the music business.
>
> We have to be aware that corporate activities are deeply related to the environment, and we at Yamaha acknowledge our responsibility to nature. We are dedicated to enriching people's lives and helping to preserve the environment as we live together harmoniously in society.

> **The Principles of Yamaha's Corporate Environmental Activities Include:**
>
> - Make efforts to develop technology and provide products that will be as sensitive as possible to the earth's animals, plants, and environment
> - Promote energy-saving activities and make effective use of resources in the areas of research and development, production, distribution, sales and service
> - Promote pollution prevention and waste minimization activities
> - Endeavour to follow environmental rules and regulations, encourage environmental protection activities, and ensure the well-being of employees and citizens by practicing sound environmental management
> - Promote continuous improvement methodologies utilizing a Corporate Environmental Compliance Team to monitor business practices and recommend to management methods for improving processes
> - Encourage environmental awareness to all employees so environmental factors are considered in its decision-making processes

Action Programme 4

Environmental matters are often in the news. Over (say) the next month, cut out items from (quality) newspapers or make notes from any relevant TV or radio items or programmes which are concerned with environmental matters. Consider the implications for the marketing function of the business, government department etc concerned.

2 Green marketing

FAST FORWARD

> **Green marketing** begins from the premise that marketing as such is not environmentally unfriendly. The products and services being marketed will necessarily become greener, to reflect more general awareness of the need to counter the effects of environmental degradation.

Green marketing brings a new factor into the traditional concerns of the modern business person.

2.1 Green consumption

The strongest reason for bringing the environment into the business equation is the consumer, and the need to make responsiveness to, and responsibility for, the consumer the central principle of marketing activity. The consumer must be the driving force behind changes in marketing and business practices. If new practices do not meet consumer needs, they will fail.

Key concept

> Green consumption can be defined as the decisions related to consumer choice which involve environmentally-related beliefs, values, attitudes, behaviour or choice criteria.

The following evidence indicates that green consumption is important.

- Surveys indicate increased levels of environmental awareness and concern
- Increasing demand for, and availability of, information on environmental issues
- Green product concepts and green substitute products
- Value shifts from consumption to conservation
- Effective PR and marketing campaigns by environmental charities and causes

The consumer demand for products which claim ecological soundness has waxed and waned with initial enthusiasm replaced by cynicism as to 'green' claims.

(a) **Marketing advantages**

Companies like Body Shop have cleverly exploited **environmental friendliness** as a marketing tool. Supermarkets now stock bleaches or cleansing products which are supposed to be 'kind to nature'.

(b) **Bad publicity**

Perhaps companies have more to fear from the impact of **bad publicity** relating to the ecological effect of their activities than positive environmental messages. An example from the USA was the consumer campaign to boycott tuna from companies whose methods of fishing endanger the lives of dolphins. This has led to changed fishing techniques.

(c) **Limits to willingness to change**

Consumers may not want to **alter aspects of their lifestyles** for the sake of environmental correctness. For example, vehicles are a prime source of carbon dioxide emissions, and simple ways to reduce pollution would be a lowering of speed limits or reduction in car usage. While this has been implemented in the USA, it appears to be out of the question in Europe. In the UK, encouraging a switch to public transport to restrict car usage is controversial.

(d) **Education of consumers**

Finally, consumers may be **imperfectly educated** about environmental issues. For example, much recycled paper has simply replaced paper produced from trees from properly managed (ie sustainably developed) forests. A recent debate, in the USA, relates to the ecological friendliness of disposable nappies. Manufacturers argue that the total effect on the environment of disposable nappies is less than that of the non-disposable kind. They argue that the environmental impact of washing (in terms of energy use, water pollution and so on) is greater than that of making and disposing of a disposable nappy.

In order to maintain good public relations, some companies may have to educate consumers as to the relative environmental impact of their products.

Action Programme 5

Make a list of all the products or services you can think of which use 'green-ness' as a major selling point.

2.2 Barriers to green marketing

There are a number of possible barriers to green marketing.

(a) **Costs**

Costs are likely to be incurred in developing more environmentally friendly products and services.

(b) **Technical and organisational**

Technical and organisational barriers have to be overcome: for instance, in developing practical applications of green energy sources, and in reshaping workforces into new ways of carrying out their roles and promoting new attitudes to their jobs.

(c) **Conflicts between objectives**

Many of the problems which will need to be addressed are **complex** and there are **conflicts** between the alternatives available. How do we choose between fuels which create acid rain, and those which produce atomic waste? What about the human consequences of dismantling environmentally unfriendly industries in areas where there are no alternative sources of employment?

(d) **International implications**

Many of the policies pursued by a particular enterprise will have implications for the environment in countries beyond national boundaries.

(e) **Lack of visibility**

Changes which promote beneficial effects, eg on the ozone layer, may well be resisted as they have no visible effects.

(f) **Timescale**

The fact that problems are generally created, and have to be treated, over a relatively long time scale creates difficulties in promoting policies and mobilising groups to implement them.

The main problems faced by those seeking to implement these green policies include the lack of certainty about the nature of the problem and about the effectiveness of the remedies proposed. In some cases, companies have introduced supposedly environmentally friendly policies and products simply as a means of paying token allegiance. One possible consequence of this is **moral fatigue**. The public may become tired of the whole idea, or sceptical about the truth of claims to greenness.

2.3 Developing the policies

Green marketing requires that managerial principles are related strictly to customer satisfaction. This requires a **green managerial orientation**.

- Rethinking the balance between efficiency and effectiveness
- Rethinking attitudes to and relationships with customers
- Rethinking the balance between our needs and our wants
- Redefining customer satisfaction

- Refocusing onto the long-term objective, rather than shorter or medium-term
- Rethinking the value chain
- New corporate culture

2.4 Processes for green marketing

While a process for green marketing can follow the same framework as a conventional marketing process, differences will occur in four areas.

- **Information** which is fed into the process
- **Criteria** against which performance is measured
- **Values** against which objectives are set
- Extent to which the process needs to involve the **whole organisation**

2.5 Marketing information

At the heart of green marketing is an appreciation and thorough understanding of the ways in which the company impacts on the customer, society and the environment. An **audit** of company performance in these areas is required. Customer needs, and their sensitivities to environmental issues, need to be researched, along with the activities, strategies and policies of competitors.

2.6 Marketing planning

> **FAST FORWARD**
>
> Marketing plans need to be re-considered in the light of **environmental priorities**.
> - Financial, strategic product/market and technical objectives
> - Markets
> - Strategies and action plans – eg market share, customer satisfaction, competitor comparisons
> - Performance and technical aspects of product performance and quality

All these aspects have to be fitted within a view of the company's **performance** taking account of environmental responsibilities. In addition, the traditional **criteria** for evaluating success or failure, and the parameters within which they operate, will have to be re-drawn.

Timescales may have to be **lengthened** considerably, since products are now evaluated in terms of their long-term effects, as well as the impact of the processes used in their production.

Green marketing **evaluates the marketing mix** in terms of **four Ss**.

S atisfaction of customer needs

S afety of products and production for consumers, workers, society and the environment

S ocial acceptability of a product, its production and the other activities of the company

S ustainability of the products, their production and the other activities of the company

2.7 Competitors and suppliers

Since greenness will be an important **competitive factor**, it will be important for companies to have information about their performance in comparison with major competitors and to be assured that their suppliers are meeting green standards.

2.8 A model of the green marketing process

The green marketing process requires the matching of those **internal variables** which the company can control with the structures of the **operating environment** which the commercial decision-maker faces. *Peattie* (1992) describes these as internal and external **green Ps** to be used as a checklist to diagnose how well the company is succeeding in living up to targets for green performance: Figures 12.1.

Figure 12.1: Elements of green marketing

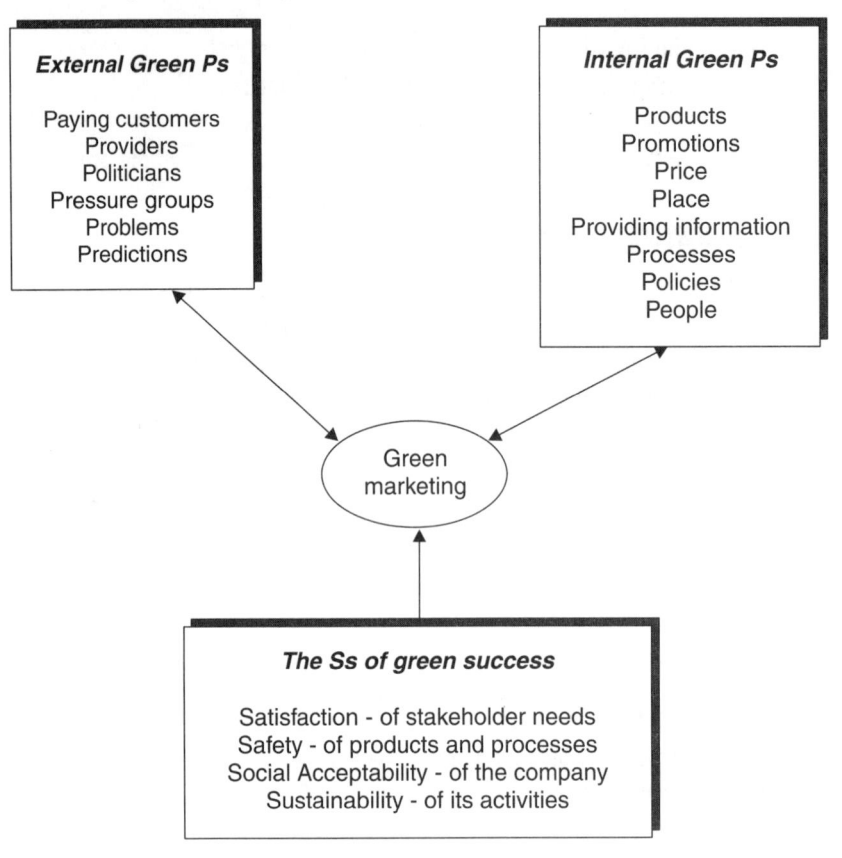

External Green Ps

Paying customers
Providers
Politicians
Pressure groups
Problems
Predictions

Internal Green Ps

Products
Promotions
Price
Place
Providing information
Processes
Policies
People

Green marketing

The Ss of green success

Satisfaction - of stakeholder needs
Safety - of products and processes
Social Acceptability - of the company
Sustainability - of its activities

Marketing at Work

Creative marketing responses to **environmental and ethical issues** in 2006 include:

- Genesis Energy (New Zealand). In response to soaring energy costs, Genesis launched a direct marketing campaign emphasising to customers that the company was there to help them save money on energy bills. They sent out a leaflet of energy-saving tips printed in fluorescent ink (so they could be read with the lights off).

- Oroverde (Tropical Rainforest Foundation) sent out a package to potential donors reminding them of the threat to tropical rainforests from land clearing by burning. The package included a 'paint by numbers' picture of the rainforest – but only one colour ink: black.

- The Disney media group severed its 10 years promotional alliance with McDonald's whereby Disney merchandise was bundled with kids' 'happy meals'. Industry sources said one reason for the (mutually agreed) split was Disney's concern over association with fast food, under increasing pressure over childhood obesity. Meanwhile, McDonald's itself has launched ranges of healthy choice salad and 'deli' options worldwide.

2.9 Cultural support for green marketing

Resistance to green marketing within many companies is likely to remain strong. It may be necessary for marketers to **market internally** ideas for these changes. New products, new communications strategies and messages, new clean plant and technology, new appointments of staff skilled in these areas, and very broad changes in organisational culture will all have to be sold to powerful individuals and groups within organisations.

Green marketing needs to be accepted not just into the present policies of the company, but in the way it plans and acts far into the future. Companies must institutionalise the ideas and to **change the company's culture**.

- Build a basis for understanding by disseminating information
- Formulate systematic plans for the implementation of green marketing
- Set aside resources
- Require demonstrations of managerial commitment
- Encourage participation and contributions throughout the company
- Sustain an internal PR programme creating a healthy response to green ideas

Exam tip

> The impact of environmental concerns on the part of stakeholders and pressure groups, and the consequent effect upon marketing activities, is an important topic. It will always be examined in a specific context – in June 2004 it appeared twice (a chemical company and a vehicle manufacturer). In June 2005, candidates were asked to consider the implications of the natural environment for a vehicle manufacturer: think about practical issues such as dwindling oil resources, pollution, energy efficiency, scrap metal recycling...

Action Programme 6

Consider the environmental impact on marketing in the following contexts. You may want to investigate each of these areas and discuss them with fellow students or colleagues.

(a) Primary industries (eg food production)
(b) Consumer goods manufacturing
(c) Industrial or business-to-business production
(d) Retailing
(e) Service providers
(f) Not-for-profit sector
(g) Small businesses

PART C   THE MACRO-ENVIRONMENT

Chapter Roundup

- **Environmental issues** have become more important over the last 10-20 years, with the emergence of the green movement and green economics.
- Environmental issues will have direct and indirect impacts on both marketing practices and on businesses in a more general sense.
- **Corporate social responsibility** (CSR) is based on the moral and ethical duties of businesses to the societies with which they interact, and on the business benefits of ethical and sustainable practices (especially given the high profile of such concerns).
- A distinction can be made between **private costs/benefits** and **social costs/benefits**: social costs, in particular, are not always taken into account by the market mechanism, and become **externalities**.
- **Pollution** is a major or social cost or externality, and has been extensively legislated and controlled in recent years.
- Emphasis is moving away from 'end of pipe' pollution control to **preventing problems at source**. Faced with growing legislation and public pressure, companies have begun to develop new standards themselves, called **environmental management systems**.
- **Green marketing** begins from the premise that marketing as such is not environmentally unfriendly. The products and services being marketed will necessarily become greener, to reflect more general awareness of the need to counter the effects of environmental degradation.
- Marketing plans need to be re-considered in the light of **environmental priorities**.
    - Financial, strategic product/market and technical objectives
    - Markets
    - Strategies and action plans – eg market share, customer satisfaction, competitor comparisons
    - Performance and technical aspects of product performance and quality

Quick Quiz

1   Give three examples of ways in which green pressure groups have exerted pressure on businesses.

2   What are the two ideas upon which social responsibility is based?

3   *Fill in the blank*

    .... involves developing strategies so that the company only uses resources at a rate that allows them to be replenished.

4   Private costs – social costs = ?

5   A public good is a good produced by the public sector.

    True ☐
    False ☐

6   List five benefits of an environmental management system.

7   Fill in the blanks

    S ....

    S ....

    S ....

    S ....

    are the four Ss of green marketing.

8   Give three examples of ways in which governments have attempted to deal with pollution.

Answers to Quick Quiz

1   - Gathering information
    - Direct action
    - Partnership and consultancy

2   - The moral and ethical responsibilities of business
    - The benefits to business of enlightened self-interest

3   Sustainability

4   Externalities

5   False. It is a good whose benefits cannot be restricted to particular customers.

6   Any five of:
    - Reduced insurance premiums
    - Earlier conformance with legislation
    - Reduced fines
    - Cost savings
    - Better public relations
    - Reduced likelihood of environmental accidents
    - Increased staff motivation
    - Improved ability to attract and retain staff

7   - Satisfaction of customer needs
    - Safety of products
    - Social acceptability of products
    - Sustainability of products

8   - Fees
    - Regulations
    - Permits

PART C   THE MACRO-ENVIRONMENT

Action Programme Review

1. Every stage of a product's life is affected by environmental issues – how it is made, what it made of, how it gets to the customer, what it is used for, what is the effect of its use, and how it is disposed of. 'Green' issues have affected the **product** itself ('ozone-friendly', 'dolphin-friendly'), its **packaging** (recyclable), its **price** (organically produced vegetables are more expensive, for example), and its **promotion** (BMW used the appealing idea that their cars are almost totally recyclable for the next generation of car drivers).

2. Similar alarms have been expressed about **ozone depletion**. Alternatives to CFCs are being developed to act as solvents in the electronics industry and coolants in refrigerators. The use of CFCs for blowing polystyrene foam (used as insulation by the building industry) has been banned in some countries and is being phased out in many others.

   Global warming (climate change) is a 'hot' issue, with public concern mobilised by pressure groups (in support of the international Kyoto Protocol which sets voluntary targets for developed countries to reduce their greenhouse gas emissions).

   Recycling is already widespread and the demand for products and packaging made from recycled materials, or from materials which can be recycled, is increasing steadily. Car manufacturers such as Mazda and Citroen are using plastic components to reduce vehicle weight and recycling used components.

   In addition to these concerns about the impact of production and consumption on the environment, there are also related concerns about the ways in which these affect **human and animal welfare**. The mistreatment of animals in food production, and concern of the inhumanity of certain kinds of animal husbandry techniques, has produced a strong reaction amongst consumers. Vegetarianism is on the increase, and this has had a significant impact on the demand for meat. There has also been an impact on the sales of cosmetics and other products in which animals are used in product testing.

   The above can have a very direct impact on aspects of marketing. You might also have thought of problems relating to waste, food scares, climatic changes, energy resources and social issues in general.

3. Item (b) is an external cost of the project, since increased columns of traffic are harmful to the environment. Item (c) is a private benefit for the firm. Item (d) would only be an external benefit if a building is better for society than the use of open land, which is unlikely. Item (a) is correct as the benefits to local shops are additional to the private benefits of the sports firm and as such are external benefits.

4. Your own research.

5. The possibilities are endless! A few examples:

   - The Body Shop cosmetics
   - 'Environmentally friendly' detergents
   - No 'CFC' aerosols
   - Organic produce
   - Ethical investments

6. Your own research.

> Now try Question 20 at the end of the Study Text

The technical and information environments

Chapter topic list

1 Technology, industry and society
2 Technology and employment
3 Developments in ICT
4 The Internet
5 Technology and marketing

Syllabus content

- 3.7 Explain the importance of the technical and information environments and their actual and potential impacts on organisations, employment, marketing and communications

PART C THE MACRO-ENVIRONMENT

Introduction

This chapter emphasises how important the technological environment is in marketing. First we discuss what technology actually means – not just equipment but the way in which equipment is used and the organisation of people and machines in work processes. Technology has some direct impacts on marketing including determining how goods are supplied, how marketers communicate and how markets operate.

As well as having some direct impacts, technological innovation is a key factor in **economic growth**. However, its effect on the economy is not easy to predict. It is clearly not the only factor that influences economic growth, and its influence is uncertain, since the precise usefulness of an invention cannot always be predicted in advance. The marketer will try to influence how technology is diffused.

Technology can have various other indirect influences, including influences on an organisation and employment patterns, and we discuss these in the last two sections of this chapter.

The second half of the chapter is given to examples of specific technological developments which are of significance to the marketer, particularly developments in information and communication technology (ICT). The Internet, which we have mentioned earlier, is very important in this context.

We draw the chapter together by summarising the most important effects of technological developments on the marketing environment.

1 Technology, industry and society

1.1 What is technology?

FAST FORWARD

Technology includes apparatus, the techniques with which the apparatus is used, and the organisation of those techniques into social structures.

Key concept

Technology consists of the apparatus (eg tools, equipment); techniques (ways of using tools, work methods); organisation (social arrangements for productive ends).

The **technological determinist** argument states that technology alone has an internal dynamic which dictates how work is done. However, there are some choices offered to users.

(a) **Equipment design**

One issue concerns the amount of **control** built into the machine. Examples from aircraft design indicate that pilot boredom (and hence errors) result if humans are given too little to do, or cannot intervene.

(b) **Innovation**

Technical innovation is promoted for a variety of reasons, not only to do with the production process. Much information technology has been used to increase management information.

(c) **Work organisation**

There are still choices in the way in which work is organised around the technology.

Despite fears that technology would 'replace' human inputs, the impact of automation on work has been varied. *McLoughlin and Clark* argue that technology generates its own imperatives and skills.

13: THE TECHNICAL AND INFORMATION ENVIRONMENTS

(a) Technology reduces complex tasks needing manual or **action-centred** skills (with significant exceptions like the construction industry).

(b) Technology generates more **intellective** skills (ie problem-solving, data interpretation). This, among other factors, can enhance the quality of working life.

1.2 Process re-engineering

Investment in technology can be wasted, if the fundamental processes of the business remain unaltered. In other words, the **apparatus** might change and even the **techniques**, but not the **organisation** behind it.

This might be a reason why, despite all the investments in information technology, the productivity of office workers has not matched the dramatic improvements in manufacturing productivity in recent years.

1.3 Technology and growth

> **FAST FORWARD**
>
> Technology is an important but not the only factor in **economic growth**. In theory, technology could be found to advance the production possibility curve to the right.

Economists use the **production possibility curve** (Figure 13.1) to describe the choices which are made in conditions of scarcity. This means that, if an economy's total output is limited, society will have to make sacrifices, producing one type of good (say, food) rather than other goods. The significance of technology is that it enables the economy to produce more goods and services in total than before. Thus it involves economic growth, with the production possibility 'frontier' moving from AB to CD.

Figure 13.1: Production possibility curve

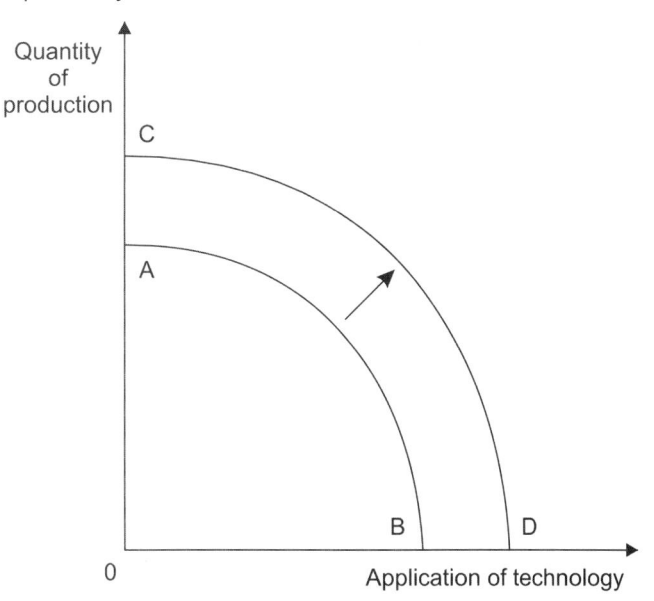

1.4 Technological change

David S Landes *(The Unbound Prometheus)* states: 'The Englishman of 1750 was closer in material things to Caesar's legionaries than to his own great-grand-children'. Landes mentions the role of technology in economic growth as follows.

(a) Quantitative gains in productivity (ie more outputs per unit of input) have occurred.

(b) 'Modern technology also ... turns out objects that could not have been produced in any circumstances by the craft methods of yesterday.'

PART C   THE MACRO-ENVIRONMENT

(c) 'Finally to this army of new and better products ... should be added the great range of exotic products ... now available at reduced prices thanks to improved transportation'.

'These material advances have in turn provoked and promoted a large complex of economic, social, political and cultural changes which have reciprocally influenced the rate and course of technological development'. These changes have included the following.

(a) **Industrialisation** (eg movement of labour and resources from agriculture to industry)
(b) **Modernisation** (urbanisation, reduction in death rates, centralising government and so on)

Some people cite post-industrialisation as a development. Increases in manufacturing productivity release resources for the service sector of the economy.

1.4.1 Importance of technical change

The significance of technological change is manifold.

(a) Schumpeter, an economic theorist, argued that 'fundamental technical innovations undergird the long-term pattern of booms and contractions which has characterised the Western economy as a whole'.

(b) 'Technical change is central to the maintenance of the vitality of the modern economy. It is not simply that innovation leads to growth and wealth; innovation is indispensable if the economy is not to stagnate' (Yearley, *Science, Technology and Social Change*).

Almost every activity in a modern industrial society has developed in some way through technological change.

Information technology has changed from a specialised industry dominated by a few companies whose 'product' included machines, software and lucrative service contracts, to one in which there is a huge number of almost identical products trying to win on a number of competitive strengths.

Marketing at Work

In the UK, cinema attendances were once well over 20 visits per person per year. This number fell to 1.5 by 1990 (when there were 88.7 million cinema visits). This has largely been caused by television, a new technology, which, like IT, has also reduced in cost since its invention.

Television itself has been subject to competition from video and DVD and now from web- and pod-casting. **New technology** has also greatly increased the number of television channels potentially available. In March 2004 the magazine *Total TV guide* listed over 90 satellite, digital and cable channels in addition to the five terrestrial channels. Of the channels listed, 14 were dedicated film channels.

1.4.2 Social impacts of technological change

The impact of recent technological change also has potentially important social consequences.

(a) Whereas people were once collected together to work in offices, home, mobile and remote working will become more important, supporting **virtual teams** and organisations.

(b) Certain sorts of skill, related to **interpretation of data** and **information processes**, are becoming more valued than manual or physical skills.

(c) Technology increases manufacturing productivity, so that more people will be involved in **service jobs**. These require greater inter-personal skills (eg in dealing with customers).

(d) More information is available more readily than ever before. This has many effects, from greater consumer awareness and increased competition (eg through readily available price comparison) to social isolation (eg through virtual team-working and internet-home-shopping) and global culture.

Action Programme 1

The (fictitious) Republic of Rukwa is a largely agricultural society. For foreign exchange, it is dependent on the exports of kwat. Kwat is a grain which can only be grown in Rukwa's climate. It is, however, widely in demand in Western markets as a 'health' food. Kwat is grown by peasant farmers on small plots of land on banks of the River Ru. At present, the harvested Kwat is transported by ox-drawn barges down the River Ru to port Ruk for export. The process is slow, owing to bottlenecks on the river. Rukwa has no other natural resources. The government is thinking of several alternatives to ease this situation.

1. Build a high speed road, and use foreign loans to buy lorries and four-wheel drive vehicles for farmers
2. Build a railway, with imported steel and engines
3. Widen the River Ru at key points, and purchase outboard motors for the barges

What do you think is right or wrong with all these options?

[*Key skill for Marketers: Problem solving*]

1.5 Consumer adoption of innovation

Innovation in the market place can take many forms, from radically new products incorporating new technology to changes in packaging. The **diffusion of innovation** model normally applied to consumers is as follows: Figure 13.2.

Figure 13.2: The diffusion of innovation model

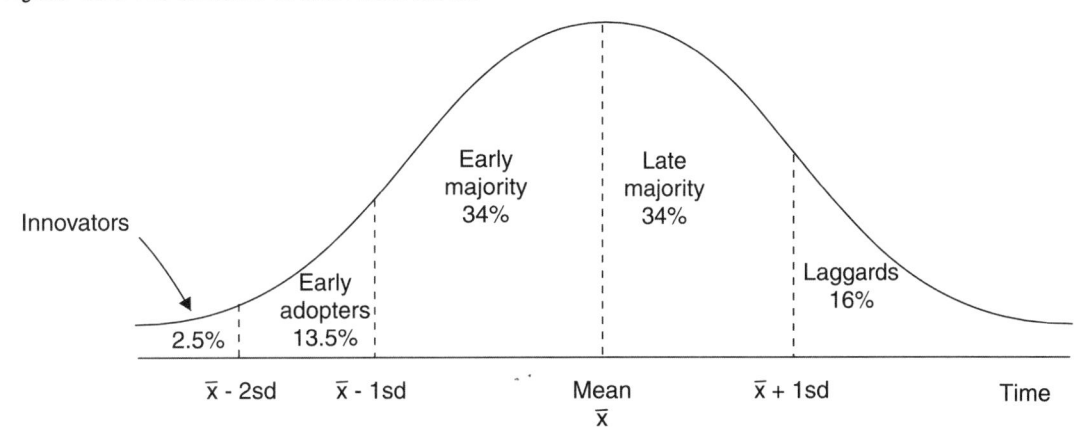

Innovators 2.5% | Early adopters 13.5% | Early majority 34% | Late majority 34% | Laggards 16%

x-axis: $\bar{x}$ - 2sd, $\bar{x}$ - 1sd, Mean $\bar{x}$, $\bar{x}$ + 1sd, Time

DIFFUSION MODEL	
Innovators	These are eager to try new ideas and products and often in close contact with change agents like sales staff and other opinion leaders. Often perceived to be risk takers, prepared to try and willing to pay often premium prices for 'being the first'.
Early adopters	They too are willing to change and are often opinion leaders themselves. They are likely to have greater exposure to the mass media than later adopters and certainly more willing to change. They are likely to seek out information actively about new products in specialist journals etc.

DIFFUSION MODEL	
Early majority	A more conservative segment who tend to purchase a new product just ahead of the average time, but who will have given it some thought before the purchase.
Late majority	These are slower than the average and sceptical about new products. They are very cautious purchasers likely to need some persuading.
Laggards	These are the smaller group of traditionalists who are unwilling to change. They may be forced to change only when their previous choice is obsolete and no longer available.

1.5.1 Diffusion and marketing strategy

Marketers usually want to ensure a rapid diffusion or rate of adoption for a new product. This allows them to gain a large share of the market prior to competitors responding. A penetration policy associated with low introductory pricing and promotions designed to facilitate trial are associated with such a strategy.

In some markets, particularly where research and development cost has been high, where the product involves 'new' technology or where it is protected from competition perhaps by patent, a skimming policy may be adopted. Here price is high initially, usually representing very high unit profits. Sales increase in step with price reductions, in line with available capacity or competitors' responses.

How far this applies to new technologies, however, is uncertain. Businesses must create customers for the new technology.

(a) In industry markets, the diffusion process will be enhanced if customers can be convinced of the technology's success, if it does not involve unacceptable risk.

(b) Companies might wish to ensure rapid adoption of the technology, and so raise barriers to entry to imitators or competitors. Again this might require creating customer need.

(c) However, it is not easy to know the possible applications of a new technology and how a customer can be created.

Marketing at Work

It is not possible to offer a general law as to whether technological change and the diffusion of innovation supports a particular industry structure, as there are so many contradicting examples. Take the example of personal computers. There is a great choice of brand of PC on the market. The computer industry which was dominated by IBM has fragmented. However, many computers share common technology, both in hardware (Intel) and in software (Microsoft).

In these cases, the old computer industry has been effectively split into at least two. Proprietary software (which only runs on one machine) is no longer desirable. Some commentators, however, argue that there is a real danger of near monopoly; **Microsoft** has been accused of trying to squeeze out competitors, by 'bundling' its own products into the software it sells to manufacturers. The Windows updates have been promoted heavily – perhaps to make it hard for competitors to keep up.

2 Technology and employment

FAST FORWARD

New technology might require new work practices, flexible manning, sub-contracting and so on.

Technological development perhaps has three different effects on employment.

- It **requires new skills**, so creates new jobs for the new machinery

- It **destroys old jobs** and replaces people with machinery (for good or ill)
- It **increases productivity**, so freeing up resources and labour for other activities

Action Programme 2

Provide an example of each of the effects listed above.

Technological development affects **employment patterns** over the whole economy, as new industries and activities develop.

2.1 The nature of work

Shoshana Zuboff, in her book *In the Age of the Smart Machine*, predicted the far-reaching effects that ICT is now having on work and management practice. Computerising a process both:

(a) **Automates**: tasks are performed with the minimum of human judgement and intervention and according to set routines; *and*

(b) **Informates**: as the process is controlled by computer, human beings can only monitor it **indirectly** by observing the data that the computer displays on, say, a VDU screen.

How might this affect management?

(a) **Skills needed**

Effective production control in a computerised environment depends on the ability of the workforce to interpret and manipulate abstract data, and to do this they need an overall theoretical knowledge of the system. A critical, questioning attitude towards data presented on the screen is needed also.

(b) **Decision making**

Dealing with problems thrown up by data on a screen requires an ability to discuss them in a co-operative way, and so decisions may be arrived at by consensus. Traditional management practice requires that managers control information, and that managers alone take decisions.

(c) **Employee empowerment**

Information technology itself is becoming more user friendly, which may lead to employees gaining more control over their own work. With the growth of database technology, routine transactions can be taken over by the machines, so that human beings can be freed to make use of the wealth of information easily available.

(d) **Cost cutting**

Computerisation has largely been seen as a means of cutting costs. Cost savings are easily identified. However, Zuboff argues that few organisations consider that information, intelligently used, can be a means of adding value.

2.2 Other effects on work operations

Zuboff's argument is that information technology can both liberate as well as control. However, there are other features relating to people's working lives that might also be briefly considered.

(a) **Redeployment**

Technology, by automating routine operations, might mean that staff are redeployed elsewhere. A much-touted example is the desire of UK banks to push more employees into

PART C   THE MACRO-ENVIRONMENT

'sales' or 'customer service' type jobs. This might have the effect of eventually restoring the degree of social interaction in office jobs.

(b) **Expert systems**

Technology might be used to support up front operations, devolving decision-making. This has been mentioned in the context of delayering. The organisation hierarchy, as it were, is on computer. Expert systems, in particular might have this effect. An expert system is a computer system which contains a base of knowledge, which it can use to answer queries. (Expert systems have been used for medical diagnosis, for example). Expert systems contain a knowledge base, a sort of question and answer session and a program to display reasoning.

3 Developments in ICT

> **FAST FORWARD**
>
> There have been major **ICT developments** in production, point of sale, e-commerce and office support and communications systems.

Recent developments in technology have made significant changes to the business and information environments within which organisations operate.

Marketing at Work

A key technological development that is currently being tested by various companies is a **mobile phone** containing a **credit card**.

The new development is risky since there is no method of including the card that seems significantly better than all other possibilities. One method being investigated is having the phones emit an infrared beam directly to a cash register; another is having a special chip in the phone that can be scanned; another just involves the use of text messaging.

The Japanese credit card company, Nicos, has linked up with mobile network provider NTT DoCoMo, in an attempt to develop the infrared system. The main obstacle they face is the preference of the Japanese for cash purchases; 5.6% of personal spending is by credit or debit card compared with 31% in the United States. As cell phone penetration is high in Japan (approaching 80%), including a credit card as one of the phone's facilities may make credit card use seem much more natural.

A further option being investigated is turning mobile phones into credit card acceptance terminals. This may have particular potential in developing markets such as India with many small shop or stall keepers who have previously found the cost of installing a traditional credit card terminal to be too high.

Developing this sort of project is much easier in Japan because of the close relationships between network providers and handset manufacturers.

Despite the risks, the potential benefits are huge. These developments are good for credit-card companies because it's easier for customers to buy on credit; mobile phone companies benefit because the phones become more of an essential; for consumers credit card use is more interactive and they don't have to carry as much around.

Far Eastern Economic Review, 14 August 2003

3.1 Production systems

Production management information systems provide information to help with the planning and control of production. One application which is frequently computerised is **production planning**, involving the provision of a production plan to meet the requirements of customers and stockists. Computer systems are also being used in an increasing number of contexts in advanced manufacturing environments.

Stock control systems or modules range from simple **batch processing** systems that update a stock file from daily movement records, to **online (real-time)** systems providing instant, up-to-date information on stock availability. A good stock control system should reduce working capital that would otherwise be tied up in stocks.

3.2 Point of sale devices

More and more large retail stores are introducing **Electronic Point of Sale (EPOS)** devices using bar coding, which act both as cash registers and as terminals connected to a main computer. This enables the computer to produce useful **management information** such as sales details and analysis and stock control information very quickly.

The provision of immediate sales information (for example, which product sells quickly), perhaps analysed on a branch basis permits great speed and flexibility in **decision-making** (certainly of a short-term nature), as consumer wishes can be responded to quickly.

Many retailers have now introduced Electronic Funds Transfer at the Point of Sale systems (EFTPOS). These are systems for the electronic transfer of funds at the point of sale. Customers in shops and at petrol stations can use a plastic card (usually a credit card or debit card) to purchase goods or services, and using an EFTPOS terminal in the shop, the customer's credit card account or bank current account will be debited automatically. EFTPOS systems combine point of sale systems with electronic funds transfer.

3.3 E-commerce applications

We will look at the Internet separately in Section 4 of this chapter.

3.4 Office support systems

3.4.1 Decision support systems

Key concept

> **Decision support systems** are usually taken to mean systems which are designed to produce information in such a way as to help managers make better decisions.

Decision support systems (DSS) are a form of management information system. Managers use decision support systems to assist in making decisions when there is uncertainty about the likely impact of different actions. DSS range from fairly simple information models based on spreadsheets to expert systems.

Decision support systems do not make decisions. The objective is to allow the manager to consider a number of alternatives and evaluate them under a variety of potential conditions. Managers using these systems often develop scenarios to refine their understanding of the problem and their possible actions.

3.4.2 Executive information systems

An executive information system (EIS) provides senior executives with access to key facts and figures related to business performance. An EIS is therefore likely to have the following features.

(a) Provision of **summary-level data**, captured from the organisation's main systems (which might involve integrating the executive's desktop PC with the organisation's mainframe)

(b) A facility which allows the executive to **'drill down'** from higher levels of information to lower

(c) **Data manipulation facilities** (for example comparison with budget or prior year data, trend analysis, 'what-if?' functionality)

(d) Graphics and templates for **user-friendly presentation** of data

3.4.3 Expert systems

Expert systems are computer programs which allow users to benefit from existing knowledge and information. An expert system is a program that relies on a database holding a large amount of specialised data, for example on legal, engineering or medical information, or tax matters. The user keys in certain facts and the program uses its information on file to produce a decision about something on which an expert's decision would normally be required.

Expert systems can give factual answers to specific queries, but they can also indicate to the user what a decision ought to be in a particular situation. In this respect, expert systems can be a form of decision support system for managers.

3.5 Communications

3.5.1 Electronic mail (email)

Email reduces the need to send letters or faxes, place memos in pigeon-holes or despatch documents by courier.

Typically information is posted by the sender to a central computer which allocates disk storage as a mailbox for each user. The information is subsequently collected by the receiver from the mailbox.

(a) Senders of information thus have documentary evidence that they have given a piece of information to the recipient and that the recipient has picked up the message.

(b) Receivers are not disturbed by the information when it is sent (as they would be by face-to-face meetings or phone calls), but collect it later at their convenience.

Each user will typically have password protected access to his own inbox, outbox and filing system. He can prepare and edit text and other documents using a word processing function, and send mail using standard headers and identifiers to an individual or a group of people on a prepared distribution list.

Email has now replaced mail and fax for many business communications. **Email marketing** (on a permission basis) is a growing direct marketing and customer service tool.

3.5.2 Computer Telephony Integration (CTI)

Key concept

> **Computer Telephony Integration** (CTI) systems gather information about callers such as their telephone number and customer account number or demographic information (age, income, interests etc).

The information is stored on a customer database and can be called up and sent to the screen of the person dealing with the call, perhaps before the call has even been put through.

Thus sales staff dealing with hundreds of calls every day might appear to remember individual callers personally and know in advance what they are likely to order. Order forms with key details entered already can be displayed on screen automatically, saving time for both the sales staff and the caller. Alternatively a busy manager might note that an unwelcome call is coming in on the 'screen pop' that appears on her PC and choose to direct it to her voice mail box rather than dealing with it at once. As another example, a bank might use CTI to prompt sales people with changes in share prices and with the details of the investors they should call to offer dealing advice.

CTI has a key application in **Customer Relationship Management** (CRM), as it enables the marketing organisation to integrate customer data and contacts with customers.

3.5.3 Mobile communications

In theory it is now possible to do any kind of office activity outside the office, on the move, although limitations in battery power (a technology lagging far behind others described in this book) impose restrictions.

The mobile services available are increasing all the time. Here are some examples.

(a) **Messaging services** include voice mail, short message service (SMS text messaging) and paging services. SMS marketing is a 'hot' marketing tool, particularly in youth markets.

(b) **Call handling services** include call barring, conference calls and call divert.

(c) **Corporate services** include integrated numbering (a single contact number for both the phone on their desk and for their mobile), and virtual private networks that incorporate mobile phones as well as conventional desktop phones, so that users can dial internal extension numbers directly.

(d) **Internet access** is possible, although the speed of transmission when downloading information is relatively slow at present, but improving.

(e) **M-commerce** applications are being developed, allowing promotions to be sent (via SMS text messaging) to customers and purchases made via e-commerce sites or direct download.

3.5.4 Electronic data interchange

Key concept

> **Electronic Data Interchange (EDI)** is a form of computer-to-computer data interchange, and so another form of electronic mail.

Instead of sending reams of paper in the form of invoices, statements and so on, details of inter-company transactions are sent via telecom links, avoiding the need for output and paper at the sending end, and for re-keying of data at the receiving end.

Until recently different makes of computer could not easily 'talk' to each other. The problem of **compatibility** between different makes of computer was a serious one, and some form of interface between the computers had to be devised to enable data interchange to take place. This is less and less of a problem as businesses adopt common standards and set up sites on the **Internet.**

Joining an **EDI network** (there are several) is quite expensive, but many smaller companies are encouraged to do so by their suppliers and/or customers. Many of Marks and Spencer's suppliers have been converted to EDI.

3.5.5 Electronic funds transfer

Electronic Funds Transfer (EFT) describes a system whereby a computer user can use his computer system to **transfer funds**. For example it can make payments to a **supplier**, pay salaries into **employees'** bank accounts, or transfer funds from one bank account to another account by sending electronic data to his bank. Since businesses keep most of their cash in bank accounts, electronic funds transfer must involve the banks themselves.

- A system for the electronic transfer of funds **internationally between banks** themselves is known as **SWIFT** (the Society for Worldwide Interbank Financial Telecommunications). If X in the USA wishes to make a payment to a company in, say, Germany, and if his USA bank and the German company's bank are members of the SWIFT network, the settlement between the banks themselves can be made through the SWIFT system.

- Interbank settlements by the clearing banks **within the UK** are also made by electronic funds transfer, using the **CHAPS** system (Clearing House Automated Payments System).

PART C THE MACRO-ENVIRONMENT

- Many large companies now pay the salaries of employees by providing computer data to their bank, using the **BACS** (Bankers' Automated Clearing Services) or BACSTEL service. It has been estimated that switching to BACS can save 90% on transaction charges.

Exam tip

> The examiner has emphasised the importance of technology and ICT developments in a range of environments: the travel industry (Specimen paper), the recruitment industry (June 2004) or the mail-order clothing business (December 2006). Questions will NEVER be general – they will ALWAYS have a specific context. In December 2004, various examples of ICT were presented, and candidates were asked to comment on them in the context of an organisation of their choice.

4 The Internet

FAST FORWARD

> The **Internet** is the technology that allows any computer with a telecommunications link to exchange information with any other suitably equipped computer. The Internet can be used for marketing, sales and distribution purposes.

Terms such as 'the net', 'the information superhighway', 'cyberspace', and the 'World Wide Web' are used fairly interchangeably.

4.1 Current uses of the Internet

The scope and potential of the Internet are still developing. Its uses already embrace the following:

(a) **Dissemination of information**

(b) **Product/service development** – through almost instantaneous test marketing

(c) **Transaction processing**

(d) **Relationship enhancement** – between various groups of stakeholders, but principally between consumers and product/service suppliers

(e) **Recruitment** and job search – involving organisations worldwide

(f) **Entertainment** – including music, humour, games and some less wholesome pursuits!

4.2 Growth of the Internet

Internet usage has grown substantially in recent years.

(a) Many households are now establishing **multiple Internet access points** eg Digital TV set, PCs, WAP phones.

(b) **Changes in the telecoms market** are likely to mean that Internet connection time will become cheaper.

(c) Digital television and WAP enabled **mobile phones** permit the Internet to be accessed without the necessity to use a personal computer.

(d) For many, the preferred Internet interface is not the PC but the **PDA (Personal Digital Assistant)**.

(e) **Internet kiosks** are becoming increasingly common in shopping centres and cafes.

The Internet is not expanding at the same rate in every sphere of business. The rate of growth is influenced by:

(a) The degree to which the customer can be persuaded to believe that using the Internet will **deliver some added-value** – in terms of quickness, simplicity and price.

(b) Whether there are 'costs' which the **customer** has to bear – not exclusively 'costs' in the financial sense, but also such psychological 'costs' as the isolated on-line shopping experience.

(c) The **market segment** to which the individual belongs. The Internet is largely the preserve of younger, more affluent, more technologically competent individuals with above-average amounts of disposable income.

(d) The **frequency of supplier/customer contact** required.

(e) The availability of **incentives** which might stimulate Internet acceptance. For example, interest rates on bank accounts which are higher than those available through conventional banks (Egg), the absence of any charges (Freeserve), the creation of penalties for over-the-counter transactions (Abbey National), and the expectations of important customers (IBM's relationships with its suppliers).

Marketing at Work

In many areas, **the Internet** is still increasing in significance, although often at a slower rate than some optimists first envisaged.

Internet banking has proved relatively successful and now forms a significant niche in the banking sector. Both 'Internet only' and High Street banks have seen steady growth in the number of customers using web-based facilities to operate their accounts.

At the same time, many customers of traditional banks are not yet ready to abandon the channels they used in the past: even with Internet and telephone banking, many still visit their bank branches regularly.

4.3 Features of the Internet

There are several features of the Internet which differentiate it from what has gone before.

(a) **Changing models**

The Internet challenges traditional business models – because, for example, it enables product/service suppliers to interact directly with their customers, instead of using intermediaries (like retail shops, travel agents, insurance brokers, and conventional banks). Businesses are finding that they can cut out the middle man, with electronic banking, insurance, publishing and printing as primary examples.

(b) **Benefits for small companies**

Although the Internet is global in its operation, its benefits are not confined to large (or global) organisations. Small companies can move instantly into a global market place, either on their own initiative or as part of what is known as a 'consumer portal'. For example, Ede and Ravenscroft is a small outfitting and tailoring business in Oxford: it could easily promote itself within a much larger 'portal' called OxfordHighStreet.com, embracing a comprehensive mixture of other Oxford retailers.

(c) **Economies of information**

The Internet offers a new economics of information – because, with the Internet, information is free. Those with Internet access can view all the world's major newspapers and periodicals without charge.

(d) **Transaction costs**

The Internet reduces transaction costs and thus stimulates economic activity. According to one US calculation, a banking transaction via the Internet costs 1 cent, 27 cents at an ATM (automated teller machine) and 52 cents over the telephone. Infomediaries can enable significant savings to be enjoyed by small-scale or even single customers.

(e) **Speed**

The net supplies an almost incredible level of speed – virtually instant access to organisations, plus the capacity to complete purchasing transactions within seconds. This velocity, of course, is only truly impressive if it is accompanied by equal speed so far as the delivery of tangible goods is concerned.

(f) **New networks of communication**

Networks have sprung up between organisations and their customers (either individually or collectively), between customers themselves (through mutual support groups), and between organisations and their suppliers.

(g) **New business partnerships**

Small enterprises can gain access to customers on a scale which would have been viewed as impossible a few years ago. For example, a university can put its reading list on a website and students wishing to purchase any given book can click directly through to an online bookseller such as Amazon.com. The university gets a commission; the online bookseller gets increased business; the student gets a discount. Everyone benefits except the traditional bookshop.

(h) **Transparent prices**

Potential customers can readily compare prices not only from suppliers within any given country, but also from suppliers across the world.

(i) **Personal attention**

Even if personal attention is actually administered through impersonal, yet highly sophisticated IT systems and customer database manipulation.

(j) **Marketing segmentation**

Approaching such segments may be one of the few ways in which e-commerce entrepreneurs can create **competitive advantage**. As *Management Today* (March 2000) puts it:

'The starting point must be a neat niche, a funky few, a global tribe. You need to understand your particular tribe better than anyone else. The tribe is the basic unit of business... The good news is that there are lots of tribes out there – and some are enormous. It's just a question of identifying them, understanding them and meeting their needs better than anyone else.'

(k) **Flexibility**

The web can either be a separate or a complementary channel.

(l) **Presentation**

Presentation is continuously improving from single text and graphics to sophisticated multi-media sites.

(m) **Interactivity**

The level and power of interactivity is also increasing.

(n) **Pricing**

A new phenomenon is emerging called dynamic pricing. Companies can rapidly change their prices to reflect the current state of demand and supply.

These new trends are creating **pressure** for companies. The main threat facing companies is that prices will be driven down by consumers' ability to shop around.

Marketing at Work

The success of the **Internet auctioneers** e-Bay has highlighted how the Internet can provide additional mechanisms for doing business. Auctions can serve various purposes. They can establish a price for items that do not have a clear market price, such as antiques. They can be used to sell products that it would be difficult to sell through more traditional channels such as last minute deals on flights. They are also a mechanism for distributing products to a number of customers.

4.4 Websites

Most companies of any size now have a website.

Key concept

> A site is a collection of web pages providing information in text and graphic form, any of which can be viewed simply by clicking the appropriate button, word or image on the screen.

Action Programme 3

What are the key elements of effective customer service through the web?

4.4.1 What makes an effective web site?

Surveys carried out by *Marketing Week* over the last couple of years have highlighted many common features, both good and bad, about brand websites. In general, unsurprisingly perhaps, technology brands such as IBM and Microsoft tended to have more appealing websites than fast-moving consumer goods (FMCG) and luxury goods brands.

The surveys found that the best websites generally score highly in the following areas:

- Detailed product information
- Information about how the brand could fulfil consumers' wants or needs
- Good use of sound and vision media
- Links to related sites and brands
- Tailoring of content to users' age and nationality
- Detailed information about local markets

A major drawback with a number of websites was that they were not **personalised** enough. For instance, distinctions made in Gillette's TV campaign between the targeting of women (highlighting product safety and attractiveness) and the targeting of men (highlighting hygiene) had not been reflected in its website; there were no separate sections for men and women.

Other significant shortcomings included:

- Navigation of sites being difficult
- Sites taking too much time to load (often because they contained too many images)

- Limited transaction capability
- Lack of focus on developing customer relationships
- Failure to offer free samples, or prizes for completing consumer surveys
- Inconsistency between offline and online offers
- Location at obscure addresses, making the brand difficult to find
- Lack of a website address on products or advertising
- Lack of links to other products
- Local subsites not being as advanced as the main site

Action Programme 4

Note details of three advertising campaigns that are currently going on, and visit the relevant websites.

(a) Do the websites link with, and reflect, the messages being given by the advertising campaign?
(b) Which of the above strengths and weaknesses do the sites possess?
(c) Are there any other major strengths and weaknesses that you can identify?

[Key skill for Marketers: Using ICT and the Internet]

4.4.2 Internal communication: intranets

The idea behind an **intranet** is that companies set up their own mini version of the Internet, using a combination of the company's own networked computers and Internet technology. Each employee has a browser and a server computer distributes corporate information on a wide variety of topics, and also offers access to the global Net.

Potential applications include daily company newspapers, induction material, online procedure and policy manuals, employee web pages where individuals post up details of their activities and progress, and internal databases of the corporate information store.

Most of the cost of an intranet is the staff time required to set up the system, which is often quite small. The **benefits** of intranets are:

(a) Money can be saved from the elimination of storage, printing and distribution of documents that can be made available to employees on-line.

(b) Documents on-line are more widely used than those that are kept on shelves, especially if the document is bulky (for instance company information handbooks, finance manuals and procedures manuals) and needs to be searched. This means that there are improvements in productivity and efficiency.

(c) It is much easier to update information in electronic form.

(d) Wider access to corporate information should open the way to more flexible working patterns. For instance if bulky reference materials are available on-line then there is little need to be in the office at all.

4.5 Marketing applications of the Internet

> **FAST FORWARD**
>
> The Internet can be used for a broad range of promotional applications, including direct marketing; sales promotion; customer loyalty programmes; media and public relations; relationship marketing; partnership development; customer service; market research; and corporate identity.

The Internet can be used for a broad range of promotional applications.

Advertising	- Dedicated corporate websites, banner/button advertising, ranking on Internet search engines (to increase site exposure)
	- The forecast global penetration of the Internet over the next few years would give it a significantly larger audience than any of the television networks, print media outlets or other advertising vehicles
	- Studies show that brand awareness increases some 5% after using banner advertising
Direct marketing	- Email messages sent to targeted mailing lists (rented, or developed by the marketing organisation itself)
	- 'Permission marketing' (targeting consumers who have opted to receive commercial mailings)
Direct response advertising	- Immediate contact (information/transaction facilities) to follow up customer responses to TV/radio/print advertising
Sales promotion	- On-line prize draws and competitions
	- On-line discounts (offset by lower transaction costs)
	- Downloadable or emailed discount vouchers
Customer loyalty programmes	- Value-added benefits that enhance the Internet buying experience
	- User home page customisation
	- Virtual communities (chat rooms etc)
	- Free e-cards/SMS messages
Media/press relations	- Online media/press kits
	- Emailed media releases
	- 'About us' and 'contacts' pages
	- Technical briefings and articles on key issues
Public relations	- 'About us' and 'FAQ' (frequently asked question) features
	- News bulletins (eg for crisis or issues management)
	- Publicity/information for sponsorships, exhibitions and events
	- Sponsorship of popular/ useful information sites
Relationship marketing	- Customisation of Web pages and targeting of offers/promotions
	- Email follow-up contacts
	- E-zines: special interest newsletters published on the Web, or distributed by email direct to subscribers and mailing lists
Grass roots marketing	- Generating word of mouth promotion and recommendation among customers
	- Online chat or message board forums and 'introduce a friend' schemes/incentives
	- **Viral marketing'** (so-called because it simulates the way a virus works!): giving visitors communication tools which they send to others, requiring them to visit the site: eg electronic postcards, greeting cards and links ('Send this page to a friend')

| **Direct distribution** | - Of products (through online shopping) and services (including access to information databases)
- Products can be **ordered** via the Net
- Some can also be **delivered** via the Net, by downloading direct to the purchaser's PC: examples include music, computer software, Clipart, product catalogues and instruction manuals |
|---|---|
| **Partnership development** | - Strategic promotional collaborations with synergistic content-specific sites or 'portals' (search engines, Web directories or other high-traffic sites such as Yahoo! or MSN) |
| **Customer service and technical support** | - Email contact
- FAQs (frequently asked questions)
- Access to databased information
- Online messaging or voice interruption for interactive support |
| **Market/customer research** | - Gathering information on customers and visitors for the purposes of market segmentation, personalisation/customisation of future contacts
- Site monitoring
- Online or emailed feedback questionnaires and surveys |
| **Corporate identity** | - Website and email messages must be designed to create a unified and coherent marketing message alongside all other marketing messages for **marketing synergy** |

Marketing at Work

Airlines

The impact of the web is seen clearly in the transportation industry. Airlines now have a more effective way of bypassing intermediaries (ie travel agents) because they can give their customers immediate access to flight reservation systems. In the UK, EasyJet became the first airline to have over half of its bookings made online.

Travel agents

The web has also produced a new set of online travel agents who have lower costs because of their ability to operate without a High Street branch network. Their low-cost structure makes them a particularly good choice for selling low margin, cheap tickets for flights, package holidays, cruises and so forth. These low-cost travel agents have been joined, furthermore, by non-travel-agents who simply specialise in opportunistic purchasing (eg lastminute.com).

Tesco

In another arena, Tesco is already the world's largest Internet grocery business, but other companies are rapidly developing new initiatives. Waitrose@work allows people to order their groceries in the morning (typically through their employer's intranet communication system) and then have them delivered to the workplace in the afternoon: this approach achieves significant distribution economies of scale so far as Waitrose is concerned.

Financial services

The impact of the Internet is especially profound in the field of financial services. New intermediaries enable prospective customers to compare the interest rates and prices charged by different organisations for pensions, mortgages and other financial services. This means that the delivering companies are losing control of the marketing of their services, and there is a downward pressure on prices, especially for services which can legitimately be seen as mere commodities (eg house and contents insurance).

4.6 Virtual companies and virtual supply chains (VSC)

Key concepts

A **virtual organisation** is a collection of separate companies or units who work together from dispersed sites, using networked computers, ICT tools and shared access to data.

A traditional **supply chain** is made up of the physical entities linked together to facilitate the supply of goods and services to the final consumer.

A **Virtual Supply Chain (VSC)** is a supply chain that is enabled through e-business links (eg the web, extranets or EDI).

The **virtual organisation** concept has been around since the mid-1990s. Initially, companies attempted to work together using fax and phone links. The concept only really became a reality when Internet technology came into common usage. Companies are now able to work together and exchange data in real time, using on-line tools. For example, engineers from five companies could design a product together on the Internet.

Many companies have become, or are becoming, more 'virtual'. They are developing into looser affiliations of companies, organised as a supply network.

Virtual Supply Chain networks have two types of organisation: producers and integrators.

(a) **Producers produce goods and services.** They have core competencies in production schedule execution. Producers must focus on delivery to schedule and within cost. The sales driver within these companies is on ensuring that their capacity is fully sold through their networking with co-ordinators. Producers are often servicing multiple chains, so managing and avoiding capacity and commercial conflicts becomes key.

(b) **Integrators manage the supply network** and effectively 'own' the end customer contact. The focus of the integrating firms is on managing the end customer relationship. Their core competence is in integrating and controlling the response of the company to customer requirements. This includes the difficult task of synchronising the responses and performance of multi-tiered networks, where the leverage of direct ownership is no longer available, and of often outsourced services such as warehousing and delivery.

Many of the most popular Internet companies are integrators in virtual organisations, eg Amazon.com and Lastminute.com. These organisations 'own' customer contact and manage customer relationships for a range of producers.

4.7 Problems with the Internet

To a large extent the Internet has grown organically without any formal organisation. There are specific communication rules, but it is not owned by any one body and there are no clear guidelines on how it should develop.

Other significant issues include:

(a) **Weak infrastructure**

This includes slow modems in most domestic households. Clicking slowly through an electronic catalogue soon becomes tiresome, and the conventional, paper-printed version can suddenly seem very user-friendly.

PART C   THE MACRO-ENVIRONMENT

(b) **Security fears**

More people are worried about security breaches over the Internet than about orthodox credit card fraud. Advances in electronic cash systems, including NatWest's Mondex card and plans to create 'E-money', 'Cybercash' and 'Digicash' may help.

(c) **Viruses**

Viruses are pieces of software which infect programs and data, possibly damaging them, and which replicate themselves. Virus scare stories are popular with many newspapers, and may mean that customers are cautious about taking up offers of free software, or opening Emails that they fear could contain viruses.

(d) **Delivery problems**

However convenient it may be to order two cases of wine through a computer screen, they cannot be 'zapped' straight into the customer's cellar. Though they have been ordered electronically, they will arrive in a humdrum delivery van, and it may not be convenient to be at home to receive them. Moreover, the speed of ordering is seldom matched by the speed of delivery.

(e) **The Internet customer profile**

Historically, Internet customers were predominantly male (for example, three quarters were male in 1997). However, rising numbers of women are now accessing the Internet, and the figure now differs by only a few percentage points on average, country by country by 2% in the UK, for instance, and numbers are now even in the US. As this change has occurred very rapidly businesses may not yet have adjusted to the new market of the 'female surfer' and may be operating on the assumption that the old demographic is still valid (promoting training and beer online instead of women's wear and cosmetics, for example). Similarly, the percentage of young people using the Internet, particularly in the developing world, is increasing rapidly.

Marketing at Work

An example of **technological failure** showing the importance of the wider organisational processes for the success of technology is provided by the *Taurus* project.

Taurus was a project, funded by various institutions in the City of London and managed by the Stock Exchange, to computerise certain aspects of share trading and registration. There was an existing computer system, Talisman, but for various reasons it was regarded as being no longer suitable.

However, the plans to develop a new computer system failed, at a cost to City institutions of about £500m and great damage to London's reputation as a financial centre. What went wrong? There was nothing inherently impossible about the task: automated settlement has been achieved in other financial centres in Europe.

(a) One reason was poor project management with inadequate control.

(b) The system was designed to replicate existing structures. Not to do so would have taken away business (and profits) from share registrar companies. The design was made unnecessarily complex in order to cater for all the vested interests. This, then, is an instance of the neutralisation of technology's possible benefits by wider social and organisational choices.

5 Technology and marketing

FAST FORWARD

Technology affects marketing management in three principal ways:
- New ways of **producing** goods and services
- New ways of **distributing** goods and services
- New ways of **communicating** with target markets

Exam tip

> In the exam, you might be asked to comment on the significance of the Internet to the marketer. This was certainly the case in both June and December 2004. It is a fundamental topic in the understanding of the modern marketing environment.

Evidence of new **possibilities** brought about by new technology are all around us. For the marketer, completely new markets may be opened up (eg interactive CD-ROM players or MP3 players) while cost reductions may allow existing markets to expand very rapidly (eg mobile phones).

As we have seen there are many examples of the ways in which technology is opening up new **communication** and promotion possibilities.

(a) Cable and satellite television channels offer new **specialised programming** to highly targeted audiences, with the possibility of interactive television shopping, which in its most developed form allows customers to respond to advertisements through the television itself.

(b) ICT is making **direct marketing** (by mail/phone/email) a very powerful communication medium.

(c) Technology itself can be used as a **competitive weapon**. Shared computerised airline booking systems can guide a customer who has to change planes to the preferred alternative.

ICT can also be used to facilitate the identification of **customer needs**. On-line monitoring, for example, allows marketers to gather data about the **actual** preference and buying patterns of web consumers (rather than a less reliable researched approach). On-line questionnaires and surveys can also be sued to gather **customer feedback**.

5.1 Technology and the micro-environment

Technological developments in the macro-environment can influence a firm's **micro-environment**. Let us take the example of information technology in relation to the five competitive forces.

TECHNOLOGICAL DEVELOPMENTS AND THE FIVE COMPETITIVE FORCES	
New entrants	IT can increase entry barriers if a lot of investment in new technology is needed or if shared systems lock customers and suppliers together. However, it may obviate the need to establish operations in different locations.
Bargaining power of suppliers	Power can be eroded if customers can easily compare supply terms. However, power can be enhanced by sharing and electronic data interchange arrangements with customers.
Bargaining powers of customers	IT can raise switching costs, and can enable easier analysis of customer needs.
Existing and substitute products and services	IT is often the substitute product itself, but can also help in supplying knowledge more easily.
Competitive rivalry	IT can aid differentiation and focus, but can also lead to co-operation with rival businesses sharing the same databases.

PART C   THE MACRO-ENVIRONMENT

Action Programme 5

Have a look at the websites of an online bookseller and a major publisher.

(a) How do the websites draw the first-time searcher's attention to particular titles?

(b) How easy is it for casual browsers to navigate the websites?

(c) Are there special features of relevance to heavy buyers, or buyers that are regular customers of the site?

[*Key skill for Marketers: Using ICT and the Internet*]

Chapter Roundup

- **Technology** includes apparatus, the techniques with which the apparatus is used, and the organisation of those techniques into social structures.

- Technology is an important but not the only factor in **economic growth**. In theory, technology could be found to advance the production possibility curve to the right.

- In organisations, technology can influence **organisation structures** by creating new jobs, requiring new skills. Technology can be a force for both **centralisation** and **decentralisation**.

- **New technology** might require new work practices, flexible manning, sub-contracting and so on.

- There have been major **ICT developments** in production, point of sale, e-commerce and office support and communications systems.

- The **Internet** is the technology that allows any computer with a telecommunications link to exchange information with any other suitably equipped computer. The Internet can be used for marketing, sales and distribution purposes.

- The Internet can be used for a broad range of promotional applications, including direct marketing; sales promotion; customer loyalty programmes; media and public relations; relationship marketing; partnership development; customer service; market research; and corporate identity.

- Technology affects marketing management in three principal ways:

    - New ways of **producing** goods and services
    - New ways of **distributing** goods and services
    - New ways of **communicating** with target markets

Quick Quiz

1. Technology consists of: ?

2. What is this, and what does it illustrate?

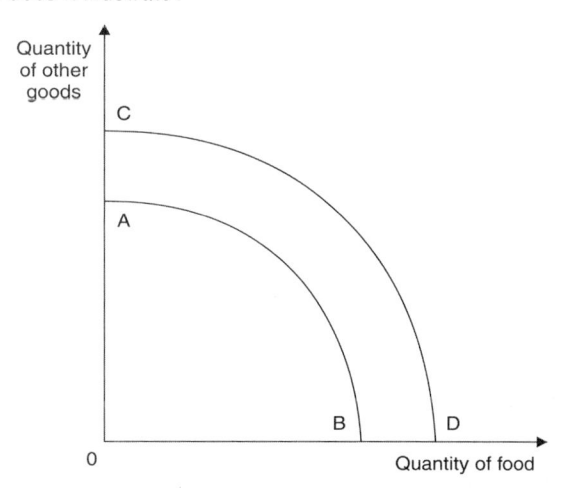

    [Graph showing production possibility curves with axes "Quantity of other goods" (vertical) and "Quantity of food" (horizontal). Inner curve from A to B, outer curve from C to D.]

3. Give three effects of technology on total employment.

4. *Fill in the blank*

    .... is a computer system which contains a base of knowledge which it can use to answer questions.

5. JIT planning stands for:

    A Job integrated technology planning
    B Just in time planning
    C Joint innovative techniques planning
    D Jocose impercipient theriac planning

6. Give four examples of features of an Executive Information System.

7. *Fill in the blank*

    .... systems gather information about callers such as their telephone number and customer account number or demographic information.

8. List some promotional uses of the Internet.

Answers to Quick Quiz

1.
   - Apparatus (tools, equipment)
   - Techniques (methods of using tools, work methods.
   - Organisation (social arrangement for productive ends)

2. The production possibility curve illustrating how technology enables the economy to produce more goods and services than ever before.

3.
   - Requires new skills
   - Destroys old jobs
   - Increases productivity

4. Expert system

5. B Just in time planning

PART C THE MACRO-ENVIRONMENT

6
- Provision of summary data
- Ability to drill down to lower levels of information
- Data manipulation facilities
- User-friendly presentation of data

7 Computer Telephony Integration

8 See Section 4 of this chapter for *lots* of ideas.

Action Programme Review

1   There is often no right answer, but here are some ideas.

   (a) Will the foreign exchange earnings from Kwat justify the infrastructural investment at all? After all, the government will have to use the foreign exchange earnings to pay interest on loans. Option 3 might be the least risky here.

   (b) Does the country have an educational and technical infrastructure to support the technology? Road vehicles need spare parts and trained service personnel. Spare parts might be an additional drain on foreign exchange. Again Option 3 might be the least risky.

2   Here are some possible candidates, but you could have possibly thought of others.

   (a) Information technology requires programming skills. Although systems analysis has antecedents in operational research, programming and screen design are relatively new disciplines.

   (b) The replacement of the horse and cart by the train and motor car reduced the activities of blacksmiths and other horse-related trades (but created jobs in garages).

   (c) Most Western economies are becoming orientated towards the service sector. In the UK, there are now more employees employed in service industries than in manufacturing.

3   The following factors will be important.

   (a) Rapid response time. If the website is not fast, the transient potential shopper will simply click on to another.

   (b) Response quality. The website must be legible, with appropriate graphics and meaningful, relevant information supplied.

   (c) Navigability. It is important to create a website which caters for every conceivable customer interest and question. Headings and category-titles should be straightforward and meaningful, not obscure and ambiguous.

   (d) Download times. Again, these need to be rapid, given that many Internet shoppers regard themselves as cash-rich and time-poor.

   (e) Security/Trust. One of the biggest barriers is the fear that information they provide about themselves (such as credit card details) can be 'stolen' or used as the basis for fraud.

   (f) Fulfilment. Customers must believe that if they order goods and services, the items in question will arrive, and will do so within acceptable time limits.

   (g) Up-to-date. Just as window displays need to be constantly refreshed, so do websites require frequent repackaging and redesign.

   (h) Availability. Can the user reach the site 24 hours a day, seven days a week? Is the down-time minimal? Can the site always be accessed?

   (i) Site effectiveness and functionality. Is the web site intuitive and easy to use? Is the content written in a language which will be meaningful even to the first-time browser (ie the potential customer)?

4   Your own research.

5   Your own research.

Now try Questions 21 and 22 at the end of the Study Text

Environmental challenges

Chapter topic list

1. Changes in the macro-environment
2. Changes in employment patterns
3. Environmental issues
4. E-commerce
5. The Single European Market and EMU
6. Globalisation

Syllabus content

- 3.8 Assess the potential significance of environmental challenges to marketing in the future eg globalisation; single currency; information and communication technology; and environmental decline

PART C   THE MACRO-ENVIRONMENT

Introduction

> In this chapter we consider challenges that are likely to have significant impacts on the environment in which marketing takes place in the future.
>
> We start by summarising the principal types of change that might affect each element of the macro-environment.
>
> We then move on to consider certain recent and current developments in more detail. We shall first show that changes in working patterns, principally labour flexibility and the changing role of women in the marketplace are significant because of the changes in attitudes that they have meant. These changes affect the products bought and also the ways in which those products are promoted.
>
> Other issues affect not only the products sold but also the ways in which resources are used. Environmental issues have led to changes in regulations and attitudes which must have an influence on the marketing process.
>
> Lastly we discuss the influences on firms to widen their environments and specifically to take account of international concerns. One such pressure is the improvement in communications brought about by the use of the Internet. European Union developments, the single European market and currency are also of significance. Lastly we consider the degree to which these influences have led to globalisation of organisations, and the effect of globalisation on the way organisations are structured and on their approach

1 Changes in the macro-environment

In this section we examine some main themes of change in the various elements of the macro-environment.

1.1 Social change

FAST FORWARD

> **Social change** involves changes in the nature, attitudes and habits of society.

Social changes are continually happening, and trends can be identified. For example:

(a) **Rising standards of living**

These may result in wider ownership of consumer and luxury goods, which have implications for those industries.

(b) **Society's attitude to business**

In the European Union countries, increasing social obligations and responsibilities are being heaped on to companies, not least with respect to **environmental protection** and ethical conduct (towards customers, employees etc).

(c) **The workforce**

There has also been a decline in blue collar jobs and an increasing proportion of people employed in clerical, supervisory or management jobs. Growth in productivity has led to an expansion in leisure time. Women have increasingly entered the workforce and, more particularly, managerial levels.

(d) **Ethnic diversity**

Europe, in particular, has shown a huge growth in population diversity in the last decade.

Marketing at Work

'McCann Worldgroup's multicultural agency MMG (Multicultural Marketing Group) has launched a new project focusing on **multicultural youth** living in Australia, as more mainstream advertisers try to crack this lucrative market.

'The research project, undertaken by the agency's research arm The Multicultural Eye, will survey 13-24 year olds from different ethnic backgrounds about their behaviours, influences, media consumption and spending habits.

'The project's findings will allow marketers to gain insights into this diverse and emerging market.

"A lot of mainstream marketers are trying to crack into the multicultural youth market. The research will highlight issues such as familiarity with the English language, social behaviour and key influences. It will explore the question: do we treat them for marketing and communication purposes as any other mainstream youth?"

'According to the 2001 Census, 15% of 15-24 year olds living in Australia were born overseas, with 16% indicating they speak a language other than English at home. This does not include the children and grandchildren of people born overseas – an increasing sector of society that speak English, but are strongly influenced by an ethnic culture.

'MMG's Youth Project will provide comprehensive insights into this group of consumers, targeting second and third generation youths of Italian, Greek, Asian and Arabic descent. Participants are expected across all religions and socio-economic groups, with surveys conducted through face-to-face groups and an online component.'

Shannon Russell, 'McGann Worldgroup targets Aussie ethnic youth, *B&T*, 27 April 2007

Although the impacts of cultural change may be indirect, they can nevertheless be very significant. They can affect not only demand, but also labour supply (increasing concern over work-life balance for example).

1.2 Economic change

1.2.1 The business cycle

As we saw in Chapter 10, an important indicator of economic activity is the **business cycle**.

(a) Some economists suggest that economic activity is always punctuated by periods of growth followed by decline, simply because of the nature of trade.

(b) Some industries prosper when others are declining. They are called **counter-cyclical** industries.

1.2.2 Economic trends: regional, national and international

Three levels of economic trend analysis need to be considered; regional trends, national trends and international trends. Many of these trends are often factors over which an organisation has no direct control, but which should be considered in the organisation's strategic plans.

A company's **local geographical environment** is important. It might be located in a growth area full of modern thriving industry, or it may be located in an area of urban decay. The economic future of the area will affect amongst other things wage rates, availability of labour, disposal income of local consumers, unemployment, the provision of roads and other services.

'National' economic trends are relevant to the individual characteristics of the firm's 'home' market and any overseas markets it trades in (exports, overseas production). Most advanced industrial economies have seen a shift from manufacturing to services such as retailing, education, health, tourism and communications. A large proportion of economic activity is taken up by services, such that the world economy is projected to be dominated by services.

World trends might seem remote to the small or medium-sized business, but they can in fact have an important influence on the future of any company with plans to trade abroad, as importers or exporters. In general, ICT developments have supported the increasing globalisation of trade, through e-commerce, off-shooting and so on.

1.3 Political change

Given that organisations must operate within a political environment, it is political **change** that complicates the task of predicting future influences, and planning to meet them. **Political risk** is the risk to an investment or business arising from the political decisions taken by the government or as a result of the activities of its citizens.

Management ought to be aware of the following.

- Whether political change could have a **significant impact** on their organisation
- What **form** of **influence** the political change might have
- What the **extent** of the **consequences** of any such change might be
- What the **likelihood is** of the change taking place
- How the organisation can **plan to cope** with the change, should it occur

Political risk is particularly relevant with regard to **overseas investment**, especially in large infrastructure projects overseas.

In some countries, cultivation of the right political contacts (**guanxi** in China) is essential for decisions to be made in your favour. There is a fine line to be drawn between aggressive lobbying and corruption.

Political instability (with risks of wards or civil violence) may also be a factor.

Action Programme 1

For a business of your choice, identify the most significant areas of political risk.

1.4 Natural environment

Environmental impacts may be direct:

- Changes affecting costs or resource availability
- Impact on consumer demand
- Impact on power balances between competitors in a market
- Regulation of areas of business activity
- New threats and opportunities

These may also be indirect aspects, for example, pressures from customers or staff as a consequence of concern over environmental matters.

14: ENVIRONMENTAL CHALLENGES

1.5 Technological change

Technological change is rapid, and organisations must adapt themselves to it. Technological change can affect the activities of organisations as follows.

(a) **Type of products or services that are made and sold**

Consumer markets have seen the emergence of home computers, compact discs and satellite dishes for receiving satellite TV. Industrial markets have seen the emergence of custom-built microchips, robots and local area networks for office information systems. Technological changes can be relatively minor, such as the introduction of tennis and squash rackets with graphite frames, fluoride toothpaste and turbo-powered car engines.

(b) **Way in which products are made**

There is a continuing trend towards the use of modern labour-saving production equipment. The manufacturing environment is undergoing rapid changes with the growth of advanced manufacturing technology.

(c) **Way in which services are provided**

High-street banks encourage customers to use 'hole-in-the-wall' cash dispensers, and shops are now using computerised point of sale terminals at cash desks.

(d) **Way in which markets are identified**

Database systems make it much easier to analyse the market place.

(e) **Way in which employees are mobilised**

Computerisation encourages delayering of organisational hierarchies, but it also requires greater workforce skills. Technology frequently requires changes in working methods.

Organisations that operate in an environment where the pace of technological change is very fast must be flexible enough to adapt to change quickly and must plan for change and innovation, perhaps by spending heavily on research and development.

2 Changes in employment patterns

FAST FORWARD

Changes in **employment patterns** including increased labour flexibility and homeworking, may mean expensive purchases are deferred, and products developed which take account of changed financial circumstances or are of use to the homeworker.

2.1 Employment patterns

Current European trends in employment patterns include the following.

(a) **Increasingly flexible workforce**

Workers no longer expect a job for life, and are prepared to work long or flexible hours rather than the traditional '9 – 5'.

PART C   THE MACRO-ENVIRONMENT

(b) **Increased use** of **part-time and temporary labour** and **outsourcing**

Advantages of using part-time labour
Easier to match working hours to operational requirements
Easier to accommodate personal circumstances of key staff
Productivity of part-timers higher than of full-timers working for the same period
Absence levels of part-timers lower
Pool of trained employees available for possible switching to full-time work
Easier to recruit staff
Alternative to paying expensive overtime rates

As costs have been cut, some organisations have employed temporary or contract staff to cover busy periods. Use of non-permanent staff means that employment matches activity, whilst costs are also saved in that non-permanent staff would not be paid for holidays or paid other benefits. A more extensive use of this policy can be seen in the major trend towards **outsourcing**: contracting projects or functions to external organisations (often off-shore, to take advantage of lower labour costs).

(c) **Knowledge workers**

An increased proportion of the workforce being 'knowledge workers', workers who use, process and produce knowledge. One aim of expanding higher and vocational education is to produce graduates able to cope with this new environment.

(d) **Homeworking and remote working**

Advances in communications technology have, for some tasks, reduced the need for the actual presence of an individual in the office. This is particularly true of tasks involving computers. The worker can, for example, do keying-in tasks at home. The keyed-in data can be sent over a telecommunications link to head office. This approach is being adopted in publishing and journalism and there are other examples as well.

However, where tangible goods are involved in workers' activities, barriers to homeworking still remain, because of the costs of transporting the goods.

ADVANTAGES OF HOMEWORKING	
Organisation	**Individual**
Cost savings in space	Commuting time saved
Larger pool of labour	Work organised flexibly round domestic commitments
If use freelance homeworkers, no need to pay sick and holiday pay, or for periods when there is no work	Easier to concentrate on work at home?
PROBLEMS WITH HOMEWORKING	
Organisation	**Individual**
Difficult to monitor	If homeworkers are freelance, poor employment rights and career prospects
Team working is problematic	Isolation

2.1.1 Marketing responses

Marketers need to consider their responses to these changes. For example:

(a) Mortgages which take account of the short-term nature of prospective borrowers' employment contracts

(b) Computers which are aimed at combined leisure/business uses

(c) Financial services tailored to the needs of the self-employed

The worry for businesses is that whilst writers such as Handy identify the need for people to have a **'portfolio'** of skills, many people do not welcome the insecurity that current labour market trends imply.

They might be likely to defer expensive purchases such as cars or houses, owing to uncertainty about their ability to meet the long-term commitments.

2.2 Women at work

> **FAST FORWARD**
>
> The enhanced **role of women** in many professions has meant increased markets for some products traditionally aimed at men and convenience products; and changing portrayals of women in advertising.

A longer-term change in the culture surrounding organisations in many countries is that related to female employment. This trend is related to:

- The growth in part-time jobs
- The rise in childbearing age
- Economic necessity, as unemployment has increased among the male population
- Policy challenges to discrimination and support for equal opportunity

2.2.1 Employer responses

In addition to responding to legislative provisions, some employers have begun to address the underlying problems of equal opportunities, with measures such as the following.

(a) Putting **equal opportunities** higher on the agenda by appointing Equal Opportunities Managers (and even Directors) reporting directly to the Personnel Director

(b) **Flexible hours** or **part-time work**, 'term-time' or annual hours contracts (to allow for school holidays) to help women to combine a career with family responsibilities. Terms and conditions, however, must not be less favourable

(c) **Career-break** or **return-to-work schemes** for women

(d) **Fast-tracking school-leavers**, as well as graduates, and posting managerial vacancies internally, gives more opportunities for movement up the ladder to women currently at lower levels of the organisation

(e) **Training** for women-returners or women in management to help women to manage their career potential

(f) **Awareness training** for managers, to encourage them to think about equal opportunity policy

(g) The provision of **workplace nurseries** for working mothers would be a boon to many female workers; employers however appear reluctant to bear the cost

2.2.2 Marketing responses

The changing role of women is also reflected in attempts by marketers to target the growing number of career women. Consider the following responses by marketers.

(a) Advertising is today less likely to portray women as housewives.

(b) Women are purchasing more traditionally male products. For example, many car manufacturers target professional women with cars whose specification is likely to appeal to them.

(c) Products have emerged to make working women's lives easier, for example ready prepared meals.

3 Environmental issues

FAST FORWARD

Ecological issues that may impact particularly over the next few years include resource depletion, genetic diversity and pollution problems. **Green marketing** may be one response to these concerns.

The marketing concept will undoubtedly be increasingly affected by environmental issues in the future. There is already a considerable impact on marketing policies.

3.1 Resource and biodiversity depletion

(a) **Resource depletion**

This may influence business operation through impacts on the availability of raw materials through damage to soil, water, trees, plant-life, energy availability, mineral wealth, animal and marine species.

(b) **Genetic diversity**

This may not seem immediately important for business. However the development of many important new plants, animals, medicines and the new bio-technology which enables commercially valuable materials of all kinds to be synthesised depends crucially on the availability of wild species from which resources of all kinds can be drawn. In the development of high-yielded and disease-resistant plants, for example, wild species are a critical resource.

(c) **Energy saving**

Energy saving programmes are under way in most of the countries of the developed world, involving the development of more efficient industrial equipment, and projects such as combined heat and power systems serving neighbourhoods or industrial plants. New energy efficient products are also being developed. Legislation which would penalise the use of certain scarce or potentially wasteful energy sources, for instance a carbon tax, may well encourage the demand for energy efficient products.

(d) **Alternative energies**

In addition, significant investment is now being made into research and development of alternative fuels and energies such as water, wind or solar power and vegetable fuels.

3.2 Pollution

Pollution concerns are, of course, at the centre of most worries about the environment.

(a) **Water**

Businesses are finding themselves under more and more pressure to curtail the impacts of their activities on the water table, the seas and the oceans. Concern over the quality of drinking water, to which this has been linked, has generated a massive increase in the size of the bottled water market in the UK. In the late 1980s, growth rates were around 20% per annum.

(b) **Air**

The quality of air has been much discussed, owing to the effect of motor car exhaust, and the general impact of road vehicles - clearly this may well have a bearing upon distribution policies.

(c) **Land**

Concerns about the pollution of land, through landfill policies and the long-term damage wrought by industry upon the land it occupies, are all likely to require some policy changes over the next few years.

(d) **Noise**

Noise pollution is also likely to become more important, and this can have far reaching impacts on the operation of all manner of businesses.

(e) **Waste**

Waste is causing just as much alarm, whether it is nuclear waste from power stations or industrial or domestic waste in landfill sites or water systems. There is increased legislation by governments to control waste disposal. New international agreements, arrived at by governments concerned, for example, about the effects of waste dumping on marine life and on beaches also lead to domestic legislation.

3.3 Climate change

Whether excess carbon dioxide in the atmosphere has caused serious climatic change resulting in 'unnatural' weather is still open to debate, but political consensus has now shifted to take 'global warming' very seriously. Potentially, the consequences could be profound, with average temperatures increasing and sea levels rising, with disastrous effects on agriculture and flooding of low lying areas.

Many nations have accepted the Kyoto Protocol (an international treaty to address climate change). The Protocol sets voluntary targets for the reduction of carbon dioxide emissions. Non-signatories (such as the USA and Australia) argue, however, that implementation would damage their economies. Alternative strategies include investment in new energy technologies and reforestation.

3.4 Recycling

This practice is already widespread and the demand for products and packaging made from recycled materials, or from materials which lend themselves to recycling, is increasing steadily. Car manufacturers such as Mazda and Citroen are using plastic components to reduce vehicle weight and are recycling used components. New legislation (based on EU directives) addresses key areas such as the obligation of manufacturers/suppliers to arrange for the recycling of waste products in the electronics and electronic equipment market.

PART C   THE MACRO-ENVIRONMENT

3.5 Animal welfare

In addition to concerns about the impact of production and consumption on the environment, there are also concerns about animal welfare. The mistreatment of animals in food production and concern about the inhumanity of certain kinds of animal husbandry techniques have produced a strong reaction among consumers. Increased vegetarianism has reduced the demand for meat in the UK, amongst other changes. There has also been an impact on the sales of cosmetics and other products in which animals are used in product testing.

Related to this, there have been a whole series of food scares, some of which have been related to the ways in which food is produced. Concerns about **food safety** and **dietary health** are closely linked to concerns about the use of chemicals and drugs in intensive husbandry and crop production, as well as the forms of feeding which have been employed. The scare over 'mad cow disease' has been linked to the use of recovered proteins from waste meat products in the production of animal feed.

3.6 Green pressures on business

As we saw earlier, pressure for better environmental performance is growing. Consumers are demanding better environmental performance from companies. Consumers are applying environmental criteria in many purchase considerations.

Marketing at Work

During 1995, Greenpeace activists boarded Shell's decommissioned oil rig, Brent Spar, in an attempt to force the company to reconsider the decision to sink the rig in mid-Atlantic rather than demolish and dispose of it on land. Shell's U-turn on the matter was prompted to a great extent by the beginnings of a consumer boycott of its products in Europe, particularly in Germany.

Deutsche Shell was caught out very badly, underestimating as it did the level of public feeling on the subject. It was forced to abandon a high-profile corporate environmental and community project advertising campaign which it had just launched. However, this case also demonstrated the importance of getting your information right. Greenpeace was forced to apologise eventually because it had substantially overestimated the amount of dangerous pollutants still contained within the Brent Spar rig. Shell's original plan is now accepted as being the most environmentally sound.

More recent **environmental conflicts** have concerned the Japanese whaling industry, for example.

4 E-commerce

> **FAST FORWARD**
> The **Internet** offers several commercial advantages, but also has several limitations, which may limit the appeal of **online shopping** and e-commerce.

4.1 Electronic commerce and the Internet

The Internet allows businesses to reach potentially millions of consumers worldwide and extends trading time to seven days, around the clock.

Companies have had to develop new means of promoting their wares through the medium of the Internet, as opposed to shop displays or motionless graphics. Websites can provide sound and movement and allow interactivity, so that the user can, say, drill down to obtain further information or watch a video of the product in use, or get a virtual reality experience of the product or service.

For many companies this will involve a rethink of current promotional activity.

14: ENVIRONMENTAL CHALLENGES

Marketing at Work

As an example of available **environmental data** – and how such data can be effectively presented – check out the following analysis of worldwide consumer broadband (Internet) usage, published in B&T magazine (Australia), 12 May 2006.

Global Broadband Application Rates

Consumers with a broadband Internet connection around the world

Tier	Country	%
First tier	South Korea	62%
	Hong Kong	57%
	Netherlands	51%
	Canada	51%
	Japan	50%
	Sweden	43%
	China*	41%
Second tier	US	39%
	UK	35%
	France	31%
	Australia	28%
Third tier	Germany	21%
	Italy	21%
	Spain	19%
	Poland	12%
	India*	3%

Source: *Forrester's NACTAS 2006 Benchmark Survey, Forrester's Consumer Technographics* * Q2 and Q4 2005

*Metropolitan China and Metropolitan India

4.2 Possible strategies

There are four possible broad strategies that a company may adopt towards e-commerce.

(a) **Do not sell products through the Internet at all**

Reselling would also be prohibited. Provide only product information on the Internet. This may be an appropriate strategy where products are large, complex and highly customised, such as aircraft manufacturing.

(b) **Leave the Internet business to resellers**

The business would not sell directly through the Internet (ie do not compete with resellers). This can be appropriate, for instance, where manufacturers have already assigned exclusive territories to resellers.

(c) **Restrict Internet sales exclusively to itself**

The problem with this is that most large manufacturers do not have systems that are geared to dealing with sales to end users who place numerous, irregular small orders.

PART C   THE MACRO-ENVIRONMENT

(d) **Open up Internet sales to everybody**

The market would decide whom it prefers to buy from.

If the decision is made to enter into e-commerce a new e-business needs **support and long-term commitment from high-level management**. Ideally such a project should be sponsored by the chief executive or a board-level director.

Strategy	Comment
Outsource to your customers	What do we do for our customers that they would rather do for themselves and could probably do better? Examples: www.cisco.com, www.dell.com.
Cannibalise your own business	If there were an Amazon.com in our market, what would it be doing? Examples: www.barnesandnoble.com, www.wsj.com.
Host your competitors	How can we create a marketplace that includes our competitors, but that we own? Examples: www.sabre.com, www.jewellery.com.
Build one-to-one customer relationships	How can we make each customer feel that we built our organisation just for them? Examples: www.My.yahoo.com, www.fireflyfans.net, www.netgrocer.com.
Make first contact	What is the first step our customers take in the chain of events that leads them to buy from us? How can we make contact with them? Example: www.autobytel.com.
Be a process integrator	What other things do customers need or do when they buy from us? Example: www.autobytel.com.
Catch rites of passage	What major life changes are customers going through when they come into contact with us? How can we help? Examples: www.usnews.com, www.citibank.com.
Create a community	What interests do our customers share? How can we create a place that people with those interests will keep coming back to? Example: www.em.avnet.com.
Create a niche portal	How can we make our site the portal our customers go to first? Example: www.tesco.net.
Pirate your value chain	How can we take over the roles of others in our value chain? Example: www.dell.com.
Re-intermediate on information value	How can we boost the value we add through information? Example: www.marshall.com.
Go pure cyberspace	What if we made the digital world our first priority and the physical world second? Example: www.amazon.com.
Be a fast follower	What are our competitors doing that looks likely to be successful? How can we do the same thing faster? Example: www.barnesandnoble.com.
Think dream not transaction	What dream do our customers start with that leads them to buy from us? How can we realise that dream? Example: www.expedia.com.
Beat the physical world	What can we do in the digital world that would be impossible or not feasible in the physical world? Example: www.benjerry.com.
Leverage the froth	What simple ideas would capture most media and public attention, even if short-lived? Examples: www.travelocity.com, www.lastminute.com.

Strategy	Comment
Change the pricing model	Would our customers benefit from a different way of pricing, perhaps micro-payments or auctions? Example: *www.priceline.com*.
Convert atoms to bits	What physical world core competencies do we have that could be applied to the digital world? Example: *www.ups.com*.

Marketing at Work

Interactive digital TV offers similar e-commerce services to the Internet as part of its package of services. Contact can be made using a remote control, although the amount of information available is lower because of limited bandwidth. High start-up costs have restricted the number of suppliers, but in the UK there are several possibilities. Arguably many of the users that these cater for are people who do not have full Internet access.

The most popular service is Sky Digital's open service. A number of retailers place content on this site; they have to pay a fixed rent and a proportion of all sales revenue for the privilege. Initial indications suggested that many new customers have been attracted. HSBC registered 80,000 customers within 3 weeks of which 20,000 were new. Domino Pizza had 10,000 requests in the first 10 days.

Businesses who wish to explore this market have to decide whether to advertise interactively or seek a deeper involvement, offering new interactive services or e-commerce facilities for a limited number of products.

4.3 Constructing an effective strategy for e-commerce

Upgrade customer interaction	Creation of automated responses to frequently asked questions, setting fast response standards, using email to communicate and ensuring website navigation is easy
Understand customer segments	Classifying each segment according to how likely it is to use e-commerce route, whether a personalised service relationship is desirable and what benefits customers need
Understand service processes	Understanding which processes can be automated and which transactions would consumers prefer to use the web for rather than say the phone
Define the role	Live interaction will be useful if cross-selling and conversion of enquiries into sales are possible, if trust is being built, or if customers prefer human contact
Decide technology	Deciding whether to run pilot programme first, or go for full integration straightaway
Deal with the tidal wave	Strategies for large initial response include having sufficient capacity for worse-case scenarios and using user-friendly technologies
Create incentives	Discounts to get consumers to switch to lowest cost channels, and disincentives for continuing to use existing channels
Decide on channel choices	Whether to offer a choice of channels (face-to-face, post, phone, Internet)

PART C   THE MACRO-ENVIRONMENT

Exploit the Internet	Tailor-made sites for significant customers, proactive product/service offerings, mechanisms for turning browsers into buyers and creating communities of users
Implement	'Strategy is nothing until it degenerates into work.'

4.4 Important aspects of strategy implementation for e-commerce

The following aspects are very important.

(a) **Organisation and culture**

When organisations move into an electronic age, some people (and functions) **increase their corporate influence**, whilst others move into the shadows. The increasing use of technology is unsettling, especially for senior people (ironically, employees lower down the hierarchy are likely to be much more comfortable about technological innovation). The Internet promotes **freedom of information**, both upwards and downwards; this, for some managers, is equated with a loss of authority.

(b) **Systems and infrastructure**

Implementation of e-commerce often requires **integration of service systems**, particularly call centres, the web, and CRM processes. This in turn may require a company to **review its whole decision-making patterns** and make some difficult choices about existing 'legacy' procedures.

(c) **Training**

Effective e-commerce implementation requires both **staff and customers** to be **trained**. Dealing with electronic interaction demands different skills from those which are appropriate to staff who focus on voice communications. Dealing simultaneously with written and verbal interaction is likely to call for a new skill set.

(d) **Looking to the customers**

This is well summarised by Mike Harris, Chief Executive of Egg, explaining the need to **avoid rehearsed, scripted and bureaucratic approaches** which give the impression that technology is driving the interaction rather than the need to relate to people.

4.5 B2B, B2C, C2B, C2C, P2P

Key concepts

There are various different types of commerce over the Internet.

B2B is business-to-business

B2C is business-to-consumer

C2B is consumer-to-business

C2C is consumer-to-consumer

P2P is peer-to-peer

B2C is just a name for traditional retailing activities of businesses to customers, carried out over the Internet.

4.5.1 B2B e-commerce

B2B activities include:

- Sale and transfer of goods before they reach the end-user
- Supply chains and joint ventures

- Subcontracting
- Distribution and marketplaces
- Support services

According to the market research firm Jupiter MMXI, the key factors for success in the B2B market are a high volume of transactions, backing from the industry leaders and real-world integration, linking online services with offline services such as telephone service and local customer support.

The B2B sector has seen major growth over the last few years.

(a) Major companies are setting themselves up as e-businesses. In November 1999, both Ford and General Motors announced that they were switching a major portion of their procurement and supply chain management to the web.

(b) IBM now requires all its suppliers to quote and invoice electronically – no paper documentation is permitted.

(c) Many firms are using the Internet to exploit the transparency of supplier prices, and to maximise their purchasing benefits from the availability of world-wide sourcing. Robert Bosch, the German kitchen appliance manufacturer, requires all its suppliers to have web-based catalogues and prices.

(d) Companies are also increasing their customer service through the web. Dell, the computer company, has created **extranets for its major business customers**, enabling them to receive personalised customer support, their own price lists, and some free value-added services.

4.5.2 C2B e-commerce

The importance of C2B is growing. The key feature of C2B activity is that the consumer takes the initiative to contact the business, rather than the business contacting the customer.

The development of C2B has huge implications for how marketing is carried out. It moves companies away from deciding what they want to sell and persuading consumers by a vigorous marketing campaign, and towards focusing on what consumers want to purchase. Key priorities will be trying to reach more easily often disparate groups of consumers.

4.5.3 C2C and P2P

C2C is where the consumer sells to another consumer using the business as an intermediary. The eBay and Yahoo auctions are examples of C2C transactions.

P2P transactions are any transactions that transfer money from one individual to another. Systems are being developed that will handle money transfers without the need for clearance. This market has a lot of potential, as there is a great deal of demand for payments to be made by email.

The best-known example of P2P is Napster, the company that allowed the exchange of music over the Internet and effectively bypassed the record companies.

4.6 M-commerce

Key concept | **M-commerce** is mobile commerce.

M-commerce has developed out of wireless access to the Internet through consumers' hand-held devices. As a result consumers can now shop from anywhere, not just a set shopping or computer location.

Marketing at Work

At the Palisade Shopping centre in New York, customers can opt to receive **personalised messages** from stores whilst they are in the shopping mall. PDAs are also proving a more popular means of obtaining product information by both customers and sales staff than the predecessor Interactive kiosk systems.

Systems have been developed that can help customers locate the products that they are after.

4.7 Disadvantages of e-commerce

E-commerce involves an unusual mix of people – security people, web technology people, designers, marketing people – and this can be very difficult to manage. The e-business needs supervision by expensive specialists.

At present, in spite of phenomenal growth the market is still fuzzy and undefined. Marketing, distribution, database development and customer services costs have proved very high for some companies.

4.7.1 Lack of trust

Above all, however, the problem with e-commerce is one of **trust**. In most cultures, consumers grant their trust to business parties that have a close **physical presence**: buildings, facilities and people to talk to. On the Internet these familiar elements are simply not there. The seller's reputation, the size of his business, and the level of customisation in product and service also engender trust.

Internet merchants need to elicit consumer trust when the **level of perceived risk in a transaction is high**. This is not always so (eg books) and research has found that consumers who have built up trust in an Internet merchant will ignore such concerns.

Internet merchants need to address issues such as fear of **invasion of privacy** and abuse of customer information (about their **credit cards**, for example) because they stop people even considering the Internet as a shopping medium.

Conventional thinking says that a company should pay no more to bring in a customer than the stream of profits that the customer will subsequently generate. Yet in the e-commerce context, investors have often rewarded companies for **customer acquisition** without asking any questions about how quickly those customers may disappear.

Similar turbulence is affecting the B2B world. Traditional manufacturing companies around the world, sensing the **potential benefits from automating transactions** with suppliers and customers, have rushed into e-commerce. Many have formed alliances to create their own on-line market place, especially in the automobile, aerospace and chemicals industries. By pooling their buying power, the organisations behind these alliances hope to have **more control** over their activities. This leaves the small, purely Internet-based commodity/component exchanges struggling to attract the volume of transactions needed to make them viable.

Marketing at Work

Flightbookers, a travel company, has very successfully developed its own **e-business**. It has a wide range of flights on offer, but the service has expanded to include car hire and hotels. The company is developing a pro-active package that will enable customers to assemble their own hire-hotel package. Another service is an aid to the last minute holiday booker, who states preferred destination and maximum amount prepared to pay; when something becomes available the company emails him.

Through advertising the company is seeking to develop its own brand values in order to ensure continued customer loyalty. The company is trying to exploit gaps but is aware that competitors will soon catch up: 'Every month in Internet time is worth a multiple in years.'

5 The Single European Market and EMU

FAST FORWARD

The **Single European Market** and **European Monetary Union** have had major influences over the last few years.

The single European market is, in theory, supposed to allow for the free movement of labour, goods and services between the member states of the EU.

(a) **Physical barriers** (eg customs inspection) on goods and service have been removed for most products. Companies have had to adjust to a new VAT regime as a consequence.

(b) **Technical standards** (eg for quality and safety) should be harmonised.

(c) **Governments should not discriminate** between EU companies in awarding public works contracts.

(d) **Telecommunications** face **greater competition**.

(e) **Financial services** can be provided in any country.

(f) Measures are being taken to **rationalise transport services**.

(g) There is **free movement of capital** within the community.

(h) **Professional qualifications** awarded in one member state should be recognised in the others (though French fears about competition currently preclude this).

(i) The EU is taking a co-ordinated stand on matters related to **consumer protection**.

However, there are still many areas where harmonisation is a long way from being achieved. Here are some examples.

(a) **Company taxation**

Tax rates, which can affect the viability of investment plans, vary from country to country within the EU.

(b) **Indirect taxation (sales tax)**

Whilst there have been moves to harmonisation, there are still differences between rates imposed by member states.

(c) **Differences in prosperity**

There are considerable differences in prosperity between the wealthiest EU economy (Germany), and the poorest (eg Greece). The UK comes somewhere in the middle. This has meant grants are sometimes available to depressed regions, which might affect investment decisions and different marketing strategies are appropriate for different markets.

(d) **Differences in workforce skills**

Again, this can have a significant effect on investment decisions. The workforce in Germany is perhaps the most highly trained, but also the most highly paid, and so might be suitable for products of a high added value.

PART C THE MACRO-ENVIRONMENT

(e) **Infrastructure**

Some countries are better provided with road and rail than others. Where accessibility to a market is an important issue, infrastructure can mean significant variations in distribution costs.

The picture is further complicated by continuing enlargement of the EU. Hungary, Poland, Slovenia, Estonia, Latvia, Lithuania, Malta, Cyprus and the Czech Republic joined the EU in 2004, for example.

Further expansion will potentially open up marketing opportunities for businesses operating in new and existing member countries, with perhaps more benefits being derived by new members. The more alarmist elements of the press in certain countries have been highlighting the supposed 'flood of immigration', which they predict will occur when the new countries join and their labour forces have rights of movement within the EU. Additionally, there are security fears (sparked by terrorism, and outbreaks of bird 'flu in 2006) about the membership of countries such as Turkey.

Exam tip

> The impact of the EU enlargement was examined in December 2003, along with other international developments such as global summits. Make sure that you have a good general knowledge of major international political events and consider when you're reading about them how they will impact upon the marketing environment of businesses in your own country and abroad.

Action Programme 2

How do you think the existence of a single European currency (the euro) affects your company's administration?

5.1 European economic and monetary union

European economic and monetary union (EMU) was a long-standing objective of the EU.

Key concepts

> **Monetary union** can be defined as a single currency area, which would require a monetary policy for the area as a whole.
>
> **Economic union** can be described as an unrestricted common market for trade, with some economic policy co-ordination between different regions in the union.

Although the whole package of measures included in European EMU is not paralleled anywhere else in the world, there have been many international monetary unions. There are three main aspects to European monetary union. Note that Denmark and the UK are not party to these arrangements.

(a) **Common currency**

A common currency is now used for normal everyday money transactions by everyone in the monetary union.

(b) **European central bank**

A European central bank has the role of issuing the common currency, conducting monetary policy on behalf of the central government authorities, acting as lender of last resort to all European banks and managing the exchange rate for the common currency.

(c) **Centralised monetary policy**

This applies across all the countries within the union. It involves the surrender of control over aspects of economic policy and therefore surrender of some political sovereignty by the government of each member state to the central government body of the union.

EMU became a reality on 1 January 1999, when the **euro** became the official currency of participating countries: euro coins and banknotes entered circulation from 1 January 2002. The UK retains the right to opt in or to opt out, depending on the government's decision at the time.

Action Programme 3

How might European economic and monetary union (EMU), and a single European currency, affect the following UK businesses?

(a) A package holiday firm, mainly selling holidays to France and Germany.
(b) An exporter of power station generating equipment to developing countries in Asia.
(c) An importer of wine from Australia.

Do this exercise twice, firstly on the assumption that the UK participates in EMU, swapping sterling for the euro, and secondly on the assumption that it stays outside of EMU.

6 Globalisation

FAST FORWARD

Globalisation is 'the increasing integration of internationally dispersed economic activities' (*Boddy*)

6.1 Drivers of globalisation

There are strong forces in the business environment drawing companies towards global marketing strategies, the most important of which are as follows.

(a) **Demographic, cultural** and **economic convergence** among consumer markets and increasing homogeneity in the needs of industrial customers worldwide

(b) **Increased need** for **investment** and research to ensure long-term competitiveness, longer lead times involved in bringing products to market and the growing return needed for this process

(c) The **growing importance** of **economies of scale** (purchasing, manufacturing, distribution)

(d) **Changes** in **regional economic cooperation** resulting in freer movement of goods and capital

(e) The **impact** of **technology** on manufacturing, transportation and distribution

(f) The **deregulation** of **national markets**, in areas such as air transport, financial services, telecommunications and power generation

Marketing at Work

Guinness has shown how companies can make significant profits in **Africa** despite high costs and infrastructure problems. Nigeria is the third largest market for Guinness in the world after Britain and Ireland. Guinness's success in Nigeria has been partly due to the success of an advertising campaign, featuring Michael Power, a James Bond like figure who appears in feature films financed by the company.

Guinness has also brewed various products with a taste, alcoholic strength and consistency tailored to Nigeria. The company has used local ingredients, principally sorghum, a common cereal in West Africa, which gives a drink a sweeter flavour. Other innovations include Malta Guinness, a non-alcoholic beer that appeals to a society in which born-again Christianity and strict interpretations of Islamic laws are significant factors.

Guinness has also benefited from perceived high barriers to entry. The company has negotiated downturns in the Nigerian beer market over the last twenty years. By already having a presence in the market, it has been best placed to take advantage of upswings as soon as they occur, by for example, buying and renovating run-down breweries.

Financial Times, 12 February 2004

6.2 Globalisation issues

We will be looking at globalisation mainly from a marketing point of view: that is, the decisions an organisation may take to enter global or international markets.

However, you should be aware that the trend towards globalisation also raises some general issues.

(a) Globalisation is argued to have beneficial effects, including:

 (i) Stimulation of local economies

 (ii) The creation of employment, leading to greater prosperity

 (iii) Transfer of technologies and skill development to developing countries

 (iv) Improvement of human rights and labour conditions via ethical trading initiatives

 (v) An incentive to positive international relations

 (vi) Improved choice and competitive pricing for consumers

(b) However, if you watch the television (particularly around G8 summits) you will realise that not everyone regards globalisation positively! Detractors argue that it:

 (i) Exploits developing countries labour markets, creating increased foreign debt (and the 'off-loading' of obsolete or poor quality goods by rich country producers).

 (ii) Exports pollution, urbanisation and other forms of environmental damage to rural economies

 (iii) Undermines domestic governments' attempts to manage their economies

 (iv) Causes unemployment in uncompetitive domestic labour markets

 (v) Squeezes small, localised businesses out of markets

(c) Economic power imbalances are a matter of on-going concern. There is continuing debate about the value of development aid and the international debt of developing nations. It has been argued, for example, that the writing-off of debts (now reluctantly agreed to by the G8 group of eight developed nations) damages the international banking system and developed countries. (The debts were unrepayable in any case, and without further positive investment, no gains would necessarily be made.) One of the arguments for globalisation is that international trade and skill transfer is a more effective approach to supporting developing economies than debt relief or development aid.

Exam tip

Some of these issues of developing economies were specifically raised in the compulsory case study in December 2006. A useful reminder to keep up-to-date with the international news, think widely about issues – and stay on your toes in the exam!

6.3 Some differences between domestic and international marketing

Sound marketing principles are generally applicable universally. However, there are major environmental differences between home and overseas markets and therefore marketing principles need to be adapted accordingly. The major differences between domestic marketing and international marketing are given below.

6.3.1 Reasons to consider global or international marketing (IM)

Firms may be pushed into IM by domestic adversity or pulled into IM by attractive opportunities abroad. More specifically, some of the reasons firms enter into IM are the following.

(a) **Chance**

A company executive may recognise an opportunity while on a foreign trip or the firm may receive chance orders or requests for information from foreign potential customers.

(b) **Mature or declining home market**

IM may provide for sales growth since products are often in different stages of the product life cycle in different countries.

(c) **Intense competition in the domestic market**

Competition sometimes induces firms to seek markets overseas where rivalry is less keen. This was a major reason in Gillette's decision to begin marketing razor blades outside its US home markets.

(d) **Diversification**

Many companies enter into IM to diversify away from an over-dependence on a single domestic market.

(e) **Technology**

Technological factors may be such that a large volume is needed either to cover the high costs of plant, equipment, R&D and personnel or to exploit a large potential for economies of scale and/or experience. For these reasons firms in the aviation, ethical drugs, computer and automobile industries are often obliged to enter several countries.

(f) **Disposal of discontinued products**

IM can facilitate the disposal of discontinued products and seconds since these can be sold abroad without spoiling the home market.

(g) **Foreign opportunities**

Many firms are attracted into IM by favourable opportunities such as the development of lucrative Middle Eastern markets, marked depreciation in their domestic currency values, corporate tax benefits offered by particular countries and the lowering of import barriers abroad.

PART C THE MACRO-ENVIRONMENT

6.3.2 Barriers to global or international marketing

	Domestic	International
Cultural factors	National price Usually no language problems Relatively homogeneous market Rules of the game understood Similar purchasing habits	Diverse national prices Many language barriers Fragmented, diverse markets Rules diverse, changeable and unclear Diverse purchasing habits
Economic factors	Uniform financial climate Single currency Stable business environment	Variety of financial climates, ranging from very conservative to highly inflationary Currencies differing in stability and real value Multiple business environments, some unstable
Competitive factors	Data available, usually accurate and easy to collect. Competitors' products, prices, costs and plans usually known	Formidable data collection problems Many more competitors, but little information about their strategies
Legal factors	Relative freedom from government interference Political factors relatively unimportant	Involvement in national economic plans Government influence on business decisions Political factors often significant
Technological factors	Use of standard production and measurement systems	Training of foreign personnel to operate and maintain equipment Adaptation of parts and equipment Different measuring systems

Walsh gives a number of reasons for and against involvement in IM.

FOR AND AGAINST IM	
For	**Against**
Higher profits abroad	Profits affected by developments abroad
Increases in sales volumes allow reductions in unit costs	Need to adapt product/limit economies of scale
Extension of product life cycle	Better long-term strategy to develop new products
Disposal of excess production	May attract anti-dumping duties
Disposal of obsolescent goods	
Levelling out of seasonal fluctuations	
Diversification of risk	
Enhancement of prestige	

However, before getting involved in IM, the company must consider both strategic and tactical issues.

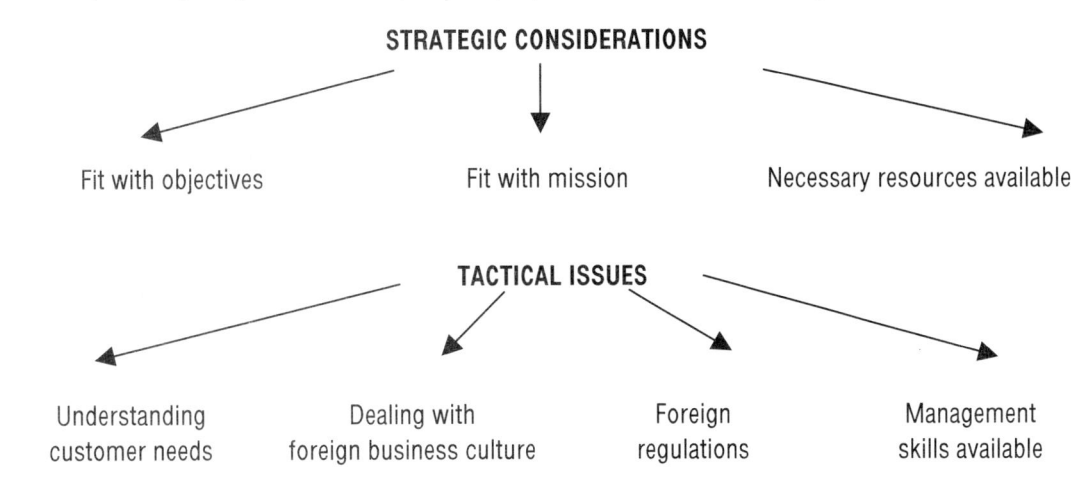

STRATEGIC CONSIDERATIONS

- Fit with objectives
- Fit with mission
- Necessary resources available

TACTICAL ISSUES

- Understanding customer needs
- Dealing with foreign business culture
- Foreign regulations
- Management skills available

6.4 Which markets should the company enter?

In making this decision the firm must start by establishing its objectives. Here are some examples.

- What **proportion of total sales** will be overseas?
- What are the **longer-term objectives**?
- Will it enter one, a few, or many **markets**?
- What **types** of country should it enter (in terms of environmental factors, economic development, language used, cultural similarities and so on)? The major criteria for this decision should be as follows.

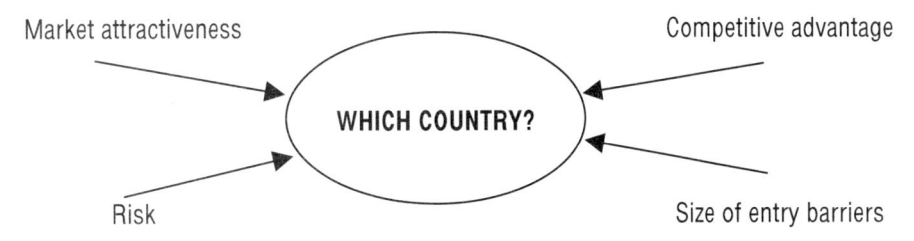

WHICH COUNTRY?
- Market attractiveness
- Competitive advantage
- Risk
- Size of entry barriers

Some products are extremely sensitive to the environmental differences, which bring about the need for adaptation; others are not at all sensitive to these differences, in which case standardisation is possible. A useful way of analysing products internationally is to place them on a continuum of environmental sensitivity. The greater the environmental sensitivity of a product, the greater the necessity for the company to understand the way in which its products interact with economic, socio-cultural and other environmental variables.

Environmentally sensitive
Adaptation necessary.

- Fashion clothes
- Convenience foods

Environmentally insensitive
Standardisation possible.

- Industrial and agricultural products
- World market products, eg denim jeans

PART C   THE MACRO-ENVIRONMENT

Marketing at Work

Tan Wang Cheouw, a Singapore businessman, made his fortune trading electrical goods in Russia and Kazakhstan. In the mid 1990s he switched to selling coffee in the East European market, initially through his own MacCoffee instant brand, but subsequently diversifying into other hot drinks, cereals and candy. His company's profits rose by 33% in 2002.

Much of the company's success has been down to its **advertising**. This has included:

- Racy television commercials featuring an attractive model serving coffee to Ukraine's most popular boy band
- Advertising on trams, taxis, roadside banners and on the back of scooters
- Sponsoring game shows, pop albums, soccer matches and sailing competitions
- Providing free cups of coffee to skiers.

Much of this advertising is carefully targeted to emphasise the unique qualities of the MacCoffee brand. This is important as in Russia there are at least 35 brands of coffee that, like MacCoffee, carry an eagle and an American flag. In addition it seems that the Russian market is much more brand conscious.

The advertising strategy is proving expensive; the price of television advertising has increased greatly over the last few years. However these costs also represent a barrier to entry, demonstrating the importance of being first in the market. Currently therefore Tan is seeking to expand into Middle Eastern countries, where there is at present little competition.

Far Eastern Economic Review, 15 May 2003

Exam tip

You should look out for further developments in the areas we have discussed in this chapter, or any new areas which become important in the marketing environment. Some may not reflect long term trends, but suddenly-emerging crisis: examples include the outbreak of SARS virus (the subject of the June 2005 case study), worldwide terrorism, the 'bird flu' (2006), rises in energy costs and so on.

Chapter Roundup

- **Social change** involves changes in the nature, attitudes and habits of society.
- Changes in **employment patterns** including increased labour flexibility and homeworking, may mean expensive purchases are deferred, and products developed which take account of changed financial circumstances or are of use to the homeworker.
- The enhanced **role of women** in many professions has meant increased markets for some products traditionally aimed at men and convenience products; and changing portrayals of women in advertising.
- **Ecological issues** that may impact particularly over the next few years include resource depletion, genetic diversity and pollution problems. **Green marketing** may be one response to these concerns.
- The **Internet** offers several commercial advantages, but also has several limitations, which may limit the appeal of **online shopping** and **e-commerce**.
- The **Single European Market** and **European Monetary Union** will have major influences over the next few years.
- **Globalisation** is 'the increasing integration of internationally dispersed economic activities' (*Boddy*)

14: ENVIRONMENTAL CHALLENGES

Quick Quiz

1 Give three examples of homeworkers.

2 Give five examples of ways in which employers have addressed equal opportunities issues.

3 Which of the following are possible e-commerce strategies?

    A   Do not sell products through the Internet at all
    B   Leave the Internet business to resellers
    C   Restrict Internet exclusively to itself
    D   Open up Internet sale to everybody

4 B2B commerce is:

    A   Business-to-business commerce
    B   Branch-to-branch commerce
    C   Back-to-back commerce
    D   Barter-to-barter commerce

5 Economic unit is a single currency area, requiring a monetary policy for the area as a whole.

    True ☐
    False ☐

6 What are the three main aspects of European Monetary Union?

7 What is the main cultural difference that international marketers need to take into account?

8 Give four examples of forces in the business environment that are leading firms towards international marketing.

Answers to Quick Quiz

1
- Traditional outworkers (home typists)
- Itinerants (salesmen)
- Personal services (hairdressing, music teaching)

2 Any five of:
- Appointment of equal opportunities managers
- Flexible hours
- Career break/return to work schemes
- Fast tracking women school leavers
- Training in management
- Awareness training
- Workplace nurseries
- Recruitment activities
- Modification of premises for disabled users

3 All of them

4 A   Business-to-business commerce

5 False. The definition is of monetary union.

6
- Common currency
- European central bank
- Centralised monetary policy

PART C THE MACRO-ENVIRONMENT

7   In society some groups will accept international products, but local product variations will be needed for other groups.

8   Any four of:

- Demographic cultural and economic convergence
- Increased need for investment
- Growing importance of economies of scale
- Changes in regional economic co-operation
- Impact of technology
- Deregulation of national markets

Action Programme Review

1   Your own research.

2   Here are some ideas – you probably have more.

- Financial reporting – Euros not sterling
- Confusion in salary structures and payscales as sterling payments are converted to Euros
- Administrative matters relating to share capital
- Conversion of trade debts into Euros

There are of course wider macro economic issues to consider, as the single currency affects interest rates, comparative prices, and relationships with other currencies such as the dollar.

3   We can offer no definitive solution, but here are some points to consider.

(a)   For companies trading primarily *within* the EU, such as the package holiday firm, participation in EMU will mean a reduction in exchange rate volatility - businesses will be able to compete on the essentials of cost and productivity. An analogy is the USA - although there are many 'states' there is only one currency. Most of British trade is with EU countries.

(b) and (c)

Companies trading outside the EU would remain subject to exchange rate risk, based on the Euro rather than sterling. It all depends on how the European Central Bank manages the currency - if the Euro becomes a 'hard' currency, like the Deutschmark, then exports will cost more to overseas customers, but imports from overseas suppliers might be cheaper. Many internationally traded goods, such as oil or aircraft, are priced in US dollars anyhow, so the impact will be indirect.

Of course, if the UK stays out of EMU it will not be in a position to influence the monetary policies of countries which use the Euro, although these policies will undoubtedly affect the UK economy and British businesses.

> Now try Questions 23, 24 and 25 at the end of the Study Text

Part D
Environmental information systems

The marketing information system

Chapter topic list

1. The importance of information
2. Marketing research
3. The marketing research process
4. Sources of information
5. Evaluating and presenting information
6. Marketing databases
7. Information communications technology and marketing information systems

Syllabus content

- 4.1 Explain why information is important to organisations
- 4.2 Explain the concept of a marketing information system and its key role in effective marketing decision-making
- 4.3 Explain the importance of marketing research and the information benefits it can provide
- 4.4 Identify key sources of internal and external information
- 4.5 Utilise, interpret and present secondary and primary data in identifying environment trends and estimating current demand
- 4.7 Explain the importance of information systems and the continuing impact of new technologies

PART D ENVIRONMENTAL INFORMATION SYSTEMS

Introduction

Part D of this Study Text deals with the systematic gathering of information for marketing. This chapter introduces the idea that information is vital for decision making, and gives an overview of the types of information that can be obtained through marketing research. It also discusses the various sources of information.

Information technology plays a key role in information management, and we finish off the chapter by looking at databases and marketing information systems.

Exam tip

The essential point to remember is the role that information plays in all marketing activity and decision-making. You may be tempted to take this for granted, but it is the core underlying theme of this syllabus. You may for example be asked about the information sources and research methods that would be used to produce specific data.

Remember that 'timely information adds power to the organisation's marketing efforts', and consider the following:

- The importance of 'quality' information (the topic of a June 2006 exam question).
- The uses to which information can be put to support an organisation's competitive advantage.
- The need for an information system.
- The impact of new information and communication technologies.

1 The importance of information

FAST FORWARD

Information (measurement, facts and data, analysis) is required for rational decision making, particularly for marketing, which requires a detailed, realistic understanding of the customer's needs and wants, the marketing mix and the marketing environment.

In a sense, an organisation is a **system of information flows**: Figure 15.1.

Figure 15.1: The organisation as an information system

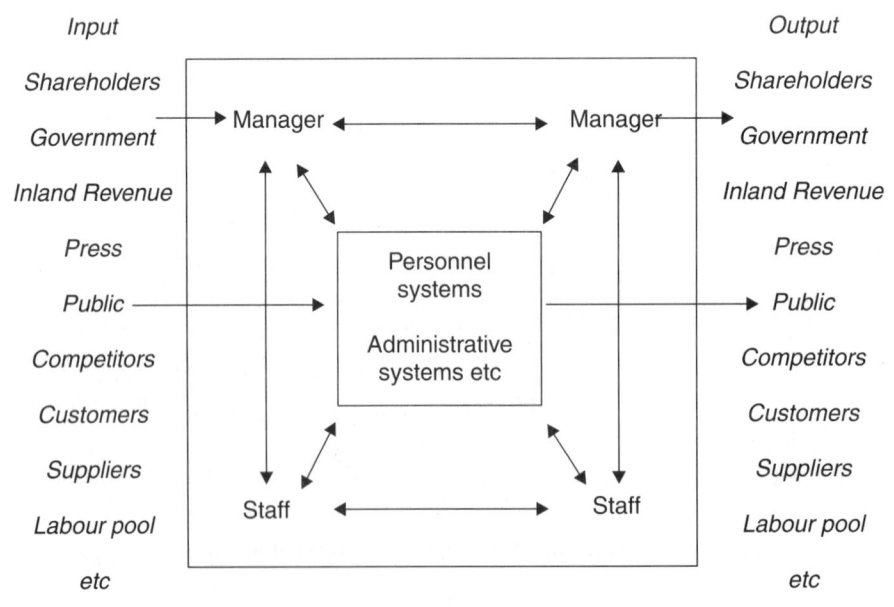

Input		Output
Shareholders		Shareholders
Government	→ Manager ↔ Manager →	Government
Inland Revenue		Inland Revenue
Press		Press
Public	→ Personnel systems →	Public
Competitors	Administrative systems etc	Competitors
Customers		Customers
Suppliers		Suppliers
Labour pool	Staff ↔ Staff	Labour pool
etc		etc

All human **action and decision-making** is based on information: about the environment, the needs or wants of the individual, the likely outcomes of the action or decision and so on.

284

1.1 Information and the marketing orientation

Peter Drucker wrote that: 'Marketing is the whole business seen from the point of view of its final result, that is from the **customer's** point of view'. A marketing orientation to business suggests that the purpose of business activity is to find out what people want, and to give it to them: to make what you can sell, not sell what you can make.

'Finding out what people want' is one key area of marketing research. You might think: 'Why does that require research? Marketers are people too: why can't we use our own experience, instincts and knowledge to make marketing decisions?'

1.2 Information and competitive advantage

Quality information (timely, sufficient, accurate, relevant, appropriately formatted) can contribute significantly to competitive advantage. It may enable the organisation to:

(a) Identify, characterise and target market segments effectively
(b) Identify new product/market opportunities
(c) Anticipate and respond to changing customer needs and wants
(d) Leverage customer and supplier relationships
(e) Anticipate and respond to threats and competitor actions

2 Marketing research

FAST FORWARD

Marketing research can operate across the extended marketing mix and the marketing environment.

Key concept

Marketing research is 'the systematic gathering, recording and analysing of data about problems relating to the marketing of goods and services' (American Marketing Association).

Marketing research is used by organisations for a number or purposes.

- Identify **changes** in the existing market price
- Build up a **bank of information**
- Improve **market awareness**, to inform negotiations with suppliers
- Help in making plans for the future and mentoring the success of current plans
- Solve *ad hoc* problems

Marketing decisions are made under conditions of uncertainty and risk. Marketing research aims to **reduce the risk** by providing information about the variables involved in the decision, and the possible outcomes of particular decisions and actions.

A wide variety of information may be relevant to marketing decisions.

	TYPES OF RESEARCH
Market	• Analysis of the market potential for existing products
	• Forecasting likely demand for new products
	• Sales forecasting for all products
	• Study of market trends
	• Study of the characteristics of the market
	• Analysis of market shares
	• Consumer attitudes
	• Influences on supply

PART D ENVIRONMENTAL INFORMATION SYSTEMS

TYPES OF RESEARCH	
Product	<ul><li>Product usage</li><li>Customer acceptance of proposed new products</li><li>Comparative studies between competitive products</li><li>Studies into packaging and design</li><li>Forecasting new uses for existing products</li><li>Test marketing</li><li>Research into the development of a product line (range)</li></ul>
Price	<ul><li>Analysis of elasticities of demand</li><li>Analysis of costs and contribution or profit margins</li><li>The effect of changes in credit policy on demand</li><li>Customer perceptions of price (and quality)</li></ul>
Promotion	<ul><li>Motivation research for advertising and sales promotion effectiveness</li><li>Analysing the effectiveness of advertising on sales demand</li><li>Analysing the effectiveness of individual aspects of advertising such as copy and media used</li><li>Establishing sales territories</li><li>Analysing the effectiveness of salesmen</li><li>Analysing the effectiveness of other sales promotion methods</li></ul>
Distribution	<ul><li>The location and design of distribution centres</li><li>The analysis of packaging for transportation and shelving</li><li>Dealer supply requirements</li><li>Dealer advertising requirements</li><li>The cost of different methods of transportation and warehousing</li></ul>

3 The marketing research process

FAST FORWARD

> Marketing and marketing research will only be relevant and cost effective if it is designed to contribute to real marketing decisions. Following logical steps will ensure the research gives data which addresses the underlying issues.

Research involves the following basic steps.

- Defining the question or problem
- Defining the range of options available
- Designing the research project
- Collecting the data
- Analysing and interpreting the data
- Presentation of findings and recommendations

3.1 Defining the problem and available options

Marketing and market research will only be worthwhile and cost effective if it is designed to address real and relevant marketing and sales issues: opportunities, threats, strengths or weaknesses, or *ad hoc* problems.

Research can be commissioned or designed as a 'one off' project to solve a specific problem (such as a rise in customer complaints, a decline in sales or loss of market share). In addition to such **ad hoc research**, there is **continuous research** designed to keep market data constantly 'topped up' to identify environmental changes and trends.

Some clarification of possible answers or options may be helpful in designing the research. If there is a decline in sales, for example, the research may focus on the likely effects of **pricing** decisions, the choice of **distribution** channels, alterations to the product, or an increase in **promotional activity**. Questions can then focus on relevant areas.

- Who buys what, in what quantity and where from?
- Who doesn't buy, and why?
- What are the shopping habits/buying power of those buying or not buying?
- What products are selling best?
- How aware are people of the promotional message?

3.2 Designing the research

Once the researchers know what question is to be answered, or problem resolved, they can determine other issues.

(a) The specific **objectives** of the research: for example, to interview customers in a region with declining sales to determine the reasons for the decline.

(b) What **data is already available** previously collected by research, available from existing records or feedback from existing marketing activities, or from secondary sources.

(c) What **type of data** is needed: secondary or primary, quantitative or qualitative or a blend of both.

(d) What **sources of data** (secondary or primary) will be most appropriate. What sample of what population will be interviewed; for example, should the question be asked of customers, or potential customers who don't buy the product, or those who consume the product and/or influence the purchase decision, but are not actually buyers?

(e) What **mechanism** will most effectively and efficiently collect the data: postal survey, personal interview, focus group?

(f) **Who** will carry out the data collection: in-house or external services?

(g) Precisely what **format**, questions and incentives the research mechanism (questionnaire, interview, discussion guide) will have. A badly worded or designed questionnaire, for example, may fail to gather the answers required.

3.3 The importance of research planning

Wasted research can be attributed to poor planning.

- Inadequate briefing of researchers
- Poor problem/question/decision definition
- Neglect of available sources, or poor selection of sources
- Poor research design, using an inappropriate vehicle or using it ineffectively
- Lack of ownership of the project

3.4 Primary and secondary research

One way of classifying research approaches is by the nature of the sources of data they use. We saw earlier in this Study Text that data can be classified as primary or secondary.

3.5 Quantitative and qualitative research

Another way of classifying research is according to the type of data gathered.

Key concepts

Quantitative research gathers statistically valid, numerically measurable data.

Qualitative research focuses on values, attitudes, opinions, beliefs and motivations.

(a) Quantitative research answers questions such as: How many? What percentage? How often? How many times? How much? Where? This is essentially *demographic*, statistical information, telling the marketer who buys what, and where, in what quantities and at what price.

(b) While quantitative data may show that 75% of men aged 18-35 drive a car, *qualitative* data might reveal how they go about choosing a car, how they feel about their car, what would make them change cars and so on. This is essentially *psychographic* information.

Quantitative data is usually gathered by survey, and qualitative data by personal interviews and discussion groups. Both types of data may be gathered from primary and/or secondary sources.

Action Programme 1

Give examples of qualitative and/or quantitative data that might be gathered in the following circumstances.

(a) The sales of a product appeared to be declining in a particular region
(b) You wanted to know whether customers would support night-time opening
(c) You were about to schedule TV advertising

Exam tip

The December 2006 question asked about the nature and implications of market research for a government agency or department. The June 2006 exam asked about the importance of conducting continuous marketing research (for an organisation of your choice). Spot the difference? Market research is not the same as marketing research! Stay alert to this pitfall in the exam!

3.6 Research objectives

Yet another means of classification is by **research objective**. There are three main kinds of research objective: exploratory, descriptive and causal.

(a) **Exploratory research**

This aims to originate ideas and hypotheses, rather than to test or measure existing ones. It is a preliminary phase before designing research to solve specific problems, and may make use of various sources of data.

(b) **Descriptive research**

This measures and estimates the frequencies with which things occur, and the degree to which variables are correlated.

(c) **Causal research**

This seeks to establish cause-and-effect relations between variables so as to explain and/or predict events. It often involves experimental research. So, for example, an organisation may trial a particular campaign with and without a certain feature (say, a response incentive) to isolate the difference made by that feature.

3.7 Limitations of marketing research

However, marketing research does not give all the answers. Some experts openly doubt the value of marketing research, citing examples of successful companies who never engage in it, and of struggling companies who have invested a great deal in it. Sometimes it is undoubtedly a waste of time – why?

(a) The design of the research took no account of the **specific decisions** that needed to be made.

(b) The research was **badly designed** and/or badly carried out.

(c) The results were **inconclusive**, so that the wrong decision was made, or the right decision was made but failed to convince the people who had to carry it out.

(d) The results were **ignored**, misinterpreted, misunderstood or misused.

(e) The research was well designed and the results were logically aimed at solving the problem but the necessary action was either **rejected** or unjustifiably deferred because it was untenable to key decision-takers. For example, the recommendation to withdraw from a particular customer communications strategy or campaign may be unacceptable to a marketing director who regards it as his creative innovation.

Marketing research makes use of a lot of data which is the result of asking people 'What do you think?', 'What would you do?', 'Would you buy?', even if the questions are not phrased quite so baldly. Are the answers received the 'right' ones? Not necessarily.

(a) Because questions tend to be **hypothetical**, respondents may be irresponsible and give an impulse response which they would reappraise and change given more time (hence the usefulness of postal questionnaires compared to on the spot interviews).

(b) Many people are **inherently conservative** when giving their opinion (especially about spending money), but may in fact be impulsive or innovative in practice.

(c) Conversely, **vanity** may make some people respond as innovators in a survey, on the basis of self-delusion, but in practice they may be very conservative when it comes to buying or using new-technology media.

(d) The **nature** of the interview or the **personality** of the interviewer may incline the respondent to give the answer he thinks the researcher wants to hear, rather than a genuine one. (People may understate the extent of their TV watching, or select the more respectable of the magazines they consume, for example.)

(e) **Insufficient information** and the artificiality of the context may result in misleading answers. (People may fail to recall a particular ad or direct mail package, for example, if it is inadequately described.)

4 Sources of information

FAST FORWARD

Secondary sources of information include:

- internal data records
- published information
- bought-in reports
- the Internet and intranets
- general environmental scanning

All these sources are available internationally.

As we saw above, **primary** sources of information are the most desirable, whatever the source: customers, consumers, supply chain partners or other businesses.

Here, we will look at **secondary** sources of information.

- **Existing data** generated and held by the organisation
- **Published information**, both general and industry specific
- Bought-in **market research reports**
- The **Internet**
- General **environmental scanning**

4.1 Internal data records

Information gathered in the course of operations and transactions may be relevant to marketing planning and control.

Such information often goes back several years, so that comparisons can be made and trends extrapolated.

4.2 Published information

We have seen that the **government** is a major source of economic, industrial and demographic information and data can also be obtained from sources such as specialist providers, professional institutions and research agencies.

While some government sources are general and others trade-, market - or profession-specific, bear in mind that general information may be applicable to your target market: keep an open mind for relevant data. Department of Transport budgets, for example, may be on the need-to-know list for car manufacturers.

Action Programme 2

Does your organisation, or individual department, have a library or libraries of published materials such as books, reference works, trade journals or newspapers? What titles are regularly stocked? How often is the information updated? How is the information categorised or indexed?

4.3 Bought-in reports

Much of the above published material is in the public domain. It is accessible and inexpensive to gather, but may need considerable analysis and processing in order to produce sufficiently targeted information for a specific organisation's needs. On the other hand, tailor-made information is only available by commissioning or undertaking primary research, which is a costly exercise.

A middle course may be to buy in reports prepared externally, whether as primary research for another organisation which is then syndicated, or as a commercial service to industry data users.

As we have seen there are a great many commercial sources of secondary data, and a number of guides to these sources are available.

There are commonly used sources of data on particular industries and markets such as Economist Intelligence Unit and Euronote publications.

4.4 Audits

Various audits generate published reports which can be bought by marketers.

4.4.1 Consumer panels or home audit panels

Consumer panels consist of a representative sample of consumers who have agreed to have their attitudes and buying habits monitored over a period of time. There are established panels for the purchase of groceries, consumer durables, cars, baby products and many others.

Consumer panels generate a vast amount of data which need to be sorted if they are to be digestible.

(a) Standard trend analysis shows how the market and its major brands have fared since the last analysis, grossed up to reflect the population.

(b) Special analyses depend on industrial preferences.

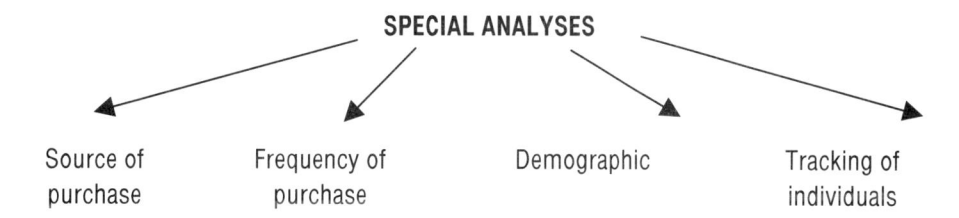

```
                    SPECIAL ANALYSES
     ┌──────────┬──────────┬──────────┐
Source of    Frequency of   Demographic   Tracking of
purchase     purchase                     individuals
```

4.4.2 Trade and retail audits

Trade audits are carried out among panels of wholesalers and retailers, and the term 'retail audits' refers to panels of retailers only. A research firm sends auditors to selected outlets at regular intervals to count stock and deliveries, thus enabling an estimate of throughput to be made. Sometimes it is possible to do a universal audit of all retail outlets. EPOS makes the process both easier and more universal.

The audits provide details of the following.

(a) **Retail sales**

For selected products and brands, sales by different type of retail outlet, market shares and brand shares.

(b) **Retail stocks**

Stocks of products and brands (enabling a firm subscribing to the audit to compare stocks of its own goods with those of competitors).

(c) **Selling prices**

The prices charged in retail outlets, including information about discounts.

Marketing at Work

In the 1980s, Coca-Cola decided to change its flavour to compete with Pepsi. Market research, **taster tests** and so forth elicited favourable responses to the change, and so the new formulation was introduced. A small group of consumers vociferously opposed the change; and this opposition spread suddenly and rapidly like an epidemic, forcing Coca-Cola to re-introduce the old formula.

It was hard to detect the reasons for this, but if some consumers perceived Coke to symbolise 'American values', then changing the formula appeared to be an assault on them.

Consumers, who had initially favoured the product, turned against it for reasons that could not be predicted by market researchers.

This case exemplifies three issues.

- The **limitations of planning** and organisational information gathering
- The unexpected **random behaviour** of the environment

PART D ENVIRONMENTAL INFORMATION SYSTEMS

- The way in which small causes (a few disaffected Coke-drinkers) can generate major consequences by feedback

4.5 The Internet

We have seen that the Internet can be a fast, efficient way to search for and access secondary data world-wide.

(a) Governments, educational institutions, libraries, commercial organisations and agencies have **home pages** on the **World Wide Web** which contain information and include links to other sites where information can be found. Well-designed sites typically have their own indexes and menus, as well as marked hypertext links that allow the browser to jump to related areas and topics.

(b) **Search engines** (such as Yahoo, Lycos, and Excite) maintain large databases of web pages, and can be used to locate relevant sites by word search.

(c) **Internet indexes** are another way of locating information on a particular subject: Yahoo is currently the biggest and most popular index available.

(d) **Newsgroups** and mailing lists (for email on selected topics of Internet) act as a kind of bulletin board service, where people post messages and articles on various topics.

It can be difficult conducting an efficient data search unless you know what you are doing. However, the Internet is friendly enough for you to be able to **browse** in areas of interest and follow links. As you discover relevant sources of information, you can add them to your favourites list to create a shortcut for regular reference.

4.6 General environmental scanning

Environmental scanning is simply the process of keeping your 'radar' switched on to what is going on in your market place. **Market intelligence** can be gleaned in many ways.

- Any newspaper, magazine, trade or academic journal
- Conferences, exhibitions, trade shows
- Personal contacts in the trade
- Personal experience and observation of the market

5 Evaluating and presenting information

FAST FORWARD

Data must be evaluated for:

- relevance
- up-to-dateness
- accuracy
- the credibility and objectivity of the source
- corroboration/confirmation
- correct methodology in sampling and data collection
- cost-effectiveness

5.1 Evaluating research data

All data collected should be **evaluated** using the following criteria.

(a) Is the data **relevant** to the purpose for which it was collected?

(b) Is it **up-to-date**?

(c) Is it **reliable and accurate**?

(d) Is the source of the data **credible** and objective, or unbiased? Look for the following.

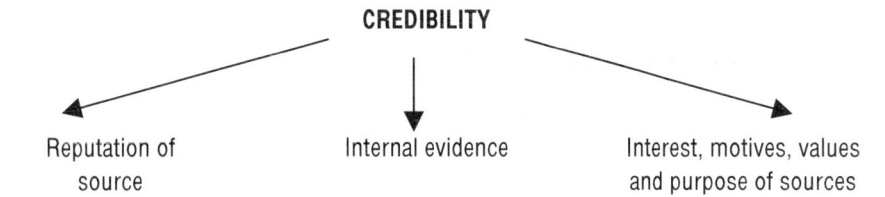

```
                    CREDIBILITY
         ↙              ↓              ↘
  Reputation of    Internal evidence    Interest, motives, values
     source                             and purpose of sources
```

(e) Is the data subject to **confirmation**, or comparison with data from other sources? Are you prepared to risk basing decisions on uncorroborated data?

(f) Is the data based on a large and representative statistical sample of the relevant population?

(g) Has the data been gathered in a way that makes it **meaningful and reliable**? Has the same question been put to all respondents? Were all terms consistently defined? Did researchers lead or suggest 'right' answers? Were the respondents influenced by the researcher, or each other, or the desire to be nice?

(h) Has the data collection and analysis been worthwhile? Has it fulfilled its purposes at a **reasonable cost** in money, time and effort?

5.2 Analysis and presentation of research findings

FAST FORWARD

> Data must be analysed and presented as **information**, accessible and relevant to the needs of the intended user.

Quantitative research quite often presents raw data: lists or tables of numbers, or ticks in boxes. This data must be analysed in order to identify key features, trends, probabilities and averages.

Qualitative research also presents raw data in the form of records of words in narrative form. This data must be analysed in order to summarise, interpret, categorise and measure the frequency of responses, for presentation in quantitative or statistical form.

The **management information**, or **decision-support** information, resulting from data analysis must be formatted for **presentation** to the target user.

- Printed tables
- Charts
- Graphs
- Narrative reports
- Oral presentation with visual aids
- Interpretation and recommendations

6 Marketing databases

FAST FORWARD

> A **marketing database** can provide an organisation with much information about its customers and target groups.

As well as using external databases, many organisations have developed their own databases. A marketing database can provide an organisation with much information about its customers and target groups. Every purchase a customer makes has two functions.

- Provision of **sales revenue**
- Provision of **information** as to future market opportunities

PART D ENVIRONMENTAL INFORMATION SYSTEMS

COMPREHENSIVE CUSTOMER DATABASE	
Contact	• Names and addresses • Contact (telephone, fax, email)
Professional	• Company • Job title • Responsibilities
Personal	• Age • Family details • Interests • Publications read
Transactions	• Products/services ordered • How often • How much spent
Call/contact history	• Sales/after-sales calls made • Complaints/queries • Meetings at shows/exhibitions
Credit payment history	• Credit rating • Amounts outstanding • Aged debts
Credit transaction details	• Items on order • Dates • Prices • Delivery arrangements
Special account details	• Membership number • Loyalty or incentive points • Discounts awarded

The sources of information in a customer database and the uses to which this can be put are outlined in Figure 15.2.

Figure 15.2: The customer database

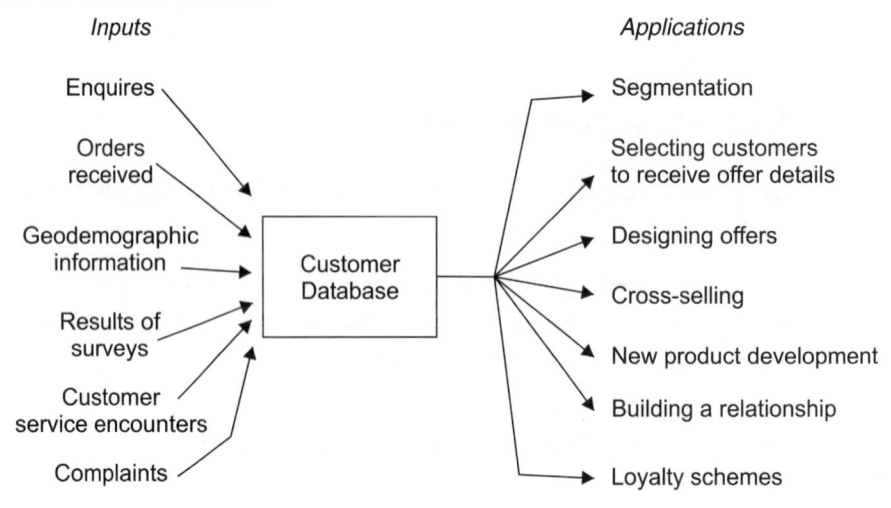

Inputs:
- Enquires
- Orders received
- Geodemographic information
- Results of surveys
- Customer service encounters
- Complaints

→ Customer Database →

Applications:
- Segmentation
- Selecting customers to receive offer details
- Designing offers
- Cross-selling
- New product development
- Building a relationship
- Loyalty schemes

(a) Customer service can indicate particular concerns of customers. For example, in a DIY store, if customers have to ask service staff where items are stored, the volume of complaints might indicate **poor signage** and **labelling**.

(b) Complaints also indicate **deficiencies in the product** or the fact that customer expectations have been poorly communicated.

(c) **Geodemographic information** relates to the **characteristics of people living** in different areas. Even simple post-code information can contain a lot of data about the customer.

(d) Other customer information can be gleaned by orders and enquiries that they place.

Information technology has been critical in the development of internal databases. It has created new marketing techniques and new marketing channels. **Database marketing** allows vast amounts of customer data to be stored cheaply and to be used to produce more accurate mailshots as well as other marketing tactics. This is important if a firm is able to gain an advantage over competitors by accessing and applying technologies that a competitor is unable to develop.

7 ICT and marketing information systems (MkIS)

> **FAST FORWARD**
>
> **Information communications technology** (ICT) has had a major impact upon the development of databases and **marketing information systems**.

Many marketing decisions are taken on a **continuous basis.** For example, decisions are taken at least annually on various aspects of the marketing mix, such as sales, advertising and sales promotion. Management need information to take such decisions. A continuous source of information is also required for control purposes. A **marketing information system (MkIS)** meets these needs. A diagrammatic representation of an MkIS is shown at the end of section 7.

7.1 Elements of a marketing information system

> **Key concept**
>
> A **marketing information system** is a set of procedures and sources used by managers to obtain everyday information about pertinent developments in the marketing environment.

The MkIS comprises all computer and non-computer systems which can help the marketer. As a result an MkIS is often built up from several different systems which may not be directly related to marketing, and will contain:

(a) The **internal reports (and accounts) database** which provides: results data, measures of current performance and sales, costs and stock information. An improvement in the timeliness, availability and distribution of reports improves the internal report system.

(b) The **marketing intelligence system** provides happenings data (what competitors are doing) and information on developments in the environment. It also scans and disseminates a wide range of intelligence.

7.2 Cost and organisational implications of MkIS

Establishing and maintaining effective MkIS requires investment.

(a) **Training** of existing and new staff will be necessary.

(b) Staff with **specialist skills** might have to be recruited and so job descriptions and specifications might need to change.

(c) Organisational considerations might include the **reallocation of duties**.

7.3 Design of MkIS

A system is only as effective as designers and users make it.

(a) Users should **understand** the systems and be in a position to evaluate and control them.

(b) The system must be regularly **reviewed** and feedback improved.

(c) The true meaning of the information provided must be clarified.

(d) The MkIS must be **flexible**.

(e) **Management's access** to the information must be easy and direct, ideally via PC or networked terminal.

(f) The **cost** of data/information gathering should be minimal.

(g) Data gathering should be **low intensity**. In other words, it should not cause excessive inconvenience to respondents or other information sources, especially customers!

(h) Data gathering should be regular and continuous since a small amount of data gathered regularly can build a considerable database. Regular data gathering produces more reliable results because it reduces the likelihood of sample bias of one kind or another.

(i) The system must allow for the easy and effective **storage and retrieval** of data.

(j) **Dissemination of information** considerations include who should receive information and how to distribute information regularly (through newsletters).

7.4 The features of an effective MkIS

As an example of an MkIS in action, let us visualise a company which has identified **quality service** as a strategic priority. To meet this goal, the MkIS must do the following.

(a) Provide managers with real time information on how customers and staff perceive the service being given, on the assumption that what is not measured can't be managed.

(b) Measure quality of both service and customer care so as to provide evidence that they do matter, the implication being that what is seen to be measured gets done.

(c) Monitor how (if at all) the customer base is changing.

(d) Perhaps provide a basis on which bonus payments can be determined, on the grounds that what gets paid for gets done even better.

7.5 Components of a computerised MkIS

A typical computerised MkIS could be described as having four components.

(a) A **data bank** will store raw marketing data, such as data about historical sales and data from market research findings.

(b) A **statistical bank** will store programs for carrying out computations for sales forecasts, making advertising spending projections, calculating sales force productivity and so on.

(c) A **model bank** will store marketing models for planning and analysis.

(d) A **display unit** (VDU screen and keyboard) will allow the marketing manager to communicate with an MkIS. Alternatively, marketing reports can be printed out in hard copy form.

Exam tip

The June 2006 exam asked for the key elements and benefits of an effective MkIS (for a national retail clothing chain eg Marks & Spencer). The examiner was particularly disappointed that students could not identify the standard elements [(a), (b), (c) and (d) in Figure 15.3.]

Figure 15.3: The market information system

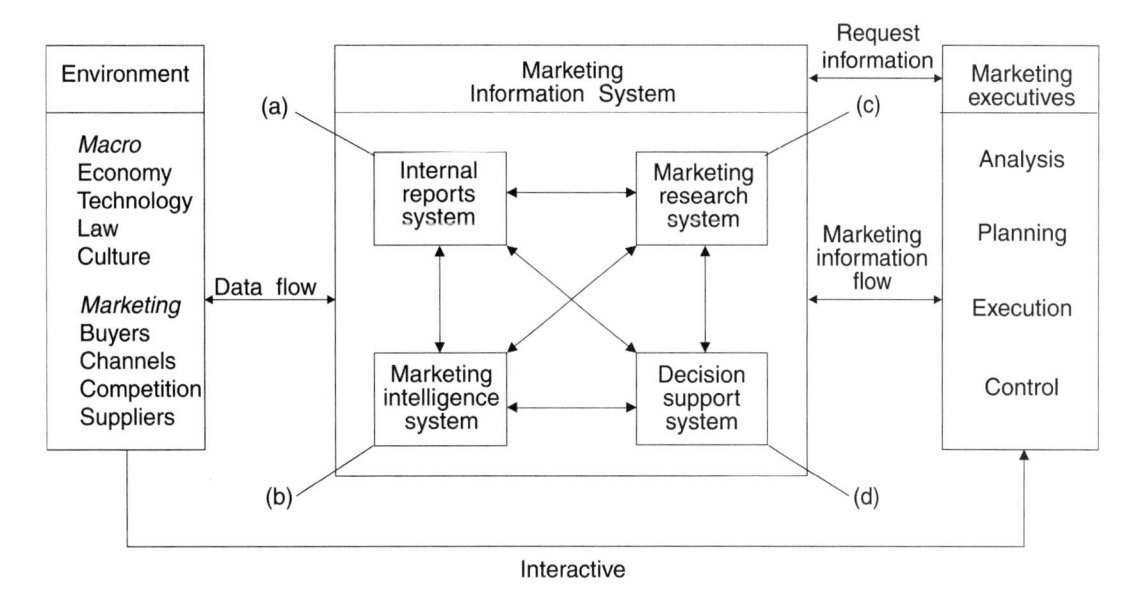

Environment	Marketing Information System		Marketing executives
Macro Economy Technology Law Culture *Marketing* Buyers Channels Competition Suppliers	(a) Internal reports system ↔ Marketing research system (c) Marketing intelligence system ↔ Decision support system (b) (d)	Request information ↕ Marketing information flow ↔	Analysis Planning Execution Control

Data flow ←

Interactive

PART D ENVIRONMENTAL INFORMATION SYSTEMS

Chapter Roundup

- **Information** (measurement, facts and data, analysis) is required for rational decision making, particularly for marketing, which requires a detailed, realistic understanding of the customer's needs and wants, the marketing mix and the marketing environment.
- **Marketing research** can operate across the extended marketing mix and the marketing environment.
- Marketing and marketing research will only be relevant and cost effective if it is designed to contribute to real marketing decisions. Following logical steps will ensure the research gives data which addresses the underlying issues.
- Secondary sources of information include:
    - internal data records
    - published information
    - bought-in reports
    - the Internet and intranets
    - general environmental scanning

    All these sources are available internationally.
- Data must be evaluated for:
    - relevance
    - up-to-dateness
    - accuracy
    - the credibility and objectivity of the source
    - corroboration/confirmation
    - correct methodology in sampling and data collection
    - cost-effectiveness
- Data must be analysed and presented as **information**, accessible and relevant to the needs of the intended user.
- A **marketing database** can provide an organisation with much information about its customers and target groups.
- **Information communications technology** (ICT) has had a major impact upon the development of databases and **marketing information systems**.

Quick Quiz

1   Define marketing research.

2   Descriptive research measures and estimates the frequency with which things occur, and the degree to which variables are correlated.

    True   ☐
    False   ☐

3   What is the difference between quantitative and qualitative research?

4   *Fill in the blank*

    ………………..consist of a representative sample of consumers who have agreed to have their attitude and buying habits monitored over a period of time.

5   Give four examples of ways that data can be presented to users.

15: THE MARKETING INFORMATION SYSTEM

6   What two functions do purchases by customers have?

7   Define a marketing intelligence system.

8   Which of the following types of research would not be relevant to marketing decisions?

   A   Product
   B   Promotion
   C   Delivery
   D   Distribution

Answers to Quick Quiz

1   The systematic gathering, recording and analysing of data about problems relating to the marketing of goods and services.

2   True

3   Quantitative research gathers numerically measurable data; qualitative research focuses on values, attitudes, options, beliefs and motivations.

4   Consumer panels

5   Any four of:

   - Printed tables
   - Charts
   - Graphs
   - Narrative reports
   - Oral presentations
   - Interpretation and recommendations

6   - Provisions of sales revenue
    - Provision of information on future market opportunities

7   A set of procedures and sources used by managers to obtain everyday information about pertinent developments in the marketing environment.

8   C   Delivery

Action Programme Review

1   (a)   Quantitative data on sales volume comparing region-on-region and year-on-year to establish amount (units, value, %) and rate of decline. Qualitative data on why consumers are less happy with the product.

    (b)   Quantitative data on volume of sales in comparable times/markets during night hours, percentage support among sample groups. Qualitative data about people's attitudes to night shopping, possible fears (related to area?).

    (c)   Quantitative data on audience figures at scheduled times, demographics of audience, cost of advertising. Qualitative data on audience response to the ad.

2   This is important information for any workplace research you may have to do – not least, for assessment of your skills in this area of the syllabus!

Now try Question 26 and 27 at the end of the Study Text

PART D ENVIRONMENTAL INFORMATION SYSTEMS

Information systems and change

Chapter topic list

1 Forecasting techniques
2 Marketing audits
3 Using SWOT analysis
4 Impact analysis
5 The product life cycle

Syllabus content

- 4.6 Explain the techniques available for forecasting future demand and coping with the challenges of environmental change

PART D ENVIRONMENTAL INFORMATION SYSTEMS

Introduction

We end the main body of this Study Text by considering how organisations can use the information available to **forecast future demand and changes**.

We firstly consider scenario building and other forecasting techniques. Scenarios take account of a variety of future factors, and essentially are designed to provide a guide on what might influence business developments. Forecasts by contrast are designed to come up with a quantified answer which is generally meant to indicate a particular course of action.

We then consider how an organisation might go about auditing its environment, objectives and activities in order to improve its own performance.

In Section 3 of the chapter we discuss analysing an organisation and its environment in terms of its own strengths and weaknesses, and the threats and opportunities it faces.

In Section 4 we briefly consider impact analysis, how major changes might affect an industry, an organisation and an organisation's strategy.

A useful technique that can be applied to individual products is product life cycle analysis, discussed in Section 5. This technique attempts to recognise stages in a product's sales history, and how these can be related to the management of the product.

1 Forecasting techniques

FAST FORWARD

There are various **forecasting techniques** organisations can use.

1.1 Scenario building

FAST FORWARD

Scenario building, looking at an internally consistent view of the future, is a particularly useful technique and can be viewed at the **industry** or **macro** level.

Key concept

Scenario building is the process of **identifying alternative futures**, ie constructing a number of distinct possible futures permitting deductions to be made about future developments of markets, products and technology.

Scenarios are used in several situations.

(a) **Contingency plans**

These can cope with the arrival of threats or opportunities which, although they may arise at any time, are of indeterminable probability. For example, a chemicals company may develop a scenario of a major spillage at one of its plants and then set up emergency routines to cope with it. They cannot assess how likely the spillage is to occur in actual practice.

(b) **As a prediction technique**

Step 1. A series of alternative pictures of a future operating environment is developed which are consistent with current trends and consistent within themselves.

Step 2. The impact of each different scenario upon the business is assessed and specific strengths and weaknesses highlighted.

Step 3. Contingency plans are drawn up to implement in the event of a given scenario coming true, or to implement now to give protection against the scenario.

1.2 Industry scenarios

Porter believes that the most appropriate use for scenario analysis is if it is restricted to an industry. An industry scenario is an internally consistent view of an industry's future structure. It is not a forecast, but a **possibility**. A set of industry scenarios is selected to reflect a range of possible futures. The **entire range**, not the most likely 'future', is used to design a competitive strategy. The process is as follows: Figure 16.1.

Figure 16.1: Use of an industry scenario

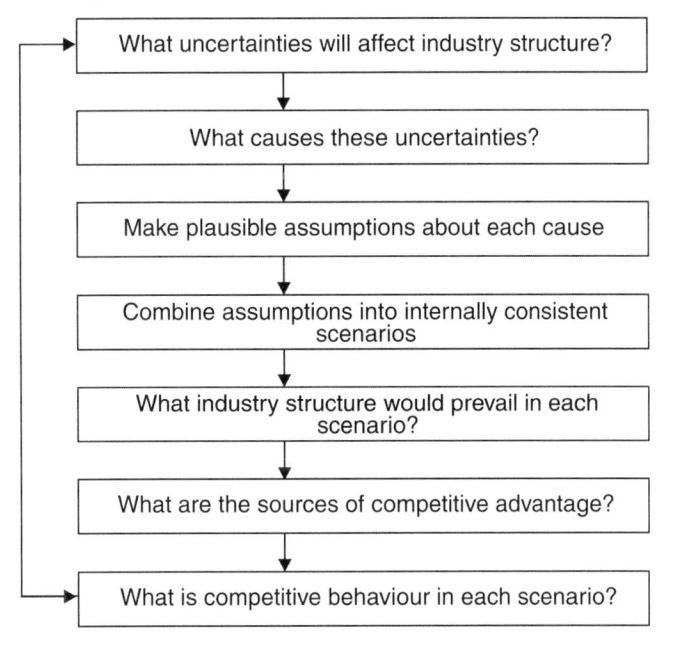

```
┌─────────────────────────────────────────────────┐
│ What uncertainties will affect industry structure? │
└─────────────────────────────────────────────────┘
                        ↓
┌─────────────────────────────────────────────────┐
│ What causes these uncertainties?                │
└─────────────────────────────────────────────────┘
                        ↓
┌─────────────────────────────────────────────────┐
│ Make plausible assumptions about each cause     │
└─────────────────────────────────────────────────┘
                        ↓
┌─────────────────────────────────────────────────┐
│ Combine assumptions into internally consistent  │
│ scenarios                                       │
└─────────────────────────────────────────────────┘
                        ↓
┌─────────────────────────────────────────────────┐
│ What industry structure would prevail in each   │
│ scenario?                                       │
└─────────────────────────────────────────────────┘
                        ↓
┌─────────────────────────────────────────────────┐
│ What are the sources of competitive advantage?  │
└─────────────────────────────────────────────────┘
                        ↓
┌─────────────────────────────────────────────────┐
│ What is competitive behaviour in each scenario? │
└─────────────────────────────────────────────────┘
```

This is not a simple process in practice, despite appearances.

(a) **Identification of uncertainties**

Identifying uncertainties in the industry's future is hard, as those uncertainties may be caused by the prospect of discontinuous change. Uncertainties hardest to anticipate are those originating outside the industry (eg microelectronics).

(b) **Independent uncertainties**

Independent uncertainties do not derive from other uncertainties in the scenario. Scenarios should only be constructed on the basis of independent uncertainties. For example, an industry might be vulnerable to both global warming and a change of government. These uncertainties are independent of each other.

(c) **Causes**

Identifying the causal factors is necessary to determine the source of uncertainties. For example, if an uncertainty is motor transport usage (and hence, say, the demand for tyres) a causal factor might be the price of petrol.

(d) **Interrelation of elements**

A scenario depends on a logical view as to how the various elements of the industry structure inter-relate.

Scenarios based on normal managerial assumptions are useful. Assumptions should be consistent with each other.

1.2.1 Analysing an industry scenario

An analysis of the scenario involves:

Step 1. Determining the future industry structure

Step 2. Developing the implications of the scenario for industry attractiveness

Step 3. Identifying implications for competitive advantage

The future industry structures identified in each scenario will have an impact on the competition in different ways. Some scenarios will highlight the probability of **price competition** and **downward pressure on prices**. Some competitors will be better than others to cope with price competition.

1.2.2 Using industry scenarios to formulate strategy

How can scenarios be used to formulate competitive strategy? In other words, what are the implications of each scenario?

- A strategy built in response to only **one** scenario is risky, whereas one supposed to cope with them all might be expensive, and might result in contradictory measures.

- Approaches to choosing scenarios as a basis for decisions about competitive strategy are as follows.

SELECTING WHICH SCENARIOS SHOULD BE BASIS OF STRATEGY	
Assume the most probable	This puts a lot of faith in scenario building process; if less probable scenario occurs, consequences may be serious
Hope for the best	Strategy is based on scenario most attractive to the firm; likely to involve wishful thinking
Hedge	Choose strategy that produces satisfactory, though not optimal results
Play wait and see	Follow others' strategies. Prudent, but sacrifices first move advantages
Influence the future	Influence demand for related products and other variables that could mean favoured scenario is more likely to occur

1.3 Macro scenarios

Macro scenarios use macro-economic or political factors, creating alternative views of the future environment (eg global economic growth, political changes, interest rates). Macro scenarios developed because the activities of oil and resource companies (which are global and at one time were heavily influenced by political factors) needed techniques to deal with such uncertainties.

Marketing at Work

Shell Corporation is a famous user of **scenarios**. Among short-term scenarios to be used as the basis of immediate contingency plans are:

(a) Nuclear destruction of the Gulf states
(b) Major tanker spillage

It is with these in mind that Shell has developed oil reserves in the USA and North Sea and has a spillage containment task force on perpetual standby.

1.4 Statistical (quantitative) forecasting techniques

Examples of statistical forecasting techniques, where the past is a relatively good guide to the future and where movement in the environmental variables is slow, are as follows.

(a) **Moving averages**

This technique removes fluctuations by averaging the results of a fixed number of periods, to eliminate seasonal variations.

(b) **Time series analysis**

In this case, data for a number of months/years are obtained, and compared. The aim of time series analysis is to identify seasonal and other cyclical fluctuations and the long-term underlying trends.

An example of the use of this approach is the UK's monthly unemployment statistics which show a **headline figure** and the **underlying trend**.

(c) **Regression analysis**

This is a quantitative technique to check any underlying correlations between two variables (eg sales of ice cream and the weather). One of these variables (eg ice-cream sales) is dependent on the other (eg the weather).

(d) **Exponential smoothing**

By this method, a new forecast for the next period's results is obtained by the following formula.

New forecast = old forecast + $\propto$ (most recent observation − old forecast)

where $\propto$ is the smoothing factor or smoothing constant. $\propto$ will be in the range 0 to 1, but its actual value is chosen subjectively depending on which value would have been most suitable in the past.

(e) **Econometrics**

This discipline is the study of economic variables and their inter-relationships, using computer models. Short-term or medium-term econometric models might be used for forecasting. This method of forecasting depends on the firm's ability to identify key 'indicators' of change, in advance of the change actually occurring and the ability to predict the span of time between a change in the indicator and a change in market demand.

(f) **Technological forecasting**

Forecasting technological changes is problematic. Discontinuous change is hard to predict, and some technological developments are hard to predict.

1.5 Qualitative forecasting techniques

Quite often the data available will be scarce. In this situation a variety of judgemental, or qualitative forecasting methods can be used.

1.5.1 Expert opinion

These techniques involve the selection of key knowledgeable people or industry players who are interviewed and asked to assign probabilities to possible future outcomes. The experts might include people such as dealers, distributors, suppliers, marketing consultants and trade associations.

1.5.2 Delphi method

The Delphi method is the most refined version of expert opinion; it can be used if there is little historical data on which to base a forecast or if results are unstable and/or uncertain. A **group of experts** are asked individually to provide their views on what will happen in the future.

(a) To begin with, each expert gives an **independent opinion**.

(b) The opinions of each expert are collated. Extreme views are discarded, and a draft **consensus** view is formulated.

(c) The draft consensus is circulated to the experts for their **further comments**, and depending on how they respond, the consensus might be amended.

(d) The process will continue until a forecast for the future has been prepared which has the acceptance of all or most of the panel of experts.

(e) When there is some uncertainty among the experts, **probability weightings** might be given to different possible future scenarios or events.

Exam tip

There were opportunities to cite the Delphi method for various forecasting activities in the June and December 2005 exams. The examiner was pleased that students had got to grips with Delphi's uses. However, where invited to discuss *two* forecasting techniques, you should pick two *contrasting* examples: Delphi plus scenario – building or trend analysis, say – rather than Delphi and expert opinion. Show your knowledge of quantitative *and* qualitative methods.

1.5.3 Executive judgement

This method of forecasting is based on the **intuition** of one or more executives. The approach is very unscientific but it has the advantages of being quick and inexpensive and it can work well if demand for the product is relatively stable and the executive in question has years of appropriate experience. Intuition is swayed heavily by recent experience, however, and so the forecast may be overly **optimistic** or **pessimistic**.

1.5.4 Marketing research

Marketing research methods include opinion surveys, analyses of market data, and questionnaires designed to gauge the reaction of the market to a product, a price and so on (all qualitative forecasting techniques). Marketing research is often very accurate in the short term but longer-term forecasts based on surveys may not be accurate because people's attitudes and opinions change.

1.5.5 Historical analogy

When past data is not available, data on **similar products** can be analysed to establish the life cycle and expected sales of a new product. Obviously care is needed in using analogies which relate to different products in different time periods but such techniques can be useful in forming a broad impression for the medium to long term.

1.5.6 Cross-impact analysis

Key trends are identified as those having high importance or high probability of occurring. The question is then asked 'If event A occurs, what will the impact be upon other trends?' The results are used to build sets of domino chains with one event triggering other events. In other words, cross-impacts are taken into account.

1.5.7 Multiple futures

Researchers build pictures of **alternative futures**, each one of which is internally consistent and has a certain probability of occurring. The major purpose of building alternative futures in this way is to stimulate management into thinking about and planning for **contingencies**.

1.5.8 Decision/hazard forecasting

Researchers identify **major events** taking place in the environment which could impact upon the organisation. Each event is rated for its convergence with several major trends taking place in society and for its appeal to major publics in society. The higher the event's convergence and appeal, the higher the probability of it taking place. The critical events identified in this way are then researched further.

1.6 The problems of forecasting

Human society is inherently complex; the world economy arises out of the interactions and activities of six billion individuals. It is hard enough to predict the weather. Meteorologists have to employ the most sophisticated computer systems to develop a viable simulation of the world's climate systems. It is not surprising that forecasts for human social and economic activity are always tentative and shaky. Often, the longer the time span, the greater the uncertainty in forecasting.

There are a number of problems involved in forecasting technological and social trends. Some of these problems arise from a misapplication of forecasting techniques; others arise from inherent uncertainties in the forecasting process. We discuss some of them below.

1.6.1 Over-simplification

The danger of regression analysis is that the relationship between two variables may only hold in a **certain range of values**. Take the example of temperature and ice cream. You would expect ice cream consumption to rise as the temperature becomes hotter, but:

(a) There is a maximum number of ice creams an individual can consume in a day, no matter how hot it is.

(b) If you continue raising the temperature, people will not be able to buy any ice creams at all, as they will have died from the heat.

(c) There may be other factors determining ice cream consumption (eg the availability of substitute products such as cold drinks).

Another possible problem with forecasting is that forecasters may **underestimate the impact** of certain factors on forecast variables. A good example is provided by traffic projections for the UK. It is well known that London's orbital motorway, the M25, was designed to take far fewer cars a day than currently use it; hence the constant traffic jams, and the controversial plans for widening it. Why might the forecasts have been so wrong?

(a) **Effect of many colours**

Planners may have underestimated the extent to which increased economic growth would lead to increased car ownership and usage.

(b) **Local traffic**

Planners may have underestimated the extent to which the M25 would be used for purely **local or short distance traffic**. It is used as a conduit between various areas in London's periphery, as well as a means for longer distance traffic to avoid going through London.

(c) **Feedback**

Critics of the government's road building schemes assert that the model is flawed in a more serious respect, in that it fails to take account of **feedback**. In other words, they say that building roads to avoid congestion is self-defeating, as roads generate more traffic: businesses relocate; people use their cars when they would otherwise have gone by train; more and longer journeys are made possible. This congestion leads to more road building which leads to more traffic usage which leads to more congestion: a sort of vicious spiral.

The underlying message therefore is that the models on which forecasts are based **over-simplify** the behaviour which they are supposed to represent.

1.6.2 Non-linearity

This brings us on to a further problem, which identifies the limitations of trend analysis. This is the concept of non-linearity, evident in **chaos theory**.

> 'Due to the instability of the marketing world, some action will have a dramatic effect well outside the limits of its 'objective' power, while other major initiatives will go largely unnoticed. We have all heard the announcements of major technological breakthroughs (remember, for instance, the rotating cylinder engine used by NSU, once hailed as a major innovation?) with no reasonable short– or medium-term commercial results. On the other hand, there are many examples of a minor adjustment to a specific product creating great success, or a chance meeting setting off a chain of events leading to major commercial effects.'
>
> Torsten Nilson (*Chaos Marketing*, 1995)

Marketing at Work

Could you see it coming?

If, at the beginning of 2001, an investor had ignored some noted Wall Street analysts and had bought 1,000 shares in Apple, maker of iPods and Macintosh computers, they would have paid about $US7,500 ($A10,500).

Today, four years later and on Apple's 30th birthday, that $US7,500 investment is worth around $US280,000. There have been two two-for-one stock splits and the shares have ranged this year between $US70 and above $US80. Had the shares been sold last January, for example, the return would have been more than $US340,000.

Far from dying, as those analysts predicted five years ago, Apple is now, in terms of market capitalisation, larger than Sony, and has greater effect on the booming global consumer electronics industry than the Japanese giant. Last year Apple's revenue was a record $US14 billion, on which it made a profit of $US3.14 billion.

It has significantly changed the lifestyle of millions, something its charismatic, difficult, demanding, inspired-visionary co-founder Steve Jobs always aimed to do. His company motto, after all, is Think Different, by which he means to think about different things to make a difference.

Apple's share of the personal computer market remains relatively small – about 5 per cent, but double what it was before the iPod – but it is among the world's most recognised brands, ranking with Heinz and Coca-Cola, and the iPod is possibly the most desired electronic device on the planet.

Gary Barket, 'Apple@30', *www.theage.com.au,* April 4, 2006

The implications of chaos theory are as follows.

(a) Certain outcomes are very sensitive to **initial conditions**. This is difficult to demonstrate simply, except to say that a series of major events (say, World War I) may have a very small and seemingly insignificant beginning (the death of a single man in Serbia).

(b) **Very complex phenomena** can be produced by the **interaction of simple factors**, but it is not always possible to predict at any one time how these phenomena will interact.

Chaos theory is being applied to a number of different disciplines, including stock market prices, and annual population patterns. It is better at interpreting past data than predicting the future.

1.6.3 Problems of macro forecasting

Given the difficulties of forecasting relatively discrete and simple matters such as ice cream consumption or traffic flows, it is surely much harder to forecast, over any period of time, wider social trends; that is, the development of the macro-environment. The reasons are similar, however.

- A **trend** might be **extrapolated beyond** the **range** where it is appropriate.
- Forecasters **underestimate** the **complexity** of the system they are modelling.
- Very minor events can have **serious long-term consequences**. Nobody at IBM predicted that the personal computer would eventually threaten the mainframe business.
- Some modellers may assume that a **possible** outcome of a system is a **certain** outcome.
- **Action taken** as a result of a forecast can **increase** the **likelihood** of an event happening. During the Cold War, both sides assumed the *other* was belligerent, and that any conflict would result in the worst possible outcome, and they planned for it accordingly.
- Forecasters may be **politically motivated** or wish to promote certain causes.

Exam tip

> The examiner has focused on forecasting in recent years, as a weak area for candidates. In December, you had to recommend a technique for forecasting the supply and demand for water in five years' time. You also had to comment on forecasting accuracy (the problem with extrapolating trends). In June 2006, you had to explain three techniques that could be used to predict environmental change.

1.7 Scenarios and forecasts compared

The table below summarises the main differences between scenarios and forecasts.

	Scenarios	Forecasts
Nature	Possibility	Prediction
Consists of	List of qualitative factors	Quantified most likely outcome based on certain assumptions
Limitations	Individual scenarios are not a complete view of all that might happen	Assumptions made may be incorrect/too strong & may take insufficient notice of uncertainties
Use in decision-making	Information to help decision between various courses of action	Indicator of likely success of particular course of action

Scenarios are meant to help management decision-making but judgement in interpreting the scenarios will still be required. Forecasts by contrast are generally designed to indicate what the decision should be.

2 Marketing audits

FAST FORWARD

> **Marketing audits** should be conducted at least once a year, and should review thoroughly an organisation's micro and macro environments.

PART D ENVIRONMENTAL INFORMATION SYSTEMS

Key concept

> 'A **marketing audit** is a comprehensive, systematic, independent and periodic examination of a company's – or business unit's – marketing environment, objectives, strategies and activities with a view of determining problem areas and opportunities and recommending a plan of action to improve the company's marketing performance.'
>
> *(Kotler, Gregor and Rodgers, 1977)*

A marketing audit does not exist in the compulsory formal sense that an external financial audit does. For proper strategic control, however, a marketing audit should have the following features.

(a) It should be conducted **regularly**, for example once a year.

(b) It should take a **comprehensive** look at every aspect of every market and ingredient in the marketing mix. It should not be restricted to areas of apparent ineffectiveness (for example, an unprofitable product, a troublesome distribution channel, low efficiency on direct selling).

(c) It should be carried out according to a set of predetermined, specified procedures; that is, it should be **systematic**.

2.1 The audit procedure

A marketing environment audit should consider the following areas.

Micro-environment	
Suppliers	The availability of resources, selling policies.
Distribution	The main distribution channels and their efficiency levels and potential for growth.
Markets	Developments in major markets, market growth, and changes in turnover and profits. Performance of different market segments.
Customers	Customer views on price, product quality and service given by organisation and its competitors. Decision processes of different types of customer.
Competitors	Objectives and strategies, market share, and strengths and weaknesses. Developments in future competition (see also Chapter 7, section 6).
Stakeholders/publics	The groups that are of particular importance, and how they have been dealt with.

Macro-environment	
Political/legal	Impact of new laws. Other developments in central and local government affecting laws and regulations in key areas, for example advertising, competition and price control.
Economic	Impact of current economic trends, particularly affecting factors influencing demand, and organisation's response.
Social/cultural	Impact of current demographic changes and action taken in response to these. Current public attitudes towards business/industry. Changes in values and lifestyle of consumers.
Technology	Current changes in technology, and whether or not organisation is at forefront of technological changes. Impact of changes, including decreases in production costs or development of substitute goods.

A marketing environment audit should be linked in with other aspects of a marketing audit.

(a) **Marketing strategy audit**

What are the organisation's **marketing objectives** and how do they relate to overall objectives? Are they reasonable?

Are enough (or too many) **resources** being committed to marketing to enable the objectives to be achieved? Is the division of costs between products, areas etc satisfactory?

(b) **Marketing systems**

What are the procedures for formulating marketing plans and management control of these plans? Are they satisfactory?

(c) **Marketing organisation audit**

Does the organisation have the structural capability to implement the plan?

(d) **Marketing functions**

A review of the effectiveness of each element of the mix (eg advertising and sales promotion activities) should be carried out.

```
                         REVIEW
        ┌──────────────────┼──────────────────┐
  Sales and price levels  Products       Distribution system
  Supply and demand       Each product   New channels
  Customer attitude       Product mix    New delivery arrangements
  Price reductions
```

(e) **Marketing productivity**

How profitable and cost effective is the marketing programme?

3 Using SWOT analysis

FAST FORWARD

> **SWOT analysis**, analysing strengths and weaknesses, opportunities and threats, enables an organisation to analyse its internal capabilities and marketing environment.

One of the most useful tools for sorting and analysing information is a SWOT analysis.

Key concept

> SWOT stands for **strengths, weaknesses, opportunities** and **threats**.

SWOT analysis is a management tool which can be used in a wide variety of situations. Its value is as a technique to help you sort information and it does not, in itself, provide ready made answers.

(a) **Strengths and weaknesses**

Strengths and weaknesses analysis involves looking at the particular strengths and weaknesses of the organisation itself and its product/service range.

(b) **Opportunities and threats**

An analysis of opportunities and threats is concerned with profit-making opportunities in the business environment, and with identifiable threats, for example falling demand, new competition, government legislation etc.

PART D ENVIRONMENTAL INFORMATION SYSTEMS

This simple technique provides a method of organising information in identifying possible strategic direction. The basic principle is that an organisation or its environment can be described in terms of features, each described as either a strength, weakness, opportunity or threat.

Action Programme 1

Explain to someone who does not work in commerce what strengths, weaknesses, opportunities and threats are.

This information is presented as a matrix of strengths, weaknesses, opportunities and threats. Effective SWOT analysis does not simply require a categorisation of information, but also requires some evaluation of the **relative importance** of the various factors.

(a) **Significance to customers**

The most important features are those perceived as significant by consumers. Listing corporate features that internal personnel regard as strengths or weaknesses is of little relevance if they are not perceived as such by the business's consumers.

(b) **Independence of factors**

Threats and opportunities are conditions presented by the external environment and they should be independent of the business.

(c) **Production possibilities**

The organisation has also to take into account its production possibilities, its ability to exploit the opportunities indicated by the analysis, and the likely returns and the risks (such as the impact of competition) involved in the possible courses of action. Sophisticated analysis uses measures such as expected value.

Figure 16.2: SWOT diagram

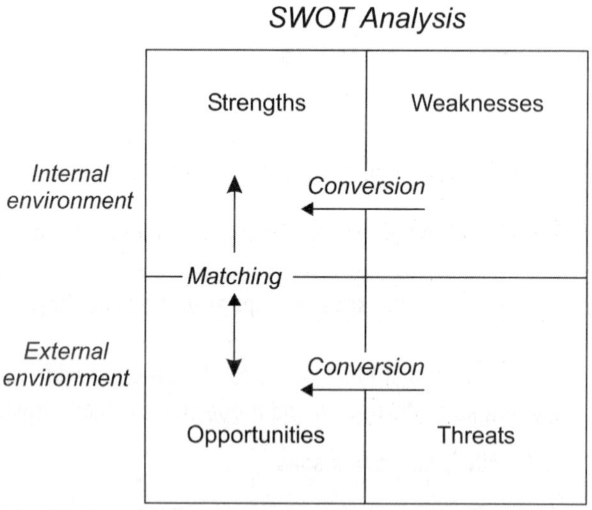

SWOT Analysis

	Strengths	Weaknesses
Internal environment		← Conversion
	— Matching —	
External environment		← Conversion
	Opportunities	Threats

SWOT analysis is often presented using a cruciform chart, as in Figure 16.2 above. This involves a tabular listing of the significant strengths, weaknesses, opportunities and threats to present the conclusions of the analysis. In the example below, the development of a single, simple potential strategy from the analysis is illustrated.

Strengths	Weaknesses
£10 million of capital available	Heavy reliance on a small number of customers
Production expertise and appropriate marketing skills	Limited product range, with no new products and expected market decline
	Small marketing organisation
Threats	**Opportunities**
Major competitor has already entered the new market	Government tax incentives for new investment
	Growing demand in a new market, although customers so far relatively small in number

Here, the company appears to face the danger of losing its existing markets and must diversify its products and markets. The new market opportunity exists to be exploited. Since the number of customers is currently few, the relatively small size of the existing marketing force would not be an immediate hindrance. A strategic plan could be developed to buy new equipment and to use existing production and marketing to enter the new market, with a view to rapid expansion.

In this example, a strategy emerges readily from our simplified cruciform chart. Reality is, of course, likely to be much less clear-cut. In practice, a combination of individual strategies and a complete analysis and evaluation of all the alternatives would be required.

3.1 Analysis of an organisation's internal capabilities

Strengths and **weaknesses analysis** is internal to the company and is intended to shape its approach to the external world. For instance, the identification of shortcomings in skills or resources could lead to a planned acquisition programme or staff recruitment and training. First, the strengths and weaknesses analysis involves looking at the findings of the position audit.

The appraisal should give particular attention to the following.

(a) **A study of past accounts and the use of ratios**

By looking at **trends**, or by comparing ratios (if possible) with those of other firms in a similar industry, analysts can identify strengths and weaknesses in major areas of the business. This is a key area of strengths and weaknesses analysis, and here, financial data and techniques of assessment provide hard data for decision making.

(b) **Product position and product-market mix**

(c) **Cash and financial structure**

If a company intends to expand or diversify, it will need cash or sufficient financial standing in order to acquire subsidiaries or for investing in new capacity.

(d) **Cost structure**

If a company operates with high fixed costs and relatively low variable costs, it might be in a relatively weak position with regards to production capacity. High volumes of production and sale might be required to break even. In contrast, a company with low fixed costs might be more flexible and adaptable so that it should be able to operate at a lower breakeven point.

(e) **Managerial ability**

While objective data should be used, the danger is that management may well overestimate their own ability or be unable to form a useful evaluation.

Typically, the analysis would use information from the following areas of company activity.

Marketing	Success rate of new product launches
	Advertising: evaluating advertising strategies and individual campaigns
	Market shares and sizes: is the organisation in a strong or weak position?
	Portfolio of business units: new, growth, mature and declining markets
	Sales force organisation and performance
	Service quality
	Customer care strategies: nature of markets targeted
Products	Sales by market, area, product groups, outlets etc
	Margins and contributions to profits from individual products
	Product quality
	Product portfolio: age and structure of markets
	Price elasticity of demand for products
Distribution	Delivery service standards – lead times for competitors and products
	Warehouse delivery fleet capacity
	Geographical availability of products
Research and development (R&D)	R & D projects in relation to marketing plans
	Expenditure on R & D relative to available assets
	Evaluation of R & D in new products/variations on existing products
	Appropriateness of R & D workload/schedules to competitor activity
Finance	Availability of short-term and long-term funds, cash flow
	Contribution of each product to cash flow
	Returns on investment from individual products
	Accounting ratios to identify areas of strength or weakness in performance
Plant and equipment and other facilities. Production	Age, value, production capacity and suitability of plant and equipment
	Valuation of all assets
Management and staff	Age profile, skills and attitudes
	State of industrial relations, morale and labour turnover
	Training and recruitment facilities
	Manpower utilisation
	Management team strengths and weakne
Business management: organisation	Organisation structure in relation to the organisation's needs
	Appropriateness of management style and philosophy
	Communication and information systems
Raw material and finished goods stocks	The sources and security of supply
	Number and description of items
	Turnover periods
	Storage capacity
	Obsolescence and deterioration
	Pilfering, wastage

When the analysis has been carried out, the following type of report might be produced.

Strengths

(a) Marketing, products and markets
   (i) Products A, B and C are market leaders
   (ii) Product D, new product launch, high profit potential
   (iii) Good brand images
   (iv) Good relations with suppliers and dealers
   (v) Good packaging and advertising appeal

(b) Production
   (i) New factory in North West, fully operational for next year
   (ii) Thorough quality inspection standards

(c) Finance
   (i) £0.5 million cash available from internal resources
   (ii) Further £2.0 million overdraft facility, so far unused

(d) Management and staff
   (i) High skills in marketing areas of packaging, sales promotion, advertising and sales generally
   (ii) Good labour relations, except at one plant which has low productivity

Weaknesses

(a) Marketing
   (i) Products X, Y and Z contribute no profit
   (ii) Products P, Q and R are declining and will lose profitability in three years
   (iii) Sales of product D are dependent upon a high level of sales of complementary products (for example, razor blades and razors)
   (iv) No new products, except for D, have been successfully launched in the last two years

(b) Research and development
   (i) No major new products have been derived from R & D for two years. Becoming too dependent on acquisition for additions to product range
   (ii) Little control over R & D budget

(c) Production
   (i) Plant at most factories has an average age of 8.7 years
   (ii) New developments could threaten ability to compete
   (iii) High level of spoiled goods on lines 3, 7, 9 at one location
   (iv) Low productivity on all lines at one plant

(d) Management and staff
   (i) Poor labour relations at plant with low productivity
   (ii) Senior executives approaching retirement with no clearly recognisable successor
   (iii) Success of the organisation too dependent on senior executive charisma

3.2 Analysis of an organisation's marketing environment

The internal appraisal highlights areas within the company which are strong and which might therefore be exploited more fully, and weaknesses where some 'defensive' planning might be required to protect the company from poor results. Following the position audit and the environmental analysis, external appraisal aims to identify profit-making **opportunities** which can be exploited using the company's strengths. Analysis would also anticipate environmental **threats** (a declining economy, competitors' actions, government legislation, industrial unrest etc) against which the company must protect itself.

This is the opportunities and threats part of SWOT analysis.

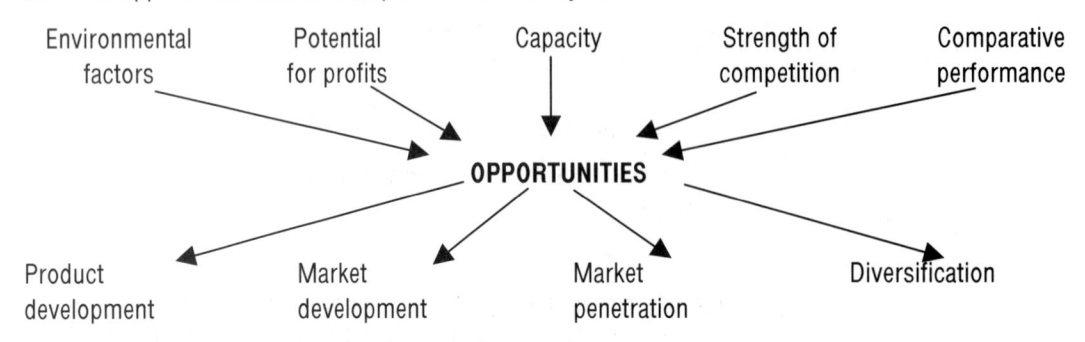

Environmental factors → Potential for profits → Capacity → Strength of competition → Comparative performance

OPPORTUNITIES

Product development ← Market development ← Market penetration ← Diversification

Threats involve the following issues.

- **Threats** to the **company** or its **business environment**
- **Competitors' position** in relation to these threats
- The company's **capacity to resist threats**, corrective action, contingency strategies

Action Programme 2

Can you think of examples of political, economic, social and technological factors which might offer opportunities or be a source of threats?

Exam tip

The Specimen Paper gave an indication of the level of detail you may face in questions on this area, asking about the threats and pressures posed to the travel industry by technological change and competitive uncertainty. This was repeated in June 2004, when the 40 mark scenario question asked candidates to produce an outline SWOT. This might have seemed like a huge task, but the marking scheme will generally give an idea of how much detail is expected. For example, 8 marks for a SWOT analysis would tend to indicate that at least two (but certainly no more than four) factors are expected under each of the four SWOT headings. Remember that strengths and weaknesses are 'internal'; threats and opportunities are 'external'.

ENVIRONMENT ANALYSIS REPORT

Opportunities

(a)	Political		
	(i)		Deregulation of the distribution market in the UK has allowed competitors to enter the marketplace, previously the domain of the state-owned monopoly supplier. This increases our range of potential customers in the UK and makes us less dependent on exports.
	(ii)		Removal of EU trade barriers has increased the size of the marketplace.
	(iii)		Expansion into Eastern Europe will enable access into new markets.
(b)	Economic		
	(i)		Relatively weak state of sterling is helping exports.
	(ii)		UK economy coming out of recession, so customer confidence ('feel-good factor') improving.
(c)	Social		
	(i)		We have an excellent 'green' image already and can capitalise on this. Our reliance on US markets has contributed to our being well ahead in this area.
	(ii)		We are well thought of as a 'local' employer through our attention to social responsibility issues.
(d)	Technological issues		
	(i)		Our new marketing database will allow good targeting of customers, especially as new companies set up following deregulation.
	(ii)		UK/US standards are being adopted in Asian markets, so we can compete there with existing products.
(e)	Competition		
	(i)		Our reputation as a key supplier of the former state-owned monopoly gives us a head start against new start-up competitors.

Threats

(a)	Political		
	(i)		Lack of agreement on standardisation across Europe means that French/German derived standard may be adopted in preference to ours (UK/US agreed).
	(ii)		'Black market' in certain Eastern European states needs to be overcome in some way, given our ethical stance.
	(iii)		Uncertainty in run up to UK general election will affect the development of the sector in the UK.
(b)	Economic		
	(i)		Any strengthening of sterling resulting from improvement of UK economic position will make exports less attractive on price alone.
	(ii)		Increased competition from suppliers based on Pacific Rim makes it difficult for us to compete there and in the US on price.

PART D ENVIRONMENTAL INFORMATION SYSTEMS

ENVIRONMENT ANALYSIS REPORT

Threats

(c) Social

    (i) Increased focus on health and safety from EU is increasing cost of compliance and related overheads.

    (ii) Cost of maintaining 'green image', important in UK and US, will damage our potential in Eastern Europe where some competitors (and customers) are unconcerned with such issues.

(d) Technological

    (i) Our main competitors control their distribution process more fully than we do in this area, as they have invested in new computer systems.

(e) Competition

    (i) The two competitors to the former state-owned monopoly which were awarded licences first have merged, thereby pooling their R&D resource. There are suggestions that they will develop or buy their own manufacturing operation rather than buy from companies like us.

Action Programme 3

For an organisation of your choice, identify from its annual accounts, press coverage and relevant websites the main opportunities and threats that it has faced over the last few years. Consider also whether the information suggests that the opportunities and threats are likely to change in the near future.

4 Impact analysis

FAST FORWARD

> **Impact analysis** means analysing the effect of a significant change on the industry, the industry's competitive forces and a firm's competitive strategy.

Key concept

> **Impact analysis** is used to analyse the effect upon a business of developments in its environment.

There are various types of impact analysis.

4.1 Competitor analysis

This represents a comparison of the impact of various environmental factors on a range of competitors within a market. Factors to be considered may span the broad range of macroeconomic influences covered in Part C of this book. The analysis aims to assess whether the broad impact in terms of sales, profits or market position will be positive or negative and the relative strength of the impact on each competitor.

4.2 Business impact analysis

This represents an analysis of the effect of a range of environmental factors on the major types of sales, the selling price and costs of a single business. These environmental factors may include developments in substitutes, changes in the age composition of the population and the consequences of the increased use of information technology.

4.3 Trend impact analysis

This aims to assess the impact up-to-date and the likely future impact of individual environmental factors such as changes in the prices of complementary goods.

4.4 Cross analysis

This involves the assessment of the effect of a change in one variable on other variables.

4.5 Refocusing

One aim of impact analysis is to cause managers to ask whether, when responding to environmental factors, they should aim to change fundamentally the way business is done or whether they should make more limited changes in operations or approaches to marketing.

Marketing at Work

The death of the book?

For many years, people have speculated that ICT would lead to the death of print media. For example, Encyclopaedia Britannica announced in 1998 that it was going to put its entire output on CD-ROM and no longer publish the huge multi-volumed encyclopaedia for which it is known. There are now on-line free and subscription based encyclopaedias (eg. wikipedia) with nno tangible 'product' changing hands at the point of sale at all. Meanwhile 'e-books' can be downloaded to PCs, PDAs and even I-Pods!

Yet companies such as Dorling Kindersley produce both books and digital media. For many leaning activities, the sequential multi-reference approach of a text is better.

BPP's i-Learn and i-Pass CD-ROMs for accountancy students are published as additional products, not as substitutes for Study Texts.

5 The product life cycle

FAST FORWARD

Business should be aware of what stage of the **product life cycle** its products have reached, and plan to improve its existing products or develop new ones as appropriate.

Many firms make a number of different products or services. Each product or service has its own financial, marketing and risk characteristics. The combination of products or services influences the attractiveness and profitability of the firm. The profitability and sales of a product can be expected to change over time. This can be shown as a product life cycle: Figure 16.3.

Key concept

The **product life cycle** recognises distinct stages in a product's sales history.

5.1 Stages of a typical product lifecycle

Figure 16.3: Product lifecycle

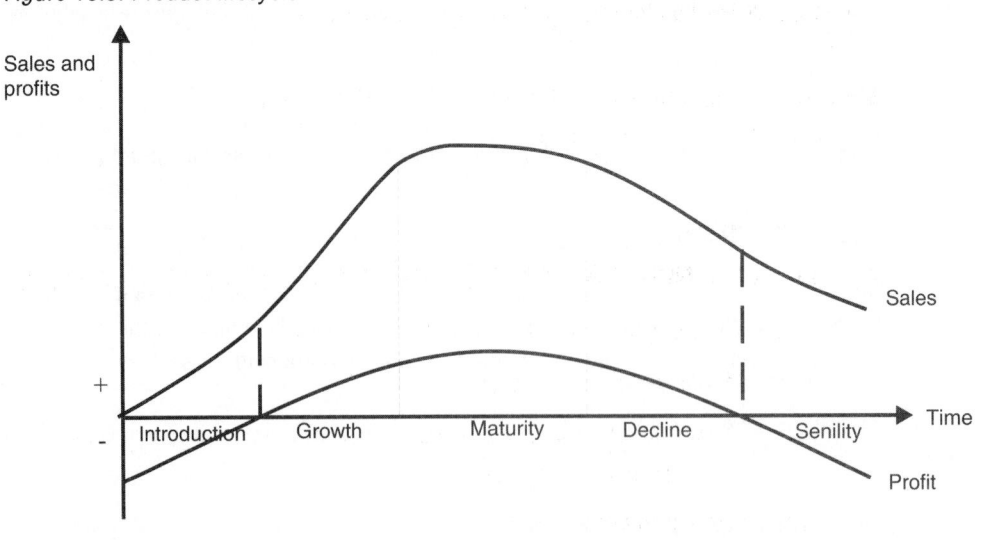

Stage 1: Introduction

(a) A new product takes time to find acceptance by would-be purchasers and there is a slow growth in sales. Unit costs are high because of low output and expensive sales promotion.

(b) There may be early teething troubles with production technology.

(c) The product for the time being is a loss-maker.

Stage 2: Growth

(a) If the new product gains market acceptance, sales will eventually rise more sharply and the product will start to make profits.

(b) Competitors are attracted. As sales and production rise, unit costs fall.

Stage 3: Maturity

The rate of sales growth slows down and the product reaches a period of maturity which is probably the longest period of a successful product's life. Most products on the market will be at the mature stage of their life. Profits are good.

Stage 4: Decline and senility

Some products reach a stage of decline which may be slow or fast. Eventually, sales will begin to decline so that there is over-capacity of production in the industry. Severe competition occurs, profits fall and some producers leave the market. The remaining producers seek means of prolonging the product life by modifying it and searching for new market segments. Many producers are reluctant to leave the market, although some inevitably do because of falling profits.

Stage 5: Senility

Senility occurs when sales are so low that losses are made on the product.

Marketing at Work

GlaxoSmithKline has for many years produced **Zantac**, an anti-ulcer drug. Patents expire after a defined period.

The company had been anticipating this development for a while and has invested in new drugs to provide income when returns from Zantac fall.

5.2 The relevance of the product life cycle to marketing planning

In reviewing outputs, planners should take the following actions.

(a) **Review existing products**

   They should undertake a regular review of existing products, as a part of marketing management responsibilities.

(b) **Obtain information**

   Information should be obtained about the likely future of each product including analysis of past trends, the history of other products, market research and an analysis of competitors. The future of each product should be estimated in terms of both sales revenue and profits.

(c) **Discuss estimates**

   Estimates of future life and profitability should be discussed with any experts available to give advice, for example research and development staff about product life, management accountants about costs and marketing staff about prices and demand.

Once the assessments have been made, appropriate **marketing mix decisions** can be made. The choices are:

(a) **Continue** selling the product, with no foreseeable intention of stopping production

(b) **Initiate action to prolong a product's life**, perhaps by advertising more, by trying to cut costs or raise prices, by improving distribution, or packaging or sales promotion

(c) **Plan to stop producing** the product and either to replace it with new ones in the same line or to diversify into new product-market areas

5.3 Difficulties of the product life cycle concept

(a) **Recognition**

   How can managers recognise where a product stands in its life cycle?

(b) **Not always true**

   The traditional S-shaped curve of a product life cycle does not always occur in practice. Some products have no maturity phase, and go straight from growth to decline. Some never decline if they are marketed competitively (eg certain brands of breakfast cereals). Research has indicated that the model is most likely to be relevant for products of mass consumer demand.

(c) **Changeable**

   Strategic decisions can change or extend a product's life cycle.

(d) **Competition varies in different industries**

   The financial markets are an example of markets where there is a tendency for competitors to copy the leader very quickly, so that competition has built up well *ahead* of demand.

PART D ENVIRONMENTAL INFORMATION SYSTEMS

Chapter Roundup

- There are various **forecasting techniques** organisations can use.
- **Scenario building**, looking at an internally consistent view of the future, is a particularly useful technique and can be viewed at the **industry**
- or **macro** level.
- **Marketing audits** should be conducted at least once a year, and should review thoroughly an organisation's micro and macro environments.
- **SWOT analysis**, analysing strengths and weaknesses, opportunities and threats, enables an organisation to analyse its internal capabilities and marketing environment.
- **Impact analysis** means analysing the effect of a significant change on the industry, the industry's competitive forces and a firm's competitive strategy.
- Business should be aware of what stage of the **product life cycle** its products have reached, and plan to improve its existing products or develop new ones as appropriate.

Quick Quiz

1   *Fill in the blank*

    .... is the process of identifying alternative futures which indicate future developments of markets, products and technology.

2   Give the main steps involved in industry scenario building by completing the boxes.

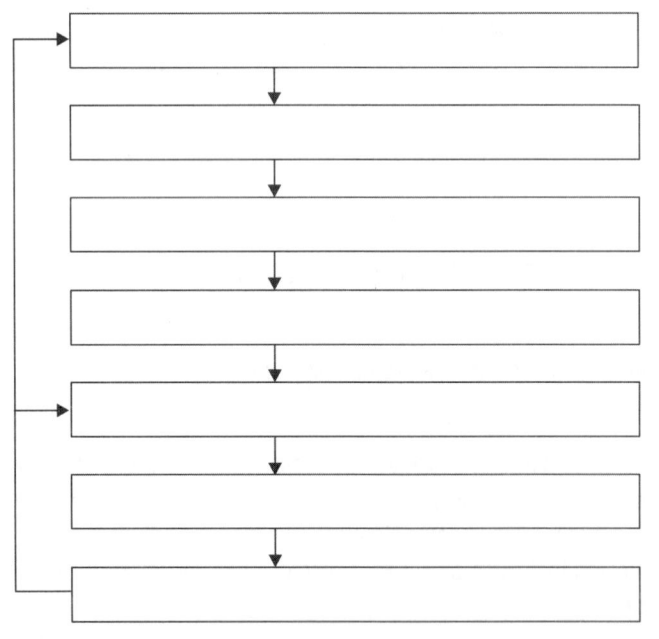

3   Which of the following is likely to be the least satisfactory method of choosing scenarios as a basis for strategy decisions?

    A   Influence the future
    B   Hope for the best
    C   Hedge
    D   Play wait and see

322

4   The Delphi method involves the collation of views of experts to obtain a consensus.

    True ☐
    False ☐

5   Give four examples of problems with macro forecasting.

6   *Fill in the blanks*

    A marketing audit is a

    - ……………………………………
    - ……………………………………
    - ……………………………………
    - ……………………………………

    examination of a company's marketing environment.

7   What is the difference between strengths and weaknesses on the one hand, and opportunities and threats on the other hand?

8   Which of the following is not a stage in the product life cycle?

    A   Introduction
    B   Growth
    C   Consolidation
    D   Maturity
    E   Decline
    F   Senility

Answers to Quick Quiz

1   Scenario building

2

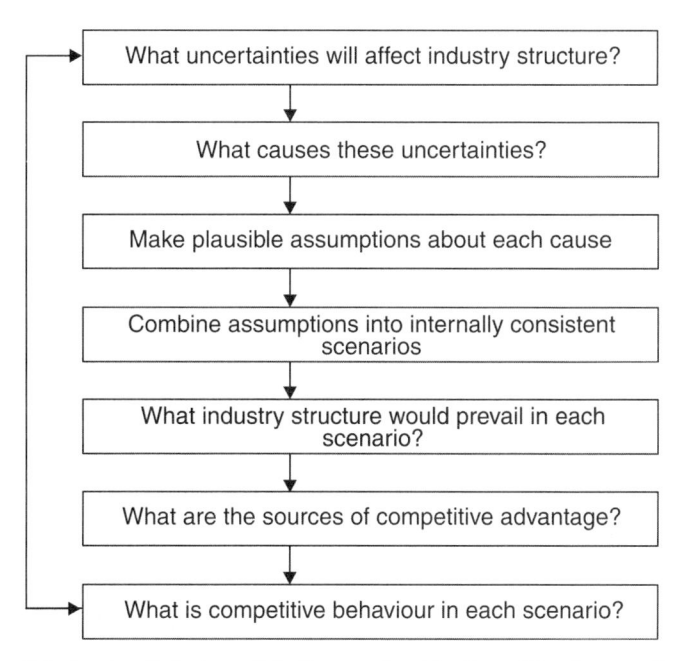

```
┌─→ What uncertainties will affect industry structure?
│         ↓
│   What causes these uncertainties?
│         ↓
│   Make plausible assumptions about each cause
│         ↓
│   Combine assumptions into internally consistent scenarios
│         ↓
│   What industry structure would prevail in each scenario?
│         ↓
│   What are the sources of competitive advantage?
│         ↓
└──  What is competitive behaviour in each scenario?
```

3   B is least satisfactory. It is the most subjective of the four methods, relating more to what the firm would like to happen, rather than what will happen.

PART D ENVIRONMENTAL INFORMATION SYSTEMS

4 True

5 Any four of:
- Extrapolation of a trend beyond its appropriate range
- Over-simplification of the system modelled
- Minor events having long-term consequences
- Assumption that a possible event is a certain one
- Forecasts being self-fulfilling if action is taken
- Bias of forecasters

6
- Comprehensive
- Systematic
- Independent
- Periodic

7 Strengths and weaknesses refer to the organisation itself, opportunities and threats refer to the situation in the external environment.

8 C Consolidation

Action Programme Review

1 (a) A **strength** may be a particular skill or distinctive competence which the organisation possesses and which will aid it in achieving its stated objectives. Examples may include experience in specific types of markets or specific skills possessed by employees, or factors such as a firm's reputation for quality or customer service.

(b) A **weakness** is simply any aspect of the company which may hinder the achievement of specific objectives. This may be, for example, limited experience of certain markets/technologies, or the extent of financial resources available.

(c) An **opportunity** is simply any feature of the external environment which creates conditions which are advantageous to the firm in relation to a particular objective or set of objectives.

(d) A **threat** is any environmental development which will present problems and may hinder the achievement of organisational objectives. An opportunity to some firms may constitute a threat to others.

2 Opportunities and threats may arise in the following areas.

(a) **Political**: legislation involving, for example, pollution control or a ban on certain products would be a **threat** to various industries, but also an **opportunity** for selling, eg, lead-free petrol and suitable cars. Taxation incentives, rent-free factory buildings, or investment grants might be available for exploitation. Government policy may be to increase expenditure on housing, defence, schools and hospitals or roads and transport and this gives **opportunities** to private companies and the relevant government organisations alike. Political upheaval might damage market and investment prospects, especially overseas.

(b) **Economic**: unemployment, the level of wages and salaries, the expected total market behaviour for products, total customer demand, the growth and decline of industries and suppliers, general investment levels etc. At an international level, world production and the volume of international trade, demand, recessions, import controls, exchange rates.

(c) **Social**: social attitudes will have a significant effect on customer demand and employee attitudes. Social issues such as environmental pollution, women's roles, and the need to solve social problems offer **opportunities** for new products and services. Demographic change and population structure will provide continuing product **opportunities**. There are recognised opportunities for growth in the personal pensions market. Unemployment will strongly affect the total spending power of consumers. This has been a chronic and long-term **threat** in certain parts of the UK.

(d) **Technology**: new products appearing, or cheaper means of production or distribution will clearly have profound implications in these types of analysis.

3   Your own research.

> Now try Questions 28, 29 and 30 at the end of the Study Text

PART D ENVIRONMENTAL INFORMATION SYSTEMS

Question and Answer bank

QUESTION BANK

1 Organisations

(a) Using a representative example, prepare a slide presentation explaining the strengths and weaknesses of one of the following forms of organisation:

    (i) A voluntary sector organisation
    (ii) A private sector organisation   **(10 marks)**

(b) Explain the potential marketing advantages possessed by a small business compared to a public limited company.   **(10 marks)**

2 Types of organisation

Write brief notes on the advantages and disadvantages of the following.

(a) Partnerships   **(10 marks)**
(b) Limited companies   **(10 marks)**

3 Marketing

(a) Give a brief definition of marketing.   **(4 marks)**

(b) Explain the distinction between the marketing concept, the product-orientation concept and the sales-orientation concept.   **(16 marks)**

4 Mission statements

The managing director of TDM plc has recently returned from a conference entitled 'Strategic planning in the 21st century. Whilst at the conference, she attended a session on Corporate Mission Statements. She found the session very interesting but it was rather short. She now has some questions for you.

'What does corporate mission mean?'

'Where does our mission come from and what areas of corporate life should it cover?'

'Even if we were to develop one of these mission statements, what benefits would the company get from it?'

You are required to prepare a memorandum which answers the managing director's questions.

    (20 marks)

5 Challenges and change

You are to give a presentation to a group of marketing managers on the topic: 'Challenges and change in the marketing environment'.

Prepare notes for this presentation, paying particular regard to:

(a) The nature of change in the marketing environment
(b) An overview of four or five major challenges
(c) An outline of the specific marketing challenges posed by two of them

    (20 marks)

QUESTION BANK

6 Sectors

(a) Compare the main characteristics and objectives of public sector, private sector and voluntary sector organisations. **(10 marks)**

(b) In reference to the private sector, examine, using examples:

    (i) The drivers for change in that sector
    (ii) The role of the marketer in the change process **(10 marks)**

7 Turbulence

The marketing environment is often characterised by turbulence and uncertainty.

(a) Explain the term **environmental turbulence** in this context. **(4 marks)**

(b) Identify, with justification, **four** potential sources of turbulence in an industry of your own choice. **(12 marks)**

(c) What are the problems of using past trends to predict future behaviour? **(4 marks)**

8 Systems

(a) Explain what is meant by an open system. **(6 marks)**

(b) In the context of a business of your choice, define its micro environment and explain what distinguishes this from its wider environment. **(14 marks)**

9 Stakeholders

(a) Define the terms internal, connected and external stakeholders. **(6 marks)**
(b) Discuss how stakeholder analysis can affect organisational behaviour. **(14 marks)**

10 Pressure groups

You have been asked to give a talk covering the means by which consumer or environmental groups may seek to influence business decisions and the role which marketers can play in accommodating the genuine concerns of such groups.

Prepare slides to accompany your talk summarising the main points that you will cover. **(20 marks)**

11 Learning environment

The importance of a learning environment

If organisations are to survive, achieve profit and grow, their rate of learning has to be equal to, or greater than, the rate of change in their environment.

This requirement is straightforward to state, simple to agree with, but often difficult to effectively implement. Those who have recognised the importance of being 'continuous learning' organisations include Microsoft, Intel and GlaxoSmithKline.

Continuous learning requires systems to scan and monitor the external environment and then respond positively to the changes which are occurring. Benchmarking and competitor analysis should be undertaken to provide comparison with internal indices of achievement in key result areas, such as market standing and innovation.

The key of encouraging continuous learning is to encourage employees to behave as if they were not part of a traditional organisational hierarchy. The customer does not experience the organisation as a chain of command but as a one-to-one relationship with an individual employee. The quality, or otherwise, of this experience may largely determine whether the customer becomes a repeat buyer.

Customers have 'moments of truth' with all organisations. This may be when they call customer service for advice, or are met at reception or most critically when they complain. Customers will talk about the bad experiences to over a dozen others, so reinforcing the negative perceptions. Boards of Directors have no direct control over these 'moments of truth', of which there may be many each working day, and they should not seek to control day-to-day operations in an effort to do so.

Directors should be taking active steps to learn from their customers and focus on the effectiveness of their 'customer facing staff'. The former must be identified together with their needs, wants and perceptions of what constitutes value-for-money relative to the offerings of competitors. The latter either create or destroy the reputation of the business, irrespective of its mission, its social responsibilities, its promotional budget and its values.

(Drawn from ideas in *'The Fish Rots from its Head'*, Bob Garratt, Harper Collins, 1997)

(a) Select two of the following terms used in the article. Explain the meaning of each and briefly indicate their significance to the marketer.

    (i) Social responsibility
    (ii) Competitor analysis
    (iii) Key result areas
    (iv) Board of Directors **(2 × 5 marks each)**

(b) The article stresses the need for 'continuous learning' at a rate which exceeds the rate of change in the environment.

    (i) Prioritise the main types of environmental change you would recommend an organisation monitors in an industry or country of your choice. **(10 marks)**

    (ii) Giving examples, suggest sources and methods to help predict the environmental changes taking place. **(10 marks)**

(c) How would you organise and control day-to-day marketing operations to ensure that 'customer facing staff' produces positive rather than negative moments of truth for key stakeholders?

(10 marks)

12 Five forces

You have been asked to provide a summary report to your product managers on the subject of Michael Porter's five force structural analysis.

(a) Explain to them the relationship between the five forces and long-run profitability in the market concerned. **(14 marks)**

(b) Recommend one strategy that could help maintain profitability in the face of these five forces.

(6 marks)

13 Environmental influences

Various areas of the environment are said to influence policies of both business and non-business organisations. One classification identifies these environmental influences as being political/legal, economic, social/cultural and technological. Describe how they influence the policy-making of organisations. **(20 marks)**

14 Demography

'If demography has its way, Asian and other developing economies should continue growing for decades to come.' (Economist 13/9/97)

(a) Prepare a brief for a group of international marketers on the long-term importance of demography to the future growth of any economy. **(10 marks)**

(b) Outline other key factors that determine a country's real rate of economic growth. **(10 marks)**

15 Family life cycle

(a) What do you understand by the following terms?

　　(i)　Lifestyle
　　(ii)　Reference groups
　　(iii)　Family life cycle **(6 marks)**

(b) Comment on how lifestyle may vary over three stages of the family life cycle. **(9 marks)**

(c) Suggest two useful information sources to consult on this aspect of the environment. Comment on the content of one of these sources. **(5 marks)**

16 Business cycles

(a) With the aid of a diagram explain the concept of the business cycle. **(10 marks)**
(b) Draw up a table which shows the main features of each phase of the business cycle. **(10 marks)**

17 Worldwide policies

Economic policies around the world are converging on four basic realities:

(a) Emphasis on market mechanisms rather than the state
(b) Provision of a stable economic framework
(c) More outward looking trade
(d) Encouraging partnerships and stakeholder involvement

Draw on your knowledge of the marketing environment syllabus to discuss the nature and significance of **two** of the above realities to marketers. **(20 marks)**

18 Economics and legislation

You are to prepare a presentation for departmental colleagues in your organisation (or an organisation of your choice) relating to one of the following areas:

(a) The economic environment – objectives, policy, performance and future prospects
(b) The legislative environment – key developments affecting consumers and competition

(20 marks)

QUESTION BANK

19 Legal terms

Distinguish the meaning of the following pairs of legal terms and briefly state their importance to the marketer.

(a) Standards and statutes (10 marks)
(b) Product liability and trade descriptions (10 marks)

20 Levels of awareness

What effects are increasing levels of environmental awareness likely to have on the marketing activities of a food manufacturer? (20 marks)

21 Advances

(a) Identify two recent advances in technology and discuss the benefits they have brought to the consumer. (10 marks)

(b) How have recent developments in technology helped companies improve their marketing operations? (10 marks)

22 Impact

(a) What is the significance of technical change to the marketer? (8 marks)

(b) Comment on the impact of technical change on the natural environment and suggest what direction marketing activity must take if future growth is to become sustainable. (12 marks)

23 Globalisation

What is meant by globalisation in:

(a) Products? (4 marks)
(b) Organisation structure? (8 marks)
(c) Markets? (8 marks)

24 Elements

Discuss the impact of the following environmental elements on the marketing operations of a large retailer.

(a) Changing lifestyles of women (10 marks)
(b) Population begins to age rapidly (10 marks)

25 Working at home

'There are virtually no technical barriers, no legal barriers and no cost barriers to having people working at home – the only barriers are human ones.' (Financial Times Report)

Your Marketing Director has read the above quotation and wishes you to prepare a briefing paper for a working party that has been set up to consider the issue. This brief should address the following:

(a) The meaning of the statement
(b) How the human barriers may be overcome
(c) Any marketing opportunities arising
(d) The implications of also shopping from home

(20 marks)

26 Benefits of technology

You are advising the Board of a hotel and leisure organisation and you have responsibility for computer-based technology in the organisation. The Board wants to ensure that its information systems provide the best possible service for customers and that information which is generated enhances decision making in the organisation.

You are required to prepare a report on the benefits of information communication technology in this type of organisation.

(20 marks)

27 Information sources

You have been appointed to the newly created co-ordinating role of 'Marketing Information Officer' in a medium-sized organisation.

Produce a report with the following headings, illustrating how you would fulfil this role.

1. How to classify different information sources
2. The key features of an effective information system
3. Examples of sources used in the micro and macro environments
4. Two representative examples of the uses of such information
5. A short appendix on any ethical issues arising for the organisation

(20 marks)

28 Opportunities and abilities

(a) Discuss what is meant by the term marketing opportunities. **(12 marks)**

(b) Discuss the internal factors that an organisation should consider when deciding whether or not to pursue a marketing opportunity. **(8 marks)**

29 Forecasters

Your government has approached an independent group of economic forecasters to undertake a SWOT analysis of the national economy.

Prepare a short series of relevant slides to support the forthcoming presentation of this analysis.

(20 marks)

30 Major bank

As a marketing manager you are given responsibility for improving customer service levels in your branch of a major bank which is a provider of financial services to the public at large. In this context your manager has emphasised the importance of having good information systems.

Required

Prepare notes for a presentation to staff on the following points.

(a) The elements of a good marketing information system in this context **(8 marks)**
(b) The importance of good information systems in providing customer service **(12 marks)**

ANSWER BANK

1 Organisations

(a) The strengths and weaknesses of voluntary sector organisations will be illustrated here with reference to employment training schemes.

   (i) **Voluntary sector organisation**

   Strengths

   - There are **no shareholders** who would expect a short-term return on their investment.
   - There is less chance of **conflict** between social goals and profit goals.
   - Voluntary organisations may be **trusted** more by users than a comparable private sector organisation, for whom users may be suspicious of the company's profit motives.
   - There may be greater **dedication** from staff who share the voluntary organisation's vision.
   - 'Staff' may be prepared to give their services for **free**.

   Weaknesses

   - The absence of a profit motive may lead to **unfocused** management whose results are difficult to monitor.
   - There may be a reluctance to act in a **business-like way**, thereby resulting in poor services to users.
   - Users may **not** expect to **pay** for services provided, but overhead costs must still be covered.
   - Voluntary workers may be **less committed** to their job as they will not lose pay for poor performance.

   (ii) **Private sector organisation**

   Strengths

   - Profit objectives give a **focus** for management and can be easily monitored.
   - The need to earn profits focuses management's attention on **value creation**. Without satisfied users of its service, the company will not survive against competition.
   - Private companies have been effective at **improving customer service** in many sectors and this could be brought to bear on the employment training sector.
   - The discipline of an **employment contract** can maximise the performance of employees.

   Weaknesses

   - **Costs** may be **higher** as shareholders require an adequate return.
   - There may be conflict between the objectives of **shareholders** and the objectives of **users**.
   - **Social considerations** are less likely to be taken into account by a private company.
   - Many users may **mistrust** the **service** being provided by a private sector company.

ANSWER BANK

- People are **less likely** to **volunteer** their services for a private company, compared to a voluntary sector organisation.

(b) Small businesses have many potential marketing advantages over public limited companies. The following are particularly important advantages.

(i) **Overheads** costs may be lower as a result of having no headquarters staff overheads, among other costs. These cost savings can be passed on to customers, giving a big advantage in price sensitive markets. This effect is noticeable in the market for small building work.

(ii) Because there is less bureaucracy in a small company, it can **respond more quickly** to changes in the marketing environment. It can therefore exploit market niches before their larger competitors move in.

(iii) The relative lack of bureaucracy can also facilitate the development of **innovative products**, for which a larger company may have not had the courage to pursue.

(iv) Small business owners are generally **closer** to their customers and may have better knowledge of the marketing environment than decision makers in large organisations whose knowledge comes through lengthy research processes.

(v) Small businesses can often claim to offer a **personal service** where each customer is known by name. In some markets this can be a big advantage.

2 Types of organisation

(a) **The partnership**

A partnership exists when two or more people **carry on business together**, owning the business property jointly and sharing the profits in an agreed ratio (without the business being incorporated as a company). Each partner puts in capital, and usually also his own efforts into the business, and a partnership may employ a number of other individuals.

The **advantages** of a partnership are as follows.

(i) Individuals can combine their **skills** which might be the same or complementary and efforts in a joint enterprise.

(ii) Partners can combine their **capital** and so provide more finance for the business than each partner could do individually as a sole trader.

The **disadvantages** of a partnership are as follows.

(i) The success of the business depends on the partners being able to **work together** in agreement and with complete trust in each other.

(ii) Important decisions, needing agreement by all the partners, might be **slow** to reach.

(iii) Unless the partnership is an LLP (Limited Liability Partnership), partners are **personally liable** for the debts of the business to an unlimited extent, which can make being a partner as risky as being a sole trader.

(iv) Effective planning and control of the partnership often depend on **good organisation**.

(b) **Limited companies**

Companies are organisations incorporated under the Companies Acts. They have a **separate legal identity** from the persons who own it (shareholders) and with limited companies, the liability of shareholders for the debts of the business is limited to their investment in the share capital.

Companies may be **private** or **public**. Many private companies are managed by their proprietors (owner-directors).

The advantages of the company as a business organisation are as follows.

(i) The shareholders have **limited liability**, and so their risk is less than for sole traders or partners.

(ii) The ownership and management of companies can **alter frequently** without the company itself necessarily being affected.

    (1) Shareholders can sell their shares, and new shareholders can acquire shares.
    (2) Management can be changed.

(iii) Companies can **raise finance** by **issuing new shares**. Public companies have access to investment capital through the Stock Market.

(iv) To grow into a large business, an organisation must have **adequate sources of finance** and it is usually only the company or state-owned enterprise that has access to suitable sources.

The disadvantages of the company as a business organisation are as follows.

(i) The company is subject to the **regulations** of the Companies Act 1989 (public companies are also subject to the rules of the Stock Exchange).

(ii) Shareholders and managers (and other employees) might have **differing objectives**.

(iii) Management (the board of directors) is only **periodically accountable** to the owners.

(iv) The performance of the business is subject to **public scrutiny**, since the accounts of companies must be filed (albeit in the case of small companies in a modified form).

3 Marketing

(a) 'Marketing is the **management process** which identifies, anticipates and supplies **customer requirements** efficiently and profitably.' It covers not only selling activities, advertising and sales promotions, but also product design, production, production control, quality control, after-sales service and credit for customers. More succinctly, marketing can be seen as creating the environment in which selling will take place.

(b) (i) The marketing concept may be defined as a **management orientation** where customer needs are considered of paramount importance. Since technology, markets, the economy, social attitudes, fashions, and the law are all constantly changing, customer needs are likely to change too. The marketing concept assumes that changing needs must be identified, and products or services adapted and developed to satisfy them.

    (ii) A **product-orientated firm** is one that believes that if it can make a good quality product at a reasonable price, then customers will inevitably buy it with a minimum of marketing effort. The firm will probably concentrate on product developments and improvements, and production efficiencies to cut costs.

    If there is a **lack of competition** in the market, or a shortage of goods to meet a basic demand, then product orientation should be successful. However, if there is competition and over-supply of a product, demand must be stimulated, and a product-orientated firm will resort to the 'hard-sell' or 'product push' to 'convince' the customer.

    (iii) A **sales-orientated firm** is one that believes that in order to achieve cost efficiencies through large volumes of output, it must invest heavily in sales promotion. This implies that potential customers are by nature sales-resistant and have to be persuaded to buy, so that

ANSWER BANK

the task of the firm is to develop a strong sales department, with well-trained salespersons. The popular image of a used car salesman or a door-to-door salesman would suggest that sales orientation is unlikely to achieve any long-term satisfaction of customer needs.

Assessment

An implication of the marketing concept is that an organisation's management should continually be asking 'What business are we in?'

(i) With the **product concept** and **selling concept**, an organisation produces a good or service, and then expects to sell it. The nature of the organisation's business is determined by what it has chosen to produce, and there will be a reluctance to change over to producing something different.

(ii) With the **marketing concept**, an organisation commits itself to supplying what customers need. As those needs change, so too must the goods or services which are produced. An example is the Hollywood film industry's reassessment of what business it was in, from 'movies' to entertainment, so that it started to operate TV and video companies, working with TV, instead of competing with it.

The marketing concept should be applied by management because it is the most practical philosophy for achieving any organisation's objective. By applying the marketing concept to product design, for example, the company might hope to make more attractive products, and achieve sales growth.

4 Mission statements

To: Managing Director
From: Anne Accountant
Date: 29 February 200X

Subject: Mission Statements
Contents: Introduction
Mission statement and strategic planning
Originating a mission statement
The scope of mission statements
The benefits of mission statements

Introduction

A **mission** can be defined as a business's basic function in society. It is often visionary, open-ended and has no time limit for achievement. It is possible however to reach a more expanded definition of mission to include four elements.

(a) **Purpose**. Why does the company exist, or why do its managers and employees feel it exists?

   (i) To create wealth for shareholders, who take priority over all other stakeholders
   (ii) To satisfy the needs of all stakeholders (including employees, society at large, for example)
   (iii) To reach some higher goal and objective ('the advancement of society' and so forth)

(b) **Strategy**. This provides the commercial logic for the company, and so defines

   (i) The business the company is in
   (ii) The competence and competitive advantages by which it hopes to prosper

(c) **Policies and standards of behaviour**. Policies and strategy need to be converted into everyday performance. For example, a service industry that wished to be the best in its market must aim for standards of service, in all its operations, which are at least as good as those found in its competitors. In service businesses, this includes simple matters such as politeness to customers, speed at which phone calls are answered, and so forth.

(d) **Values**. These relate to the organisation's culture, and are the basic, perhaps unstated beliefs of the people who work in the organisation. For example, a firm's moral principles might mean not taking on an assignment if it believes the client will not benefit, even though this means lost revenue. An example of this can be found in the standards of professional ethics required of accountants.

A **mission statement** is a document embodying some of the matters noted above. A mission statement might be a short sentence, or a whole page. It is intentionally unquantified and vague, and is sometimes seen as a statement of the guiding priorities that govern a firm's behaviour. Mission statements are rarely changed, as otherwise they have less force, and become mere slogans.

(a) **Purpose**

  (i) The firm's purpose might be described in terms of more than just self interest. A pharmaceutical company might define its corporate mission as 'the well-being of humanity'.

  (ii) The firm's responsibility to its stakeholders should be set out.

(b) **Strategy**

  (i) The statement should identify the type of business the firm is engaged in.

  (ii) The statement should perhaps identify the strategy for competitive advantage the firm intends to pursue.

(c) **Values**

  (i) The statement should identify values that link with the firm's purpose.
  (ii) The values should reinforce the corporate strategy.

(d) **Behaviour standards**

  (i) Defined standards of behaviour can serve as benchmarks of performance.
  (ii) Individual employees should be able to apply these standards to their own behaviour.

(e) **Character**

  (i) The statement should reflect the organisation's actual behaviour and culture, or at least its aspirations for improved behaviour and culture.

  (ii) The statement should be easy to read.

Objectives, on the other hand, are the embodiment of a mission statement in a commercial context. They specify the meaning of a mission in a particular period, market, or situation.

Originating a mission statement

A mission statement originates at the **highest levels** of the organisation. It is possible that, given a mission statement is meant to inspire as well as direct, a process of consultation with employees should take place to determine what the mission statement should be, or to assess what would be laughed out of court. A company which declared its commitment to customer service in a mission statement, but whose practices for years had been quite the opposite, would have problems in persuading employees to take it seriously. The fact that the employees were consulted about the current ethos in a formal procedure would make the mission statement more effective. The mission statement would be introduced as part of an attempt to change the culture of the organisation.

The scope of mission statements

All areas of corporate life can be covered by a mission statement. This is because it is broadly based, and as a statement of an organisation's values and objectives, it should affect everyone in the organisation.

That means its scope is wide-ranging. If it did not affect everybody in each department, from managing director to clerk, then its power would be lessened, and its purpose poorly satisfied.

For example, if a company's mission highlights the provision of **good quality products and services**, then this does not only include the way in which products are made and services delivered, but the way in which commercial relationships are conducted. Given that a successful business requires, in the long term, good commercial relationships, 'quality' applies to these as well.

The benefits of mission statements

The benefits of mission statement are that they:

(a) **Describe** what the **company** is about

(b) Provide a **guiding philosophy** where there are doubts about the direction a company should take, or a decision an individual manager or employee should make

(c) **Display** the **area** in which the company is operating

(d) **Enable** the **communication** of a common culture throughout the whole organisation

(e) **Stimulate debate** as to how the mission can be implemented

5 Challenges and change

> **Tutorial note**. Remember that you have been asked to make a presentation. This answer is based on car manufacturers.

(a) **Challenges and change in the marketing environment of car manufacturers**

　　(i)　The car market is not stable. It is constantly changing.

　　(ii)　The more successful car makers are those that have successfully responded to change in their marketing environment.

(b) **Main sources of change**

　　(i)　**Customer preferences**. There has been change in the features and benefits that buyers seek from a car. In most Western countries, an emphasis on speed and performance has been replaced by an emphasis on safety and economy.

　　(ii)　**Change in composition of buyers**. In most Western countries, there has been change in the make-up of new car buyers. In particular, more women are now buying new cars in their own right. There has also been an increase in the numbers of affluent young people buying new cars.

　　(iii)　**Change in social attitudes**. Cars are increasingly being seen as an anti-social element with increasing levels of congestion and air pollution.

　　(iv)　**Changes in government policy**. Partly in response to the above, cars have attracted increasing attention from politicians, with threats of increased taxation and reduced freedom to use cars as motorists would desire. The government's decision as to whether or not to join the Euro is also important.

　　(v)　**Changes in channels of distribution**. The number of independent distributors of cars in the UK is decreasing, giving more power to the newer larger dealer organisations. At the same time, new forms of online competition have emerged to challenge established dealers' position in the market.

(c) **Outline of two of the most important challenges facing car manufacturers in the UK**

(i) **The development of the euro zone**. In 1999, most countries of the EU became part of a common currency zone, with the UK remaining outside. One aim of the development of the euro has been to harmonise prices of goods throughout the EU. The presumption is that if goods are priced in all countries in the same currency, variations between different countries will become more transparent and will eventually be reduced.

The development of transparent euro pricing poses a significant challenge for manufacturers who sell cars in the UK. Car prices in the UK are currently significantly higher than in most other EU countries, according to a number of sources. Transparency of prices would logically lead to **erosion** of the margins that car manufacturers are able to earn in the UK.

An immediate challenge to car manufacturers comes from importers who specialise in sourcing new cars from low price EU markets and passing some of the cost saving on to buyers in the UK. This undermines established car dealers and also undermines the brand position of a company.

(ii) **Threats to the UK system of tied car dealers**. In the UK, car dealers are generally tied to a manufacturer by an agreement which many would regard as quite restrictive. The car manufacturer can insist on independent dealers' showrooms being equipped to a certain specification. It can also insist that **no competing brands** are stocked, either of new cars or of replacement parts. Approved dealers may have to agree not to sell on new cars for distribution through non-approved dealers. This system has suited car manufactures well because it has allowed them considerable control over their product from the point that it leaves their factory to the point of purchase.

The challenge to car manufacturers comes from a review of the system of tied dealerships which will be initiated by the European Commission. The present system is allowed under a temporary dispensation. The challenge for car manufacturers is to show that the system continues to offer benefits to the public. These include comprehensive after-sales service, stocking a wide range of spare parts and higher levels of safety as recalls of defective cars can be made more easily.

If the dispensation is not extended, car manufacturers must face the challenge of not being able to restrict their cars to sale by approved dealers only. This would mean that any dealer could sell any other manufacturer's cars. It might also mean that supermarkets and other non-motor retailers would become more active in the sale of new cars.

6 Sectors

(a) **Public sector**

Characteristics. It is difficult to define public sector organisations as a whole because they embrace quasi-public sector organisations (eg non-departmental public bodies). Main characteristic is ownership by government; often bureaucratically run; high level of accountability.

Objectives. Typically set performance objectives (eg number of operations performed by a hospital), subject to a budgetary constraint. Profit objectives are less common.

Private sector

Characteristics. Wide range of business units, from sole trader to public limited company. Based on owners holding equity in the business and taking risks. Limited companies have separate legal identity from owner of the business.

ANSWER BANK

Objectives. Essentially motivated by profits, although growth objectives may also exist (possibly as a means towards achieving profit objective). There are also informal objectives held by managers.

Voluntary sector

Characteristics. A diverse range of organisations, many covered by the provisions of the Charities Act. Some organisations comprise groups of amateurs joining together for a cause. Others, eg Oxfam, are professionally managed. This group is funded largely by donations and some trading activities and government grants.

Objectives. Their main objective is to advance the cause which is the reason for their being. Profit objectives not important, except for some trading activities. Managers of larger voluntary sector organisations may develop their own informal objectives.

(b) (i) **Drivers for change in the private sector**

These are the main drivers for change in its broadest sense.

- **Political** – new legislation, eg on employment rights, requires companies to change their practices.
- **Economic** – periods of recession and prosperity drive a need for retrenchment and new product development.
- **Social** – changing social habits and demographics render some existing products less useful, while requiring new innovatory products (eg more ready prepared meals for busy households).
- **Technological** – new technologies can make established products redundant (eg typewriters). New technology, eg the internet, can become a norm in a sector, requiring all companies to change their working practices if they are to remain competitive.

(ii) **Role of the marketer in the change process**

These are the main roles:

- To collect information about environmental change and to analyse and disseminate this information through a marketing information system
- To facilitate internal change (eg working with HRM departments in training front-line staff to use new on-line services)
- To communicate change to customers so that they feel reassured and not alienated by new product, new distribution methods etc

7 Turbulence

(a) **Environmental turbulence** refers to a state where the environment is changing, often in an unpredictable way. The implication of turbulence is that the key defining characteristics of the environment (eg household incomes, technology, social trends) will be different next year compared to what they are today. The presence of turbulence makes forecasting difficult.

(b) **Four potential sources of turbulence in the UK car industry**

(i) **Change in legislation governing relationships with dealers.** In the UK, car manufacturers have benefited from a 'block exemption' which allows them to restrict the activities of their franchised dealers. With the end of this exemption, new forms of distribution are likely to emerge. There is a possibility of retailers such as Tesco entering the market to sell cars, potentially causing turbulence.

(ii) **High value of sterling**. This has created problems for UK manufacturers of cars as it makes their cars more expensive in overseas markets. Further turbulence is provided by the fact that a strong exchange rate makes imported cars cheaper.

(iii) **Recycling requirements**. An EU directive requires car manufacturers to take responsibility for disposal of their cars at the end of their life. This may create uncertainty in the costs involved, especially for smaller car manufacturers.

(iv) **Change in taxation on cars**. In 2002, new rules for taxing company cars came into force. This created turbulence by changing the pattern of demand for new cars. Fuel-inefficient cars suffered while sales of small, cleaner cars increased.

(c) **Past trends and future behaviour**

In some environments characterised by stability, past performance can be a very good guide to future behaviour. However, the number of industry sectors where this is true has shrunk. Increasing turbulence in environments implies that the environment tomorrow will be quite different to the environment as it exists today. It follows that past performance based on previous environmental conditions may have little bearing on performance under a new set of environmental conditions.

8 Systems

(a) A system can be defined as a series of **interdependent components**, where change in one component has an effect – direct or indirect – on other components. For example, a central heating system is one where a change in one element – temperature – activates a thermostat, which in turn activates a boiler until the system reaches its desired operating temperature. An **open system** is one where it is not possible to define all the elements of the system. The marketing environment is such a system, in which many indirect factors, eg changes in technology, consumers' attitudes and overseas competition, can affect the marketing activities of a company within this system.

The following report is prepared with specific reference to the car manufacturer Toyota.

(b) **Defining the micro environment**

An environment for any system can be defined as anything which is **external** to that system and therefore not a functioning part of it. Various levels of an organisation's environment can be defined in terms of their **proximity** to the system itself. The **micro-environment** of Rover can broadly be defined as comprising all those individuals and organisations whose activities can **directly impinge** on the company itself. By contrast, Toyota's **macro-environment** comprises **general forces** and pressures which may not affect the company immediately and directly, but may eventually do so.

The micro and macro environments can be contrasted with reference to the **competitive environment**. Other competitors and customers directly impinge on a company and therefore form part of its micro-environment. By contrast, proposed new fair trading legislation does not directly affect a company, but it can ultimately affect the relationships between a company and its customers. It therefore forms part of a company's macro-environment.

The micro-environment of Toyota includes the following elements.

(i) Customers, both current and potential
(ii) Suppliers, both current and potential
(iii) Pressure groups
(iv) Regulatory agencies
(v) Intermediaries (eg car dealers)

ANSWER BANK

9 Stakeholders

(a) All organisations have stakeholders: these are individuals and groups who are **affected** by or **affect** the **performance** of the organisation in which they have an interest. Typically they would include employees, managers, customers, suppliers, creditors, shareholders (if appropriate), pressure groups and society at large. The table below provides a useful method of classifying the different stakeholder groups.

Internal stakeholders	Connected stakeholders	External stakeholders
• Employees	• Customers	• Pressure groups
• Management	• Suppliers	• Government
	• Creditors	• The community
	• Shareholders	

Internal stakeholders are individuals **directly connected** with the organisation, since they are its employees. Their aims, objectives and activities are likely to have a major impact on how the organisation operates.

Connected stakeholders are individuals who have a **direct connection** with the **organisation's performance** whether as financial backers, customers, part-owners, suppliers or distributors and so on. Their position both affects and is affected by the decision taken by the internal stakeholders.

External stakeholders are generally groups, such as central and local authorities, pressure groups, professional associations and society at large, which operate largely at **arm's length** from the organisation but still often have a stake in its performance (for example, if it pollutes the atmosphere).

(b) **Variety of stakeholder interests**

Stakeholder analysis provides a useful approach to understanding organisational behaviour since it focuses attention not only on the **different individuals** and groups that interact with the organisation, but also on the **variety of interests** which these individuals and groups may pursue and which may have a direct bearing on the firm's performance.

Employees, for example, tend to be principally concerned with issues such as wage levels, working conditions, job security and personal development, whereas owners (eg shareholders) are more likely to stress the importance of a satisfactory return on their investment, the need for efficient management and management accountability. While at times the objectives of these two groups may be relatively consistent, at other times they are likely to conflict, and this will present an organisation's management with the dilemma of how to balance the conflicting interests.

The resolution of this problem is likely to be reflected in management decisions and would normally be conditioned by a variety of factors, including the relative bargaining strength of the parties involved and the structure of the relationships between them.

Stakeholder influence on management

Stakeholder influence on management – and hence on organisational decisions and behaviour – can operate at a variety of levels. At the **strategic level**, for instance, the firm's mission and objectives, and the strategies to achieve these, are likely to be constrained primarily by the interest of its **owners** (eg shareholders), as interpreted by the individuals chosen to manage its affairs (eg directors). But is also likely that the other stakeholders, most notably customers and creditors, will exercise an important influence.

Similarly, at both the **planning** and **operational levels**, a complex pattern of stakeholder influence is likely to be experienced, ranging from general requirements to operate within a particular legislative framework laid down by the government (eg on health and safety at work) to more specific influences emanating from customers requiring products of a particular quality in a particular place at a specific time.

Other factors

The attractiveness of the stakeholder approach to organisational analysis should not be allowed to mask the wide range of other factors which can help to explain organisational behaviour. In particular it is important to recognise the influence of a firm's **external environment** on the attitudes and activities of its managers. Factors as diverse as a change of government, technological development, economic recession and demographic change can all be influential in explaining why organisations behaved in particular ways at specific times. These factors are not necessarily linked to the activities of specific stakeholders. In short, the stakeholder approach can only provide a partial guide to understanding behaviour and should be used as one tool amongst many by the organisational analyst.

10 Pressure groups

Slide 1

Definition of pressure groups

Groupings of people who join together to try to:

(a) Influence activities and decisions of individuals, organisations or governments
(b) Represent interests of their members

Slide 2

Types of pressure groups

(a) Interest or protective groups, protecting interests of particular sections

Examples – trade unions, professional bodies

(b) Cause or issue groups promoting particular issues

Examples – environmental protection, animal rights or penal reform

Slide 3

Techniques used by pressure groups

(a) Direct lobbying of management to achieve or prevent particular course of action
(b) Pressuring government, eg to achieve changes in legislation
(c) Media campaigns to raise public awareness and gain support
(d) Direct appeals to public to get them to pressurise businesses
(e) Commissioning research to strengthen case for or against particular cause

Slide 4

Possible reactions of businesses

(a) Polite dismissal
(b) Negotiation and consultation
(c) Accommodation of the pressure group's point of view

ANSWER BANK

Slide 5

Role of marketing in accomodating pressure group

(a) Publicising their response both directly and via the media
(b) Communicating their decision both internally and externally
(c) Promoting benefits of their decision especially via advertising or public relations
(d) Instigating changes in product design and/or packaging
(e) Developing enhanced public image

Slide 6

Conclusion

Pressure group's activity may change buyer behaviour

∴ Short-term costs of responding < Long-term benefits

11 Learning environment

(a) (i) **Social responsibility**

Commercial organisations survive and succeed by making satisfactory levels of profits for their shareholders. Customers are crucial to bringing in revenue to a company, and hence allowing it to create profits. But in seeking revenue from customers, a company may find itself undertaking actions which are harmful to society in general. Its actions may meet with approval from customers in the short term (expressed by their willingness to buy) but be harmful to them in the longer term (eg cigarettes). **Social responsibility** is about marketers recognising the consequences of those of their activities that go beyond the immediate effects on their revenue generating customers.

Significance to the marketer

The first challenge for the marketer is to recognise the possible **harmful consequences** of their actions on society (eg increased pollution, safety issues, implications for social exclusion). Marketers must realise that if socially irresponsible action is not kept in check, **regulators** may limit or ban the offending marketing actions, making it difficult for them to serve their target customers. It must also be realised that many profitable customers may **refuse** to buy from companies that are perceived to be acting in an anti-social way. For example, some customers of Shell boycotted the company following its attempt to dump the Brent Spar oil platform at sea.

(ii) **Competitor analysis**

It is too easy for marketers to look inwardly at their organisations and become product-focused. Marketing-led organisations focus on their customers by gaining a thorough understanding of their **needs** and **buying behaviour**. An essential part of this involves identifying and understanding the **competitors** that enter a potential customer's choice set. A customer judges competitors on the basis of the organisation's **image**; the **features** of the products they offer; their ease of **availability**; **value for money** and the extent to which they satisfy their needs. Products may at first sight seem quite different to anything that a company offers, but in fact they could be competing to satisfy a similar level of basic need.

Significance to the marketer

Marketers must identify who their **main competitors** are, including potential new competitors, who may be able to satisfy customers' needs just as well as itself (eg supermarkets have become competitors for many banks' services). After identifying who the competitors are, a company should undertake a **comparative analysis** (or benchmarking) of its own products against the competitors. Various criteria should be used to assess the attractiveness of product of competitors in the eyes of potential buyers.

(iii) **Key result areas**

The key results for most commercial organisations is to earn a sufficiently high level of profits for its shareholders. However, profitability represents the cumulative effects of many marketing related activities and it is useful for managers to have guidance on **targets** and **actual performance** in each of these areas. Some key result areas will be financially based and feed directly through to profitability (eg sales levels, margin, acquisition cost per customer). However, there are many more indicators which do not have any immediate relationship to financial accounting, but may be crucial in maintaining a competitive and profitable position in the market place. These typically include customer **satisfaction levels**, **complaint levels** and comparative ratings by consumer panels.

Significance to the marketer

The marketer must gain a thorough understanding of the factors that lead to long-term **profitability**, even though these may not have an immediate financial impact. Routine measurement must be undertaken, both internally and in comparison to **competitors' performance** in these areas (eg Are competitors achieving higher levels of customer satisfaction?).

(iv) **Board of Directors**

Directors are appointed by shareholders to act as the **governing body** of a limited company. The Companies Acts have given company directors a number of rights and responsibilities that essentially require that they act within the law for the best interests of shareholders. One director would normally be appointed as Managing Director with additional rights and responsibilities. The Board of Directors is the ultimate source of authority within a company, although many decisions of a day-to-day nature may be delegated to a Chief Executive Officer, or other employees of the company. Major issues would normally require approval of the Board of Directors.

Significance to the marketer

Marketers must recognise the **authority** vested in the Board of Directors on behalf of shareholders. The board has responsibility for all functions within a company, although one member of the board may be given specific responsibility for marketing. Nevertheless, the Board of Directors would expect to be involved in major proposals from the marketing department which could significantly affect the nature of the company and its ability to comply with Companies Acts legislation.

(b) (i) This section is answered with respect to the UK car market. The following type of environmental change are listed in their order of priority.

(1) **Competitor analysis**. The company should understand the effects of new low-cost car manufacturers competing for traditional markets. Many Far Eastern brands, such as Lexus, have now grown in status.

(2) **Technological developments**. A company should remain abreast of new technologies and seek to incorporate them ahead of its main competitors (eg additional safety equipment).

(3) **Buyer's preferences**. The attributes sought in a new car change over time (eg there is now more emphasis on safety and less on speed). Companies should ensure that they monitor and respond to these changes.

ANSWER BANK

- (4) **European Monetary Union**. The single European currency may bring pressure to harmonise prices within Europe.
- (5) **Government regulation**. The company should understand and try and anticipate the UK and EU governments' attitudes towards potentially anti-competitive practices, such as discriminatory pricing and tied dealership networks.
- (6) **The economic environment**. Car buying is closely related to the economic cycle and the company should monitor and respond to changes in the level of economic activity. As the economy recovers, it should ensure that it has sufficient stocks of new cars.

It should be noted that the above priorities may change from time to time. For example, monitoring the attitudes of regulatory agencies has become a major issue but was of less significance (although still important) in earlier years.

(ii) The following sources of information and methods of environmental analysis relate to the most important types of environmental change facing a company in the UK car market.

- (1) **Competitor analysis**. Monthly reports are produced by the Society of Motor Manufacturers and Traders which show the market share of each manufacturer within the UK market. This will give an indication of current and recent trends, but needs to be supplemented with other sources of intelligence about what is likely to happen in the future. Regular scanning of the car trade press may give some indication of likely future competitor activities.
- (2) **Technological developments**. The most useful source of information about technological change may come through scanning the trade press, for cars and related engineering sectors. Attending major car shows will give some indication of recent developments. An examination of futuristic 'concept cars' may give clues to future developments.
- (3) **Buyers' preferences**. There are now many sources of information about buyers' preferences. 'Off-the-shelf' sources such as Mintel may contain information specific to car buying. A company can supplement this with its own specially commissioned research among car buyers, and by scanning consumer magazines such as 'Which?'.
- (4) **European Monetary Union**. The company should monitor the quality business press to gain an understanding of the impact of the euro within the existing euro area. This can be supplemented with information for the company's own contacts and sales agents throughout Europe.
- (5) **Government regulation**. Following the quality press will give some indication of the general direction of government thinking. For more precise feedback, the company could employ lobbyists to enter into a two-way dialogue with key government influences.
- (6) **The economic environment**. ONS statistics available on-line will give an indication of changes in the pattern of consumers' expenditure. More detailed information relevant to specific sectors is provided by organisations such as GfK, who also measure consumer confidence, an important indicator of future economic conditions.

(c) Evert Gummerson described all employees of an organisation as **'part-time marketers'**. This recognises the fact that no matter how hard a marketing department tries to undertake marketing activities, it is often front-line operations staff who can thwart their plans.

ANSWER BANK

These are some commonly used methods by which companies organise and control their day-to-day marketing operations to ensure favourable reactions from customers to the action of 'customer facing staff'.

(i) **Mission statement**. Make quite sure that all employees share a vision that is realistic and achievable.

(ii) **Recruitment**. Ensure that criteria used to recruit staff relate to customers' preferences rather than being a matter of administrative convenience. For example, an ability to smile may be more important than formal qualifications.

(iii) **Training**. Make sure staff have the necessary training for them to be able to perform their job well. Inadequate training soon becomes apparent in the eyes of customers. For example, restaurant waiting staff who are asked to deputise in a hotel reception without having had training in reception procedures may be unable to deliver an acceptable level of customer service.

(iv) **Monitoring and feedback**. Staff should be regularly monitored, not in a confrontational 'snooping' manner, but as part of a process of continual improvement. Results should be shared with employees. Good performance should be rewarded. Poor performance should be discussed with employees and, where necessary, appropriate training undertaken.

(v) **Customer expectations**. Finally, it should be noted that employees may be seen by customers to be failing because customers' expectations are too high. If a company is not able to provide training and resources for front-line staff to deliver a high quality of service, they should not raise expectations in advertising.

12 Five forces

(a) Michael Porter identified a five forces model which affects the intensity of competition within an industry. Their relationship to long-term profitability in the market concerned is discussed below.

(i) **The power of suppliers**

The power of suppliers is likely to be high where input materials are **scarce**, and/or there is **collusion** between suppliers to restrict supplies of a vital input. During the mid-1990s there was a world shortage of computer chips which led to the profits of computer manufacturers being closely dependent upon their ability to obtain this vital component of their product. Some companies are totally dependent upon one supplier, for example British train operating companies must rely on Network Rail for the provision of track facilities. In this case the impact on a firm's profitability is limited by **regulatory control** of the supplier. Even in the absence of regulatory controls, the impact of suppliers on long-term profitability is likely to be moderated by the emergence of **substitute** products and/or suppliers.

(ii) **The power of buyers**

Buyers can exercise considerable power over suppliers in markets where buyers are **large** in size and **small** in number relative to suppliers. The loss of sales to such key buyers can severely harm the long-term profitability of a supplier. In the UK grocery sector, it has been noted that four retail chains now control about three quarters of all grocery sales. It follows that a manufacturer of grocery products must normally ensure that their products are stocked by the big four retailers, if they are to have any chance of building sales volumes. Manufacturers have frequently accused retailers of having a 'take it or leave it' attitude to suppliers, where they will only buy on terms which give minimal profits to the supplier.

ANSWER BANK

(iii) **The threat of new entrants**

Markets are frequently transformed by the emergence of **new competitors** who challenge existing business practices. They may come from within the business sector, but are based in overseas markets and bring their expertise and **economies of scale** to challenge the existing companies (eg Aldi and Netto moving into the UK retail grocery sector). At other times, companies from a different industry sector can challenge existing companies with **lower costs** and a **more customer-friendly product** (eg retailers moving into banking in the UK during the late 1990s). In both cases, the threat to existing companies' profitability is likely to be more short-term than long-term. Over time, existing companies can respond to a challenge through cost cutting and/or product modification.

(iv) **The threat of substitute products**

The long-term profitability of many industries has been challenged by **substitute products**, eg typewriter manufacturers were challenged by the appearance of computers. Unless a company embraces the new technology which underlies the substitute product, the effects on long-term profitability could be catastrophic.

(v) **Intensity of rivalry**

Profitability is affected by the level of **competitive activity** between companies operating in a market. In some markets (eg estate agents in some towns) there may be a tacit acceptance of each other's position. At other times, much more aggressive competition through price cutting and promotion can be good for customers, but reduce the long-term profitability of all firms involved.

(b) A strategy of **differentiation** could help to maintain profitability in the face of these five forces, for the following reasons.

(i) A **differentiated product** gives a company a relatively unique product, possibly allowing it a price premium.

(ii) Customers may show great levels of **loyalty**, even when new competitors emerge.

(iii) If the product is aimed at small **niche markets**, it may be a less attractive target for new market entrants who seek the biggest market possible.

(iv) Through differentiation, a company can incorporate **new developments** in technology and stay one step ahead of its competitors.

To be effective, a differentiation strategy must be based on a **continuous assessment** of a firm's **strengths** and **weaknesses** relative to its **opportunities** and **threats**. **Changing customer tastes** must be monitored and **new products developed** where a company has a competitive opportunity. Only by continually adapting its differentiated product will a company achieve long-term profitability.

13 Environmental influences

(a) **Political/legal factors**

(i) Political factors can take the form of **direct legislation or controls**. An example is the Broadcasting Act which put up for auction the franchise for independent television companies. Other political activities are regulation and control (the desire by politicians to be seen to be 'doing something').

(ii) Other political factors include:

(1) Wars

(2) Alliances between states (eg 'tied' aid)

(3) Political parties' ideological preferences (eg in favour of privatisation)

(iii) The government can aid business by providing a more stable operating environment and by direct financial assistance. Examples of such assistance include the following.

(1) Setting or targeting appropriate interest and exchange rates

(2) Providing education and training relevant to business either directly through the state educational institutions or via grants to firms and local technical and educational councils

(3) Protection of intellectual and physical property through making the laws (eg patents, theft) and enforcing them

(4) Economic planning of key industrial areas, for example information technology

(5) Acting as a customer to the private sector, for example when purchasing from the aerospace and defence industries

(6) Giving incentives for capacity expansion, for example capital allowances and investment grants

(7) Giving support to emerging business, for example the Business Expansion Scheme

(8) Creating entry barriers by restricting the activities of foreign businesses in the country, or by imposing import tariffs

Conversely, the government can act as an **impediment** to business. Governments may be the source of instability and lead to costs, in addition to tax, being incurred on organisations. There is an argument that the commercial logic which drives competitors and markets can be learned by an adaptive organisation and hence allowed for. The government can be less easily anticipated. Examples of the government acting as an impediment to business include the following.

(1) **Creation of legal regulations** which are costly to comply with

(2) **Distortion of markets** by the use of indirect taxation and discretionary production licenses

(3) **Uncertainty and volatility** in financial markets occur when governments change their policies in response to political pressure

(4) **Imposition of restrictions** such as monopolies and mergers controls and equal opportunities legislation may limit business activities

(5) **Putting short-term political advantages** before long-term national benefit

(6) **Acting solely** on behalf of sectional interests

(b) **Economic factors**

This factor manifests itself through markets, customers, investors, suppliers, labour, competition, price levels and, indirectly, legislation and government policy.

(i) Markets are **continually changing**. Old markets can decline and new ones emerge. As organisations sell their products to markets, changes must influence the organisation's decisions about what products to sell and where to sell them.

(ii) The availability of capital and investors willing to put money into an organisation will influence the **spending decisions** of the organisation. An organisation will not raise money to invest if the profits from the investment are insufficient to pay sufficient interest or dividends on the money raised.

(iii) The **supply and cost of raw materials** or energy can influence an organisation. If raw materials are in scarce supply, it might be necessary to switch to a substitute material. If the raw material is a commodity with large fluctuations in price, it might be prudent to buy forward to remove uncertainties in a future buying price. High energy costs might persuade an organisation to close down factories.

(iv) The **availability of labour**, its skills and cost, are an aspect of the economic environment. An organisation may site its operations in areas where labour is either cheap or well-paid, skilled and productive.

(v) An organisation with **competitors** must always be aware of their activities, so as not to be out-manoeuvred in the market.

(vi) **Government legislation and policy** are clearly influential. Fiscal policies will determine rates of taxation and government grants, as well as government spending as a customer. Monetary policies will affect the cost of borrowing. Membership of the EU has influenced the choice of markets for many British companies, because of lower tariffs.

(vii) **Inflation** inevitably influences an organisation's decisions with respect to buying, rewarding labour and investors, setting prices and so on.

(c) **Social/cultural factors**

(i) **Health and safety of products** and their impact. The last twenty years have seen increased pressure against cigarette smoking in Europe and the United States. In consequence of this tobacco companies have been forced to diversify either away from tobacco into packaging and insurance or to find different markets for tobacco products.

(ii) **Careful handling** of the product. The nuclear industry has to handle waste carefully. The chemical industry has to avoid the risk of leakages.

(iii) **Pollution** of the environment. This can be audible, visual or toxic. Airlines must control noise of operations and fly aircraft that comply with noise levels, Oil refineries must be screened for view and emissions from chimneys and waste outlets controlled.

(iv) **Trade relations**.

(v) **Treatment of employees**.

(vi) **Avoidance of sharp practice**. Companies must behave acceptably towards customers, creditors and employees.

(vii) **Fashion changes**. In the West there is a strong lobby against the use of sealskins and other animal skins for fashion garments.

(viii) The **needs** and **expectations of customers** in relation to the organisation's products will influence the organisation. Customers may expect an organisation to offer cheap price goods or alternatively quality goods for a high price (for example Rolls Royce); they might expect certain standards of service from a nationalised industry. Organisations should try to fulfil their customers' expectations.

(d) **Technological factors**

(i) New technology might affect methods of **production** (the development of robots), **storage** (containerisation), **sales** and **distribution** (some years ago, the development of supertankers).

(ii) **Computerisation** has transformed information systems in organisations, the nature of office working, and the techniques available for management decision making.

ANSWER BANK

(iii) New technologies may alter an organisation's **requirements for staff** (numbers, education and skills). Already in Britain, the long-term decline in manual working seems apparent.

(iv) **New types of product** become available for selling to customers. Consumer products which have emerged in recent years are home computers, DVD recorders and digital watches.

(v) Technology also affects the **availability and price of energy**.

(vi) Various researchers (such as Woodward) have suggested that an **organisation's structure** is determined by the technology it uses.

(vii) Researchers at the Tavistock Institute (for example Trist) suggested that the behaviour of employees at work is influenced by their **technological surroundings**.

14 Demography

(a) **Briefing for ABC Ltd export department: The importance of demography to economic growth**

Demography is the study of populations in terms of their size and characteristics. Among the topics of interest to demographers are the age structure of a country, the geographic distribution of its population, the balance between males and females and the likely future size of the population and its characteristics.

A number of reasons can be identified why demographic factors can affect the future growth of an economy.

(i) Firstly, on the demand side, demographic change influences the **size of the market** that is available within a country. For example, demographers can predict changes in the proportions of the population that are dependent and those who have their own income. A country with a high proportion of elderly or young people is less likely to have a workforce which will generate consumer spending. The high proportion of young people in many less developed countries is one reason why these countries have less wealth: dependent children and adults consume wealth rather than create it.

(ii) Secondly, demographic trends have **supply side implications**. Countries grow by having a pool of highly trained and motivated labour to create wealth. The high levels of dependency referred to above also have the effect of reducing the number of people available to work.

Other factors that need to be taken into account in studying the link between demographics and economic growth include the following.

(i) The **ethnicity** of the population: many countries are notable for how different ethnic groups contribute to economic growth, for example it has often been commented that the Chinese community in Indonesia has been an important vehicle for economic growth in that country.

(ii) **Household structure**: different types of household structures can encourage or inhibit members from gaining educational qualifications and being free to gain employment outside the family unit.

(iii) **Regional distribution** of the population: there is evidence that countries with widely dispersed populations are in a weaker position to create wealth than countries with major metropolitan areas.

(b) In addition to demographic factors described above, the following factors contribute to real economic growth (that is, growth in the underlying value of a country's output, after allowing for inflation):

(i) **Government regulation of the economy**. There is argument about what role government should have in stimulating economic growth, with some free market theorists arguing for a

ANSWER BANK

'hands off' approach as the best means of stimulating growth through competition. However, governments are essential to **protect investors** against practices which could impede growth, for example governments protect patents and the rights of inward investors. Many governments have contributed to growth by supporting key industry sectors with start-up grants.

(ii) An adequate technological and business **infrastructure**. There is evidence that businesses have a number of infrastructure prerequisites if they are to survive and grow. These include efficient road and rail communications; telecommunications; an effective banking system and a well developed distribution system.

(iii) **Education**. Many studies have shown the impact of education on long-term growth. For countries to gain competitive advantage in new and growing markets, rather than being stuck with declining industries, they need to train people for **tomorrow's skills**. This has been seen to good effect in the 'tiger economies' of the Far East which based much of their growth in the 1990s on a workforce which had developed skills in electronics. The same is also true of Ireland.

(iv) **Availability of natural resources**. Countries have grown by exploiting their natural resources, which may be minerals (eg gold mining in South Africa); agricultural based (eg New Zealand) or sights and climate (eg Switzerland and the Canary Islands).

(v) **Entrepreneurship**. To secure growth, it is not sufficient to have in place all of the above. Entrepreneurs are necessary to bring together the resources and to create value in the eyes of customers. The success of many far eastern countries has been attributed to the presence of an entrepreneurial culture, which may be absent in many Eastern European countries.

15 Family life cycle

(a) (i) **Lifestyle** refers to the overall **pattern** of **behaviour** and attitudes held by an individual. This can be quite independent of such factors as income and occupation which have traditionally been used to categorise buyers.

There are many ways of classifying individuals' lifestyles, for example 'healthy', 'conformist', 'ostentatious' and 'adventurous'. They can be difficult to measure but stereotypical pictures of these people can help in targeting.

(ii) **Reference groups** are those individuals and groups referred to when going through the buying decision process. The **values** of the reference group influence an individual's evaluation of choices available. Reference groups can be direct/primary (eg the influence of colleagues at work or college) or they can be secondary and indirect (eg the influence which a pop star or football player can have on a purchase decision).

(iii) **Family life cycle** describes the stages that families go through in terms of the impact on expenditure. From single adult to married couple with no children; then with children; followed by no children again and finally a solitary survivor. The total disposable income of a family is likely to differ significantly between stages, as are product preferences. Of course, not all families go through this idealised cycle (for example divorce and remarriage can alter the traditional pattern).

(b) Variation in lifestyle between:

(i) Single adulthood
(ii) Young married couple with no children
(iii) Married couple with dependent children

(i) **Single adulthood**

For many people, this is a period of **high disposable income**, because although income may represent the low point of a career ladder, there are typically few financial commitments. With no family responsibilities, this group is able to indulge itself in activities of hedonistic value, for example attending pop concerts or eating out frequently. An individual may still be trying to establish their identity and may purchase aspirational branded products for this purpose. With no family responsibilities, lifestyle may be dominated by preoccupation with the needs of today rather than planning for the future.

(ii) **Young married couple with no children**

This again is a relatively prosperous period with two incomes and no costs associated with dependent children. Such individuals can often afford to indulge themselves with **luxury purchases**, such as overseas holidays and fashionable clothing. However, this group is more likely to have established its identity, and purchases for the purpose of enhancing an image may begin to decline. On the other hand, they may become more **future oriented**, for example by taking out mortgages and savings schemes.

(iii) **Married couple with dependent children**

At this stage, an individual's disposable income may fall as children **consume resources**. As well as money, children will consume resources of time. Less time and money will be available for pursuing other lifestyle activities. Caring for children, for example attending school functions and buying clothes for the children lead to a lifestyle which is less hedonistic and self-centred.

It should be noted that all three stages described above are stereotypical and that circumstances and resources can influence the transition from one stage to the next.

(c) **Social Trends** is an annual publication of the UK Office for National Statistics. It brings together information from a number of sources (eg registers of births, marriages and deaths; Department of Health statistics) to present a snapshot of the lifestyles of the UK population. The following contents are particularly useful for understanding lifestyles.

(i) The allocation of household financial budgets
(ii) The amount of time that members of households spend taking part in various activities
(iii) The composition of households
(iv) Per capita consumption of a range of goods and services
(v) Educational qualifications obtained
(vi) Timing and rate of marriage

16 Business cycles

(a) Levels of business activity vary over time. On some occasions businesses may face **boom** conditions with rapidly rising demand for the goods and services they produce. At other times the reverse may be the case, with demand falling and businesses experiencing difficult trading conditions. Such variations in demand and therefore output often occur in a **cyclical** fashion with growth in national output (ie national income) followed by a slow-down in growth which ultimately turns to a fall in national income before a recovery occurs once again. This cyclical pattern of economic activity is known as the **business cycle** or **trade cycle** and can be illustrated as in the diagram below.

ANSWER BANK

Figure 1: The business cycle

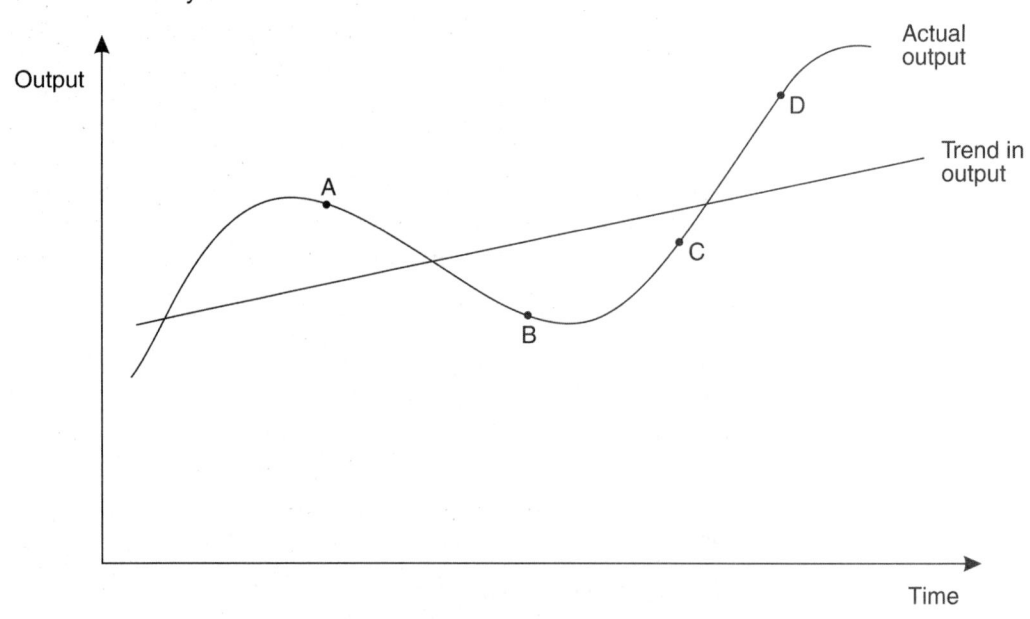

The diagram indicates that the typical business cycle has four main phases, known as **recession**, **depression**, **recovery** and **boom**. At point A, the economy is entering the **recession** phase, characterised by falling levels of demand, declining business confidence, a disinclination to invest in new projects, a reduction in stock levels and ultimately the shedding of labour (ie rising unemployment) and the closure of some firms.

Where no stimulus to demand exists, economic activity may decline even further culminating in a **depression** within the economy (point B) with its associated problems of high unemployment, low business confidence and low levels of consumer demand.

When depression occurs it may be relatively short-lived or could last for some time before confidence returns to the economy and demand starts to rise. At point C the economy enters the **recovery** phase with rising levels of output and income and (subsequently) increased employment. As businesses become more confident about future prospects, investment tends to increase and businesses are able to achieve high levels of profits as sales and prices recover.

A continuation in these trends can push the economy into the **boom** phase (D) with its high levels of spending, output, investment, business confidence and business profits, together with a tendency towards rising price levels (ie inflation) as consumption tends to outstrip the economy's capacity to meet the demand. Ultimately, the boom phase may give way to a recession and the cycle begins once again at higher levels of average output.

(b) A summary of the main features of the business cycle is shown in the table below.

Key variables	Cyclical phase			
	Recession	Depression	Recovery	Boom
Demand	Falling	Very low	Rising	Rising fast
Unemployment	Rising	High	Eventually falling	Falling
Investment	Falling	Very low	Recovering	High
Business confidence in future	Declining	Very low	Starting to recover	High
Profitability	Falling	Very low	Rising	High
Prices	Stabilising	Stable or falling	Stable or rising slowly	Rising

Key variables	Cyclical phase			
	Recession	Depression	Recovery	Boom
Capacity	Over-capacity starting to occur	Significant over-capacity	Rising use of idle capacity	Output capacity reached

The essential point to remember is that the different variables are inter-related. For example, falling levels of demand depress business confidence and cause a reduced level of investment, a reduction in the labour force and subsequently a decline in profitability which if unstoppable can move the economy into a depression. By the same token a recovery in demand tends to feed positively into business confidence, investment, profitability, employment and so on, and can culminate in boom conditions before the economy goes into the next phase of the cycle. It should also be noted that despite periodic slumps and booms, the long-term trend in output tends to be consistently upward (see Figure 1), indicating that national income (or output) normally rises over time in the long run. Accordingly, while successive falls in national income may mark the onset of a recession at a particular point in time, these levels of national income may still be higher than those measured in some recent previous periods, including periods characterised as booms.

17 Worldwide policies

Impact of recent economic policies on marketers

(a) **Emphasis on market mechanisms rather than the state**

This can be seen in many countries through such actions as:

(i) Deregulation of previously regulated markets

(ii) Privatisation of state owned organisations

(iii) Creation of many 'arms' length' agencies of government

(iv) Encouragement of individuals to rely on their own means, rather than those of the state (eg in respect of pensions)

These have been worldwide trends during the last two decade, although the pace of change has varied between countries. In the former Soviet Union, the pace of change has been much more dramatic than in the USA which has traditionally had a large private sector.

The changes represent **opportunities** and **challenges** for marketers. Companies which previously enjoyed protected markets have had to learn new disciplines of marketing, turning their attention away from production planning to meeting customers' needs.

Many private sector organisations have profited from shifts away from government domination of the company. Many public utility services, for example, are now provided by **profit seeking private organisations** which must understand and practice marketing.

Many new positions for marketers have been created within government organisations, as these are increasingly being set customer focused performance targets.

(b) **Provision of a stable economic framework**

The international economy, and the economies of individual countries have a habit of going through cycles of **prosperity** and **recession**. Growth which is too rapid may bring about inflation and high interest rates which eventually trigger a recession, which in turn will be self correcting. There have been many 'boom and bust' cycles in the past, but now it is suggested by some that we have mastered the art of national and economic management to avoid a repeat of this cycle. There is some evidence for this, for example the slowdown in the Asian economies during the late 1990s did not lead to the global recession which many people had expected to be a consequence. However, despite this, economic cycles continue to exist at national level, even though their impact may not be as severe as in the past.

A **stable economic framework** is of great significance to the marketer as it reduces the riskiness inherent in marketing planning. In industries where production lead times are great, the risk of a company having insufficient or excessive supply because of an inaccurate forecast about the marketing environment is reduced. Rather than spending a lot of time developing short-term opportunities, a stable economic environment allows a marketer to **plan long-term** and to develop products which will deliver **long-term value** to customers.

(c) **More outward looking trade**

The average share of nations' GDP which enters international trade increased during the 1990s. This came about as a result of the World Trade Organisation's efforts to **reduce international trade barriers** and countries' desires to exploit the benefits of comparative cost advantage. It has been recognised that countries with a relatively open trade policy are likely to be the most successful in terms of GDP per head.

There have been differences between countries in the rate at which they have become more outward looking on trade. Some countries, such as Singapore and Hong Kong have a long tradition of **open borders** and have therefore not had to look outwardly much more than they did previously. On the other hand, countries such as China have remained relatively inward looking.

More outward looking trade presents challenges and opportunities for marketers. The challenge is to **think globally**. With the rapid development of worldwide communications, especially the Internet, it is becoming easier for overseas suppliers to attack a firm's traditional domestic market. This improvement in communication also allows marketers to go on the offensive in overseas markets, which with the reduction in tariff barriers have become more attractive.

(d) **Encouraging partnerships and stakeholder involvement**

There is a growing trend towards co-operation rather than confrontation in business relationships. This is manifested in such ways as **efficient, co-operatively managed supply chains**, **joint problem solving** between buyer and seller, and greater **consultation** with interested stakeholder groups, such as employees, consumer groups and local communities. There have been many examples of where two co-operating companies have collectively achieved more than each of them would if they acted alone.

Some commentators have noted, however, that many partnerships are entered into quite opportunistically and many fail after a short time. Where partnerships become firmly rooted, they can also lead to allegations of **anti-competitive practices** by regulatory bodies.

For the marketer, consideration must be given to ways in which it can enter partnerships in order to gain a competitive advantage in its market place. In the airline sector, most airlines would lose some of their competitive advantage if they did not belong to a global partnership (eg the Star Alliance). On the other hand, many companies have succeeded in niche markets without the possible complications of global partnerships (eg many 'low-cost' airlines have succeeded without membership of a global alliance).

18 Economics and legislation

(a) **The economic environment**

The economic environment of Yahoo! comprises the micro– and macro-economic environments.

The **micro-economic environment** comprises the **customers, competitors, suppliers, intermediaries and government regulators** that the company encounters in its day-to-day activities. In this environment, the objective of the company is to be a successful competitor which makes an adequate return for its shareholders by delivering good value services to its customer.

The company's policy has been to develop a **sustainable competitive advantage**. It aims to achieve this through **product development**, a **reputation for reliability** and by **promoting these benefits** to consumers. The company has grown to a point where it can benefit from **economies of scale** relative to its competitors.

Performance to date has been below the initially high expectation of the company. The company grew rapidly on the back of the 'dot.com' boom of the late 1990s, and the general economic prosperity of that period. In this economic environment, the company succeeded in capturing large numbers of users, and, more importantly, large numbers of advertisers who pay to place banner adverts on the company's websites. When the dot.com bubble burst in 2000, the company was badly affected. Many investors lost confidence in the sector. Many of the company's advertisers either went out of business, or cut back the amount of spending on advertising with Yahoo! The fall of many dot.com companies also coincided with the slowdown in the global economy, resulting in less expenditure by consumers and businesses. Directly and indirectly this has had an effect on Yahoo!

In the longer term, Yahoo! has established a service which is superior in many ways to its competitors, many of whom have gone out of business. The economic environment of Yahoo! should improve when the **global economy recovers** and it finds itself facing fewer competitors.

(b) **The legislative environment**

Yahoo! finds itself operating in a very uncertain legal environment. In principle, an Internet Service Provider such as Yahoo! is **subject to** the **laws** of the countries that it operates in. To this extent, the legal environment impacts on it in a number of important ways.

(i) The company's dealings with its customers, intermediaries and employees are governed by the **law of contract**. Increasingly, statutory intervention has affected the company's relationships with these groups (eg the Consumer Protection Act and Unfair Contract Terms Act affects the company's dealings with private customers).

(ii) The company uses the law to **protect its trade mark** against imitation services.

(iii) The company must **comply with the UK Data Protection Act 1998**, just like any other business which records personal data about customers.

However, there are also many issues in the company's legal environment which do not apply to conventional companies, and which pose threats and opportunities for the company. Some of these are listed below.

(i) It is not always immediately clear where a **contract** is made using the Internet, and therefore which country's judicial system should apply.

(ii) The **law of libel** is very unclear. Some countries' legal systems have held an Internet Service Provider to be liable to libellous messages that they carried, regardless of whether they were responsible for designing the content of the message.

(iii) Issues are continuing to emerge about the **legality** of holding personal information, for example through the use of 'cookies'. Again, the question of which country's legal jurisdiction applies is raised.

(iv) There is increasing concern about the potential **anti-competitive** effects of large **multi-media organisations** which can restrict the availability of films and other resources which are considered to be an essential part of a nation's culture.

(v) The EU has implemented a proposal for an **'electronic signature'** which will provide a legally binding signature in place of a written signature which is traditionally required for some forms of documentation (eg house purchase).

19 Legal terms

(a) **Standards and statutes**

Standards act as guidelines by which goods and services companies operate. To achieve significance, the meaning of a standard must be widely known, so that buyers and sellers can refer to the standard as a common basis for negotiation. Sometimes, buyers may insist on purchases meeting a specified standard. Also, governments can insist that products sold in a particular market meet a specified standard. The standard itself could have been developed by a government agency or an independent agency. The British Standards Institute (BSI) is a widely used source of product standards.

Statutes, by contrast, become mandatory on all people affected. While a firm may have some discretion in deciding whether to adopt a standard, it may be compelled by statute, for example, in the use of ingredients for its food markets.

For the marketer, statutes constrain marketing decisions. Because they normally apply to all companies in a market, they cannot be used to gain competitive advantages. However, failing to meet statutory requirements can lead to prosecution of a firm and adverse publicity surrounding it. Firms often adopt standards voluntarily to gain a competitive advantage. For example, many buyers of some products are willing to pay premium prices for goods which meet BSI standards.

(b) **Product liability and trade descriptions**

Product liability refers to a company's **responsibility** to all users and others who come into contact with its products. The company is said to owe a **duty of care** to avoid injury. For example, a toy company which sells a dangerous toy owes a duty of care not only to people who buy its toys, but also to anybody who eventually uses them.

Trade description refers to the manner in which traders **describe goods** offered for sale. In the UK, legislation makes it an offence for a company to give inaccurate descriptions of its products, for example in relation to performance, price or quality.

For marketers, product liability requires new products to be comprehensively tested for the uses described by the company. If a product is not deemed to be safe to use in all situations, the company must make this quite clear in its publicity material.

The cost of failing in this respect can be heavy fines and compensation claims, as well as long-term harm to its image.

20 Levels of awareness

Increasing levels of environmental awareness are manifested in many ways. Environmental concerns receive increasing coverage in the media and an organisation that is revealed as pursuing environmentally harmful policies may suffer from a poor public image. **Pressure groups** may be formed to campaign against bad practices, often lobbying government for a change in legislation. Finally, the increasing awareness of individual consumers lead some segments of buyers to switch their purchases from an organisation that they see as bad to one that they see as good.

The effects of increasing levels of environmental awareness on a food manufacturer can be examined by looking at how they affect the main areas of marketing activity. These are listed below.

Market research

As a first step, the company should set up a research programme to understand better the environmental expectation of food purchasers. In particular, it should identify the following points.

(a) What **specific 'green' factors** do buyers look for when choosing a particular type of food? For example, how important is the fact that carrots have been grown without the use of insecticides?

(b) To what extent are the **environmental credentials** of the food supplier, as opposed to the credentials of the product, important in influencing consumer choice?

(c) What **segments of the population** are particularly conscious of environmental concerns and motivated to make purchases on this basis?

(d) What are the company's **competitors** doing to try and satisfy environmental concerns?

Product development

(a) Following thorough market research, product development should try and develop foods which **satisfy consumers' identified needs** (for example, developing cheeses which are free of artificial preservatives).

(b) It is important that products are **tested** to ensure that they provide a comparable level of performance in line with consumers' expectation. Although consumers may prefer environmentally friendly foods, they may be unhappy about accepting products that perform significantly worse (eg many buyers may not tolerate a preservative-free cheese which goes mouldy very quickly).

(c) There can be **publicity advantages** to firms who are first to develop new environmentally sensitive products. There may also be cost savings.

Pricing

Research should have established what, if any, **price premium** customers are willing to pay for an environmentally friendly product.

Promotion

(a) Promotion for the environmentally sensitive food must be carried out **sensitively** and avoid allegations that the company is merely 'cashing in' and exploiting environmental concerns.

(b) As well as promoting specific products, a company will find it important to **promote its image** as a caring company that is concerned for the environment.

Distribution

(a) A company that has sold its food through large volume supermarket chains may find these are unable or unwilling to handle products that have been reformulated in an environmentally friendly manner. Short shelf lives and variable product quality may be incompatible with the operations and quality standards of a major supermarket chain. A food manufacturer may therefore have to consider using **alternative, more specialised retailers**.

(b) Research should have shown where the segment of environmentally aware customers is most likely to shop. If they do not typically patronise its traditional outlets, it may have to seek **new outlets**. For example, many buyers of organic foods prefer to buy their food from specialised small retailers rather than supermarkets.

ANSWER BANK

21 Advances

(a) **Home banking** is a recent technological advance which allows bank customers to **communicate** with the bank's computer network **online** via a screen (for example, a home computer linked to a television monitor) or by telephone. This has brought a number of benefits to consumers.

The service is relatively flexible, allowing various facilities such as statement requests, balance and transaction enquiries and automated bill payments. New services, such as foreign currency orders, may be added. Obviously, cash withdrawals still generally need to be dealt with at branches or at automated teller machines (ATMs).

As home banking is generally based on computer programmed procedures, reliability is high compared with banking transactions involving bank staff members. Furthermore, the convenience of 24-hour operations, the time saved by not having to visit bank branches so often and reductions in the number of banking transactions which need to be dealt with by post are all benefits to the home banking user.

Consumer choice is preserved in that there remains the choice of carrying out transactions at bank branches as usual. Cost savings made through reductions in numbers of branch-based transactions should feed through to consumers in lower account charges.

Electronic facsimile transmission is another advance which has brought various benefits to consumers. The main users of fax machines are still businesses, but it is likely that the number of private individuals with fax machines will increase in the future, helped by the fact that it is not necessary to install a dedicated telephone line for the machine.

Consumers' choice of methods of transmitting messages is widened by the availability of fax machines in cases where the receiver of the message also has a fax machine. Where the sender or recipient has no machine, it would be possible to use a fax bureau although there is then a loss of convenience.

Fax machines allow printed messages to be transmitted at the speed of a telephone call. The cost compares favourably with the alternative of letter post if the message is relatively short. The speed is of particular advantage for messages to be sent overseas.

The main disadvantage for the consumer compared with letter post is the loss of quality resulting from the digital scanning of the document to be sent by facsimile. The loss in quality will be much lower where the message can be down-loaded directly from a computer file.

(b) Marketing involves the **identification, anticipation** and **supply** of customer requirements efficiently and profitably. Each of these elements of marketing has been aided by developments in technology in recent years.

Market research seeks to **identify customer requirements**. The production of market forecasts and sales forecasts has been made easier by computerisation of data collection and analysis methods. The computer spreadsheet (eg Excel) provides a very flexible tool for producing such forecasts.

Efficiency of communication with customers and potential customers through direct marketing methods has been greatly enhanced by telecommunications and word processor technology. More potential customers now have telephones and mailshots can be tailored to meet the anticipated requirements of particular customers.

The **efficient anticipation** and **supply** of customer requirements is aided by a number of developments. An example is the linking of sales terminals with inventory systems such as that used in Argos retail outlets, where terminals record the level of unsatisfied demand by counting the number of orders for goods which are out of stock. Computerised integration of sales processing and inventory systems enables sales analyses to be produced more accurately and more quickly for marketers' use, as well as improving financial control. Automation of warehouses is appropriate for some products, and this improves inventory control greatly.

In conclusion, although recent technological advances have been extremely rapid, there is undoubtedly some way to go in the process of harnessing these advances in a wider number of businesses to the benefit of marketing.

22 Impact

(a) Technical change affects the marketing of different products to differing extents. For example, technological change has had a relatively limited impact on the marketing of funeral services, but has had a dramatic effect on the marketing of telecommunications-related services.

Technical change is of significance to firms in the following ways.

(i) Technology allows **new products** to be developed and made available to the public. The market for cellular telephones is a product of technological innovation.

(ii) New methods of producing existing products can allow **costs** to be reduced and **new market opportunities** opened up. For example, aviation technology has reduced airlines' costs, thereby opening up new markets for long-haul travel.

(iii) **New promotional opportunities** are presented by technological developments. Satellite television and the Internet are examples of new media which are now available for firms to promote their products with.

(iv) Closely related to new promotional opportunities are **new distribution opportunities**. Powerful databases and inventory tracking systems have allowed companies to handle distribution more efficiently, and in many cases to be able to deal directly with customers rather than acting through intermediaries.

(v) Customers' **expectations of quality** are constantly increasing and new technology allows firms to provide goods and services which are of a higher and consistent standard of quality.

(b) Firm's marketing decisions can affect the natural environment in a number of ways.

(i) The **falling costs** of producing many goods has resulted in **increased demand** for them. For example, the cost of producing cars has fallen in real terms, on account of improvements in manufacturing efficiency. This has resulted in more cars being produced, thereby consuming **more natural resources**, such as iron and aluminium. Against this, technical change has also allowed products to be made with fewer natural resource requirements. In this way, cars are designed to be just as rigid as previously, but use less steel. Increasingly, technology is allowing components of cars to be recycled, or made of renewable materials.

(ii) During **consumption** of a product, further natural resources are consumed. For example, during the use of a dishwashing machine, electricity is used and waste chemicals discharged into water courses. Again, technical change has been a double-edged sword. While it has allowed for new products to be made available to the market (and thereby pose a threat to the natural environment), change has also allowed products to be much more friendly towards the environment. So dishwashers now consume less water and electricity than previously.

(iii) Once consumers have finished with a product, there is usually some **residual waste** (eg packaging materials, scrap cars, waste detergents). Disposal of this waste can pose a threat to the natural environment, for example through pollution of water courses. Technical change has on the one hand created problems for the natural environment (by stimulating sales of product in the first place). But it is also allowing **new solutions** for waste disposal. New techniques are being developed to recycle used products in a cost-effective way (for example, waste glass and metals are increasingly recycled).

(iv) **Distribution decisions** affect the natural environment. While a consistent and reliable supply chain may involve having a small number of suppliers and centralised warehouses, the implications of this can include greatly increased traffic movements and consequent pollution. Technology has again partly offset some of these problems, for example through the use of more fuel-efficient lorries.

In practice, it can be very difficult to assess the impact of technical change on the natural environment, because many innovations have both benefits and disadvantages. For example, the introduction of cars which use unleaded fuel may reduce the harmful effects of lead in the environment, but increase the problems of benzene which has been linked with cancer.

Growth for the nation as a whole, as well as for individual firms, may be unsustainable if natural resources become exhausted, and only obtainable at a very high price. In this context, marketers can take a number of steps to bring about sustainable growth for their company, as follows.

(i) By developing products which use **sustainable resources**, a company will not be faced with suddenly escalating input costs. In many cases the development of an environmentally friendly version of a product will not adversely affect its technical performance or costs, thereby not endangering its market performance. (For example, aerosols not containing CFCs perform comparably to those containing harmful CFCs).

(ii) Where **product performance** is **reduced**, firms should seek to **promote** the **benefits** of using a product made from sustainable resources. Many segments of markets may be happy to sacrifice performance in return for knowing that their purchases are not harming the natural environment.

(iii) Firms should **anticipate proposed legislation** to protect the environment and be ready to adopt new measures and gain a lead on competitors who only change to new product designs when forced to by legislation.

(iv) Where market growth appears to be unsustainable, firms can develop **alternative products** which are more sustainable. For example, the growth of private cars in cities may be unsustainable, so some car manufacturers have invested in urban public transport systems.

(v) The public at large is becoming increasingly critical of firms who do not pay due consideration to the natural environment. By adopting a more environmentally friendly approach to the way it does business, a firm can develop a **more favourable image** and avoid, in the extreme, consumer boycotts.

23 Globalisation

(a) A **global product** is one that is sold throughout the world. It is a standard product although it might be marketed in different ways in each country. Examples include:

(i) Oil
(ii) Foreign exchange
(iii) Aeroplane engines
(iv) Certain brands of soft drinks (eg Coca Cola)

(b) **Organisation structure**

Global or boundary-less corporations have come into being for the following reasons.

(i) Companies now produce and sell in a **wide variety of countries**.

(ii) To serve these various markets, a company can **invest** in **more than one country**.

(iii) Companies make decisions primarily with regard to their **global ambitions**, and do not take their legal nationality into account.

There is thus an increasing number of stateless corporations, whose activities transcend national boundaries, and whose personnel come from any country. However, it is debatable how global many of these organisations are.

(i) Most multinationals, other than those based in small nations, have **less than half** of their employees abroad.

(ii) Ownership and control of multinationals remain **restricted**. This is partly because of the way in which capital markets are structured.

(iii) **Top management** is rarely as multinational as the firm's activities.

(iv) National residence and status is important for **tax reasons**. Boundary-less corporations are not recognised as such by lawyers or tax officials.

(v) The bulk of a multinational's **research and development** is generally done in the home country, where strategic decisions are made.

(vi) Where capital is limited, 'global' companies stick to the **home market** rather than developing overseas ones.

(vii) Finally, profits from a global company must be **remitted** somewhere. Firms like Reuters are quoted on a number of stock exchanges worldwide, but they are exceptional.

(c) **Global markets**. It is sometimes asserted that the 'free world as a whole can be viewed as a global market'. In other words, goods can be made and sold anywhere in the world, and competition can exist between firms from any country. The growth of trade and the movement towards trade liberalisation should encourage this view.

However, the existence of global markets should not be taken for granted in terms of all products and services, or indeed in all territories.

(i) Some services are still subject to **managed trade** (eg some countries prohibit firms from other countries from selling insurance) and there are some services which by their very nature can never be exported (eg haircuts, visits to stately homes) from the home territory, although they can be provided to visitors.

(ii) There is unlikely ever to be a global market for **labour**, given the disparity in skills between different countries, and restrictions on immigration. Companies can best respond by relocating, but this is not always a viable commercial option.

The global market for some items is much more extensive than for others. The market for oil is truly global. Oil is produced in many countries and consumed everywhere.

24 Elements

(a) (i) **Impact of changing lifestyles of women on the marketing operations of a large retailer**

There is an increasing level of employment among women, especially full-time employment among career-oriented women.

Likely impact on a large retailer

Women are increasingly financially rich, but 'time-poor'. Retail formats are therefore increasingly emphasising convenience in the services they offer and the products they sell. In the grocery retail sector, this is manifested in extensive ranges of prepared foods and the

ANSWER BANK

resurgence of 'convenience' stores in town centres and at petrol stations. Home delivery and home shopping offers new opportunities.

(ii) **Delayed marriage**

Women are tending to delay marriage and to spend less time out of the labour market bringing up children.

Likely impact on a large retailer

Women are now increasingly buying goods and services which were previously considered a male preserve. As an example, the proportion of BMW cars sold to women has increased. Career women may represent important new or growing segments for many companies. The desire of many career women to return to work soon after childbirth can lead to opportunities for retailers offering child care related facilities, for example a crèche attached to a store.

(iii) **Changing role of women in the family**

As a result of the above changes, women's traditional subservient role at home has been challenged.

Likely impact on a large retailer

Change in family structures leads to changes in decision making for a wide range of goods and services. Purchases such as furniture, overseas holidays and groceries are increasingly likely to be based on a joint decision. Women are increasingly likely to have their role as buyer of groceries replaced by a man. For retailers, promotion, services offered and product ranges must reflect the preferences of all members of the decision making unit.

(iv) **Higher educational achievements of women**

More women are participating or have participated in higher education.

Likely impact on a large retailer

Retailing has traditionally relied on a pool of unskilled and poorly paid female labour. With rising expectations and abilities, their pool may dwindle, so retailers must consider operating systems which require fewer but better paid staff.

(b) **Impact of an ageing population on the marketing operations of a large retailer**

The ageing of the population in many Western countries is manifested in many ways.

(i) An increase in the proportion of the population **aged 65** and above
(ii) A particularly great increase in the number of **'very old'** people (aged 80+)
(iii) A fall in the proportion of the population which is **aged 16 and under**

Impacts on a large retailer

(i) **Product ranges** offered must reflect the changing structure of the population. A fashion retailer, for example, should devote more space to meeting the needs of the elderly, rather than the young population which is growing at a slower rate.

(ii) **Store design** should reflect the needs of the elderly, for example clear labelling for those who may be visually impaired. Elderly segments tend to prefer traditional values rather than fashionability for its own sake.

(iii) Elderly segments may prefer an emphasis on **personal service** provided by more mature employees, and home delivery services.

(iv) An increasing proportion of elderly people are retiring with **private pensions** which allow them to lead a comfortable lifestyle. Price may become less important than quality of service received.

(v) Retailers must avoid lumping all elderly people into one segment (and indeed, all people of any age group). The elderly includes **sub-groups** which are diverse in their income, mobility and attitudes and each should be targeted with appropriate product offers.

(vi) The falling relative number of children in the population, and the reduction in family size which this implies, will lead to parents demanding **higher quality goods** and **services** for their children, as rising real household incomes are distributed among fewer children.

(vii) Finally, the ageing of the population has implications for the **recruitment** of staff by retailers. The large pool of young people who are prepared to accept poorly paid jobs will diminish. Retailers should exploit the opportunities provided by the large elderly segment which many employers have found to offer a reliable, loyal and flexible source of labour.

25 Working at home

(a) The technology to enable home working has been developed considerably during the past two decades. **Telecommunications technology** has allowed information to be passed quickly and cheaply between workers regardless of their location. The likely future trend is for the cost of information transmission to fall and the reliability and capacity to increase. However, it should be noted that this statement applies primarily to workers whose main work processes revolve around knowledge management. Where tangible goods are involved in workers' activities, **barriers** to home working may still **remain**. The cost of transporting goods has, if anything, been increasing. The opportunities for outsourcing manufacturing production, for example, have not been as great as for the outsourcing of knowledge management. Even in the case of knowledge workers, problems in monitoring home workers' performance and developing motivation remain.

(b) Human barriers to home working focus on the potential difficulty of motivating teams of workers and supervising individual workers' performance. However technology has the potential to overcome some of these problems. Where tasks are straightforward and repetitive, workers can be monitored with simple **performance measures**. For a telephone operator working at home, the time taken to answer an incoming call can be routinely measured. A sample of calls can be recorded and the worker assessed for the quality of their interaction with a customer. **Mystery customers** may phone up employees and test the quality of service provided.

In the case of non-routine work, for example editing of technical manuals, performance can best be measured by the tangible **results** produced. In these circumstances it may be more appropriate to pay workers by results rather than per hour. However, this may not appear attractive to many people who see the certainty of a regular pay cheque.

The problem of **team working** remains a problem. There have been numerous attempts to create virtual communities using video conferencing facilities. However doubt remains about whether the quality of group interaction which emerges from this is of the same standard as face-to-face interaction.

(c) There are numerous marketing opportunities arising from an emphasis on home working. Where a company faces a highly variable pattern of demand, it may use a large pool of home workers as a standby resource to be brought on line at times of peak demand. This would be less expensive than retaining staff in a central office and would allow a higher quality of response to customers.

Staff who work at home may be **less stressed** than those who have to spend a long time commuting and make arrangements for child minders etc. This may be reflected in a higher standard of service received by customers.

Home working may **reduce** a company's **costs**, thereby allowing it to pass on lower prices to customers.

(d) Home workers who use information technology to work from home may also be expected to use the **same technology** to **shop** from home. They will probably be more familiar and confident with the technology than the general population. Because they are at home more than their office-based colleagues, they will have fewer problems accepting deliveries from Internet-based shopping companies. However, there is the opposite argument that home workers will seek variety in their lives and will be more likely than most to get out of their home. Shopping in High Street shops represents such variety.

26 Benefits of technology

REPORT

To: The Board
From: Anne Adviser
Date: 7 December 200X
Subject: The benefits of information communication technology

Introduction

The organisation now uses computers and communications technology to manage almost all of its activities. For example:

(a) Bookings for rooms or leisure activities can be made by customers over the telephone or at any of our hotels from any other hotel.

(b) Catering supplies are managed using a constantly updated central stock control system and electronic data interchange with our suppliers.

However, it is in the **retrieval of information** and **manipulation** of it for use that computers have had their most profound impact. Various types of application are commonly cited in support of this, notably decision support systems, executive information systems and expert systems. I shall take the first two as examples.

(a) **Decision support systems**

The term 'decision support system' (DSS) is usually taken to mean computer systems which are designed to produce information in such a way as to help managers to make better decisions. It is now often associated with information **at the touch of a button** at a manager's personal computer or workstation. DSS can describe a range of systems, from fairly simple information models based on spreadsheets to expert systems.

A decision support system **integrates** many of the functions supplied by information systems so that managers may use them more easily and on a wider range of both structured and unstructured problems. Examples of the types of decisions which they might support include a decision on whether to lease or buy company cars; an examination of options as to capital structuring and consequences of alternatives; and decisions on the introduction of a share option scheme.

(b) **Executive information systems**

An EIS is likely to have the following features.

(i) Provision of **summary-level data**, captured from the organisation's main systems (which might involve integrating the executive's desk top micro with the organisation's mainframe)

(ii) A facility which allows the executive to **drill-down** from higher levels of information to lower)

(iii) **Data manipulation facilities** (for example, comparison with budget or prior year data, trend analysis)

(iv) **Graphics**, for user-friendly presentation of data

(v) A **template system**. This will mean that the same type of data (eg sales figures) is presented in the same format, irrespective of changes in the volume of information required.

At the heart of an executive information system is a **corporate model**, which holds key information about the organisation. A **database** is used to store the underlying data and the corporate model holds such information as organisational structure including performance indicators such as ratios, and reporting cycles as appropriate. This model provides the interface between the database and the executive, who as a result does not have to define how information should be displayed. The corporate model contains rules as to how the information should be presented and aggregated. The model can be amended if required.

(c) **Customer/client service**

Future developments in customer or client service are likely to take advantage of the link between telecommunications and computers (the so-called **information superhighway**) and set up direct interactive links between customers at home and service providers. **Multimedia** applications offer enormous opportunities in marketing applications where we want to show off our wares.

At present, however, the most important computer application in this area is one that has been mentioned already, the **database**.

The database concept is based on considering what data can be provided and then suiting that to the needs of particular applications, rather than beginning with the needs of particular applications.

Thus, for example, a bill for an overnight stay at one of our hotels provides not just a figure to post to the accounting system but a huge amount of useful information for marketing purposes: what services customers buy, with what frequency, where they live (how far they are willing to travel to make use of our facilities), what credit card they use, and so on.

If the bill is entered into (or is accessible by) a database this provides a comprehensive file of data for a number of different users. Each user will have access to the same data for their own processing applications, and at the same time if required. This removes the need for duplicating data on different files and it means, for example, that customer information will always be up-to-date and as full as possible.

Thus, because they allow previously disparate information to be linked up, databases allow customers' needs to be monitored far more closely than ever before and so served and satisfied far more precisely than ever before.

The information has always been there. Computers have made it available and useable.

27 Information sources

Plan for Managing Information within the company

These are my proposals for how information should be managed within the company. My report identifies five key areas.

1 **Classification of information resources**

The company collects information from a number of sources. The main sources are

- **Routinely collected internal sources**, eg analysis of sales invoices, customer comments and complaints

- Marketing intelligence gathered through our **monitoring** of the **local press**, trade press and sales personnel's reports
- **One-off market research exercises** undertaken by ourselves
- Ongoing **customer satisfaction surveys** handled by an external research agency

2 **Key features of an effective information system**

An effective information system must have the following characteristics.

- **Speed**. We must be able to collect, analyse and disseminate information before it becomes out-of-date and irrelevant.
- **Reliability**. We must be able to trust that the results are subject only to a reasonable amount of variation and sampling error.
- **Cost effectiveness**. We must balance the need for reliable, up-to-date information with the need to keep our data collection costs down.

3 **Examples/sources used in the micro and macro-environment**

Micro-environment

- Internally collected sales data
- Industry association routine monitoring studies
- Consultants' reports on our industry sector
- Competitors' briefings and annual reports

Macro-environment

- HM Treasury statistics on retail price inflation, growth in GDP and government expenditure
- Consultants' and industry association reports on the broader economic outlook for our industry
- Solicitors' briefing notes on how new legislation may affect our industry
- *Financial Times* for country and industry – specific reports

4 **Example of uses of this information**

Sales data

We routinely record information about our sales, but currently do not analyse it sufficiently. In future we should conduct greater analysis to spot trends, which we can then act upon. We should analyse trends in terms of:

- Types of customer
- Types of product
- Geographical location of customer
- Time of year

GDP data

We should establish more clearly a link between changes in GDP and changes in our volume of sales. We can try to establish this link by analysing historical data. In future, we can study government forecasts of GDP and adapt our output accordingly.

5 **Ethical issues**

We must **maintain integrity** in our **use of data** and ensure that it is not used for purposes other than those which the information provider intended. We must abide by the Data Protection Act

1998. In cases where ethical issues do arise, we should establish a small committee (including possibly an impartial external member) to adjudicate on such issues.

28 Opportunities and abilities

(a) **Marketing opportunities**

A marketing opportunity exists whenever there is a **gap between demand and supply**. When there is an unfulfilled demand, an opportunity exists for an enterprising marketer to fulfil this by supplying suitable goods and services at the right time, at the right place and at the right price. For example, in the UK a demand may exist for beer outside normal pub opening hours, especially during hot weather. A pub which opens earlier can make a profit by fulfilling this demand, ie exploiting this marketing opportunity.

The tightening of the drink/drive laws in Europe led to an increase in demand for low alcohol beers and lagers which provided a marketing opportunity for those brewers who were able to identify and close this gap between demand and supply.

In hot weather demand increases and thereby provides a marketing opportunity for increased sales of cold drinks and ice-cream.

Marketers need to recognise that **demand changes over time**, due to changes in the so-called **environmental factors** (Political, Economic, Sociological, Technological) and competition. Increased concern over health in the western world has provided marketing opportunities for all sorts of diets, sporting equipment and health clubs, as well as for books on how to keep healthy and a great variety of lotions and potions.

Equally, demand for existing goods and services will normally diminish over time due to technological advances and/or changes in fashion. To stay in business therefore, a company needs to modify its goods and services or provide new goods and services in order to meet changing customer wants and needs.

Alternatively a company may identify new markets for existing goods and services, for example a demand for British bread in Paris and a demand for British stores such as Marks and Spencer and Sainsbury in France.

Awareness of opportunities

Companies need to be continuously on the **lookout for marketing opportunities** if they wish to grow. Marketing growth opportunities have been classified by Ansoff as falling under four general categories:

(i) Market penetration: Existing products for existing markets (more of the same)
(ii) Market development: Existing products for new markets
(iii) Product development: New products for existing markets
(iv) Diversification: New products for new markets

Would-be marketers and firms wishing to stay in business must be capable of both **recognising and exploiting marketing opportunities**, ideally **before competitors** do so. They must also be capable of **analysing these opportunities** so as to quantify demand and to determine an appropriate marketing mix. These requisites imply an adequate and continuous supply of marketing information ideally formalised in a MkIS (Marketing Information System).

In summary, a marketing opportunity exists whenever circumstances allow an organisation to take advantage of demand from a particular group of people or indeed from other organisations.

(b) Having identified a marketing opportunity an organisation has to decide whether it is capable of **exploiting** it. In making this decision the organisation has to assess its resources both currently and in the future. Clearly an organisation is constrained by its resources and will normally have set overall objectives in light of these. An organisation's internal capabilities can conveniently be categorised using the normal business functions framework, as follows.

(i) **Financial capabilities**

Clearly there are limits to what an organisation can afford. An organisation's financial capability might be defined as its cash reserves, working capital and its capability to borrow money to invest.

(ii) **Production capabilities**

An organisation is constrained in the types of goods or services it can supply by the limitations of its plant, machinery and the skills of its operatives.

(iii) **Marketing capabilities**

A company's marketing capability is limited by its **marketing mix**, namely its **products, prices, promotion and place** (distribution outlets). Within the promotion element, an organisation may only have a certain number of salespeople, with limited product knowledge, limited selling skills and limited contacts. Marketing managers' expertise may not be particularly broad. For these sorts of reasons an organisation operating in industrial markets, if faced with an opportunity to move into consumer markets, may decide that it does not possess the right marketing capabilities to achieve this.

(iv) **Personnel capabilities**

An organisation employs a limited number of staff, each of whom has limited expertise and skills. It may not be able to expand its staff quickly enough (or be able to train existing staff into acquiring new skills) to take advantage of a short-term marketing opportunity such as a sudden rise in demand for heating equipment during a particularly cold spell in the weather.

The above examples show that it is extremely important that a company **analyses its internal capabilities**. Failure to recognise the constraints imposed by limitations in these capabilities could lead to the grasping of a wrong marketing opportunity with catastrophic results.

29 Forecasters

SWOT analysis of the national economy

Strengths (internal features)	Weaknesses (internal features)
Stable political system	Declining industrial base
Sophisticated economic and financial system	Underinvestment in education and training
Good communications network	Underinvestment in technology and infrastructure
Increasingly flexible labour market	Relative underinvestment in research and development
Relatively stable multi-cultural society	
Stable legal system	Skills shortages in some sectors
Membership of supranational and inter-national politico-economic organisations (eg WTO, EU)	Burden imposed on public finances of growing dependant population
Highly developed marketing infrastructure	Productivity levels in some industries
	Tendency for price inflation

ANSWER BANK

Opportunities (external features)	Threats (external features)
Development of markets with enlargement of European Union	Overdependence on imported manufactures
Growth potential in Eastern Europe	Threat from low-wage producers (especially Far East manufacturers)
Attraction of further inward investment to UK	Exchange rate instability
Increased opportunities in global information technology and communications	Political and economic uncertainty over question of single European currency
Increased tourism opportunities	Costs of implementing internationally agreed environmental standards
Market development in Southern Africa	
	Danger of increased protectionism in retaliation to common external tariff

30 Major bank

(a) Slide 1 | The Marketing Information System (MkIS)

Note. This presentation will explain what is meant by an MkIS and how it is made up.

Slide 2 | Definition

An **MkIS** is used to collect, analyse, disseminate and store data relevant to the needs of the organisation. It is part of the Management Information System (MIS) of the organisation.

Slide 3 | MkIS Kotler model

The marketing information system

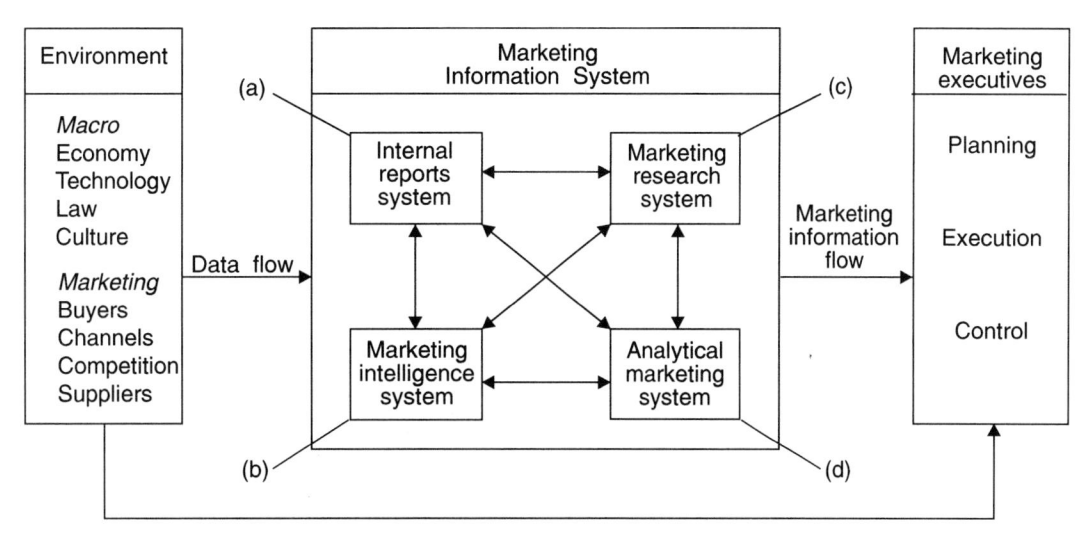

[Diagram: The marketing information system showing Environment (Macro: Economy, Technology, Law, Culture; Marketing: Buyers, Channels, Competition, Suppliers) feeding Data flow (a) into the Marketing Information System which contains Internal reports system, Marketing research system, Marketing intelligence system, and Analytical marketing system, with Marketing information flow (c) going to Marketing executives (Planning, Execution, Control), with feedback loops (b) and (d).]

Notes. The system is based on a flow of information. Data comes in from the external environment (macro and micro) and information feeds out to management to assist planning, implementation and control. This constant flow of information is vital to support marketing decisions taken on a continuous basis. For example, an upturn in economic activity may boost consumer confidence leading to an increase in the demand for mortgages. The four constituent parts of the MkIS will be considered in more detail.

ANSWER BANK

Slide 4 | Internal reports system

Notes. The **internal reports system** provides the following.

(i) Results data
(ii) Measures of performance
(iii) Sales, cost and stock information

Slide 5 | Marketing intelligence system

Notes. A marketing intelligence system allows the systematic collection of **qualitative and quantitative research**.

(i) It provides up-to-the-minute event data
(ii) It provides information on developments in the environment
(iii) It scans and disseminates a wide range of intelligence

Slide 6 | Marketing research system

Notes. Such a system studies marketing problems, opportunities and effectiveness

Slide 7 | Analytical marketing system

Notes. There are various types of **analytical marketing systems**, all of which use models to explain, predict and improve the marketing process.

Slide 8 | Management information

Notes. The flow of information from the MkIS will assist managers with **planning and control**. It will help them to make the right decisions given the prevailing influences within the wider environment. The bank will therefore be better able to provide the financial services the public want, in a form that they need. This of course leads to higher levels of customer service.

(b) Slide 9 | An effective internal report system is vital in providing customer service

Notes. The system will provide results data and show accurate measures of **current performance levels** (number of complaints, frequency of complaints, categories of complaint). These can then be compared to target and any corrective action taken. Information on sales levels will allow comparisons to be made against competitors. Is our market share falling? Information on the stock of leaflets and brochures should avoid stock-outs. Standard customer data should be held, including contact details, bank services used etc to build a comprehensive customer record database. To allow any necessary corrective action to be taken speedily, all reports need to be produced on time and made available to the staff/managers who need them.

Slide 10 | An effective market intelligence system is vital in providing customer service

Notes. The system will provide **information on competitor activity**. This will enable the bank to keep up with its competitors and will ensure that it counters any new financial initiatives they may take. The performance of the bank should be benchmarked against that of its competitors. The system will gather intelligence on new developments and changes within the financial markets generally. This will include intelligence data on customer service trends, not only in banking but also in related sectors, such as insurance. It will scan and disseminate information from the wider environment which might impact on the business and will facilitate intelligence feedback from internal sales staff about customer service problems, types of enquiry etc.

Slide 11 | *An effective marketing research system is vital in providing customer service*

Notes. Marketing research takes three basic forms:

(i) **Internal**

    (1) Company records (including centralised data)
    (2) Employee knowledge

(ii) **External (published)**

    (1) Government statistics
    (2) Financial sector magazines, journals and newspapers
    (3) Published reports, conference and seminar papers
    (4) Books covering financial services

(iii) **Primary research**

    (1) Own survey
    (2) Commissioned via MR agency

Information from any of these sources can be used to improve the quality and quantity of product targeting of offerings and can lead to an improvement in customer service levels. Specifically, questionnaires can be used to gauge existing customer satisfaction levels and to determine whether levels are improving. Recurrent problems can be identified and it will be possible to establish whether complaints tend to come from the same people or whether they come from a cross-section of the public. Questionnaires could be used to determine the type of financial services people actually need and to provide information on how competitors' offerings are perceived. Focus groups can provide information on issues such as image and the public's perception of the bank.

Slide 12 | *Modelling techniques*

Notes. The analytical marketing system uses **models** to explain, predict and improve marketing processes. They can be extremely useful in markets such as financial services where there are a large number of inter-dependent variables. Their role in anticipating and predicting outcomes can have a positive bearing on future levels of customer satisfaction.

Slide 13 | *Organisational implications*

Notes. For the MKIS to be effective, some **organisational changes** may be required.

(i) Additional training
(ii) Recruitment of staff with specialist skills
(iii) More streamlined structures

If handled properly, the resulting increase in efficiency should result in improved customer service.

Slide 14 | *Summary*

Notes. A good MkIS will allow target levels of customer service to be achieved by providing timely, relevant and accurate data to assist the bank in anticipating and satisfying customer needs.

ANSWER BANK

Specimen paper

SPECIMEN PAPER

The Chartered Institute of Marketing

Certificate in Marketing

Marketing Environment

5.23: Marketing Environment

Time:

Date:

3 Hours Duration

This examination is in two sections.

PART A – Is compulsory and worth 40% of total marks.

PART B – Has **SIX** questions; select **THREE**. Each answer will be worth 20% of the total marks.

DO NOT repeat the question in your answer, but show clearly the number of the question attempted on the appropriate pages of the answer book.

Rough workings should be included in the answer book and ruled through after use.

© The Chartered Institute of Marketing

Certificate in Marketing

5.23: Marketing Environment – Specimen Paper

PART A

An Overview of the Marketing Environment

Marketing has become a fundamental business philosophy applied within increasingly competitive markets. In fact it is being adopted by large sections of the **private**, **public** and **voluntary sectors** alike. In each, it is the needs of the customer that provides the springboard for marketing activity. Marketers in all types of organisation must identify or anticipate these needs and then develop products or services that will satisfy them through an exchange process.

The organisation itself may constrain the extent to which it can effectively satisfy the identified needs. Most private businesses, for example, are limited by the need to earn a satisfactory level of profit for their **shareholders** and if prospective sales or returns from an activity fall short of this requirement they are unlikely to be continued. However, it may also be argued that the more effectively a business satisfies customer needs, the more likely it will achieve a **competitive edge** over rivals and realise its financial objectives.

Public sector organisations pursue social objectives, but are also likely to be resource constrained and will need to account the interests of various interested groups in achieving value for money.

Marketing management is in essence concerned with mobilising the resources of the organisation so that they successfully meet the changing needs of the internal and external stakeholders on whom they depend. It is not just the customer who is the focus of attention but often a range of interested groups who all may make a critical contribution to the organisation.

The sum total of these changing needs, pressures, constraints, threats and opportunities are commonly referred to as the organisation's marketing environment. Much of this environment is beyond the direct control of the marketer but marketing activities may influence significant elements in the micro environment.

A key to a true marketing orientation is the ability to adapt to changes in the organisation's marketing environment. Where opportunities or threats cannot be easily influenced, they can be monitored, forecast and assessed for their implications. Such knowledge can provide a powerful edge for the more proactive organisation.

Adapted from The Business and Marketing Environment by Palmer and Hartley. McGraw-Hill, 3rd Edition

SPECIMEN PAPER

PART A

Question 1.

a. Define **two** of the following terms highlighted in the article and provide a **bullet point summary** of their significance for the marketer:

   i) Voluntary sector.

   ii) Competitive edge.

   iii) Shareholders.

   (10 marks)

b. Given the suggestion in the article that the private business is limited by the need to earn a satisfactory profit, brief your Marketing Manager on the nature and significance of objectives pursued in the private sector as compared with those pursued in the public sector.

   (12 marks)

c. The case states that much of the marketing environment is beyond the direct control of the marketer. Provide a summary of the merits and the means of understanding the changes taking place in this environment.

   (10 marks)

d. Identify **four** critical stakeholder groups of The Chartered Institute of Marketing and state one critical contribution made by each to its effectiveness.

   (8 marks)
   (40 marks in total)

SPECIMEN PAPER

PART B – Answer THREE Questions Only

Question 2.

a. Why is it important for a firm to monitor its industry environment?

(8 marks)

b. Identify the means or sources available to monitor its industry and competitors.

(8 marks)

c. List **four** good reasons for not colluding with competitors.

(4 marks)
(20 marks in total)

Question 3.

Write a memorandum to your immediate manager outlining **three** social or lifestyle trends that have led, over the last two decades, to significant changes in your society. Include an appendix outlining the marketing implications of these changes for either a public or private sector organisation of your own choice.

(20 marks)

Question 4.

a. List **four** government economic objectives and their equivalent economic indicators.

(4 marks)

b. State the current numerical value of the indicators you have identified in a country of your choice.

(4 marks)

c. Select **one** government economic objective and discuss what policies would be used to help achieve it and any marketing implications that might arise from its implementation.

(12 marks)
(20 marks in total)

Question 5.

The Marketing Director is concerned at the apparent unreliability of quantitative forecasts concerning the likely state of the economy in the first decade of the new century.

Your Manager has delegated you the task of preparing a report to explain and evaluate the following alternative techniques:

a. Environmental audit.

b. Delphi technique.

c. Scenarios.

(20 marks)

Question 6.

The travel and tourism industry appears to be entering into a new age of technological change and competitive uncertainty.

a. Outline threats and pressures currently facing the industry within its marketing environment.

(12 marks)

b. Provide a summary of the potential marketing opportunities for the industry arising out of information communication technologies, such as, digital television and the Internet.

(8 marks)
(20 marks in total)

Question 7.

Prepare a series of slides highlighting, with appropriate examples, the significance to marketers of **three** of the following aspects of environmental information systems:

i) Information.

ii) Marketing research.

iii) Secondary data.

iv) Marketing information system.

(20 marks)

SPECIMEN PAPER

Answers to Specimen paper

1

(a) (i) **Voluntary sector**

The voluntary sector comprises organisations that do not operate for profit, but to satisfy a social objective of some sort. They often provide goods and services to users without charge, and often rely on volunteers to provide labour inputs. However, voluntary sector organisations often charge for services and pay staff.

Significance for the marketer

- Voluntary sector organisations can have high levels of loyalty from the public
- Users/consumers may favourably evaluate the services of a voluntary sector organisation
- Nevertheless, voluntary sector organisations are increasingly having to compete with other types of organisations for funding

(ii) **Competitive edge**

An organisation is said to have a competitive edge where it has a distinct advantage (in the eyes of customers) compared to other organisations providing similar goods and services.

Significance for the marketer

- Must identify the nature of a competitive edge and exploit it
- A competitive edge can be eroded very quickly by competitors – marketers must continuously explore new ways of maintaining a competitive edge
- Must understand emerging competencies of competitors
- A competitive edge must be relevant to the needs of customers

(iii) **Shareholders**

Shareholders own a share of the equity capital of a company. This entitles them to a share of the profits of the company and a share of the voting to decide policy of the company, (although the Articles of Association may limit voting rights). Shareholders also share the risk of a company, although this risk is often limited to the value of their paid-up shares.

Significance for the marketer

- Marketing plans need the broad approval of shareholders if they are going to be capable of implementation
- Communication activity is often aimed at shareholders
- Shareholders are often targeted as customers for the company's products

(b) These are the main areas in which objectives pursued by the private sector are likely to be different compared with those pursued by the public sector.

- *More diverse objectives*

    Private sector organisations are essentially driven by profit and sales objectives. Public sector organisations must additionally set social objectives and performance objectives (eg a hospital is likely to specify the number of each type of operation to be carried out).

- *Qualitative v quantitative objectives*

  Public sector organisations are more likely than private sector organisations to set qualitative service objectives, although this distinction is often blurred between the two sectors.

- *Transparency of objectives*

  Private sector organisations often like to keep many of their objectives secret, in order to confuse competitors. Public sector organisations are accountable to a much wider range of stakeholders and therefore objectives need to be more transparent for all to see.

- *Time period of objectives*

  A range of objectives are set by organisations, from short to long-term. It is often said that public sector objectives are influenced by the political election cycle.

(c) The main merit of understanding the marketing environment which is beyond the direct control of the marketer lies in the ability it gives the marketer to anticipate change. With such an understanding of the environment and how it is continually evolving, an organisation can be prepared to adapt to environmental change rapidly.

These are some of the means by which an organisation can understand the changes taking place in its environment:

- Gathering, analysing and disseminating environmental intelligence in order to create a 'learning organisation'. Intelligence can be gathered through such sources as trade journals, conferences, sales personnel feedback etc. This approach is only as good as the vigour with which information is analysed and disseminated.

- Retain specialist consultants who are specialist in a particular aspect of the environment eg technology, social trends. The company must be able to incorporate such advice within an organisational knowledge base.

- A marketing information system can provide early warning signals of change in the environment, for example through long-term changes in the sales level of particular products. Collecting information in this way (as in the previous two ways) can be expensive and a balance has to be struck between the value of the information and the cost of obtaining it.

(d) **Four stakeholder groups of the CIM**

1. *Members*

   The CIM exists to serve members. The continuing financial and moral support of members is critical to the organisation's continuing success and relevance.

2. *Customers*

   CIM provides services (eg training courses) to non-members. The revenue generated by these activities can be critical to avoid deficits on overhead costs occurring.

3. *Education establishments*

   Many colleges provide tuition to satisfy the examination and the Professional Development requirements of CIM. Without the support of these establishments the educational mission of CIM will be greatly weakened.

4. *Suppliers*

   Like most organisations, CIM buys in supplies from a number of sources. Withdrawal of services of key speakers at conferences organised by CIM may be seen as critical.

2

(a) **Reasons why it is important for a firm to monitor its environment**

A number of areas of concern can be identified:

- Need to monitor trends in customer preferences. By spotting emerging trends, the firm can switch its resources to products with a growing demand, and away from those which are going out of fashion.

- Need to monitor competitors. New sources of competition can emerge to threaten the firm, both from within the industry sector and from beyond.

- Need to monitor supplier activities. New competitive sources of supply may emerge (eg from lower cost Far Eastern products). Suppliers may develop new technologies which the firm can incorporate into its own production methods.

- Need to monitor government attitudes to the sector. Policy statements may lead to new legislation which affects the industry. The firm can seek to amend new legislation where this is harmful to the industry. Where legislation is actually passed, the firm can prepare for its implementation ahead of its competitors.

(b) **Means and sources of information**

Sales personnel. These are close to industry trends and the firm should arrange and collect, analyse and disseminate intelligence gathered by sales personnel.

Industry Associations. Most industry sectors have a trade association which disseminates intelligence through newsletters and seminars.

Retained consultants. The firm may pay a consultant to keep a watching brief over developments in the industry sector. A consultant may be able to do this more effectively and efficiently than relying solely on the firm's own personnel.

Media cuttings. The media (newspaper, TV, radio, Internet) can be regularly trawled for emerging trends. A firm may engage a specialist agency to do this.

Analysis of the firm's own data. Routine analysis of sales figures, disaggregated by product type and market segment may give a clue about emerging trends within the industry.

(c) **Reasons for not colluding with competitors**

- The firm may face a fine from a regulatory agency if it is found to be in breach of legislation prohibiting anti-competitive behaviour.

- An investigation may itself waste valuable management time, so it is advisable to avoid suspicion of collusion.

- Collusion with other companies implies restricting some aspect of a company's marketing plan. It may in the long term be more profitable for the company to pursue its marketing plan single-mindedly.

- Collusion can be unstable where one gains a cost advantage over the others.

3

Three social changes/lifestyle which have had effects on society

1. A growing number of individuals are becoming money-rich, but time-poor. This has affected society's attitudes in a number of ways, for example with respect to childcare, the value of family life and the desire for immediate gratification.

SPECIMEN PAPER ANSWERS

2. As individuals become financially more secure, their motivation to buy products typically changes from a need for necessities to a desire for the unusual and challenging. Society now places greater merit on goods and services which are purchased for their aesthetic, rather than purely utilitarian value.

3. There has been increasing concern by many groups within society on the benefits from healthy living. Society no longer regards as abnormal those individuals who prefer not to smoke/drink alcohol/regularly exercise.

Marketing implications for a grocery retailer

Businesses have responded to the changes identified above in a number of ways.

1. The growing number of money-rich, time-poor households presents new opportunities for businesses to provide convenient solutions to this group at a premium price. Many of the major UK retailers have identified this opportunity and developed home delivery services. Somerfield stores was an early retailer to develop a home delivery service which delivers customers' shopping to their home or place of work. Subsequently, many retailers have further developed this service proposition, most notably by allowing shoppers to do their shopping using the Internet from the convenience of their home or office.

   Additionally, grocery retailers have responded by developing new products which are attractive to busy people, such as gourmet ready-prepared meals.

2. The move from satisfying basic needs to more esoteric higher level needs has implications for the product ranges offered by grocery retailers. Many have responded by offering more exotic ranges of fruit and vegetables. In addition, many retailers have offered menu advice and themed food areas to make it easier for customers to put together the ingredients for authentic foreign cuisine.

3. Consumers' increasing interest in healthy lifestyles has been reflected in a range of products which offer health benefits. Many grocery retailers have developed their own label ranges of 'low-fat' products. Further developments have occurred with low cholesterol and low salt products. Many retailers stock low alcohol wines as an alternative to traditional wines.

   Many grocery retailers have sought to capitalise on growing interest in healthy living by linking themselves with health promotion organisations, an this has resulted in in-store promotions and jointly produced information pamphlets.

4

(a) **Four government objectives/economic objectives**.

   1. Maintain a stable level of prices with the economy. The economic indicator for this is the level of inflation, in the UK most commonly measured using the Retail Prices Index (RPI).

   2. Maintain a stable exchange rate. The indicator for this is the value of the nation's currency in terms of other foreign currencies.

   3. Maintain economic growth. This is indicated by the rate at which Gross Domestic Product (GDP) is expanding or contracting.

   4. Maintain a low level of unemployment. This is typically indicated by the number of people currently out of work and/or claiming unemployment, expressed as a percentage of the total working population.

(b) **Numerical value of indicators for the UK, first half of 2003**

   1. **Stable prices**. The annual level of inflation, measured by the Retail Prices Index (RPI) during the year to June 2003 was 2.9%.

2. **Exchange rates**. During the first half of 2003, the value of sterling was in the range 1.6-1.7 US dollars and about 1.38-1.55 Euros.

3. **Economic growth**. Forecast economic growth for 2003 was 2.0% to 2.5%.

4. **Employment**. During this period, the total number of people unemployed, based on the ILO definition from the Labour Force Survey, was 1,474,000 in May/June 2003, representing 5.0% of the workforce.

(c) **Government policies to maintain a stable exchange rate**

The following steps are typically taken by governments to maintain stability in a nation's currency.

- Adjust interest rates – a higher interest rate will attract 'hot' money and thereby increase the value of the currency. Lowering interest rates will have the opposite effect. Implications for marketing: The use of interest rates is quite a blunt tool. Higher rates may have the effect of reducing consumers' discretionary expenditure, and hence their ability to purchase a company's products. Higher interest rates may also affect a company's costs where it has borrowed heavily.

- Reduce government expenditure and hence the need for government to borrow money. Implications for marketing: This will have a general deflationary effect and may lower the general level of consumer demand in the economy. Also, many companies supplying to government (eg road builders) may be directly affected by cutbacks in government expenditure.

- Reduce inflationary pressures within the economy, for example by increasing personal taxation where excessive spending by consumers is causing inflationary pressures. Implications for marketing: As noted above, this might reduce consumers' expenditure.

- Encourage exports and inward investment, while trying to provide substitutes for imports. Implications for marketing: Firms may capitalise on export assistance schemes.

- Sometimes, governments have taken direct action to control prices, and hence maintain a stable currency. These actions include limits on wage rises and the need to seek prior approval for price rises. Implications for marketing: These actions can have serious implications for marketers, and may make it difficult to adjust prices in accordance with market demands.

5

Evaluation of alternative forecasting techniques

(a) *Environmental audit*

This is a comprehensive, systematic, independent and periodic examination of a company's marketing environment, objectives, strategies and activities. It is undertaken with a view to determining problem areas and opportunities and recommending a plan of action to improve the company's marketing performance.

The environmental audit is not itself a framework for decisions. It is essentially a set of procedures by which an organisation explicitly asks questions, about the internal and external environments in which marketing operates, as well as the performance of the marketing functions themselves (such as the firm's distribution and proving effectiveness). It is usually undertaken by an independent and objective external organisation or individual.

To be effective, an environmental audit requires the availability of good quality, timely information. A self-audit could be undertaken, but at the risk of a loss of objectivity. The process of undertaking an environmental audit can be costly and time consuming so a company must ensure that it makes effective use of this technique.

(b) *Delphi technique*

This technique involves a number of experts, usually from outside the organisation, who (preferably) do not know each other and who do not meet or confer while the process is in play. A number of pictures, or scenarios of the future are drawn up by the company. These are then posted out to the experts. Comments are returned and the scenario(s) modified according to the comments received. The process is run through a number of times and the scenario being amended on each occasion. Eventually a consensus of the most likely scenario is arrived at.

It is often considered that this technique is more accurate than relying on any one individual, because it involves the collected wisdom of a number of experts who have not been influenced by dominant personalities. Nevertheless, the effectiveness of the result is dependent on the quality of the individuals who participate. It can become a slow and cumbersome process.

(c) *Scenarios*

Scenario building is an attempt to paint a picture of the future. It may be possible to build a small number of alternative scenarios based on differing assumptions. This qualitative approach is a means of handling environmental issues that are hard to quantify because they are less structured, more uncertain and may involve very complex relationships.

Scenario building among senior management will help individuals to confirm or moderate their views. A new perspective may be taken on forthcoming events. A wider perspective may be taken by individuals who may become more sensitive to the environment and the impact it can have on business. A more cohesive view may be adopted by senior management which may help strategy formulation and planning.

The scenarios may be built up over a number of meetings which may be either totally unstructured or semi-structured, with each meeting focusing on different aspects of the environment. The approach may be used at different levels of management in a large organisation; a multinational company may build scenarios at the global, regional and country level.

Scenario building is a useful technique for visualising possible future marketing environment, and has been used by the UK Government's Foresight Programme, which attempts to bring together experts from industry, academia, and government in an attempt to identify and evaluate trends in technological developments. However, it must be remembered that scenario building in itself will not make decisions about which actions a company should take.

6

(a) **Threats and pressures currently facing the travel and tourism industry**

- Threats of terrorism. Following the events of September 2001, many potential customers have been deterred from travelling. While there was some recovery in demand following the events, many people remain concerned about the effects of further unexpected terrorist activities. Terrorism also has the effect of increasing travel companies' costs (eg through higher insurance premiums), thereby reducing their profitability.

- Declining natural resources. Travel and tourism continues to harm the natural environment, for example, through the use of fossil fuels and the over-development of tourism destinations. It is a challenge for the industry to try and deter governments from imposing more restrictions on the operation of travel related services.

- Alternatives to travel. It must be remembered that for most leisure travel and tourism services, consumers may often quite happily substitute a non-travel related service.

Following the events of September 2001, many consumers deferred their holidays and instead spend money on new items for their home.

- Virtual tourism. Furthermore, information technology is allowing many aspects of tourism services to be experienced without leaving home. Video-conferencing has the potential to reduce the need for business meetings. Within the personal leisure sector, virtual tours of a destination may reduce the desire to actually visit the destination.

- New forms of competitors emerging. The Internet has enabled new forms of virtual competitors to appear. Many intermediaries have emerged to challenge traditional travel agencies.

(b) **Potential marketing opportunities for the travel and tourism industry arising out of information technologies**

These are the main ways in which information technology will offer opportunities for the industry.

- Information technology can allow new types of services to be offered to consumers – self-select package holidays, for example.

- New technology can allow existing services to be produced more cheaply, thereby widening their market through being able to charge lower prices. In this way, more efficient web-based booking systems have allowed new markets for air travel to develop.

- Technological developments have allowed new methods of distributing tourism services. New intermediaries such as Expedia.com have emerged and increasing levels of Internet access at home has led to many more consumers booking online.

- New opportunities for companies to communicate with their target customers have emerged, with many travel companies using computer databases to target potential customers and to maintain a dialogue with established customers. This has been achieved through database-driven direct mail, telemarketing and increasingly, Internet-based marketing.

7

Significance to marketers of environmental information

(i) *Information*

Information is the link between an organisation and its operating environment. It comprises quantitative and qualitative data about phenomena which have an impact on the organisation. To be useful, information must be collected, analysed and disseminated with an appropriate level of speed and accuracy. What is appropriate depends upon the task in hand. Information requirements in a fast-moving market such as computer hardware are likely to be quite different to information required to assess demand for a new underground railway.

We need to distinguish between the terms 'knowledge' and 'information'. Even though in some senses they may be used interchangeably, many writers have suggested that the two concepts are quite distinct. In fact, knowledge is a much more all-encompassing term which incorporates the concept of beliefs that are based on information … Information only becomes knowledge in the hands of someone who knows what to do with it.

(ii) *Marketing research*

Large organisations operating in complex environments need to adopt a structured approach to their information collection activities. Marketing research is one aspect of these collection activities. Data collected should be as up-to-date and relevant to a problem as time and cost constraints allow.

The stages of the marketing research process can be described in a simple, linear format. A model exists for this process, which begins with the definition of the research problem and ends with the presentation of the findings. This process follows the basic pattern of enquiry that is adopted for other forms of scientific or academic research.

The trigger for marketing research can usually be related to a gap in the market information which is currently available to a firm. For example, a company may have comprehensive information on the current market for its products, but lacks information on new market opportunities for which its product range could be adapted.

Very often, marketing research activity fails because the 'problem' to be researched has been inadequately thought through and expressed as a research brief. For example, a company may be facing declining sales of a product and commission research to investigate customers' liking of the product's features relative to competitors' products. However, the real problem may be to understand the macroeconomic environment which may explain why sales of that category of product are declining.

(iii) *Secondary data*

Data sources are traditionally divided into two categories according to the methods by which they were collected. Secondary research is often referred to as desk research. Its distinguishing feature is that it is second-hand to the user, as it was collected previously for some other purpose. Data could be second-hand because it has already been collected internally by the organisation, although for a different primary purpose. Alternatively, the information could be acquired second-hand from external sources.

Most organisations would approach a research exercise by examining the available sources of secondary data.

Internal information, on products, costs, sales etc may be accessed through an organisation's Marketing Information System. Where such a system does not exist formally, the information may still be available in relevant departmental records, though it would probably need to be re-worked into a format that market researchers can use.

Secondary research can be a useful starting point for a research exercise. If somebody else has collected data or published a report in a closely related area, it is often much cheaper to buy that report rather than starting to collect data afresh. Reports by organisations such as the Economist Intelligence Unit (ECU) may at first sight seem to be very expensive, but set against the cost of undertaking the research from scratch, their cost begins to look relatively good value. Secondary research can be carried out internally by a company's own employees, although some specialist knowledge is required in knowing which sources of information are likely to be useful. Undertaking unnecessary primary research when similar information is available through secondary sources is an expensive and time-consuming exercise.

(iv) *Marketing information system*

Many analyses of organisations' information collection and dissemination activities take a systems perspective. The collection of marketing information can be seen as one sub-system of a much larger management information system.

A marketing information system has been defined by Kotler as a system that '.... Consists of people, equipment and procedures to gather, sort, analyse, evaluate and distribute needed, timely and accurate information to marketing decision-makers'.

A marketing information system can conceptually be seen as comprising four principal components, although in practice, they are operationally inter-related.

- Internal data, particularly important in respect of operational and control functions.

- Marketing research is that part of the system concerned with the structured collection of marketing information.
- Marketing intelligence comprises the procedures and sources used by marketing management to obtain pertinent information about developments in their marketing environment.
- Marketing decision support systems comprise a set of models that allow forecasts to be made.

SPECIMEN PAPER ANSWERS

List of Key Concepts and Index

A
Actual economic growth, 170
Agent, 201

B
B2B, 268
B2C, 268
Balance of payments, 184
Barriers to entry, 103
Business cycle, 175
Business process re-engineering, 43

C
C2B, 268
C2C, 268
Cartel, 112
Class, 152
Closed system, 38
Comparative advantage, 181
Competitive forces, 102
Computer Telephony Integration (CTI), 240
Concentrated industries, 111
Connected stakeholders, 40
Consumerism, 94
Contingency theory, 44
Contract, 199
Culture, 155

D
Database, 71
Demography, 142
Desk research, 67
Direct taxation, 177

E
Economic union, 272
Economies of scale, 20
Electronic Data Interchange (EDI), 241
Emerging industry, 114
Environmental complexity, 53
Environmental set, 132
Environmental uncertainty, 52
Exchange rate, 183
External data, 67
External stakeholders, 40
Externality, 219

F
Field research, 67
Fiscal policy, 177
Floating exchange rates, 184
Fragmented industry, 110

G
Green movement, 215

Gross domestic product, 167
Gross national income, 168
Gross national product (GNP), 168

I
Indirect taxation, 177
Interest group, 197
Internal data, 67
Internal stakeholders, 40
Internet, 72

L
Lifestyle, 159
Limited company, 12

M
Macro environment, 126
Marketing audit, 310
Marketing intelligence system, 295
Marketing research, 285
Marketing, 7
Micro environment, 64
Mission, 28
Monetary policy, 179
Monetary union, 272
Monopoly, 113

N
National income, 167

O
Objectives, 32
Oligopoly, 111
On-line system, 71
Open system, 38
Organisation, 4

P
P2P, 268
Partnerships, 12
Perfect competition, 110
Political party, 197
Potential economic growth, 170
Pressure group, 90
Price discrimination, 113
Primary data, 67
Private benefit, 219
Private cost, 219
Product life cycle, 319
Public good, 220
Public sector organisation, 8

Q
Qualitative research, 288
Quantitative research, 288

LIST OF KEY CONCEPTS

Rate of Natural Increase in population, 143
Real-time system, 71

Scenario building, 302
Secondary data, 67
Social benefit, 219
Social cost, 219
Sole tradership, 12
Stakeholders, 40
Strategic Business Unit, 33
Supply chain, 249
Supply side economics, 179
Sustainability, 218
SWOT analysis, 311
System, 37

Technology, 232
Turbulence, 54

Virtual company, 249
Virtual Supply Chain (VSC), 249

Index

Accountability, 6
Acid rain, 215
ACORN, 135, 154
Ad hoc research, 287
Advanced manufacturing technology, 259
Advertising, 197
Age structure (of the population), 144, 147
Amazon.com, 244
American Marketing Association, 285
Analysis of opportunities and threats, 311
Ansoff, 35
Apple Computers, 30, 31
Audits, 290
Authority, 6

B2B world, 270
BACS, 242
BACSTEL, 242
Balance of payments, 166, 184
Bargaining power of customer, 106
Bargaining power of suppliers, 107
Barriers to entry, 103, 113
Bedeian A, 56
Birth rate, 143
Board of Directors, 81
Bought-in Reports, 290
Boundary, 38
Bureaucracy, 22
Business activities, 17
Business cycle, 175, 257
Business Monitor, 69
Business process re-engineering, 43
Business to Business (B2B) sector, 269
Buying behaviour, 154

Capital requirements, 104
Capitalism, 64
Causal research, 288
Cause groups, 90
CD-ROMs, 133, 251
Chambers of Commerce, 136
Chaos theory, 308
CHAPS, 241
Charities, 18
CIS, 119
Citizens' Charter, 97
Class, 152
Closed system, 38
Coca-Cola, 291
Code of conduct, 96
Code of ethics', 218
Collusion, 112
Commercial sources, 290

Commitment, 29
Competition for customers, 102
Competitive advantage, 108
Competitive forces, 102, 120, 251
Competitor intelligence system, 68
Competitor response profile, 119
Complaints, 295
Complements, 65, 66
Complexity, 53
Computer Telephony Integration (CTI), 240
Concentrated industries, 111
Conflict of stakeholder interests, 78
Connected stakeholders, 81
Consumer groups, 94
Consumer panels, 291
Consumer protection legislation, 95
Consumerism, 83, 95
Contingency plans, 302
Contingency theory, 44
Continuous research, 287
Contract law, 199
Co-operative movement, 28
Corporate identity, 248
Corporate objectives, 33
Cost leadership strategy, 109
Cost-push inflation, 174
Cross-impact analysis, 306
Cultural change, 129
Culture, 128
Customer database, 294
Customer research, 248
Customer service, 248, 295
Customers, 106
Customers', 85
Customs, 155
Cyclical unemployment, 173

Data protection, 201
Data Protection Principles, 202
Database, 71, 259, 293, 298
Death rate, 143
Decision support systems, 239, 293
Decline, 320
Defensive groups, 90
Delayering, 259
Delegation, 6
Delphi method, 177, 306
Demand-pull inflation, 173
Demerit good, 220
Demography, 128, 142
Deregulation, 54
Descriptive research, 288
Desk research, 67
Differentiation strategy, 109

Digital television, 242
Direct Mail Services Standards Board, 205
Direct marketers, 205
Direct marketing, 247
Direct response advertising, 247
Directories, 69
Directory publishers, 71
Diseconomies of scale, 21
Distribution channels, 105
Distributors, 86
Dividend payments, 35
Drucker P, 285
Duty of care, 201
Dynamic pricing, 245

Early adopters, 235
Earnings per share, 35
EasyJet, 248
Ecology, 215
Econometrics, 305
Economic change, 131
Economic environment, 130
Economic growth, 166
Economic recession, 175
Economic trends, 257
Economies of scale, 104
Economy, 130
Electronic commerce, 264
Electronic Data Interchange (EDI), 241
Electronic Funds Transfer, 241
Electronic mail (E-mail), 240
Electronic Point of Sale (EPOS), 239
Emerging industry, 114
Employees, 86
Employment law, 206
Empty nesters, 151
Enterprise Act 2002, 115
Environmental dynamism, 53
Environmental information, 133
Environmental issues, 215
Environmental legislation, 216
Environmental management systems, 221, 228
Environmental risk screening, 216
Environmental scanning, 68, 72, 292
Environmental set, 132
Environmental uncertainty, 52
Equipment design, 232
European Economic and Monetary Union, 272
Eurostat, 71, 136
Executive information systems, 239
Executive judgement, 306
Expectational inflation, 174
Expenditure approach (to measuring national income), 168
Expenditure reducing policy, 186
Expenditure switching policies, 186
Experimental research, 288
Expert systems, 240
Explanatory research, 288
External balance, 166
External databases, 71
External economies of scale, 21
External stakeholders, 83
Externality, 219
E-zines, 247

Factor incomes, 167
Fair trading, 95
Family Expenditure Survey, 69
Family life cycle, 150
Fertility rate, 143
Fiduciary duty, 201
Field research, 67
Floating exchange rates, 184
FMCG industries, 83
Focus strategy, 109
Forecasting techniques, 177
Foreign markets, 136
Formal organisation, 5
Fragmented industry, 110
Franchises, 16
Frictional unemployment, 172
Frost & Sullivan, 71
Full employment, 166

General Agreement on Tariffs and Trade (GATT), 182
Genetic diversity, 262
Geodemographic information, 295
GlaxoSmithKline, 31, 321
Global marketing strategies, 273
Government, 290
Government economic policy, 166
Graphics, 240
Grass roots marketing, 247
Grayson, 221
Green consumption, 223
Green movement, 160, 215
Green pressure groups, 216, 264
Gross domestic product (GDP), 167
Gross national product, 168
Gross National Product, 170, 187
Growth, 36

Health issues, 160
Home pages, 292
Household Survey, 69

Human and animal welfare, 230
Human resources, 148

IBM (UK), 31
Import cost-push inflation, 174
Import substitution, 186
Incentives, 243
Industrialisation, 234
Inflation, 166, 169
Informal organisation, 5
Information flows, 284
Information sources, 133
Information superhighway, 242
Innovators, 235
Insider groups, 91
Integrators, 249
Interactive television shopping, 251
Interest groups, 90
Intermediaries, 64
Internal capabilities, 313
Internal communication, 246
Internal data records, 290
Internal economies of scale, 21
internal environment, 4, 7
Internal marketing, 80
International trade, 180
Internet, 72, 242, 252, 292
Internet growth, 242
Internet kiosks, 242
Internet uses, 242
Intranets, 246
Investment decisions, 170

JICNAR, 152

Kawasaki, Guy, 31
Keynote, 71
Komatsu, 31
Kompass, 71

Lastminute.com, 248
Legal entity, 12
Lifestyle, 159
Limited companies, 12, 14, 18
Limited liability partnership (LLP), 12
Lobbyists, 197
Loyalty programmes, 247

Macro environment, 126
Macro forecasting, 309
Macro scenarios, 304
Mail Order Protection Scheme, 205

Managerial economies, 26
Market economy, 64
Market failure, 196, 218
Market intelligence, 292, 68
Marketing audit, 310
Marketing database, 293, 298
Marketing decisions, 285
Marketing information system, 296
Marketing intelligence system, 295
Marketing orientation, 285
Marketing planning, 225
Marketing research, 306
Marks & Spencer, 241
Matsushita, 31
Maturity, 320
Media, 197
Media relations, 247
Mergers, 115
Merit goods, 220
Micro environment, 64
Mintel, 71, 133
Mintzberg, 28
Mission, 28
Mission statements, 30, 31
Mobile communications, 241
Monopoly, 113
Mortality rate, 143
Multimedia, 251
Multiple scenarios, 307

National Food Survey, 69
National income, 167
Natural resources, 171
Net national product, 167
Newsgroups, 292
Non-commercial bodies, 18
Non-government sources of information, 69

Objectives, 287
Office support systems, 239
On-line system, 71
Open system, 38
Optimum, 218
Organisational hierarchies, 259
Outsider groups, 91
Overheads costs, 22
Ozone depletion, 230

Partnerships, 12, 14
Patent rights, 105
Peattie, 226
Perfect competition, 110
Personal Digital Assistant (PDA), 242

Political party, 197
Pollution, 219, 263
Population size, 143
Porter, 102
Power, 6
Presentation, 293
Press relations, 247
Pressure groups, 84, 90
Price discrimination, 113
Price takers, 110
Primary corporate objective, 34
Primary data, 67
Primary sources, 289
Private benefit, 219
Private cost, 219
Private sector, 8
Privatisation, 195
Process re-engineering, 233
Producers, 249
Product differentiation, 104
Product liability, 201
Product life cycle, 319
Product standards, 95
Production possibility curve, 233
Production systems, 238
Profitability, 32, 34
Promotional groups, 90
Public goods, 220
Public limited companies, 22
Public relations, 197, 223, 247
Public sector institutions, 19
Published information, 290

Qualitative data, 288
Qualitative research, 288, 293
Quantitative data, 288
Quantitative research, 288, 293

Rate of Natural Increase in population (RNI), 143
Raw data, 293
Real-time system, 71
Recession, 175
Recycling, 230
Regression analysis, 305
Relationship marketing, 247
Research and development, 26
Research objectives, 288
Resource depletion, 262
Responsibility, 6
Return on capital employed (ROCE, 35
Return on equity, 35
Return on investment (ROI), 35
Risk, 285
Rivalry, 107

Sales promotion, 247
Search engines, 292
Seasonal unemployment, 173
Secondary data, 67, 292
Secondary objectives, 34
Secondary sources, 290
Semi-closed system, 38
Service industries, 17
Shareholders, 14, 85
Shares, 19
Single Market, 181
Small businesses, 22
Social benefit, 219
Social change, 128, 256
Social cost, 218, 219
Social factors (in strategic planning), 128
Social structure, 151
Social systems, 39
Social trends, 128
Social Trends, 69, 134
Sole tradership, 12, 18
Sources of data, 287
Spin doctors, 197
Stakeholders, 40, 90
Statistical sources, 135
Stock control systems, 239
Strategic business unit (SBU), 33
Strengths and weaknesses analysis, 311
Structural analysis, 102, 120
Structural unemployment, 173
Substitute, 65, 106
Subsystems, 41, 47
Supernormal profits, 113
Suppliers, 107
Suppliers', 86
Supply chain, 249
Sustainability, 218
Sustainable development, 166
SWIFT, 241
Switching costs, 105
SWOT analysis, 133, 311
System boundary, 38

Taurus project, 250
Technological change, 131, 259
Technological environment, 131, 259
Technological progress, 171
Technological unemployment, 173
Terms of trade, 171
Tesco, 248
Test of reasonableness, 200
Threat of new entrants, 102, 103
Threats, 316

Time series analysis, 305
Trade audits, 291
Trade cycles, 175
Trade unions, 18
Trade-off, 33
Transaction costs, 244
Transformation processes, 42, 43
Trend analysis, 291
Trend analysis, 308

Uncertainties, 303
Unfair Contract Terms Act 1977, 200
Unfiar contract terms
Unit objectives, 33
Unsolicited mail, 205

Value added, 34
Viral marketing, 247
Virtual company, 249
Virtual Supply Chain (VSC), 249
Voluntary codes of conduct, 95
Voluntary regulation, 207

Wage-price spiral, 174
WAP phones, 242
Weaknesses, 313
Websites, 245
Which? magazine, 216
Work ethic, 129
Work organisations, 4
World Wide Web, 242, 292

Yahoo, 292
Yearbooks, 69

INDEX

CIM – Professional Certificate in Marketing: Marketing Environment (9/07)

REVIEW FORM & FREE PRIZE DRAW

All original review forms from the entire BPP range, completed with genuine comments, will be entered into one of two draws on 31 January 2008 and 31 July 2008. The names on the first four forms picked out on each occasion will be sent a cheque for £50.

Name: _____   Address: _____

_____

_____

How have you used this Text?
(Tick one box only)

☐ Self study (book only)
☐ On a course: college _____
☐ With BPP Home Study package
☐ Other _____

Why did you decide to purchase this Text?
(Tick one box only)

☐ Have used companion Kit
☐ Have used BPP Texts in the past
☐ Recommendation by friend/colleague
☐ Recommendation by a lecturer at college
☐ Saw advertising in journals
☐ Saw website
☐ Other _____

During the past six months do you recall seeing/receiving any of the following?
(Tick as many boxes as are relevant)

☐ Our advertisement in *Marketing Success*
☐ Our advertisement in *Marketing Business*
☐ Our brochure with a letter through the post
☐ Our brochure with *Marketing Business*
☐ Saw website

Which (if any) aspects of our advertising do you find useful?
(Tick as many boxes as are relevant)

☐ Prices and publication dates of new editions
☐ Information on product content
☐ Facility to order books off-the-page
☐ None of the above

Have you used the companion Practice & Revision Kit for this subject?   ☐ Yes   ☐ No

Your ratings, comments and suggestions would be appreciated on the following areas.

	Very useful	Useful	Not useful
Introductory section (How to use this text, study checklist, etc)	☐	☐	☐
Introduction	☐	☐	☐
Syllabus coverage	☐	☐	☐
Action Programmes and Marketing at Work examples	☐	☐	☐
Chapter roundups	☐	☐	☐
Quick quizzes	☐	☐	☐
Illustrative questions	☐	☐	☐
Content of suggested answers	☐	☐	☐
Index	☐	☐	☐
Structure and presentation	☐	☐	☐

	Excellent	Good	Adequate	Poor
Overall opinion of this Text	☐	☐	☐	☐

Do you intend to continue using BPP Study Texts/Kits/Passcards?   ☐ Yes   ☐ No

Please note any further comments and suggestions/errors on the reverse of this page.

Please return to: Kellee Vincent, BPP Learning Media, FREEPOST, London, W12 8BR

CIM – Professional Certificate in Marketing: Marketing Environment (9/07)

REVIEW FORM & FREE PRIZE DRAW (continued)

Please note any further comments and suggestions/errors below.

FREE PRIZE DRAW RULES

1. Closing date for 31 January 2008 draw is 31 December 2007. Closing date for 31 July 2008 draw is 30 June 2008.
2. Restricted to entries with UK and Eire addresses only. BPP employees, their families and business associates are excluded.
3. No purchase necessary. Entry forms are available upon request from BPP Professional Education. No more than one entry per title, per person. Draw restricted to persons aged 16 and over.
4. Winners will be notified by post and receive their cheques not later than 6 weeks after the relevant draw date. List of winners will be supplied on request.
5. The decision of the promoter in all matters is final and binding. No correspondence will be entered into.